W9-AGZ-970

AMP Real Estate

EXAM PREP

The SMART Guide to Passing

Virginia L. Lawson, J.D.

THOMSON

SOUTH-WESTERN

Australia · Brazil · Canada · Mexico · Singapore · Spain · United Kingdom · United States

THOMSON

SOUTH-WESTERN

AMP Real Estate Exam Prep:
The Smart Guide to Passing, First Edition

Thomson

Prepared by Virginia L. Lawson, JD

VP/Editorial Director:
Jack W. Calhoun

VP/Editor-in-Chief:
Dave Shaut

Executive Editor:
Scott Person

Associate Acquisitions Editor:
Sara Glassmeyer

Outside Development Services:
Margaret Maloney

Content Project Manager:
Anne Sheroff

Senior Marketing Manager:
Mark Linton

Senior Technology Project Manager:
Matt McKinney

Senior Manufacturing Communications Manager:
Jim Overly

Senior Manufacturing Coordinator:
Charlene Taylor

Art Director:
Linda Helcher

Cover Designer:
Pop Design Works

Printer:
West
Eagan, Minnesota

Library of Congress Control Number:
2007920594

For more information about our products,
contact us at:

Thomson Learning Academic Resource
Center
1-800-423-0563

Thomson Higher Education
5191 Natorp Boulevard
Mason, OH 45040
USA

The author would like to thank the following reviewers for their comments and suggestions:

Gregory J. Dunn – Columbus, Georgia
Thomas Gillett – Snellville, Georgia
Barbara Krueger – New Berlin, Illinois

CONTENTS

Introduction

Additional exposure to the material and repetition will improve your confidence and help alleviate "exam anxiety." The more you know, the less stress you will have when taking the test. There is no magic wand or "smart pill" you can take, but if you follow these guidelines, we think you will be successful.

General Study Hints

Use questions in your book more than once. Write your answers on a separate sheet of paper. This will make scoring easier as you compare your answers with the answer key in the back of this book, and leave the questions unmarked for additional "practice" retakes. This will also work with your regular textbook and any other practice exams you might decide to use.

Practice taking timed tests. Duplicate the testing situation by practicing the questions under pressure. This is one of the best ways to overcome exam anxiety. Based on the time allowed on the state examination, your goal should be to complete 50 questions per hour. Missed items quickly pinpoint your weak areas and help focus your attention on them for additional study.

Research wrong answers. First, carefully read the explanation in the answer key. Determine why the correct answer is correct and the other "distracters" are not. Try not to memorize individual questions, as this may cause you to miss subtle wording differences on the exam, thereby causing you to answer incorrectly. You need to concentrate on concepts, not exact phrasing.

Pace your studying. Immediately test yourself after class discussion. Look up wrong answers. Remember that last-minute cramming before the state licensing exam may cause you to panic when confronted with difficult material or to become overly tired during the exam. Do not get behind in your studying; it is difficult to catch up.

Limit your study time. Most people more easily recall the first and last part of whatever they study, while the middle material becomes a little muddled. It is better to study for 10 to 20 minutes with breaks rather than for a solid hour.

Get a good night's sleep before the test. A proper amount of sleep will help you think more clearly and avoid errors from just being tired. "Pulling an all nighter" will just make you tired and often more confused.

Know where you are going. If you are going to a test site in another town, know how to get there and give yourself lots of extra time. Do not add to your frustration by being late!

Know the testing rules. Review your state examination guide to be sure you know how you will be tested and the general process. There are generally a few sample questions in the guide, as well as a list of content to be tested. There should also be a chart of how many questions will be asked in each general category.

Last-minute study. Your last-minute study should include definitions from your regular text for the national portion and the key point review for the Illinois portion from this booklet. If you struggle with a given topic, don't waste time trying to master it at the very end. Move on and review the material with which you are more familiar.

Test Taking Strategies

1. **Read the question.** Some students go so far as putting a huge "RTQ" on some scratch paper to remind them. It is imperative to know what is being asked. Look for words like NOT or EXCEPT or INCORRECT. In math questions, the numbers provided may be monthly, but the question is seeking an annual number. Make sure you understand the question before you look at the answers.

2. **Read the answers.** Go through the 4 choices. Look for ones that can be easily eliminated. Some students put "A B C D" on a sheet of paper for tougher questions and physically mark through incorrect answers as they are eliminated. If you can eliminate 2 answers, you now have a 50-50 chance, even if you have to guess. You might want to approach a multiple choice question as 4 separate True/False questions — you are looking for the True answer.

3. **Review your answer.** When done, review by reading the question and the answer you picked, asking yourself, "Does this completed sentence make sense?" If it is a "story problem," put yourself in the story. Does the correct answer make common sense to you? On math problems, put the answer back into the formula. Also, is the answer logical? It wouldn't make sense for a $100,000 home to have annual real estate taxes of $50,000.

4. **Make sure you immediately record your answer.** Many students find that silly mistakes, such as recording "B" instead of "D" on their answer sheet, will cost them a point or two.

5. **Manage your time during the exam.** Go through the entire exam in order, answering the questions that come easily. If you are in doubt or do not know the answer, skip it and move on. Many students use 45–60 minutes to answer about 70% of the questions. This leaves plenty of time to focus on the remaining 30%. On computerized exams, there should be an indicator of how many questions have been answered and how much time is remaining.

6. **Manage your panic.** Better yet, don't panic! As you go through the exam the first time, remember that it is normal to leave about one out of four questions blank. When you come to a question that stumps you, remember that subsequent questions may jog your memory or provide answers to earlier questions; look for that help. Remember that you can miss 1 of every 4 questions and still pass.

7. **Stay comfortable and avoid stress.** Lean back in your chair and roll your neck occasionally. If necessary, get up and stretch or use the restroom. Staying comfortable will help you stay focused on the test itself. By the way, the small camera that may be on top of your computer station is there to take your picture for licensing — it is not there spying and constantly watching you as some students believe!

8. **Math problems.** Keep all of your work for each problem in one area, circle the work, and label it with a number. That way, you can quickly review your work if needed. Start by developing the formula. For example, on a tax question you might want to write down:

Assessed Value x Tax Rate = $Taxes Paid

You will always be given two of the numbers and be asked to solve for the third:

50,000 x Tax Rate = $4,000.

To solve this formula, the $4,000 is divided by 50,000 to obtain the correct answer. However, if you panic and forget how to solve it from this point, you can replace the Tax Rate with all 4 possible answers to see which one works. Regardless, make sure your selected answer will fit into the formula and produce the correct answer.

It is possible to calculate an incorrect answer that matches one of the answers on the inches to feet, or feet to yards, misplace a decimal point, or similar common mistakes. Don't lose points over simply being careless or sloppy.

9. **Don't get stuck on any one question or problem.** Rather than dwell on a single problem, you could be answering several more questions to which you DO know the answer. Also, a later question may provide you with a clue or answer to the bypassed one. Get out of negative thinking and move on to the next question.

10. **Don't change an answer.** Unless you find an obvious mistake, such as an incorrectly recorded answer or misread question, do NOT change your original response. First instincts are correct more often than changed answers. Be 100% sure if you are going to make a change.

11. **Answer all questions.** Before handing your test in, or indicating on your computer that you are finished, be sure every question as an answer. If you are out of time, mark one answer for each randomly. It can only help your score.

12. **Congratulations — you've passed!** If so, you may want to let your instructor know. If you fail for some reason, before leaving the test site, write down questions or areas that need more study. You may forget many of these if you wait until you get home.

National Exam Outline

Topic	Number of Questions	
	Salesperson	**Broker**
Listing Property	34	31
Listing		
Assessment of Property Value		
Services to the Seller		
Selling Property	22	21
Services to the Buyer		
Advising Buyers of Outside Services		
Property Management	12	14
Leasing and Management		
Settlement/Transfer of Ownership	17	14
Tax Issues		
Titles		
Settlement Procedures		
Completion of the Transaction		
Financing	12	10
Sources of Financing		
Types of Loans		
Terms and Conditions		
Common Clauses and Terms in Mortgage Instruments		
Professional Responsibilities/Fair Practice/Administration	<u>3</u>	<u>10</u>
	100	100

Content Outline: Listing Property

A. Listing Property

1. Legal description
2. Lot size
3. Physical dimensions of structure
4. Appurtenances (for example, easements and water rights)
5. Utilities
6. Type of construction
7. Encumbrances (for example, liens, encroachments, restrictions)
8. Compliance with building codes
9. Ownership of record
10. Homeowners association documents and expenses
11. Brokerage fee
12. Property taxes

Key Point Review: Listing Property

- The process used by the owner of real property to retain the services of a real estate broker to sell or lease property
- Property is listed through the use of a listing contract
- Brokers are not employees of the seller, but rather are independent contractors
- Parties to the listing contract are all of the owners and the broker
- Sales associates are not parties to the listing contract
- There are three types of listing contracts: Open Listing, Exclusive Agency Listing, and Exclusive Right To Sell Listing
- Listing contracts must have a beginning and ending date
- An agency relationship is created between the owner and broker when a
- listing contract is signed
- A net listing is not a type of listing contract and is illegal in many states
- A multiple listing is not a type of listing contract
- Multiple listing services provide brokers a way to share listings with other
- brokers

Listing

- Agents should verify all information possible before including it in the listing contract
- Both the owner and the broker can be legally liable for inaccurate or incorrect information

Legal Descriptions

- Real property must be described in such a way that it cannot be confused with any other parcel of real property in the world
- and in such a way that it can be precisely located
- Legal descriptions vary from state to state and some states use more than one method for describing real property
- There are three methods to describe real estate: metes and bounds;
- lot and block; and government survey system
- Metes and bounds descriptions use distances and directions and must have a beginning point and an ending point that are the same point; that is, a metes and bounds description must "close"
- An example of part of a metes and bounds description would be:

"Beginning at a point at an iron pin on the east side of a private road corner to T. C. Johnson, said point being S 68° 45" E 40.5' from a stone at a corner to Williams and Wilkerson, said stone being S 89° 30" E 50', S 37° 50" E 100' from the center of the Madison Ave...."

- Lot and block descriptions are used in subdivisions that are platted
    An example of a lot and block description would be:

"Being all of Lot 7, Block E, in the Best Subdivision of Lexington, Fayette County, Kentucky, as shown on plat of record in Plat Cabinet 130, at Page 789, in the office of the Fayette County Clerk to which reference is made for a more particular description."

- Government survey system is also known as a rectangular survey system and as a geodetic survey system. Most of the United States use this system
- The government survey system uses townships, sections, principal meridians, and ranges to describe the land. An example of a government survey system description would be:

"The NE ¼ of the NE ¼ of Section 12, Township 8 North, Range 6 East of the Fifth Principal Meridian, Jefferson County, IL.

- A legal description must be included in the listing contract
- Depending on the custom in the area, the description in the listing contract may be only the mailing address
- The listing contract must clearly identify the property being listed

Lot Size

- Lot size is stated with the <u>road frontage being used as the first number</u>, e.g.,a lot size that is stated as 100' by 150' has road frontage of 100' and a depth of 150'
- Surveys determine the exact size of the lot
- Plats show lot dimensions
- An acre contains 43,560 square feet

- Deeds contain lot dimensions, but may be incorrect because newer survey techniques provide greater accuracy than older methods
- Subdivisions may require a certain lot size before an improvement can be built on the lot
- Zoning designations may require the lot to be a certain size
- Broker and seller may be legally liable for misstating lot size to a buyer

Physical Dimensions of Structure

- Structures on property are also referred to as improvements
- Steps to determine square footage:

    1. draw a diagram of the structure and divide the structure into rectangles, squares, and triangles
    2. measure the outside of the structure
    3. only measure the part of the structure that is above grade (belowground level or "below grade" should be calculated and stated as a separate measurement when listing and marketing property)
    4. place measurements on drawing
    5. calculate square footage for each rectangle, square, and triangle, then add the amounts together to find the total
    6. deduct square footage in garages, porches, patios, and other non-livable areas

- Square footage for a rectangle and square is found by multiplying length times width
- The formula for determining the area of a triangle is to multiply the base times the height and divide by two
- Broker and seller may be liable for misstating square footage of the structure

Appurtenances

- All tangible and intangible items attached to land are known as appurtenances and include rights and privileges attached to the land
- Deeds convey all interests in appurtenances on the land, unless it
- specifically excludes one or more of them
- Listings should include information about the appurtenances and whether there are costs associated with them
- Examples: easements, water rights, right to use parking spaces in shopping center
- Types of easements include: appurtenant easement, easement in gross, easement by necessity, and easement by prescription
- Types of water rights include: percolating, riparian, surface, littoral
- Water can create accretion, alluvion, avulsion, and reliction
- Doctrine of prior appropriation is applied in areas where water is scarce
- Listings should include information about the water sources on the
- property and whether or not flooding has occurred

Utilities

- Utilities include government services, e.g., sanitary and storm sewers, and private services to property, e.g., electricity, water, gas, telephone, and cable

- Property owners pay for utility services either directly to the private company or to the government through taxes and assessments
- Utility availability affects the value, marketability, desirability, and use of the property
- Listings should specifically include what utility services are available and the costs for same

Type of Construction

- Architectural styles for residential construction include ranch (one-story floor plan), one-and-a-half story, two-story, and split level. Styles have facades that may make the dwelling look entirely different from others of the same style
- Each style may include a basement that may or may not be finished into living area
- There are four types of roof styles: gable, hip, gambrel, and mansard
- Although real estate agents are not required to be construction experts, when listing a property the broker should inspect the property for obvious problems and deferred maintenance

Encumbrances (e.g., liens, encroachments, restrictions)

- A right or interest in a parcel of property held by someone other than the owner of the property
- Encumbrances are "clouds" on real property title
- An encumbrance on property prevents it from having a "clean" or "clear" title
- Encumbrances may lessen the fair market value of the property
- Property may be transferred with the encumbrance; however, the encumbrance usually remains attached to the property and the new owner is subject to it
- Encumbrances may affect the title to the property or may affect the use of the property
- Examples of encumbrances that affect title include liens, taxes, judgments, licenses
- Examples of encumbrances that affect the use of the property include easements, subdivision restrictions, governmental restrictions, and encroachments
- Encroachments are always encumbrances, but encumbrances are not always encroachments

Compliance with Building Codes

- Building codes are regulations established by the government that set minimum standards for building construction. Not all areas have established building codes.
- These codes are land use controls set by the government to protect the health, safety, and welfare of the public
- Building codes include specific codes for plumbing, electrical, and fire
- Building design, construction, location, maintenance, use, and occupancy are all items that are covered by building codes
- In areas with building codes, builders must obtain building permits before beginning construction
- A Certificate of Occupancy must be obtained before the building is occupied. The Certificate is designed to assure property owners that the building codes have been followed.

- Civil fines and criminal penalties may be imposed on builders who fail to comply with the building codes
- Listings should include all information known by the agent relating to the property and building code violations

Ownership of Record
- Ownership of land passes by deed and by will
- Title passes by deed and by will, even if the deed or will are never recorded
- Evidence of title is the deed or will and should be recorded in the public records to give constructive notice
- Constructive notice gives public notice of ownership
- Grantees have constructive notice of recorded documents even if they never see the recorded documents
- Grantees have an affirmative duty to protect their interests by looking at recorded documents
- Constructive notice is not the same as actual notice

Homeowners Association Documents and Expenses
- Homeowners associations typically have officers or a management company that enforces restrictive covenants, collects assessments, and manages common areas
- All property owners are members of the association and have voting rights
- Homeowners associations may operate as unincorporated associations, or may form corporations or limited liability companies
- Documents that govern homeowners associations depend on the form of organization, but generally include declaration of restrictions, bylaws, rules and regulations, and a master deed (for condominiums)
- Property owners are usually required to pay association fees either monthly, quarterly, or annually to maintain the common areas, including clubhouses, swimming pools, and tennis courts; management fees for the association; legal fees to enforce the restrictive covenants and collect the association fees; and other association expenses
- Association fees may become liens on the property if they are not paid
- Listings should clearly set forth information about the homeowners association, including any amounts homeowners are required to pay

Brokerage Fee
- Brokers are paid according to the terms set forth in the listing agreement
- Fees are typically paid by the seller, but may be paid by a third party or the buyer pursuant to the terms of the listing contract
- Brokerage fees may be calculated in any manner the broker and seller agree upon, except they cannot legally agree on a net listing, which are illegal in most states
- Fees are typically a percentage of the selling price, a flat fee, or fees for each service provided
- Fees are generally paid at closing for property that has sold
- Fees for leasing property are paid either at the time of signing the lease or at set periods through the lease term

- Brokerage fees are not paid unless the broker is successful in consummating the transaction by either selling or leasing the property
- Brokers may be paid the brokerage fee when a seller refuses to consummate a transaction that meets the terms of the listing contract
- All brokerage fees are negotiable between the owner and broker
- Under the anti-trust laws, it is illegal for brokers to conspire to "fix prices" for the brokerage fee

Property Taxes

- Property taxes are also known as general estate taxes and ad valorem taxes
- Ad valorem taxes are based on a property's assessed value
- These taxes are placed on property by the state and local governments for the benefit of the government
- Property taxes are the single largest source of government revenue. The assessed value is determined by the assessor, also known as the property valuation administrator. Assessed values are determined based on a comparison of values of other properties in the area
- Taxes are based on the assessed value, and they can be as much as 100% of that value
- To find the tax amount, multiply the assessed value by the tax rate
- Tax rates may be stated in dollars or mills
- Senior citizens and disabled property owners may have a reduced tax assessment
- Ad valorem taxes are always a lien on the property and have the first lien priority
- Property taxes are generally prorated between the buyer and seller at the time of closing the transaction
- Listing agents should explain to the owner that property taxes must be current when the property is sold and that unpaid taxes will affect the net proceed to the seller

Content Outline: Listing Property

B. Assessment of Property Value

1. Location
2. Anticipated changes (e.g., zoning and use)
3. Depreciation
4. Deterioration (e.g., physical)
5. Obsolescence (e.g., usefulness, outdated characteristics)
6. Improvements (e.g., additions)
7. Economic trends
8. Market data

Assessment of Property Value

- **Warning!** Assessment of property value usually relates to property taxes or special assessments levied by the government for items such as sewers, street lights, and sidewalks. This testing service, based on analysis of the examination outline, appears to use "assessment" instead of "appraisal" when discussing the value of property. Section 1(B) includes terminology and principles used in appraising and not in assessing. Those taking the test should be aware of this difference in the language. Many textbooks refer to this information as "valuation" of property

- Appraising is the process used by an appraiser to form an opinion of the fair market value of property using factual data in the market place
- States license and/or certify appraisers
- Real estate agents listing property should know the basics of appraising in order to prepare a comparative market analysis for the seller at the time of listing to give the seller some idea of the property's value
- There are various types of value placed on property, including assessed value, fair market value, insurance value, mortgage loan value, condemnation value, book value, liquidation value, value in use, and investment value
- When valuing property one must keep in mind the purpose for the valuation

Location

- Location of property is also known as its situs
- A major consideration for valuing property is its location
- Other elements are used to form an opinion of value over time, but the land's location will not change

Anticipated Changes (e.g., zoning and use)

- Value of property can change because of the expectation that changes are going to occur for the property being valued or for adjacent property that will either increase or decrease the value of the subject property. This is sometimes referred to as speculation value
- A zoning change, either for the property being appraised or for a neighboring property, can dramatically increase or decrease the property's value
- Either the use of the property or the use of a neighboring property can change the value of the subject property

Depreciation

- Depreciation occurs when improvements to property lose value for any reason
- Land does not depreciate
- Depreciation can be curable or incurable
- There are three types of depreciation: physical, functional, and external
- Depreciation can be calculated through the straight-line method by using the improvement's economic life
- Investment property is said to depreciate for tax purposes when, in fact, actual depreciation has not occurred

Deterioration (e.g., physical)

- Physical deterioration is one of the factors that leads to the property value depreciating
- Deterioration that is physical can be curable or incurable

- If repair to the improvement would be economically feasible or if it would contribute to the comparable value of the property, the deterioration is curable; otherwise it is incurable
- Physical deterioration may be caused by wear and tear and deferred maintenance, as well as by catastrophic events like fires, floods, tornadoes, and hurricanes

Obsolescence (e.g., usefulness, outdated characteristics)

- Obsolescence can be either functional or external
- Functional obsolescence occurs when elements of the structure are
- outdated, useless, or undesirable because of advances in
- construction, improvements to systems, and changes in desirability
- Functional obsolescence may be either curable or incurable
- Whether the obsolescence is curable or incurable depends on the economic feasibility of making necessary changes
- A kitchen with few cabinets and poor plumbing would probably be curable, while moving the kitchen from one location in the house to another may be incurable
- External obsolescence refers to negative factors not located on the property that are unlikely to improve
- External obsolescence is sometimes referred to as locational obsolescence
- This type of obsolescence will always be incurable because the owner cannot do anything on his property to change the adjacent property, e.g., a pig farm operating next door would be an example of external obsolescence

Improvements (e.g., additions)

- Improvements are immovable, permanently attached, objects added to the land. Improvements may not always increase the value of the real estate
- House, buildings, barns, fences, streets, sidewalks, trees, and flowers are all examples of improvements
- Improvements can also be items added to currently existing structures on the property

Economic Trends

- Value of property can be affected positively or negatively with changes in the economy
- Economic factors, including interest rates, taxes, employment levels, company relocations, and population growth in the area, all affect the value of real estate
- Property value depends on utility, scarcity, transferability, and effective demand
- In good economic times real property values tend to increase, while in bad economic times the values either stay the same or decrease
- Lower interest rates tend to increase the values of real property because there are more buyers who can qualify to purchase property, while higher interest rates stagnate or decrease property values

Market Data

- The market data approach to determining value of real property is also referred to as the comparison approach and the comparative analysis approach

- This is the primary approach to rendering an opinion on the fair market value of real property
- The market data approach compares the "subject" property to other properties in the area with similar characteristics that have sold recently
- Properties used in comparison are known as "comparables" or "comps"
- Adjustments are made to the sales prices of the comps when they are either inferior or superior to the subject
- The market data approach determines a value based on what the market will be willing to pay based on what they have actually paid for comparable properties
- An active market gives a more reliable estimate of value under the market data approach
- Another approach sometimes used in conjunction with the market approach is the cost approach
- The cost approach determines a value based on purchasing the land and reproducing the improvements on it
- The income approach, also referred to as the capitalization approach, is used to determine value of income producing property.

Content Outline: Listing Property

C. Services to the Seller

1. Responsibilities of the licensee and the listing firm
2. Property subdivision
3. Hidden defects known by the owner
4. Information about required disclosures (e.g., lead based paint)
5. Property included in and excluded from sale (e.g., land, minerals, water, crops, fixtures)
6. Personal property and real property differences
7. Net proceeds estimation
8. Completion of listing agreement, provision to seller, explanation
9. Determination that parties holding title have signed listing agreement
10. Showing of house and safeguarding property
11. Methods of marketing property
12. Presentation of offers to the seller
13. Property tax information
14. Transaction files
15. Deed restrictions and covenants
16. Forms of ownership interests in real estate, issues related to conveyance of real property
17. Fair housing laws
18. Comparative market analysis—sales comparison approach
19. Comparative market analysis—income derived from property use
20. Independent appraisal necessity
21. Inspection necessity

22. Non-ownership interests in real property (e.g., leasehold interests of tenants)
23. Planning and zoning (e.g., variance, zoning changes, and special study zones such as floods and geological hazards)

Services to the Seller

- The owner of the property retains the services of the real estate broker to sell or lease the property

Responsibilities of the Licensee and the Listing Firm

- The licensee listing the property is working for the seller
- Included in listing licensee responsibilities to the seller are:
  - educating the seller on the selling process
  - advising the seller on the fair market value of the property
  - assisting the seller in setting the listing price and advising the seller on "fix-up" and "clean-up" to increase marketability
  - advertising the property
  - promoting the property
  - placing a sign on the property
  - showing the property to prospective buyers
  - presenting offers and counteroffers to the seller
  - assisting the seller in understanding the offers and counteroffers
  - assisting the seller in making counteroffers
  - explaining the offer's terms and conditions to the seller
  - assisting the seller in meeting all contract deadlines
  - answering all questions for the seller from the contract to closing/settlement
  - attending the closing/settlement
  - answering questions which may arise after the closing/settlement

Property Subdivision

- Property subdivision is the process of dividing land into smaller
- tracts/parcels, usually for development purposes
- Subdividing land may be subject to government regulations, including planning and zoning regulations
- Plats are prepared to show the land after it has been subdivided
- Real estate licensees typically do not subdivide land for sellers, unless they are specifically in the business of developing land and hired for that purpose

Hidden Defects Known by the Owner

- Hidden defects are also known as latent defects. Latent defects are defects in the property not easily discovered by an ordinary inspection of the property
- Sellers are required to disclose known hidden defects
- Some states require agents to discover and disclose hidden defects to prospective buyers
- Patent defects are the opposite of latent defects in that they are obvious defects

Information about Required Disclosures (e.g., lead-based paint)

- Many states have seller "disclosure of property condition forms" that licensees must ask the seller to complete when listing property
- Federal law requires sellers and landlords to complete a lead-based paint disclosure form before selling or leasing residential property if the house was constructed prior to 1978
- When lead-based paint forms are required, they must be attached to sales contracts and leases
- Agents should provide the property owner with the lead-based paint forms, and, once completed, a copy of the form should be kept in the agent's file

Property Included in and Excluded from Sale (e.g., land, minerals, water, crops, fixtures)

- When listing property for sale, agents should specifically include in the listing contract personal property that is to be either included in or excluded from the sale of the real property
- Subsurface mineral rights may be severed from the surface rights
- Timber rights may be sold separately from the land
- Growing crops that are planted each season (known as emblements) are personal property and do not transfer with the land unless specifically included in the sales contract
- Fixtures are personal property that have been affixed to the real estate in such a way that they becomes part of the real estate and pass with the deed
- Trade fixtures typically do not become part of the real property
- Sales contracts should also include personal property that will be included or excluded from the sale of the property

Personal Property and Real Property Differences

- Personal property is everything that is not real property
- Personal property may be tangible or intangible
- Examples of tangible personal property include furniture, draperies, outside storage buildings that are not attached to the ground, window air conditioners that are not permanently attached to the window, slide-in kitchen ranges, and freestanding book shelves
- Examples of intangible personal property include contract rights,
- easements, licenses, and water rights
- Real property is always tangible
- Personal property may become real property
- Examples of personal property that may become real property include mobile homes that are permanently attached to the ground, built-in dishwashers, antennas, curtain rods, fences, and plumbing fixtures
- Real property may become personal property
- Examples of real property that may become personal property include dirt
- that is removed from the property, timber that is cut, minerals that are
- removed from the land, and drywall that is removed from a building
- Real property is transferred by deed

- Personal property is transferred by a bill of sale

Net Proceeds Estimation

- When presenting offers, listing agents should calculate and estimate the
- net amount the seller will receive at closing/settlement
- Informing sellers of the estimated amount of the net proceeds will enable sellers to make an informed decision on accepting or countering the offer
- Sellers often ask the listing agent to list the house for a price that will net the sellers a certain amount after the real estate commission is paid
- To determine the listing price when the seller wants to net a certain amount after the real estate commission is paid, the listing agent should subtract the commission percentage from 100% then divide the amount desired by the remaining percentage
- To calculate the net proceeds, the agent must subtract all of the seller's costs from the gross amount being paid by the buyer
- Included in the seller's costs will be the real estate commission, prorated property taxes, property transfer taxes, buyers costs that the seller has agreed to pay, and the seller's current mortgage

Completion of Listing Agreement, Provision to Seller, Explanation

- Agents should explain in detail each provision of the listing contract,
- including how it affects the seller
- The real estate commission to be paid to the listing broker should be
- clearly outlined in the listing contract
- State laws require that the listing contract have a definite term – a
- beginning date and an ending date
- Special instructions from the seller to the listing broker should be included in the contract
- To protect the broker from the seller selling the property to a person brought to the property by the broker, the broker often includes a carryover clause, which is also known as an extender clause, safety clause, or protection clause
- Terms that should be included in a listing contract include the:
  - right to advertise the property, including placing a sign on the property
  - right to place a lock box on the door
  - seller's warranty of title
  - seller's agreement to cooperate and make the property available to prospects
  - seller's agreement to pay the real estate commission
  - seller's and broker's agreement that neither will violate the fair housing laws
  - broker's agreement to give her best efforts to sell/lease the property signatures of both the seller and broker
- The entire agreement between the listing broker and seller must be included in the listing contract
- Sellers should be given a copy of the listing contract once it is signed

Determination that Parties Holding Title Have Signed Listing Agreement

- One of the most important tasks of the listing licensee is to make sure
- all parties with an interest in the property sign the listing contract
- A place to start is with the current deed; however, depending on state law,
- all of the title holders may not be on the deed.
- For example, the deed may not have the spouse's name; in the cases of death or divorce and remarriage, the correct spouse's name may not be on the deed; or when the owner has died, the owner's last will and testament may give the names of the person or people inheriting the property
- In the event of death without a will, the applicable state statute controls who owns the property
- The best procedure for the listing agent to follow is to look at all available documents, and, in the event of doubt, an attorney should be consulted

Showing of House and Safeguarding Property

- In many areas the listing agent must be present when the property is shown, but, and in other areas, he is only present at the request of the seller
- Sellers may allow the use of a lock box to give agents access to the
- property
- Listing agents should advise sellers to remove, or at least hide, valuables
- before making the property available to prospective buyers
- All agents showing property should make sure the property is locked when
- they leave
- Although vacant property may generally be shown without an appointment, agents should get an appointment to show occupied property

Methods of Marketing Property

- The listing broker should develop a marketing plan for each property listed
- Property may be marketed through the use of signage, open houses; advertising in newspapers and magazines, on television, on radio, on the internet, and by direct mail

Presentation of Offers to the Seller

- The offer is prepared by either the buyer, the buyer's real estate agent, or the buyer's attorney
- If the offer is prepared by the real estate agent, the agent must use a form
- Offers are typically presented to the seller by the seller's agent
- The custom in many areas is for the seller's agent and buyer's agent to meet with the seller and present the offer to the seller
- In the event the seller's agent and buyer's agent present the offer together, the buyer's agent is generally not permitted to be present when the seller and the seller's agent discuss the offer
- Fee for service brokerages and limited service brokers may have a contract with the seller that provides for the buyer or buyer's agent to present the offer directly to the seller without the seller's agent being present

- Buyers' agents would present offers directly to the seller if the seller does not have an agent and is acting as a "For Sale By Owner"
- If the seller accepts the offer as written, a contract is formed
- To form a contract, the offer accepted by the seller must be identical to the offer made by the buyer (this is sometimes referred to as the "mirror
    - image" rule)
- The seller may counter the offer to the buyer, reject it without a
- counter, or hold the offer and neither accept, reject, or counter it -- in which case the offer expires either on the time and date included in the offer or by a reasonable time if no date is given in the offer
- If the seller wants to make a counteroffer, the seller's agent assists the seller in making the counteroffer
- The seller's decision should be communicated by the seller's agent to the buyer's agent or directly to the buyer if the buyer does not have an agent

Property Tax Information

- A listing agent should explain proration of property taxes to the seller when listing the property and when presenting the offer
- Proration of taxes can either increase or decrease the net proceeds to the seller at closing/settlement
- If the seller has paid the taxes, the buyer will refund to the seller prepaid taxes that will accrue after the seller sells the property, thereby increasing the net proceeds to the seller
- If the seller has not paid taxes for any period of ownership, the seller will pay the buyer those amounts at the time of closing/settlement, thereby decreasing the net proceeds to the seller
- Property taxes that are owed by the seller and are unpaid must be paid at closing unless the buyer agrees to accept the property without the seller paying her share of the taxes

Transaction Files

- Most states require that the seller receive a copy of all documents he signs at the request of the real estate agent
- State laws require that the real estate broker keep files for each transaction for a set period of time
- The required period of time for keeping files varies from state to state

Deed Restrictions and Covenants

- Deed restrictions and covenants are private land use controls placed on the land by the owner
- These restrictions and covenants may be placed by the owner on one lot or may be placed as part of a general plan for an entire development
- The owner placing the restrictions and covenants on the land wants to limit the way all future owners use the land

- Deed restrictions may be recorded in the deed conveying the property, or may be recorded separately in a document called Deed of Restrictions, Declaration of Restrictions, Restrictive Covenants, or other similar title
- Once recorded in the public records, deed restrictions run with the land for an indefinite period of time
- Deed restrictions cannot be imposed on a property in violation of the fair housing laws
- Termination of restrictions and covenants may occur
  - if the document creating them has a termination date
  - by a unanimous vote of the landowners
  - over time if the restrictions are violated and no legal action is taken to enforce them
  - the neighborhood changes to the point that the restrictions are meaningless
- Once recorded, the restrictions must be followed by new owners even if they did not have actual notice of them prior to purchasing the property
- Tenants leasing in a deed restricted area must follow the restrictions even if they were unaware of the restrictions when entering into the lease
- Examples of deed restrictions include:
  - number of dwellings that can be on the land
  - types of animals that can be kept on the property
  - materials for the facade of structures
  - minimum size of the house and other improvements on the land
  - if a detached garage is permitted on the lot
  - whether or not fences are permitted, and if so, the types of fence permitted
  - paint colors for exterior of house
  - colors of roofs
  - whether or not a boat can be parked in the driveway
- These restrictions are usually enforceable by either the developer, by the homeowner's association, or by any of the property owners
- Listing agents should ascertain from the owner if listed property is subject to deed restrictions

Forms of Ownership Interest in Real Estate, Issues Related to Conveyance of Real Property

- The form of ownership of real property determines who must sign the listing contract, the sales contract, and the deed
- Real property may be owned individually or jointly
- Joint ownership, also known as concurrent ownership, may be with or without survivorship
- For a more detailed review of forms of property ownership, including what is necessary to create them and convey them, refer to Section 2(A)(3) in this exam guide

Fair Housing Laws

- There are federal, state, and local fair housing laws
- Federal fair housing laws: Civil Rights Act of 1866 and the Fair Housing

Act of 1968, with its 1974 and 1988 amendments
- The fair housing laws prohibit discrimination in matters related to housing
- Racial discrimination is prohibited under the Civil Rights Act of 1866
- Protected classes under the fair housing laws include: race, color, religion, national origin, sex, mental or physical handicap, and familial status
- Some areas have a newly created protected class of sexual orientation
- Discrimination is prohibited in selling, renting, advertising, financing, appraising, and insuring residential property
- Steering, blockbusting, panic pedaling, discriminatory advertising, and redlining are illegal acts under the fair housing laws
- All prospects for buying and leasing property must be treated the same and the same information must be given to all of them
- Terms of sales contracts and leases cannot be changed based on the fact that the buyer or tenant belongs to one or more of the protected classes
- Discrimination cases may be filed by the aggrieved party in the federal district court
- The Department of Housing and Urban Development can file a formal charge against a person allegedly discriminating in a housing transaction
- The U.S. Attorney General may initiate an action in the public interest
- Sanctions for violation of the fair housing laws include: injunctions; damages, including punitive damages; fines; and prison sentences
- Fines that may be imposed by Administrative Law Judges are: $11,000 for the 1st offense, $27,500 for the second offense within 5 years, and $55,000 for the third offense within 7 years
- There are certain exemptions under the 1968 Fair Housing Act; however, none of them apply if a real estate agent is involved in the selling or renting of a dwelling, or if discriminatory advertising has been used
- There are no exemptions under the Civil Rights Act of 1866
- Real estate licensees may be penalized by their licensing agencies for violating fair housing laws

Comparative Market Analysis – Sales Comparison Approach

- A comparative market analysis (CMA) using the sales comparison approach compares the subject property with similar properties (comps), that have sold in the same general area in the recent past
- Adjustments are made to the comps to reach an estimated fair market value for the subject property
- This is the same approach used by appraisers in their "market data" approach to appraising
- Listing agents should prepare a CMA to give the seller an idea of the fair market value of their property

Comparative Market Analysis – Income Derived from Property Use

- The comparative market analysis using the income approach is also referred to as the capitalization approach
- This approach to value is used for properties that produce income

- Present value of the property is estimated by using a capitalization rate (cap rate)
- An operating statement includes the income, vacancy rate, and expenses
- Net income is determined by subtracting the estimated vacancy losses, the fixed expenses, the operating expenses, and the replacement reserve from the estimate potential gross income
- The formula for finding value under the income approach is to divide the annual net income by the capitalization rate

Independent Appraisal Necessity

- Independent appraisers may be retained to form an opinion of the fair market value for property
- The Uniform Standards of Professional Appraisal Practice (USPAP) sets the standards to which appraisers must conform
- Lenders typically want an independent opinion of the fair market value of property on which they are making mortgage loans
- Not all appraisers are licensed or certified
- Appraisers completing appraisals for federally related entities must be licensed or certified
- Federally related transactions include mortgage loans that are sold in the secondary market to FNMA, GNMA, or FHLMC, and transactions that are FDIC insured

Inspection Necessity

- Sellers may want to have a property inspection prior to listing property
- to alert them to defects in their property
- Buyers generally have property inspections to protect themselves from defects in the property that may not be disclosed by the seller because either the seller was unaware of the defect or chose not to share the information with the buyer
- A sales/purchase contract may be contingent upon the results of a property inspection

Non-Ownership Interests in Real Property (e.g., leasehold interests of tenants)

- A tenant, also known as a lessee, has the right to possess and use the leased property for a period of time
- The leasehold estate is sometimes referred to as a lease
- Landlords, also known as Lessors, own the property and give up the right of possession during the term of the lease
- Leasehold interests are non-ownership possessory interests in land
- Leasehold interests are personal property, not real property
- There are four types of leasehold interests: estate for years, estate from period to period, estate at will, and estate at sufferance
- Easements are non-ownership non-possessory interests in land that give the holder the right to use the land for a particular purpose
- The landowner also retains the right to use the land
- Written easements run with the land

- Easements are classified as appurtenant easements, easements in gross, easements by necessity, and easements by prescription
- A license is a non-ownership non-possessory interest in land
- Licenses are personal property and not real property
- The licensee has the privilege to use the land of the licensor
- A licensee may be required to pay for the privilege or it may be free at the discretion of the licensor
- Licensors may revoke the license at any time
- Licenses terminate upon the death of either the licensor or the licensee
- Example of licenses include: using land for hunting or fishing, entering a movie theater or amusement park, or placing a billboard on property

Planning and Zoning (e.g., variance, zoning changes, and special study zones such as floods and geological hazards)

- Zoning is a governmental police power used to regulate the use of land
- Cities and counties have planning programs to provide for the orderly growth and development of land
- Municipalities often have comprehensive plans, also referred to as master plans, that are created to provide a plan for future land development
- Planning and zoning functions go hand in hand in developing land
- Changing a parcel of land's zoning may drastically change its value
- Although zoning changes may depreciate the value of land, the governmental unit making the change is not required to compensate the landowner for the decrease in value
- Zoning ordinances set out the zoning classifications and the requirements for each classification
- Zoning maps show the zoning designations for each area of the city or county
- Residential, commercial, agricultural, light and heavy industrial, manufacturing, and professional office are some of the zoning designations
- Zoning authorities have the right to grant variances to landowners who want to use their land for a purpose that does not conform to the current zoning
- Property owners may petition the zoning commission to change zoning designations for their property
- Each zoning commission has a process for property owners to request a zoning change
- Nonconforming uses may be permitted by the zoning authority
- Planned Unit Developments, also known as PUD's, are a form of mixed use zoning
- PUDs allow for higher density use of the land, thereby providing more green space
- A PUD may have single family and multi-family residential, professional office space, and small retail stores all in the same area
- Planned Unit Developments have recorded covenants and restrictions as well as property owner associations that manage the common areas
- Zoning requirements may include buffer zones, aesthetic zoning, incentive zoning, and bulk zoning

- Spot zoning is illegal when used for the sole purpose of benefiting one landowner; however, it may be legal if used for the public good
- The National Flood Insurance Act of 1968 was passed to assist property owners who have property damaged by flooding
- FEMA administers the flood program, and it has designated certain areas as flood-prone areas
- The Army Corps of Engineers has prepared maps that show the areas prone to flooding
- Property owners in the flood designated areas may buy flood insurance.
- If they choose not do so and their property is damaged by a flood, they will not receive government assistance
- To obtain federally-related mortgage financing or financing that will be sold in the secondary market for property located in the flood prone area, buyers must purchase flood insurance
- If the landowner can prove that the improvements on the property are above the 100-year flood mark, many lenders will waive the flood insurance requirement
- Flood insurance is purchased from private insurance companies
- Landowners should inspect their properties to the extent possible to determine if any geological hazards exist
- Examples of geological hazards include sinkholes, cliffs, quicksand, and underground water sources
- Sellers should make their agents aware of known geological hazards on the property when listing the property for sale

Key Term Match: Listing Property

Work on mastering real estate language by matching the following terms with the correct definition. For additional key term matching exercises, see Appendix A.

Terms

A. Survey

B. Plat

C. Acre

D. Easement by necessity

E. Encroachment

F. Easement in gross

G. Appurtenances

H. Appurtenant easement

I. Declaration of restrictions

J. Accretion

K. Annexation

L. Doctrine of prior appropriation

M. Avulsion

N. Encumbrance

O. Above grade

Definitions

1. _____ The part of the improvement that is above the ground level.

2. _____ Loss of land caused by running water, such as a stream or creek.

3. _____ The process used to determine property boundaries that is performed by a registered professional engineer or registered land surveyor.

4. _____ (1) The process of adding area to a city; (2) the process of affixing personal property to real estate.

5. _____ A water system found in dryer states that gives the government control over water adjacent to property.

6. _____ A limitation on the owner's rights in his real property.

7. _____ Everything that is attached to the real estate.

8. _____ A map of a city, town, subdivision, on other parcel of land that has been divided into lots.

9. _____ A measurement of land containing 43, 560 square feet.

10. _____ The personal right to use someone else's property.

11. _____ An easement involving adjoining parcels of land known, respectively, as the dominant estate and the servient estate.

12. _____ A recordable document, generally prepared and recorded by the developer, that states the limitations, conditions, and covenants that affect a parcel of land.

13. _____ The process of acquiring additional land because of gradual accumulation of rock, sand, and soil when the land fronts on a lake, river, or ocean.

14. _____ An easement granted by the court for ingress and egress that will prevent a property from being landlocked.

15. _____ An improvement that crosses the boundary line.

Practice Questions: Listing Property

1. An owner wants to hire a real estate broker to sell her property while keeping the right to sell it herself, will sign a/an

A. open listing.
B. exclusive agency contract.
C. net listing.
D. exclusive right to sell contract.

2. Because Mr. Seller is out of town, Broker Bob had only Ms. Seller sign the listing contract for jointly owned property. Ms. Seller said her husband would sign the deed. Is this an acceptable practice?

A. Yes, because a wife can always obligate her husband to sign the deed
B. Yes, because it is important for Broker Bob to get the property advertised.
C. No, because Mr. and Ms. Seller own the property as tenants in common.
D. No, because all owners must sign the listing contract.

3. A seller is contemplating placing his property on the market. He wants to get maximum exposure. His BEST option would be to

A. co-list his property with a number of different brokers.
B. use an open listing that would encourage all of the area brokers to sell the property.
C. list with a broker who uses the multiple listing service.
D. list the property with a different broker each week.

4. When Sally went to list property for Mr. and Mrs. Seller it was raining really hard. Sally obtained the lot dimensions and square footage of the house from the sellers, but did not look at a plat or measure the house. She prepared her listing and information for the MLS based on the unverified information from the sellers. Sally's actions were

A. appropriate, because Sally is not surveyor or an appraiser.
B. appropriate, because it is the sellers' responsibility to know the lot size and the square footage of the house.
C. inappropriate, because Sally is required by law to measure the lot to determine its exact size.
D. inappropriate, because Sally has the duty to make sure information on the listing is verified when possible.

5. Property legal descriptions include all of the following types EXCEPT

A. metes and bounds.
B. lot and block.
C. county clerk survey.
D. government survey.

6. A township has how many square miles?

A. 24
B. 640
C. 63
D. 36

7. A lot that is 186' x 244' x 210' x 242' has how many feet along the road?

A. 244'
B. 186'
C. 210'
D. 242'

8. A home is situated on a lot that is 100' x 200'. The house is a ranch with a total square footage of 2,800, including unlivable area of 450. There is a swimming pool covering 673 square feet and a driveway covering 160 square feet How many square feet of the lot are not covered by improvements?

A. 15,917
B. 20,000
C. 16,367
D. 17,200

9. When in doubt about the size of a lot, the BEST thing to do is

A. ask the sellers if they are absolutely positive.
B. ask an attorney to look at the deed.
C. ask the seller to hire a surveyor.
D. look at the property valuation records.

10. Mr. Black wanted to build a new office building containing 6,000 square feet on the first floor. His building lot is 200' by 550'. The sidewalks, parking lot, and driveway will take up 3,200 square feet. The zoning designation for the area requires at least two acres for green space. Will he be able to meet the zoning requirement?

A. Yes, because he will have about 2.3 acres for green space.
B. Yes, because he will have about 2.5 acres for green space.
C. No, because he will only have 1.9 acres for green space.
D. No, because he will only have ½ acre for green space.

11. Carlos listed a two-story brick house with a partially finished walk-out basement. He measured the house and determined that the house had 1,980 square feet on the two top floors and 876 square feet finished in the basement. The owner had finished the basement and it was as nice as the top two floors. What square footage should Carlos use in his listing for the gross living area?

A. 1,890
B. 2,856
C. 1,104
D. 1,980

12. Jacob purchased property that had hundreds of trees, three barns, and miles of fencing on it. He was concerned when he discovered that the deed did not list the trees, barns, and fences as part of the purchase price. Does Jacob have reason for concern?

A. No, because those items are appurtenances that do not need to be listed.
B. No, because it would be too hard for the seller to remove those items.
C. Yes, because those items are appurtenances that do need to be listed.
D. Yes, because the seller has 30 days to return to the property and remove the trees.

13. The type of easement that requires two parcels of property is

A. easement by prescription.
B. appurtenant easement.
C. easement in gross.
D. easement by necessity.

14. If a landowner wants to have utility service on the land, the utility company is likely to require

A. a license from the landowner.
B. written permission from the neighbors.
C. an easement by necessity.
D. an easement in gross.

15. A couple have just purchased a farm along the river. Their water rights are known as

A. littoral.
B. running.
C. riparian.
D. percolating.

16. Accretion is the process where water

A. adds land to the shore line.
B. removes land from the shore line.
C. pollutes the land and makes it unfit for farming.
D. is prevented from percolating into the ground.

17. Availability of utilities to a property may affect all of the following EXCEPT

A. marketability.
B. value.
C. use.
D. insurability.

18. Four basic architectural roof styles are

A. gable, hip, gambrel, and mansard.
B. gable, hip, slate, and gambrel.
C. hip, gable, truss, and mansard.
D. mansard, slate, truss, and gable.

19. A lien is an

A. easement.
B. encumbrance.
C. encroachment.
D. none of the above.

20. Silas has just listed a house. According to the seller, he has been sued by a former employee who has received a judgment against him. Is this information important to Silas?

A. Yes, because the employee may place a lien on the property before closing.
B. Yes, because the employee may take ownership of the house before it closes.
C. No, because employee law and real estate law are not related in any way.
D. No, because the seller has plenty of time to file an appeal before the house sells.

21. Building codes set

A. maximum standards for construction.
B. minimum standards for construction.
C. acceptable standards for construction.
D. guidelines for builders who wish to follow them.

22. After construction of a home is complete, prior to the new owner taking possession, the builder must obtain a

A. deed.
B. building permit.
C. certificate of completion.
D. certificate of occupancy.

23. Carlos met with a widow to list her late husband's property. The widow gave him a copy of the deed with only her husband's name on it and a copy of her husband's obituary. Based on this information, Carlos asked her to sign the listing contract for the estate. Carlos' actions were

A. appropriate, because the widow now owns her husband's property and is administering the estate.
B. appropriate, because the obituary was constructive notice that her husband had died.
C. inappropriate, because he does not know who owns the property and who is administering the estate.
D. inappropriate, because he needed to see a death certificate not an obituary.

24. Recording a deed

A. conveys title.
B. gives constructive notice.
C. is only required in certain situations.
D. gives actual notice.

25. Mr. and Mrs. Adams moved into a new house. Their agent had informed them there were restrictive covenants creating a homeowners association for the neighborhood and informed them of the association fees that must be paid. After meeting with the officers of the association, the Adams decided they did not want to belong to the association. Their decision

A. will be honored by the homeowners association.
B. will be honored by the association if at least 2/3 of the other property owners agree.

C. will not be honored by the homeowners association.
D. will not be honored by the homeowners association unless 75% of the owners agree.

26. The governing document for a homeowners association is the

A. master deed.
B. bylaws.
C. articles of incorporation.
D. restrictive covenants.

27. Brokerage commissions are

A. set by the local board of REALTORS®.
B. agreed upon among the brokers in a 100 mile radius.
C. negotiated between the seller and broker.
D. standard in each area.

28. A broker is charging 7% or $7,500, whichever is less. The house is listed for $155,000, and sells for $135,000 after the broker has paid $750 in advertising costs. How much commission will the broker receive?

A. $9,450
B. $10,100
C. $7,500
D. $6,750

29. Property taxes are based on the

A. fair market value.
B. purchase price.
C. assessed value.
D. contract price.

33

30. A property is assessed for $150,000 and has a fair market value of $156,000. The tax rate is 20 mills. Taxes are paid in two equal installments in June and December. How much will the homeowner pay in each installment?

A. $3,000
B. $3,120
C. $1,560
D. $1,500

31. An owner who wants to hire someone to give her an independent opinion of the fair market value of her property would call

A. an assessor.
B. an appraiser.
C. a surveyor.
D. a real estate broker.

32. One of the most important elements in the fair market value of property is its

A. prior selling price.
B. amenities.
C. location.
D. tax assessment.

33. Mr. Green has recently heard that a new automobile manufacturer is looking to relocate to his area. He knows about a 200-acre farm that is near the farm the manufacturer is looking to buy. If he buys the property with the intention of trying to sell it to the company later, he is operating on the principle of

A. appreciation.
B. highest and best use.
C. market value.
D. anticipation.

34. Ed and Bob are looking to buy investment property. It has an economic life of 15 years. The asking price is $225,000. The have agreed to pay $210,000 for the property which has a land value of $30,000. They are borrowing $175,000 from the bank. Using the straight line method of depreciation, their annual depreciation will be

A. $14,000.
B. $11,667.
C. $15,000.
D. $12,000.

35. Amanda goes out to list property. When she arrives she notices that some of the shutters on the front of the house are missing and that the guttering needs to be painted. The missing shutters and the paint are examples of

A. functional obsolescence.
B. physical deterioration.
C. external deterioration.
D. external obsolescence.

36. Marla is showing property to her buyers that has only one bathroom. The bathroom is really nice and has been recently remodeled. To reach the bathroom you must walk through the master bedroom. This room arrangement is an example of

A. incurable functional obsolescence.
B. curable functional obsolescence.
C. internal functional obsolescence.
D. physical deterioration that is incurable.

37. Property owners are getting ready to build a swimming pool that will cost about $25,000. They are selling the property next year and are confident they will be able to recover the full cost of installing the swimming pool and may even make a profit. Their analysis about the likelihood of recovering their investment for the pool is

A. correct, because swimming pools always increase the value of property.
B. correct, because the value of their property will appreciate before next year.
C. incorrect, because swimming pools do not always add dollar-for-dollar value to property.
D. incorrect, because the value of their property will depreciate before next year.

38. A clothing company in a small community has recently closed and relocated to another area. The company terminated the employment of 200 people and took 250 employees to its new location. Real estate values in the area where the company closed will likely

A. decrease.
B. not be affected.
C. increase.
D. not enough information given.

39. The subject property in an appraisal has a garage, but does not have a fence. One of the comparable properties does not have a garage, but has a fence. The comparable property sold for $152,900. A garage has a value of $9,500 and a fence has a value of $1,500. In using the comparable sales approach, how much would the value of the comparable

property be reduced.

A. $11,000.
B. $8,000.
C. $9,500.
D. $1,500.

40. When appraising a residential property for a family, the best appraisal method is

A. cost approach.
B. comparable sales approach.
C. income approach.
D. economic approach.

41. The listing agent should do all of the following for the seller EXCEPT

A. educate the seller on the selling Process.
B. advertise the property.
C. review the settlement statement with the seller.
D. arrange for the seller's homeowner's insurance to remain in effect.

42. Mario listed property in the new Marshes Subdivision and he wanted to include the lot dimensions with his listing. The BEST place for him to locate the lot dimensions is on the

A. property assessment.
B. subdivision plat.
C. independent appraisal.
D. zoning map.

43. Last year when the seller cleaned her swimming pool, she noticed a small crack in the corner near the diving board. She had the pool inspected and the repair person said the pool did not need to be fixed at that time, but probably would in the future. Does Ms. Seller need to disclose the crack in the pool?

A. Yes, because it is a patent defect
B. Yes, because it is a latent defect
C. No, because it is a latent defect
D. No, because the repair person said it did not need to be repaired

44. Under the lead-based paint federal law, a disclosure form must be completed by the seller for houses constructed

A. prior to 1978.
B. after 1978.
C. prior to 1987.
D. after 1987.

45. When Barney listed property for Mr. and Mrs. Farmer he learned that shortly after they purchased the property they sold the mineral rights to ABC coal company. According to Mr. Farmer, the mineral rights would be returned to the new owners within three years from the date of purchase. Barney's best action would be to

A. include this information in the listing.
B. ask the sellers to see their contract with the coal company.
C. discuss the matter with his principal broker.
D. leave it out of the listing because it will automatically happen in three years.

46. After the sellers purchased their property, they built a storage building in the back yard. The building has a foundation and concrete floor. When the sellers move, is it TRUE that they

A. may take the storage building if the buyer does not want to buy it.
B. may remove the building as long as they leave the concrete pad.
C. must take it with them because it is not an appurtenance in the deed.
D. must leave it with the property because it is a fixture.

47. All of the following are tangible personal property EXCEPT

A. window air conditioner.
B. water rights.
C. freestanding book shelves.
D. furniture.

48. The sellers sold their property for $185,000. They had to pay off their current mortgage of $92,000. Their expenses included 6.25% real estate commission, $250 in legal fees, and they owed $832 in prorated taxes. Based on these amounts, their net proceeds will be

A. $185,000.00.
B. $80,355.50.
C. $92,750.00.
D. $173,437.50.

49. The seller wants to net $155,000 after she pays the 5.75% real estate commission. Her agent informs her that the property should sell for 95% of its listing price. What is the BEST listing price to achieve the seller's goal?

A. $164,500
B. $156,250
C. $173,125
D. $172,675

50. Listing contracts should contain all of the following EXCEPT

A. permission to advertise.
B. signature of broker.
C. beginning date.
D. sales price.

51. Alonzo is listing a farm owned by six heirs. One of the heirs, Richard, has been living in the farmhouse and taking care of the estate. When Alzono goes to list the house, Richard signs the listing and informs Alzono that the other heirs will sign next week. Which of the following is Alonzo's next step?

A. Call the other heirs to make sure they agree to sign the listing next week.
B. Place the sign in the yard, but wait until next week to start marketing the house.
C. Tell Richard that the other heirs do not need to sign the listing because he is handling the estate.
D. Wait until all heirs sign the listing before placing a sign in the yard.

52. When listing property, the listing agent should inform the seller to do all of the following EXCEPT

A. allow anyone calling for an appointment at least 24-hours in advance to look at the property.
B. place all valuables in a safe place or remove them from the premises.
C. only allow prospective buyers accompanied by their agent to look at the house.
D. leave pets in a safe place in the house to prevent them running out the door.

53. The most effective form of advertising is the

A. yard sign.
B. internet.
C. homes magazine.
D. newspaper.

54. The party making the offer is known as the

A. offeror.
B. offeree.
C. agent.
D. licensee.

55. When accepting an offer, the acceptance must be

A. the mirror image of the offer.
B. signed by the agent.
C. delivered back to the buyer within 24 hours.
D. signed by at least one of the owners.

56. At closing, tax prorations will

A. have no effect on the seller's net proceeds.
B. will have to be paid by the seller at Closing.
C. will either increase or decrease the net proceeds to the seller.
D. will either increase or decrease the net proceeds to the buyer.

57. Property taxes for the year are $2,874.76 and are based on a 365-day calendar year. The amount of taxes for August is

A. $263.28.
B. $236.28.
C. $244.16.
D. $220.53.

58. After the closing, the broker must

A. keep all records for 7 years.
B. keep only the contract and closing statement for 5 years.
C. keep the listing contract, sales contract, and closing statement for only 3 years.
D. keep all records for the period of time required by state licensing laws.

59. Sam purchased property in a deed restricted subdivision. He has received a letter from the homeowner's association stating that he is in violation of the restrictions because he has a large antenna for his short wave radio on the end of his house. Which of the following is TRUE?

A. He must remove his antenna because it violates the restrictions.
B. He must remove his antenna because it is dangerous.
C. He can keep his antenna, because of his constitutional right to free speech
D. He can keep his antenna, because of his first amendment rights

60. Deed restrictions are an example of

A. governmental interference with our rights.
B. private land controls.
C. unconstitutional restraint on alienation.

D. governmental land controls.

61. Bill and Elizabeth owned property as joint tenants with right of survivorship. When Bill died, Elizabeth married Alex. Alex died before Elizabeth. When Elizabeth died, Alex's children

A. inherited his one-half of the property.
B. inherited no interest in the property.
C. inherited a life estate interest in the property.
D. inherited the property as tenants in common with Elizabeth's children.

62. The Civil Rights Act of 1866 only has one protected class which is

A. age.
B. race.
C. creed.
D. sex.

63. Fair housing laws are designed to

A. give everyone the opportunity to choose where they want to live.
B. balance the population in certain areas.
C. keep real estate agents from steering and blockbusting.
D. prevent discriminatory advertising in the newspapers and on the radio.

64. Redlining is a discriminatory practice of

A. real estate appraisers.
B. insurance agents.
C. real estate agents.
D. mortgage lenders.

65. The BEST use for a comparative market analysis is

A. to inform property owners of the recent sales in the area.
B. to assist the seller in deciding on a listing price.
C. to convince buyers that they are not paying too much for the property.
D. to assist appraisers in their efforts to meet the contract price.

66. An owner is trying to calculate his net operating income for his 24-unit apartment building. Each apartment rents for $850 per month. The vacancy loss is five percent, his fixed expenses are $24,480, his operating expenses are $76,500, and his replacement reserve is $5,000. Based on these numbers what is his net operating income for one month.

A. $11,568.33
B. $20,400.00
C. $126,580.00
D. $10,548,33

67. The cap rate for an office building is 8%. It has a vacancy rate of 7%, an annual gross income of $180,000 and an annual net operating income of $81,000. Fair market value under the income approach is

A. $1,157,142.86
B. $1,126,000.00
C. $1,237,500.00
D. $1,012,500.00

68. Is it true that appraisers cannot perform appraisals unless they are licensed or certified?

A. Yes, they must be licensed or certified to perform all types of appraisals.

B. Yes, an unlicensed appraiser cannot appraise property of any kind unless she works with a review appraiser.
C. No, an appraiser who has performed at least 100 appraisals, under the direct supervision of a licensed appraiser, is grandfathered and is exempt from licensing.
D. No, only appraisers that perform appraisals for federally related transactions must be licensed or certified.

69. Appraisal standards are known by the acronym of

A. FNMA.
B. USPAP.
C. USRA.
D. RESPA.

70. Buyers are relocating across country. They've visited their new city and made an offer on property. They will be unable to come back to the new city until the day of closing. Their BEST option to ascertain the condition of the property is to

A. carefully review the seller disclosure form prepared by the seller.
B. ask their agent to go through the house and make notes of the condition.
C. hire a licensed property inspector to inspect the house and to prepare a written report.
D. hire a licensed appraiser to inspect the house, establish a fair market value, and give them a written report.

71. Non-ownership interests in land include all of the following EXCEPT

A. life estates.
B. easements.
C. licenses.
D. leases.

72. Farmer Brown told the owner of the local radio station that he could place a billboard on his property. Unfortunately, at night the light on the sign is so bright it lights up his house. He has asked the radio station to do something about the light and they refuse. Can Farmer Brown make the radio station remove the billboard?

A. Yes, he gave the radio station only a license and it can be revoked.
B. Yes, because the sign is clearly a nuisance to the landowner and all neighbors.
C. No, because he gave the radio station an easement that runs with the land.
D. No, the radio station has a leasehold interest that continues for at least one year.

73. A tenant has a lease that begins on May 1st and ends on April 30th. If the tenant wants to move on April 30th, she is

A. required to give the landlord at least a 30-day notice
B. not required to give the landlord any notice before moving
C. required to give a notice to avoid losing her security deposit
D. is required to notify the landlord at least 15 days before the end of the lease.

74. When a municipality wants to provide for the orderly development of its land, it will prepare

A. a comprehensive plan.
B. a plat of the area.
C. an assessment of the land to determine its value.
D. an assessment of the land to determine if it can be developed.

75. A popular form of mixed use zoning is a

A. condominium with limited common area.
B. planned unit development.
C. restricted neighborhood with multi-family housing.
D. flood plain that has been developed with retention basins.

Content Outline: Selling Property

A. Services to Buyer

1. Relationship and responsibilities of licensees and selling firm to buyer
2. Rights of ownership, e.g., bundle of rights
3. Types of ownership, e.g., joint tenancy and tenancy in common
4. Determination of buyer's price range and eligibility for various types of financing
5. Identification of property that meets buyers' needs and specifications
6. Current market conditions
7. Showing properties to prospective buyers
8. Characteristics of property
9. Material facts concerning property, e.g., taxes, zoning, building codes and other land use restrictions
10. Physical condition of property. e.g., defects and environmental hazards
11. Psychological impact related to property
12. Income tax implications of home ownership
13. Tax implications for real estate investments
14. Required disclosure statements
15. Sales contract forms and provisions, including contingencies
16. Recommendation that buyer seek legal counsel
17. Preparation of offers and counteroffers
18. Presentation of offers and counteroffers
19. Planning and zoning, e.g., variance, zoning changes, and special study zones such as floods and geological hazards
20. Availability of home protection plans
21. Need for insurance. e.g., fire, hazard, liability
22. Policy for complying with fair housing laws

Key Point Review: Selling Property

Services to the Buyer

Relationship and Responsibilities of Licensees and Selling Firm to Buyer
- Licensees may be retained by buyers to represent them when purchasing property
- If the licensee is representing the buyer, the licensee owes fiduciary duties to the buyer
- Fiduciary duties include the duties of accounting, loyalty, disclosure, obedience, confidentiality, due care and diligence
- A buyer may be represented by the licensee when the licensee is sharing in the real estate commission being paid by the seller

- Buyers may decline representation by the agent, in which event the buyer is the customer of the agent
- Agents must be fair and honest with their customers
- Licensees may also represent both the buyer and seller in one transaction
- When licensees represent both parties in a transaction they are known as dual agents
- Informed consent is required by both the seller and buyer in a dual agency relationship
- When acting as a dual agent, the licensee owes fiduciary duties to both clients
- Dual agents cannot disclose the buyer's confidential information to the seller, or disclose the seller's confidential information to the buyer

Rights of Ownership (e.g., bundle of rights)
- Ownership rights in property are known as the owner's estate
- When taking title to property the grantee receives all of the ownership interests in the property held by the grantor
- Ownership of property gives the grantee certain rights in the property
- Rights in property include, among other things, the right to hold title, to convey title, to sell, to give away as a gift, to mortgage, to lease, to grant easements, to grant licenses, and to devise by will
- Each right is commonly referred to as a "stick." When the grantee receives all of the rights in the property from the grantor, it may be said that the grantee received the "whole bundle of sticks" or "bundle of rights"

Types of Ownership (e.g., joint tenancy and tenancy in common)
- Real property may be owned individually or concurrently
- Individual ownership is known as sole ownership or ownership in severalty
- Although an individual owns property in severalty, depending on state law, he will need his spouse's signature to convey the property
- Individually owned property is still subject to state laws relating to dower and curtesy interests, and homestead rights
- Simultaneous ownership of property by two or more people is known as concurrent ownership or co-ownership
- Types of joint ownership includes: tenants by the entirety, tenants in common, joint tenants with rights of survivorship, and community property
- Certain unities of title are required to create the different types of co-ownership
- Unities include: time, title, interest, and possession
- The type of ownership becomes important in the event of the death of one of the co-
- Owners
- Tenants in common ownership:
  - are created when two or more people hold the title simultaneously
  - each co-owner has an undivided interest in the property
  - the only unity required is that of possession
  - each owner's share does not have to be equal
  - owners are equally responsible for expenses
  - one owner may convey her title to the property, or pledge her share

- o one owner can obtain a loan, without the consent of the other co-tenants
- o when one owner dies, his share of the title passes to his estate, not to the co-owners
- Joint tenancy with right of survivorship:
  - o is created when two or more people hold title concurrently
  - o requires all four unities to be created
  - o owners interests must be equal
  - o owners are equally responsible for expenses
  - o when one owner dies, her share of the title passes to the surviving owners
  - o when one owner transfers her interest, the new owner becomes a tenant in common, with the remaining owners as joint tenants
  - o a joint tenant cannot leave his interest in the property in his will to someone other than the joint tenants – a will cannot change the survivorship element of a joint tenancy with right of survivorship (JTWROS)
- Tenancy by the entirety:
  - o co-tenants must be husband and wife
  - o only the principal residence can be held in the entirety
  - o when one spouse dies, the survivor takes the entire title
  - o one owner's last will and testament cannot change the survivorship element in a tenancy by the entirety
  - o the concurrent ownership is terminated by divorce
  - o after a divorce, the former spouses own the property as tenants in common
- Community property:
  - o applies in a few states
  - o in these states a husband and wife must take title to property as community property
  - o upon the death of one spouse, that spouse's one-half interest will descend to her heirs and not to the surviving spouse
- Life estates may be created to give a person, known as the life tenant, the right to use real property for her lifetime
  When the life tenant dies, her interest in the property is extinguished, and the property passes to the remainder interest
  Life estates may be created by reservation or grant
- A life estate *pur autre vie* creates a life estate for one person while being measured by the life of another
- Real property may have combination forms of ownership, sometimes referred to a multiple ownership
- Examples of combination forms of ownership include condominiums, cooperatives, planned unit developments (commonly referred to as a PUD), timesharing (also known as interval ownership)
- A combination form of ownership includes property that has parts of it that are owned individually and parts that are owned in common
- The interior of the condominium unit (sometimes referred to as from paint-to-paint) is owned individually or jointly, and the outside of the unit is owned "in common" with all of the property owners
- Entities other than individuals may own real estate

Examples of non-individual entities include sole proprietorships, corporations, general partnerships, limited partnerships, limited liability companies, syndications, trusts, joint ventures (also referred to as joint adventures), and real estate investment trusts (commonly abbreviated as REIT)

Documents creating non-individual entities have provisions for transferring real estate, including designation of the individual authorized to sign the deed when property is conveyed

Determination of Buyer's Price Range and Eligibility for Various Types of Financing

- In order to purchase property, the buyer must have an income, a good credit rating, not too many liabilities, and a down payment
- A review of the income and liabilities, as well as the amount of monthly payment the buyer will feel comfortable paying, should give the agent a good idea of the price range to show the buyer
- Many lenders now use credit scores to qualify buyers for mortgage loans
- Credit scores take into account the income, debts, and credit history of the borrower
- Buyers should be informed that lenders have certain income-to-debt ratios that must be met before a loan will be approved
- Agents should be familiar with various types of financing in order to answer buyer's questions, at least generally
- VA loans, FHA loans, first time homebuyer's loans, and other special programs should be discussed with the buyers to give them a familiarity with the financing process
- When beginning the home buyer process, the agent should try to identify the type of property the buyer wants to buy
- Location is often a very important consideration for buyers. The buyer chooses where he wants to live and agents must avoid unlawful steering of buyers to certain areas

Current Market Conditions

- Licensees should stay abreast of the market conditions
- Agents should make buyers aware of interest rates and whether they are increasing or decreasing

Showing Properties to Prospective Buyers

- One of the most important tasks of the buyer's agent is to locate properties to show a buyer that meet the buyer's needs
- Once properties are selected to be shown, the agent should make the necessary appointments to show the property
- When showing properties, the agent should point out the amenities and other positive factors of the property, but should also point out any negative factors
- Buyers should be given ample opportunity to preview the property
- Agents should be aware of safety factors for themselves when meeting new people to show property, as well as safety factors for their buyers

Characteristics of Property

- Characteristics of the property, both good and bad should be pointed out to the buyers
- One of the important value characteristics is whether or not the property will be transferable
- If a buyer wants to purchase a property that may not be readily transferable, that fact needs to be given them
- Utility is also an important characteristic. If the agent knows that the property will not meet the needs of the buyer, that information needs to be disclosed to the buyer

Material Facts Concerning Property (e.g., taxes, zoning, building codes and other land use restrictions)

- Agents have a duty to disclose all material facts to the buyer about the property
- Material facts do not include only facts about the improvements on the property, but also facts about the property taxes, zoning, building codes, and land use restrictions
- Agents should either supply the tax information or should refer the buyer to the taxing authority to obtain the information on property tax assessments and rates
- Zoning should be verified, either by the agent or the buyer. If the agent thinks a property may not be properly zoned, that information should be given to the buyer
- Building codes change frequently; however, it is important for the buyer to know if the structure does not meet the building codes
- Although the seller is not usually obligated to make improvements to the property to bring it into compliance with all of the building codes, buyers need to know what is not in compliance
- Agents should either provide the buyer with copies of the subdivision or deed restrictions, or should inform the buyer where they can obtain such information
- Subdivision and/or deed restrictions may severely limit how the property many be used

Physical Condition of Property (e.g., defects and environmental hazards)

- When showing property, agents should point out to the buyers any defects in the property of which they are aware
- Buyers should be made aware that there are cosmetic defects and more serious structural defects in property
- Different areas have different environmental hazards. Licensees should be aware of the environmental hazards in their particular community and make the buyers aware of those hazards
- Buyers should be given the opportunity, when making an offer on property, to include a provision for testing the property for environmental hazards

Psychological Impact Related to Property

- Properties may be stigmatized by something that has happened in the property that has no actual bearing on the condition of the property
- Examples of such stigmas include properties where murders and suicides have taken place, and where ghosts are said to reside
- State laws vary on whether or not these stigmas must be disclosed to the buyer. Some states require the stigmas be disclosed only if the buyer asks, while others require disclosure even if the buyer does not ask
- Disclosure of whether or not someone living in the house is HIV positive, or if someone has died because of an AIDS, is a violation of the fair housing laws

Income Tax Implications of Home Ownership

- See the material relating to Section 4(A) in this exam guide for a review of the tax implications of home ownership.

Tax Implications for Real Estate Investments

- Buyers of investment property should be referred to their CPAs for specific information on the tax implications of real estate investments
- See the material relating to Section 4(A) in this exam guide for a review of the tax implications of real estate investments

Required Disclosure Statements

- There are state and federal disclosure statements that agents must use
  - Agency disclosure forms are used to inform prospects, clients, and customers about agency relationships in a real estate transaction
  - Some of the forms explain agency, while others create agency
  - Agents should be familiar with their state forms
- Many states also use seller disclosure of property condition forms
  - These forms are designed to ask the seller to inform the agent and prospective purchasers about the condition of the land and its improvements as well as any information sellers may know about the title to the property
  - Seller disclosure forms have proven to be very helpful to agents in defending themselves in lawsuits, but care must be taken to let the seller furnish the information if the agent is to receive the liability protection
- Federal law requires the lead-based paint disclosure for property built prior to 1978
  - The agents duty is to furnish the form and ask the seller to complete it
  - Sellers must disclose knowledge about lead based paint in their properties, but they are not required to remove the paint

- o Agents must also deliver the form to the buyer and ask them to sign stating they received the form
- Lenders are also required to make disclosures under the Truth-in-Lending Act and Real Estate Settlement and Procedures Act

Sales Contract Forms and Provisions, including Contingencies

- Most states permit licensees to complete form sales contracts
- Agents who are not also lawyers should only complete forms and not draft forms, because drafting legal documents, without a license to practice law, is the illegal practice of law
- Agents should remember that the contracts belong to the parties, and only the parties (and not the agents) may modify the form contracts as they choose
- Sales contract forms vary from state to state and often from broker to broker; however, there are certain provisions that are typically included:
  - o Names of buyer and seller
  - o Signatures of the buyer and seller
  - o Property description
    - some areas use the address of the property
    - some areas use the full legal description
    - some areas use deed book and page references
  - o Date of the contract
  - o Sales price and how it will be paid
    - down payment
    - commercial financing or cash
    - seller financing
  - o Personal property that is to remain with the real estate, as well as personal property, to be removed by seller
  - o Earnest money deposit (also referred to as good faith deposit), how it will be held, and released
  - o Financing terms
  - o Closing date
  - o Possession date, and whether or not seller will pay rent if she stays in the property for a period of time after the closing
  - o Agency relationships
  - o Whether or not taxes, assessments, and rents will be prorated
  - o Whether or not the buyer will have property, wood destroying pests, or environmental inspections
  - o If the buyer is having any inspections, how repairs will be handled
  - o Buyer walk-through inspection prior to closing
  - o Risk of loss prior to closing (which party will carry the property insurance until closing)
  - o Default clause (what will happen if one party does not perform under the contract as agreed)
  - o Type of deed to be delivered by seller

- Sellers' warranties
- Transfer of builder and manufacturer's warranties
- Other legal terms that the parties want to include
- Whether or not the contract is assignable
- Whether or not the parties heirs, successors, or assigns are bound to perform in the event of death or other disability
- Whether or not addenda (riders or exhibits) are attached
- Contingencies, if any
  - financing
  - inspection
  - attorney approval
  - buyer selling current property
  - seller's acquisition of another property
  - buyer's transfer becoming effective
  - seller clearing title defects

Recommendation that Buyer Seek Legal Counsel

- Agents should recommend that the buyer seek legal advice before signing the offer to purchase since this document will ultimately become the sales contract
- If the buyers decline to seek legal advice before signing, the agent should include a contingency in the sales contract giving the buyers a period of time to have an attorney review the contract
- If the buyer declines to have an attorney review the contract, the agent should have the buyer sign a waiver showing the agent recommended the review

Preparation of Offers and Counteroffers

- When the buyer wants to make an offer on the property, she is known as the offeror
- The party receiving the offer, usually the seller, is known as the offeree
- Typically, the offer form is completed by the buyer's agent, although occasionally the seller will make the offer
- The buyer's agent should consult with the buyer on what terms the buyer wants to include in the offer
- When the offer is presented, if the seller wants to make changes to the terms before accepting the offer, the seller or seller's agent prepares a counteroffer
- Once the counteroffer is presented to the buyer, the buyer may make a counteroffer to the seller in which event the buyer's agent assists the buyer in writing the counteroffer
- After the original offer is written, the counteroffers are typically changes to the original offer, although a completely new offer could be written by the party making the counteroffer

Presentation of Offers and Counteroffers

- Once the offer is written by the buyer, it is presented to the seller
- In some areas, the offer is delivered by the buyer's agent to the seller's agent, and the seller's agent presents it to the seller
- In other areas, the buyer's agent and the seller's agent meet with the seller together and the buyer's agent presents the offer to the seller
- State laws generally require that the offers be delivered without delay (as soon as possible) to the seller, and likewise, that counteroffers be delivered back without delay
- When an offer is presented and countered by the seller, the counteroffer is a rejection of the original offer
  - Each time the counteroffer is countered, that is a rejection of the prior counteroffer. i.e., the party rejecting the offer by countering with his own offer must remember that the prior offer is no longer in existence and he cannot automatically go back and revive that offer if the offeror of the rejected offer does not agree to do so
- Once an offer or counteroffer is presented, it may be accepted, rejected, countered, or held
- The offeree is not legally required to respond to an offer or counteroffer
- Once the offer or counteroffer is accepted, that acceptance must be communicated to the offeror
- An offer or counteroffer may be withdrawn by the offeror before being accepted by the offeree
- Once an offer or counteroffer is accepted, an executory contract is created, and it remains an executory contract until it is performed, at which time it becomes an executed contract

Planning and Zoning (e.g., variance, zoning changes and special study zones such as floods and geological hazards)

- Buyers are very concerned about the property's zoning, because improper zoning may make it impossible to use the land for the buyer's intended purpose
- If zoning changes are required before property can be used by the buyer for a specific purpose, the buyer should consider the cost of securing a zoning change in the price that is offered to the seller
- Although zoning changes and variances are possible to obtain, a buyer should either write a contract contingent upon those changes or make certain prior to writing the offer that the changes are a certainty
- For a complete review of variances, zoning changes, and special study zones such as floods or geological hazard, please refer to Section 1(C) of this exam guide.

Availability of Home Protection Plans

- Home protection plans, also referred to as home warranties, are plans designed to protect the buyers against defects in the house they purchase. The warranties may be purchased for new construction as well as existing properties
- Homeowner's warranty plans are for a set period of time, from one year to ten years
- These plans are generally sold through the real estate agent, but may be purchased on line
- Agents selling these plans should either carefully explain the terms of the warranty, or should refer the buyer of the warranty (may be buyer or seller) to the warranty company for an explanation
- If the agents receive compensation for selling the plan, that fact needs to be disclosed to the parties to the transaction
- Some of the terms have caused confusion and led to lawsuits against the agents who sell them
- Important terms of some of the plan that need to be explained:
  - Pre-existing condition clauses
  - Deductibles
  - Specific repair services must be used
  - Prior notice before repair
  - Exclusions
  - Transferability of the plan

Need for Insurance (e.g., fire, hazard, liability)

- Some state laws say the seller retains the risk of loss if the property is damaged or destroyed during the contract period, while other states say the risk of loss passes to the buyer at the time the contract is signed. The sales contract should specifically state which party has the risk of loss from contract to closing
- Regardless of the risk of loss during the contract period, homeowners always need insurance once they own the property
- Homeowner's insurance is generally included in the owner's monthly mortgage payment as an item escrowed by the mortgage lender
- Property insurance includes: fire insurance, extended coverage insurance, hazard insurance, and liability insurance
- Fire insurance will pay the insured if the property is damaged or destroyed by fire
- Extended coverage insurance protects the insured against damage or destruction resulting from acts of God (tornadoes, hurricanes, forest fires, storms, etc), friendly fires (fireplace fires), civil commotion, and vehicles
- Liability insurance pays for personal injury claims when someone is hurt on the property

- Most homeowner's hazard insurance policies are package policies that provide coverage for the structure and its contents
- In order to obtain insurance, the party purchasing the policy must have an insurable interest
- Insurance policies pay up to the face amount, and if the loss is greater than that, the property owner must incur the loss
- Homeowner's insurance policies contain a coinsurance clause that requires the property owner to insure the property for at least 80 percent of its value

Policy for Complying with Fair Housing Laws

- Property buyers, sellers, and agent must comply with the fair housing laws
- There are state and federal fair housing laws that are designed to guarantee each person the right to choose where she wants to live regardless of her race, color, religion, national original, sex, familial status, or handicap
- Some communities have added the additional protected class for housing of sexual orientation
- Agents have the duty to know, understand, and comply with the fair housing laws
- It is also important for agents to educate their customers and clients about the fair housing laws
- In the event a customer of client does not choose to comply with the fair housing laws, the agent should immediately refuse to work with that client or customer
- Brokerages should support fair housing by having the fair housing logo on signs, business cards, and advertising

Content Outline: Selling Property

B. Advising Buyers of Outside Services

1. Inspection reports
2. Survey reports
3. Appraisal reports
4. Environmental reports

Advising Buyers of Outside Services

- Real estate agents should be aware of the outside services needed by their buyers to insure that the buyers make an informed decision on the purchase of property
- Because of liability issues, it is not advisable for an agent to recommend a certain service provider; however, the agent may provide the names and phone numbers of several service providers for the buyer to call

- It is also not advisable for the agent to order services on behalf of the buyer because, in addition to the liability issues, if the buyer refuses to pay for the service, the agent may have to pay for the service

Inspection Reports

- The standard of practice in real estate is to recommend an inspection of the property by an independent inspector
- Sales/purchase contracts that provide the opportunity for the buyer to have an inspection should also contain a provision outlining what, if anything, the seller agrees to do based on the results of the inspection
- Buyers may choose a whole property inspection, while others may choose to have only certain elements of the property inspected
- Examples of specific inspections include: roof, heating and air conditioning, electrical and plumbing systems, radon, asbestos, mold, sewer, water, and wood destroying insects and damage
- Costs of inspections are usually paid by the buyer; however, the contract can specify that the seller will pay for some or all of the inspections
- Property inspectors prepare written reports of their findings for the buyer to review
- Buyers should review the reports to ascertain what repairs, if any, they are going to ask the seller to make
- A walk through inspection (sometimes referred to as a final inspection) is often made just prior to closing to ascertain that the property is in the same condition as it was at the time of contract and to inspect repairs that have been completed
- Property inspectors may or may not be licensed or certified depending on state law and regulations

Survey Reports

- If a buyer wants to know where his boundary lines are, he must have a survey performed
- Surveys are performed by registered engineers or registered land surveyors
- In the past, lenders would not make a mortgage loan without a pinned and staked survey; however, now most of them waive that requirement
- Many lenders now require some form of plat drawing that shows the lot dimensions and the improvements on the property as well as any encroachments of the improvements onto easements, building lines, and side lines
- Lenders generally require a title policy endorsement to protect them against a survey problem, but that endorsement does not protect the buyer from a survey problem that may arise
- When a survey is actually performed, the buyer and/or lender will receive a drawing of the land with the improvements, easements, building lines, and other permanent fixtures shown on it

Appraisal Reports

- Buyers often retain the services of an appraiser to give them an independent opinion of value prior to buying property
- Appraisal standards require appraisers to have a copy of the sales contract; however, the opinion of value should not be based on the purchase price shown on the sales contracts
- When an appraisal is ordered by a lender, the appraiser is working for the lender and not the buyer

Environmental Reports

- Buyers may choose to have certain environmental evaluations made
- Agents should know the environmental risks in each area and should explain those to the buyers. Environmental risks include, among other things, radon, asbestos, mold, lead based paint, water pollution, air pollution, and landfill issues
- Once an environmental assessment is made, the buyer will receive a report from the environmental engineer which should be reviewed by the buyer
- If the buyer is chooses to have an environmental assessment, the buyer's agent should provide a contingency in the sales contract for either an abatement of the problem by the seller or some other solution for the buyer

Key Term Match: Selling Property

Work on mastering real estate language by matching the following terms with the correct definition. For additional key term matching exercises, see Appendix A.

Terms

A. Home warranty

B. Credit score

C. Duty of Disclosure

D. Duty of confidentiality

E. Purchase contract

F. Presentation

G. Informed Consent

H. Walk-through inspection

I. Fiduciary duties

J. Duty of accounting

K. Duty of obedience

L. Dual agent

M. Duty of loyalty

N. Agency disclosure form

O. Duty of due care and diligence

Definitions

1. _N_ A form mandated by the real estate licensing law that must be completed by licensee notifying buyers and sellers of agency relationships.

2. _L_ Occurs in a real estate transaction in which the real estate broker represents both the seller and the buyer.

3. _J_ The fiduciary duty of the agent to inform the principal about all monies received and disbursed by the agent on behalf of the principal.

4. _I_ Responsibilities that arise in a fiduciary relationship of trust between the agent and the principal.

5. _G_ Consent that is given after the parties understand all of the ramifications of their consent.

6. _D_ The fiduciary duty of the agent to keep all of the principal's personal information confidential.

7. _F_ The process where the real estate agent, while representing the seller or buyer, delivers, explains, and assists in responding, to an offer or counteroffer.

8. _C_ The fiduciary duty of the agent to inform the principal of land that has been divided into lots.

9. _H_ The physical inspection of property that takes place immediately prior to closing to determine that the property is in the same physical condition as when the sales contract was signed.

10. _O_ The fiduciary duty of the agent to use at least the same level of skill and effort in representing the principal as another agent would use.

11. _E_ A contract for the purchase and sale of real property.

12. _M_ The fiduciary duty of the agent to protect the interests of the principal above the interests of all others, including those of the agent.

13. _B_ A method used by credit reporting agencies to determine the creditworthiness of an individual.

14. _K_ The fiduciary duty of the agent to follow all legal instructions of the principal even if the agent does not agree with the instructions.

15. _A_ A contract between a warranty company and the homeowner in which the company agrees to repair certain items for a set period of time after the sale of the house.

Practice Questions: Selling Property

1. Fiduciary duties owed a buyer client include all of the following EXCEPT

A. courtesy.
B. loyalty.
C. confidentiality.
D. disclosure.

2. An agent may only be a disclosed dual agent when he

A. sells his own listings.
B. gets the informed consent of the seller and buyer.
C. has an agency disclosure signed by both the seller and buyer.
D. writes the offer for the buyer.

3. When an agent writes an offer for a party he is not representing, that party is referred to as a

A. client.
B. customer.
C. prospect.
D. offeree.

4. Several ownership of property means the property is owned by

A. at least two people.
B. only one person.
C. a husband and wife.
D. three or more people.

5. Willie owned a farm prior to getting married, and he lives in a state that recognizes dower and curtesy interests. He has decided to sell part of the farm to an adjacent property owner. His wife is not certain he should sell any of the farm and has said she will not sign the deed. Willie:

A. may sell part of the farm without his wife's signature because he owned it prior to his marriage.
B. may sell part of the farm as long as he doesn't sell more than one-half of it because his wife owns one-half because of the marriage.
C. may not sell any of the farm unless the buyer gives his wife a first right of refusal to buy it back if he decides to sell it later.
D. may not sell any part of the farm unless she agrees to sign the deed.

6. Types of joint ownership of property include all of the following EXCEPT

A. joint tenancy with right of survivorship.
B. tenancy in common.
C. tenancy from year to year.
D. tenancy by the entirety.

7. To create a tenancy in common, the only unity that must be present is

A. unity of title.
B. unity of possession.
C. unity of interest.
D. unity of possession.

8. Property is owned concurrently by three friends. Their ownership interests are 60%, 35%, and 5%. How do they hold title?

A. Joint tenants with right of survivorship
B. Tenancy by the entirety
C. Tenants in common
D. In severalty

9. A tenancy by the entirety may be destroyed by all of the following EXCEPT

A. divorce.
B. death of one co-owner.
C. deed of conveyance signed by both parties.
D. last will and testament.

10. Jorge has a life estate in his mother's house. This means that

A. he can live there during his mother's lifetime.
B. his mother can live there during her lifetime.
C. he can live there during his lifetime.
D. his mother can live during his lifetime.

11. A joint venture is similar to a

A. corporation.
B. limited liability company.
C. partnership.
D. sole proprietorship.

12. A condominium is a combination form of ownership because

A. it has individual and common ownership.
B. it is a multi-family dwelling.
C. it has amenities that are used by all owners.
D. it has common management.

13. When working with first time homebuyers, it is BEST to do which of the following first?

A. Ask them questions about their financial situation to decide if they can qualify for a loan.
B. Send them to a loan officer to get them pre-qualified.
C. Discuss the home buying process and answer their questions.
D. Choose a few houses they may like and make appointments to show them as soon as possible to keep them interested.

14. When there are many more houses on the market than there are buyers for those houses, this is known as a

A. buyer's market.
B. seller's market.
C. bull market.
D. bear market.

15. Margo was showing one of her listings with an unfinished basement. As she was showing the basement, she noticed a large diagonal crack on the front wall. It was very obvious and she was sure the prospects saw it, but they didn't mention it and neither did she. Not mentioning the crack was

A. appropriate, because everyone saw it, and if they buy it, the home inspector will include it in his report.
B. appropriate, because she was representing the seller and did not want to speak negatively about the seller's property.
C. inappropriate, because the prospects may not have noticed crack.
D. inappropriate, because agents should disclose material defects with properties they show.

16. One of the MOST important economic value characteristics of property is

A. transferability.
B. size.
C. neighborhood.
D. safety.

17. Purchasers were looking at a large Victorian style house to use as a bed and breakfast. The property is in a residential neighborhood and there are no other bed and breakfasts in the area. When they asked the listing agent for things they needed to consider, what should be at the top of his list?

A. Whether or not they could obtain financing
B. The name of a good home inspector for this type of property
C. Zoning designation
D. Whether nor not the house could pass a health department inspection

18. When writing an offer for an out-of-town buyer, the buyer asked about the advisability of having a radon test. In response, the listing agent said he would be wasting her money because there had never been radon in any houses in the area. Did the agent give the buyer good advice?

A. Yes, because the agent saved the buyer money by keeping her from having a useless test.
B. Yes, because the agent would have breached his fiduciary duty by letting them have a test when no radon was in the area.
C. No, because he is not qualified as an environmental engineer and should not give advice outside his area of expertise.

D. No, because he doesn't know about every house in the area and has only heard that none of the houses in the area have radon.

19. A listing agent has been informed that a ghost lives in the upstairs bathroom. This information must be disclosed

A. to all prospective purchasers.
B. if it is a material fact.
C. when state law requires it.
D. only if the buyer specifically asks.

20. At closing the purchaser wanted to know how much money he would save the first year on his income taxes because of the mortgage interest he would be paying. His agent asked him a few questions about his tax return and calculated the amount he would save. The agent's actions were

A. appropriate, because the information was extremely helpful.
B. appropriate, because one of a buyer's agents duties is to show the buyer how much money he will save.
C. inappropriate, because the buyer may have misremembered the information on his tax return.
D. inappropriate, because giving that information was the practice of accounting.

21. Agents are required to provide disclosure forms for all of the following EXCEPT

A. agency.
B. property condition.
C. fair housing.
D. lead-based paint.

22. Which of the following items should NOT be included in a sales contract?

A. Mailing address of the property
B. Social security number for buyer
C. Marital status of the seller
D. Name of the buyer's lender

23. Personal property that is going to stay with the real estate should be

A. written in the sales contract.
B. discussed between the buyer and seller at the closing.
C. attached to the real estate so that it becomes a fixture.
D. written on a separate inventory form attached to the sales contact.

24. Risk of loss in a sales contract refers to which

A. person replaces personal property that is removed during showings.
B. party carries the property insurance after the contract and before the closing.
C. person pays the seller for any damage which occurs during the home inspection.
D. agent takes a reduced commission in order to make the deal work.

25. If a buyer definitely does not want to buy a new house until he has the money from the sale of his current house, he should ask his agent to include in the sales contract

A. back-up contingency.
B. 24-hour kick out clause.

C. contingency that his house must close before this house closes.
D. contingency that his house must sell before this house closes.

26. Sellers are selling property and moving to Florida to retire. While packing to move, Mr. Seller has a heart attack and dies. Mrs. Seller does not want to move. Her agent tells her she can terminate the sales contract. Was the agent's advice was correct?

A. Yes, because the reason they were selling was to retire to Florida and which will be an impossibility now.
B. Yes, because a party to the sales contract has a right to terminate the contract in the event of death or disability.
C. No, because the agent should have told her that she could terminate the contract but would owe the buyers damages.
D. No, because death or disability will not terminate a sales contract unless it specifically includes such a termination clause.

27. When writing an offer for his buyer client Frank must exercise care, because a mistake in the contract will be interpreted against

A. the offeror.
B. the offeree.
C. the listing agent.
D. Frank.

28. Buster has just received an offer on his home He would like to accept the offer, but can not give possession as early as the buyer wants possession. His BEST option would be to

A. make a counteroffer.
B. wait for an offer that meets his timetable.
C. include a contingency that he can decide on the possession date later.
D. accept the offer and bring up the possession date closer to closing

29. Stephanie has just received a call from a selling agent that has an offer on one of her listings. She has been planning a night out with the family for two weeks and doesn't want to present the offer until tomorrow morning. She should call the

A. seller and make an appointment for tomorrow morning.
B. seller and ask for an appointment as soon as the seller can see her.
C. buyer and ask if it will be OK to wait until tomorrow morning.
D. seller early in the morning to get an appointment.

30. A seller has made a counteroffer on his apartment building that the buyer is considering. He has just received a much better offer and wants to sell the property to the second offeror. His BEST option would be to

A. accept the second offer and withdraw the counteroffer.
B. hold the second offer until the counteroffer expires.
C. withdraw the counteroffer and accept the second offer.
D. accept the second offer contingent upon withdrawing the counteroffer.

31. Rita just listed a house with a mother-in-law apartment over the detached garage. What should be her FIRST concern?

A. Verifying with the health department that the apartment is safe
B. Calling the neighbors to make sure they do not object to the apartment
C. Confirming that the zoning designation is appropriate for the apartment
D. Having a plumbing inspection to make sure the septic system works

32. A purchaser that is concerned about the age of the water heater should ask the seller to

A. have the water heater inspected prior to closing.
B. purchase a home warranty.
C. replace the water heater.
D. guarantee the dishwasher for one year after the closing.

33. Which party to the sales contract carries the risk of loss?

A. Seller
B. Buyer
C. Depends on language in contract
D. Depends on state law

34. Selma's new home has a value of $265,000. Because of the co-insurance provision in her homeowner's policy, she must carry at least how much insurance?

A. $200,000
B. $212,000
C. $265,000
D. $295,000

35. Fair housing laws are designed to

A. create diversity in all neighborhoods.
B. afford each person the opportunity to live where she chooses.
C. prevent discrimination.
D. ensure fairness in housing.

36. A buyer asked his agent to order a home inspection for him. The agent agreed to do so and called his friend at ABC Inspections. Which of the following statements is MOST true about the agent's actions?

A. The action of calling his friend was not good, but there is no problem with calling an inspector and helping the buyer.
B. The actions were risky, and the agent could be liable for any mistakes made by the inspector and for the cost of the inspection.
C. The action of calling his friend was a wise move, because that was someone he could trust.
D. The actions were appropriate, because this is exactly what a good agent should do, and the agent should be commended.

37. Once a home inspection has been completed, the BEST practice is for the

A. selling agent to review the report with the inspector and discuss needed repairs.
B. buyer to review the report with the inspector and discuss needed repairs.
C. selling agent and buyer to review the report and discuss needed repairs
D. selling agent and listing agent to review the report, discuss needed repairs, and present the seller with the list.

38. If a buyer wants to know the property boundary, he should

A. order an appraisal.
B. ask the seller.
C. ask the listing agent.
D. order a survey.

39. A buyer who wants to know the fair market value of the property she is purchasing may

A. ask her agent to do a comparative market analysis.
B. check the tax assessment for the property.
C. order an appraisal from an independent appraiser.
D. ask her lender for an estimate.

40. Audrey had read an article recently about lead based paint in houses. She is concerned because she has two small children. What is her BEST course of action?

A. Ask her agent to only show her property built after 1975
B. Include a contingency in her contract that she can have a lead based paint assessment
C. Ask the sellers of each property what they know about the property and whether or not there is lead based paint
D. Include a contingency that she can void the contract if lead based paint is discovered after her inspection

Content Outline: Property Management

A. Property Management

1.   Negotiation of property management agreements
2.   Negotiation of lease agreements used in property management
3.   Preparation of rental and lease agreements
4.   Explanation of rental and lease agreements
5.   Methods or marketing property
6.   Rental market evaluation
7.   Disclosure of material facts to lessee
8.   Obtaining tenants
9.   Showing property to prospective tenants
10. Occupancy terms
11. Applicant screening according to laws and regulations
12. Complaints and conflict resolution among tenants
13. Prorating of rents and leases
14. Operating budgets
15. Trust accounts
16. Financial statements for owners
17. Income, expenses, and rate of return
18. Environmental and safety hazards
19. Compliance with federal requirements, e.g., ADA, fair housing, lead-based paint disclosures)
20. Eviction proceedings
21. Maintenance and repair management
22. Fees, security deposits, and rent
23. Insurance coverage to protect the tenant and owner

Key Point Review: Property Management

Leasing and Management

- Property managers must be real estate licensees, unless they are exempt under narrowly defined exemptions in the state's licensing laws
- In many states, if the manager is an employee of the owner, he does not need to be a real estate licensee
- Some states have a special license classification for agents who manage real property while other states permit any licensee to manage real estate
- Owners use property managers to manage a variety of real property, including commercial, retail, professional offices, residential, condominiums, homeowner

associations, and farms.

- Because each property type has specific requirements, licensees should be specifically trained to manage the particular type of property they are retained to manage
- A resident manager may be used to manage residential property
- Property managers may manage several properties for one owner or may manage properties for several different owners
- Management duties may be broken down into three categories: financial management, physical management, and administrative management
- Managers have the responsibility to produce the highest possible net operating income while maintaining and enhancing the value of the owner's investment

Negotiation of Property Management Agreements

- Brokers, who manage real estate, must have written property management agreements with the owners
- Some state licensing laws regulate what must be included in property management agreements
- Items that are typically included are:
  - o names and address of the property owner and broker
  - o property location and description
  - o beginning and ending dates of the management agreement
  - o automatic continuation provision, if permitted by state law
  - o amount of compensation to the broker
  - o how the compensation will be calculated and paid
  - o broker's authority, including authorization for broker to make expenditures on behalf of the owner and to sign the lease agreement on the owner's behalf
  - o how security deposits and rents will be handled
  - o how reporting will be made to the owner
  - o copy of the lease that will be used
  - o signatures of the owner and broker
- The management agreement creates an agency relationship between the owner (the principal) and the broker (the agent)
- There is a fiduciary relationship between the owner and the property manager and the manager owes the owner the same fiduciary duties that she would owe in a sales transaction
- Although a broker may have licensees working for her, assisting in the management of the properties, the property management agreement is between the broker and the property owner
- Some states and some owners require the property manager and/or management company to post a surety bond, also referred to as a fidelity bond
- Brokers making a bid to become a property manager may submit a management proposal
- Some owners may retain brokers to lease the property while the owner acts as the property manager

Negotiation of Lease Agreements Used in Property Management

- Both the lessor and the lessee may have agents representing them in the negotiating process
- Agents may work as either lessor's or lessee's agents or may work as dual agents, representing both the lessor and lessee
- Because a lease agreement is a contract, typical contract negotiations between the lessor and lessee apply
- With the advice of the broker, the owner sets the terms for leasing his property, including rental amount, amount of security deposit, length of the lease, and whether or not the lease will include options
- There are two types of options that may be negotiated: (1) additional lease periods; (2) and option to purchase the property
- Property managers should advise their clients on market conditions and on specific terms that lessees may want to include in the lease
- Lease negotiations have offers and counteroffers similar to a sales transaction
- Licensees advising lessors and lessees in commercial lease transactions must be aware of the tax consequences that arise and must advise clients to seek legal and accounting advice

Preparation of Rental and Lease Agreements

- Licensees cannot "prepare" these agreements, unless they are also licensed to practice law
- Property managers may complete, but not prepare, rental and lease agreement forms
- When completing the forms, licensees should take care to fill in all blanks on the form
- Either the property owner should prepare the lease agreement form, or she should retain the services of an attorney to prepare the form
- It is appropriate for the property manager to suggest terms for inclusion that may be expected in the market place

Explanation of Rental and Lease Agreements

- Licensees should suggest to lessees that they may want to obtain either legal or tax advice before signing the document
- Brokers and property managers must take care not to practice law or accounting when explaining the forms

Methods or Marketing Property

- One of the most valuable services of the property manager is marketing the property
- The same marketing techniques apply for marketing rental property as they do for selling property
- Free rent for a month or other inducements may be effective
- Referrals from current or past tenants are always valuable
- Yard signs, as well as advertisements in the newspaper, on the radio and TV, on bulletin boards, and the internet are all methods of marketing

Rental Market Evaluation

- Property managers should have knowledge of how to evaluate the rental market in order to help the owner establish rental rates and project budgets
- The economic principle of supply and demand affects rental rates: when there are fewer people renting, the rental rates will be lower; when there are more people renting, the rental rate will be higher
- A rule of thumb for evaluating the number of renters is to assume that one-third of the households will be renters

Disclosure of Material Facts to Lessee

- As in all real estate transactions, licensees are required to disclose material facts when acting as a rental agent or property manager
- Material facts are facts that would make a difference in whether or not the lessee would enter into a lease agreement
- Failure of the property manager to disclose material facts can lead to the lessee legally terminating the lease
- Failing to disclose material facts may lead to the tenant filing a lawsuit against the owner and/or property manager
- Licensing laws require that licensees disclose material facts in all real estate transactions, and the failure to do so may lead to a penalty assessed by the regulatory agency against the licensee

Obtaining Tenants

- One of the most important duties for a property manager is to get the property rented
- A strong marketing plan should be made and followed

Showing Property to Prospective Tenants

- A positive attitude about the property when showing it is crucial
- Prior to showing the property, the property manager should preview the property to make sure it is clean, well-maintained, and well-lighted
- Property managers should not promise anything not authorized by the owner just to get a new tenant
- Managers should anticipate questions by the prospective tenants and be able to answer them
- A rental application and a copy of the lease should be available for the prospect when the property is shown
- It is important for the rental agent to be prompt and not late for a showing appointment
- If the property is currently rented, state law should be followed for gaining access to the property

Occupancy Terms

- Most states laws require written leases when property is being rented for longer than one year

- Although the best practice is to have all leases in writing, many leases are oral
- Leases may contain any term that is agreeable to both lessor and lessee
- Typical lease terms include:
    - names and signatures of the lessor and lessee
    - address and description of the property to be leased
    - term of the lease (beginning and ending dates)
    - amount of the rental payment
    - additional payments by tenants such as insurance, taxes, maintenance
    - when the rent is due and instructions for payment
    - security deposit provisions
    - how the property may or may not be used
    - lessee's agreement to pay rent and maintain the property
    - default provisions
    - termination provisions
    - lessor's warranty of quiet enjoyment
    - lessor's warranty of habitability

Applicant Screening According to Laws and Regulations

- Owners, property managers, and their staffs must be knowledgeable of the fair housing laws
- A process should be established by the property manager for screening applicants
- The screening process should be based only on the tenant's ability to pay the rent
- Tenant applications must conform to federal and state law

Complaints and Conflict Resolution among Tenants

- A complaint process should be established, either in the lease or in another written form, to inform the tenant when and how to let the property manager know there are problems
- When a problem arises with the property, the property manager should take immediate action
- Property managers must be aware of the fact that tenants may have conflicts with each other, and they must have a process for handling those conflicts
- Tenants may have conflicts with the neighbors that must be resolved by the property manager

Prorating of Rents and Leases

- Because lessors often want rent to be due and payable on the first day of the month, and because leases may not begin on the first date of the month and end on the last day of the month, rents are often prorated at the beginning and/or end of the lease
- To prorate the rent, take the monthly rent and divide it by the number of days in the month and multiply that amount by the number of days owed
- The lease should state whether a 360-day year (a banker's or statutory year) or a 365-day year (a calendar year) will be used for pro-rations
- When prorating on a calendar year basis, use a 366-day year for leap years

Operating Budgets

- Operating budgets are prepared on an annual basis using an estimate of revenue (income) and expenses
- To determine the estimated revenue, determine the potential gross income, subtract the estimated vacancy and rent loss, and add additional income
- Subtract fixed expenses from the estimated revenue to find the net operating income
- An operating budget should also establish a cash reserve fund

Trust Accounts

- Trust accounts are established by property managers to hold funds that belong to someone else
- Most often, the funds that are held are security deposits; however, other funds may be held by the property manager if authorized by the property owner
- These accounts must be separate and apart from the property manager's operating accounts
- Money held in trust cannot be commingled with the property manager's other funds
- State laws vary on the requirements for holding and dispersing money held in a trust account

Financial Statements for Owners

- Property managers must prepare periodic financial statements for owners showing the income and expenses for the property being managed
- Reporting periods vary from state to state
- Owners may request specific reporting periods and specific reports
- A profit and loss statement is the main report required by the owner
- To prepare a profit and loss statement to determine the net profit, add the total receipts for rent and other income, subtract the operating expenses to arrive at the operating income, then subtract the mortgage payment and add back in the principal reduction

Income, Expenses, and Rate of Return

- Rate of return (ROI) measures the profitability of an investment property and is stated as a percentage
- ROI may be determined before or after income taxes
- To compute the rate of return, the first step is to project the anticipated income by adding the potential gross income and any additional income (for example, income from vending machines and/or clubhouse rental) then subtracting the rent loss based on the anticipated vacancy
- The second step is to subtract the expenses from the anticipated income to reach the net operating income before debt service
- Next, subtract the debt service to find the before-tax cash flow before subtracting the income taxes
- Income taxes are subtracted from the before-tax cash flow income to determine the after-tax cash flow
- The rate of return is determined by dividing the after-tax cash flow by the equity (amount of dollars invested) and multiplying that number by 100%

Environmental and Safety Hazards

- Property managers must be aware of both potential and actual environmental hazards in and around the properties they manage
- Federal and state laws control and regulate hazardous waste and substances
- Licensees are not required to be environmental experts, but do need a general knowledge and awareness of environmental issues
- Property managers should not advise on environmental issues, but should refer both landlords and tenants to the proper governmental authorities to have their questions answered
- Environmental issues that may be encountered are radon, lead-based paint, asbestos, formaldehyde, pesticides, wetlands, underground storage tanks, mold, brownfields, and PCBs.
- Safety hazards are also of a concern to property managers
- State laws vary relating to the landlord's duties to keep property safe. Safety issues for landlords include lighting, smoke and carbon monoxide detectors, fire sprinklers, hand rails, snow and ice removal, and security

Compliance with Federal Requirements, e.g., ADA, fair housing, lead-based paint disclosures)

- Property managers should be aware of the American With Disabilities Act (ADA), the fair housing laws, the lead-based paint disclosure requirements, and other environmental laws affecting real property
- ADA prohibits discrimination in commercial properties and public accommodations
- Under ADA, people with disabilities must have full and equal access to facilities and services
- Property managers should inspect the property to determine whether it meets the ADA requirements, and advise the owner of any deficiencies
- Owners of existing properties are required under ADA to make reasonably achievable accommodations to provide access to the buildings
- Federal and state laws require that tenants of residential property be provided with a brochure explaining lead-based paint and a disclosure form signed by the owner, informing the tenant of the owner's knowledge of the presence of lead-based paint
- Lead-based paint disclosure forms must be delivered to the tenant by either the landlord or property manager for properties built prior to 1978
- The property manager has a duty to explain the lead-based paint disclosure requirement to the owner and to ensure that the disclosure form is delivered to the tenant
- Fair housing laws apply to residential dwellings
- Property managers have a duty to follow all fair housing laws
- The protected classes include race, color, national origin, religion, sex, handicap/disability, familial status
- Some areas have added sexual orientation as an additional protected class
- There are certain exemptions to the fair housing laws, but they do not apply when a real estate licensee is involved in the transaction

Eviction Proceedings

- Property managers may have the duty of evicting tenants who do not pay rent or breach the lease agreement in some other way
- Some states allow the property manager to proceed with the eviction proceedings, while others require the landlord to file the court action
- Eviction proceedings are referred to as forcible entry and detainer actions
- Forcible entry and detainer actions are lawsuits that must be filed in the appropriate court
- These actions require a notice to the tenant before they are filed
- State laws vary, but generally, once the action is filed, the court sets a date for the parties to appear for the court's determination as to whether the tenant will be evicted
- These cases may be with or without a jury, depending on state law

Maintenance and Repair Management

- The property management agreement between the owner and property manager should specifically state the manager's duties relative to maintenance and repair
- One of the greatest areas of dispute between property owners and their managers is in the area of maintenance and repair
- There are four types of maintenance: preventative, corrective, routine, and construction
- Construction includes remodeling, interior redecorating and capital improvements

Fees, Security Deposits, and Rent

- Fees that are going to be charged by the lessor should be specifically included in the lease agreement
- Property managers may charge an application fee that is used to pay for the credit report and other administrative work in processing the lessee's rental application
- A clean-up fee may be charged to refurbish the property when the lessee vacates
- Late rent fees, returned/insufficient fund check fees, and advertising fees may also be charged by the lessor
- Security deposits are designed to provide the lessor with money to repair any damage to the property by the lessee
- States have specific laws on how the security deposits must be held
- Generally, security deposits cannot be used as rent
- Many states have laws that require the landlord to take certain steps before he can retain the security deposit, even if there is damage
- State laws often require the landlord to give the tenant a written disclosure of any existing damage before the tenant moves in and when the tenant vacates the property
- Rent for residential space is typically stated as a monthly rent per unit
- Commercial rent is quoted as either an annual or monthly rate per square foot
- Rent for investment property may be quoted as a net rent, double net rent, or triple net rent
- The lease should state when the rent is due and payable
- Leases usually provide that rent is paid in advance
- Under common law, if the lease does not state when rent is due, it is due at the end of the rental period

- Some states have rent control, which regulates how much rent the lessor can charge the lessee

Insurance Coverage to Protect the Tenant and Owner

- Risk management for the owner is one of the responsibilities of a property manager
- One of the best ways to manage risk is with adequate insurance
- The property manager should recommend to the owner that she should obtain an insurance audit to make sure she is adequately insured
- There are a number of insurance coverages that owners of investment property should consider: fire and hazard; contents and personal property; liability; casualty; and consequential loss, use and occupancy. Extended coverage insurance may be added to fire insurance for additional protection
- Multi-peril policies are available on commercial properties
- If the owner or property manager have employees, they must carry worker's compensation insurance
- Leases typically recommend that that lessees carry content and personal property insurance to protect themselves
- Many commercial leases require the lessee to carry all of the insurance to protect the lessor and lessee
- Lessors often require the lessees name them as co-insured or additional loss payees on insurance policies
- Before a person can buy insurance, she must have an insurable interest in the property

Key Term Match: Property Management

Work on mastering real estate language by matching the following terms with the correct definition. For additional key term matching exercises, see Appendix A.

Terms

A. Leased fee interest

B. Use and occupancy insurance

C. Net lease

D. Lease option

E. Liability insurance

F. Leasehold interest

G. Banker's year

H. Lease agreement

I. Casualty insurance

J. Triple Net Lease

K. Calendar Year

L. Sublease

M. Extended coverage insurance

N. Fire and hazard insurance

O. Double net lease

Definitions

1. _____ Insurance that extends a standard fire insurance policy to cover damages resulting from wind, rain, and other perils.

2. _____ A lease entered into between a lessee and a third person that transfers part of the leasehold interest to the third party with a reversionary interest to the lessee.

3. _____ Insures against claims caused by injuries to people and the legal liability resulting from those injuries.

4. _____ The lessor's interest in leased property.

5. _____ A commercial lease that requires the tenant to pay a base rent plus two of the following: property insurance, property taxes, or property maintenance.

6. _____ An agreement, either oral or written, that creates a landlord and tenant relationship, giving the tenant possession of the landlord's property.

7. _____ A personal property right created by contract between the lessor and lessee that gives the lessee the right to possess and use the real property. Everything that is attached to the real estate.

8. _____ A commercial lease in which the tenant pays a base rent plus either the property taxes, the maintenance, or the property insurance.

9. _____ A basic fire insurance policy covering losses caused by fire or lightning.

10. _____ Insurance that protects a party against liability or losses suffered by a third party for personal injury.

11. _____ A commercial lease in which the tenant pays a base rent, plus the property taxes, insurance, and maintenance.

12. _____ A year with 360 days.

13. _____ A contract between a seller and buyer that gives the buyer the right to purchase the property at some point in the future upon the terms contained in the contract and giving the buyer the right to lease the property while deciding whether or not to purchase it.

14. _____ A year with 365 days or with 366 days when there is a leap year.

15. _____ Insurance for commercial property that insures against lost rent.

Practice Questions: Property Management

1. All property managers must

A. hold a real estate license.
B. have a written property management agreement.
C. work as an independent contractor for the owner.
D. have repairmen that can be available for emergencies.

2. Leases are

A. always written.
B. a contract.
C. subject to termination by landlord.
D. terminated if the property is sold.

3. Property managers should explain the lease agreement to the tenant and recommend that the tenant

A. take the lease agreement home with them to read.
B. consider seeking legal and/or accounting advice.
C. think about it for three days before signing it.
D. sign it immediately.

4. Ralph owns a retail store that he rents on a triple net lease. Under this type of lease the tenant will be required to pay all of the following EXCEPT

A. insurance.
B. debt service.
C. maintenance.
D. property taxes.

5. The BEST way to qualify a prospective tenant is to

A. find out where she currently lives to see how it compares to this property.
B. get a rental application completed and verify information.
C. call the prior landlord and ask for references.
D. talk to the prospect to get a feel for her qualifications.

6. Richard is moving into his new apartment on June 18th. The rent is $1,150 per month and will be prorated for the month of June and paid at the time of occupancy. The security deposit is $1,000 and must be paid when the lease is signed. How much will Richard pay when he moves into the property?

A. $460.00
B. $498.33
C. $1,460.00
D. $1,498.33

7. To prepare an operating budget, you must have all of the following EXCEPT

A. potential gross income.
B. vacancy rate.
C. variable expenses.
D. additional income.

8. Trust accounts are MOST often used by property managers to

A. hold security deposits.
B. pay the owner's mortgage payment.
C. pay the costs of maintaining the property.
D. pay property management fees.

9. A rate of return analysis

A. measures the profitability of an investment.
B. assumes a lower than average vacancy rate.
C. projects the owner's profits for the year.
D. shows the owner his profit and loss for a given year.

10. Byron has been managing a 4-plex for a number of years. Recently, one of the tenants has called to say the outside security light keeps going out. Byron informed the tenant that, as part of the lease, the tenants were to replace the bulbs. Byron's response was

A. appropriate, because the lease was clear on who was responsible for replacing light bulbs.
B. appropriate, because a property manager is not required to change light bulbs.
C. inappropriate, because the tenant may fall off the ladder while replacing the bulb and sue the owner.
D. inappropriate, because a light fixture that keeps blowing bulbs may be a safety issue.

11. An owner of an existing commercial building must make reasonably achievable accommodations because of the

A. American with Disabilities Act.
B. Federal Fair Housing Act of 1968.
C. Equal Employment Opportunity Act.
D. Equal Housing Opportunity Act of 1988.

12. Under the fair housing laws, the protected classes include all of the following EXCEPT

A. marital status.
B. sex.
C. creed.
D. color.

13. Which of the following is NOT one of the four types of maintenance

A. construction.
B. corrective.
C. preventative.
D. exhaustive.

14. The property manager has just shown prospective tenants an apartment in a building that was built in 1970. They have asked her if the landlord will paint all of the woodwork to cover any lead-based paint that may be present. She responds that she has not asked him but is sure he will, because the federal law requires a landlord to disclose the presence of lead-based paint and to make the property safe. Her response was

A. correct, because the federal lead-based paint law requires the landlord to keep the property safe.
B. correct, because the federal lead-based paint law requires the landlord to both disclose and repaint to keep the property safe.
C. incorrect, because the federal lead-based paint law requires the landlord to disclose the known presence of lead-based paint but does not require the landlord to repaint.
D. incorrect, because she misstated the law and promised that the landlord would do something she was not authorized to promise.

15. Murrell is managing a single family residential property for the owner. The tenant is late again paying his rent. Last month when the tenant paid his rent late, Murrell told him that the next time he was late with the rent the locks would be changed and he could not enter his property until the rent was paid. Murrell's actions were

A. appropriate, because the tenant will continue to be late unless drastic measures are taken.
B. appropriate, because he has a fiduciary duty to protect the owner's interest.
C. inappropriate, because he must follow the legal process as set forth by state law to evict the tenant and/or collect the rent.
D. inappropriate, because he should give the tenant a written notice to pay the rent before the locks are changed.

Content Outline: Settlement/Transfer of Ownership

A. Settlement/Transfer of Ownership

1. Tax implications of interest expenses
2. Real property taxes
3. Tax shelters
4. Capital improvements
5. Property taxation (e.g., ad valorem, special assessments)
6. Tax deferred exchanges

Key Point Review: Settlement/Transfer of Ownership

- The process for transferring ownership is known as the settlement or closing
- At the closing the title passes by deed from the grantor to the grantee
- Purchasers pay the seller for the property at the settlement
- Grantors are sometimes referred to as Parties of the First Part and Grantees are sometimes referred to as Parties of the Second Part

Tax Issues
- Tax rates vary and may be imposed by state, county, or city government
- Property taxes (ad valorem taxes), transfer taxes, and income taxes are all considerations at the settlement
- State transfer taxes are generally paid by the seller at the closing, although the parties to the sales contract can agree that the buyer will pay the taxes or that they will be split between the buyer and seller
- Transfer taxes must be paid before the deed can be recorded
- Certain property may be exempt from transfer tax, including: gift deeds, charitable deeds, divorce deeds, partition deeds, and tax deeds
- Some states refer to transfer taxes as a grantor's tax and some states use documentary stamps that are purchased by the taxpayer
- Property taxes are pro-rated between the grantor and grantee
- Forms are completed by the seller at the settlement that notify the Internal Revenue Service that the seller either does or does not owe capital gains taxes

Tax Implications of Interest Expenses
- Homeowners may deduct the interest paid on mortgages for their first and second homes from federal and state income taxes
- The interest expense deduction encourages people to own homes because the interest paid reduces their income taxes
- Federal tax laws allow homeowners to earn capital gains on their homes without paying income taxes if certain criteria are met:

- married taxpayers may exclude $500,000 from capital gains for jointly owned property, and single tax payers may exclude $250,000
- the homeowners must have occupied the property for two of the past five years
- Loan discount points are tax deductible because they are actually prepaid interest

Real Property Taxes
- Ad valorem taxes may be used as tax deductions to reduce gross income
- Real property taxes are based on the assessed value of the property and may be based on a calendar or fiscal year

Tax Shelters
- Real estate investment is one of the most popular forms of income shelters (tax shelters)
- Depreciation, also referred to as cost recovery, allows the owner of an income-producing asset to take tax deductions over a period of years
- This form of depreciation allows the investor to take a tax deduction without the improvements actually losing value
- Straight-line depreciation is used, allowing the owner to take the same amount each year as a deduction from net income before taxes are paid
- Improvements, not land, are depreciated
- Other deductions from income for investment properties include: accounting and legal fees, advertising, property management fees, property insurance, wages and salaries, maintenance and repairs, and property taxes
- Another tax shelter is the installment sale of real property in which the seller does not receive all of the sale proceeds in a lump sum, but rather over a period of time
- Receiving money over a period of time allows the seller to pay income taxes as the money is received and not all at one time
- With an installment sale, the seller does not receive all of her money at one time; rather, she collects it over a period of time and only pays capital gains tax as it is received

Capital Improvements
- Capital improvements are permanent additions to real estate that enhance its value and extend its useful life
- Cost of making capital improvements is referred to as a capital expenditure
- Extensive remodeling, a new roof, and additions to existing improvements are all examples of capital improvements
- Maintenance is not a capital improvement

Property Taxation (e.g., ad valorem, special assessments)

- In addition to ad valorem taxes, governmental entities may levy special assessments on property, which may be for sidewalks, sewers, roads, parks, utilities, or other government improvements
- These assessments are generally due and payable at the same time as the ad valorem taxes
- A special assessment is for a specific improvement and runs for a specific period of time
- Special assessments have the same lien priority as property taxes, and foreclosure actions can be filed to collect them

Tax Deferred Exchanges

- Unlike a primary residence, investment property that is sold is subject to a capital gains tax
- A 1031 tax-deferred exchange may be used to defer payment of capital gains on investment properties
  - Rules for tax-deferred exchanges must be followed exactly or the tax benefit may be lost
  - In a 1031 exchange, the proceeds of the sale of property must be out of the control of the seller and must be used to purchase like-kind property to replace the property sold
  - An escrow agent may hold the funds for the seller and deliver them to the closing of the new purchase
  - Real estate licensees should not advise on tax-deferred exchanges; rather, they should recommend their clients seek legal and/or accounting advice

Content Outline: Settlement/Transfer of Ownership

B. Titles

1. Need for title search
2. Title insurance (e.g., owner and mortgagee)
3. Title problems
4. Legal procedures (e.g., quiet title, foreclosure, bankruptcy, declaratory judgment)
5. Preparation of title abstracts
6. Liens and order of priority (e.g., mortgages, trust deeds, construction/mechanics liens, judgments by court)
7. Importance of recording

Titles

Need for Title Search

- Grantees take title subject-to prior interests in the property
- Prudent grantees will have a title examination, sometimes referred to as a title search, prior to taking title to property, regardless of how long the grantor has owned the property
- A title examination will reveal all recorded interests in the property
- Recording an interest in real property gives constructive notice that someone has an interest in the property

Title Insurance (e.g., owner and mortgagee)

- Title insurance protects the insured against financial loss because of a defect in the title to real estate
- There are four types of title insurance: owner's, lender's (sometimes referred to as mortgagee's), leasehold, and contract buyer's
    - the owner's policy is for the purchase price of the property and it remains in effect for that amount during the insured's ownership, and, in the event of death, the benefit passes to the heirs
    - the mortgagee's policy protects the lender for the amount of the mortgage, and it decreases as the mortgage balance decreases
    - the leasehold policy protects the lessee and/or his mortgagee against defects in the lessor's title
    - the contract buyer's policy protects the buyer against defects when she is purchasing the property on an installment sales contract (also referred to as a land contract or contract for deed)
- To obtain a title insurance policy, the property must have an insurable title
- A title examination must be performed prior to issuing a policy of title insurance to assist the company in assessing its claim risk
- There is a one-time premium, paid generally at the time of closing
- Title insurance protects only against defects that were in existence at the time the policy was written

Title Problems

- Title problems that may arise include:
    - incorrect legal description
    - lien or other third party claim against the property
    - incorrect grantor or grantee name
    - missing or incorrect marital status of the grantor
    - forgery of grantor's signature
    - the deed, or other recorded document, signed by someone other than the owner
    - all owners not signed as grantors, including missing spouses and missing heirs
    - failure to record or defective recording
    - signed by a minor or mentally disabled grantor

Legal Procedures (e.g., quiet title, foreclosure, bankruptcy, declaratory judgment)

- Most legal proceedings involving real estate are in state court; however, bankruptcy is in federal court
- Quiet title actions are filed when more than one person is claiming title to the property
    - Quiet title actions allow the court to determine who has the right, title, and interest to the property
    - Quiet title actions may be used in estate settlements, and to settle disputes in adverse possession and prescriptive easement cases
- Foreclosure lawsuits are used when someone has filed a lien on the property and the owner refuses to pay the debt
    - Foreclosure actions are judicial proceedings
    - Foreclosure actions "foreclose" or terminate all interests in the land of the parties named in the lawsuit
    - When a foreclosure is filed, a lis pendens notice should be filed in the public records to give notice of a legal action that affects the title to the property
- When a property owner files bankruptcy, his real property becomes part of the bankruptcy estate and is controlled by the bankruptcy trustee
- Depending on the type of bankruptcy and amount of debt, the bankrupt property owner may or may not be able to keep the property
- Declaratory judgment actions are sometimes referred to as "friendly" lawsuits
- When two parties agree on the facts, but disagree on how the law will be applied to the facts, a declaratory judgment may be filed to allow the court to decide the law based on the agreed-upon facts

Preparation of Title Abstracts

- A title abstract is a chronological history of the property that passes from owner to owner
- Some states uses title abstracts, while other states use title opinions, setting forth the owner and the condition of the title
- Title abstracts are prepared based on a title examination of the property

Liens and Order of Priority (e.g., mortgages, trust deeds, construction/mechanics liens, judgments by court)

- Liens on property have a priority established by law and/or recording
- Priority is important because the priority sets out who will receive payment of their liens in the event of a foreclosure or bankruptcy action
- Ad valorem taxes and special assessments have priority over all other liens
- Other than taxes and assessments, lien priority is established by recording
- A document is recorded when it is officially filed in the public records, giving constructive notice of the lien interest
- Someone taking title to the property after the lien is recorded takes the title subject to that lien interest

- Some states use mortgages to secure repayment of a mortgage loan, while other states use trust deeds
- Construction liens, also referred to as mechanic and materialman's liens, are filed by someone who has supplied labor and materials to improve the property after the property owner refuses to pay for the labor and/or materials
- A judgment lien may be filed after a lawsuit in which the Plaintiff has been awarded money and the Defendant refuses to pay the lien
- There are two types of liens: general and specific

Importance of Recording

- Recording is extremely important because it establishes the lien priority and gives public notice of ownership and interest
- Once an interest is recorded, it is presumed that anyone taking interest in the property is aware of the recorded notice
- If a buyer buys property that has a lien recorded against it, the lien stays with the property and the new owner would have to pay the debt in order to get the lien removed

Content Outline: Settlement/Transfer of Ownership

C. Settlement Procedures

1. Purposes and procedures of settlement
2. Obligations of settlement agent
3. Calculations regarding proration/prepayment
4. Warranties associated with deeds (e.g., grant, quit claim)
5. Settlement statement (HUD-1 form)
6. Other settlement documents (e.g., deed, bill of sale, note, deed of trust)
7. Real Estate Settlement Procedures Act
8. Transfer tax

Settlement Procedures

Purposes and procedures of settlement
- Settlement, also referred to as the closing, is the time when the title changes hands from the sellers to the buyers
- All agreements between the parties should be completed at this time
- Settlements are generally conducted by either a title company or an attorney
- Settlements can either occur face-to-face between the buyer and seller or in escrow, where the parties are not together for the closing

Obligations of Settlement Agent
- The settlement agent is the person who conducts the closing
- Settlement agents represent the lender when the buyer is obtaining a mortgage

- Although the settlement agent is not typically representing the parties to the transaction, he has have an obligation to close the transaction as set forth in the purchase contract
- Some states require the settlement agent to be an attorney, while other states allow anyone to conduct the closings
- The settlement agent may be legally liable for damages because of mistakes on the closing statement and other mistakes arising from the closing documents
- Settlement agents are responsible for the accuracy of all documents prepared and used at the closing

Calculations Regarding Proration/Prepayment

- Property taxes, government assessments, homeowner's associations, insurance and rents are examples of items that are prorated at the settlement
- Items paid in advance by the seller will be credited to the seller and debited to the buyer on the closing statement
- Items that are owed by the seller, but not paid, will be debited to the seller and credited to the buyer on the closing statement
- The settlement agent must prorate items based on either a 360-day or 365-day year
- Either the contract, custom in the area, or state determines whether a 360-day or 365-day year will be used
- A settlement agent must ascertain how many days to use for the calculations

Warranties Associated with Deeds (e.g., grant, quitclaim)

- Deeds may or may not contain warranties of title
- When a covenant of warranty is included in the deed, the grantor is agreeing to defend the title against claims that may be made against the title
- Warranties are for a specific period of time and for a specific purpose
- Covenants included in warranty deeds include: covenant of seisin, covenant against encumbrances, covenant of quiet enjoyment, covenant of right to convey, covenant of further assurance, and covenant of warranty forever.
- A general warranty deed is the best, because the grantor warrants that she will defend the title forever against any and all defects without limitation
- A special warranty deed contains the same warranties as the general warranty deed, but limits the time period to that of the grantor's ownership
- The grant, bargain, and sale deed may or may not contain warranties
- Western states use the grant deed, and warranties are not included in the deed, but rather are provided by state statute
- A quitclaim deed has no warranties
- The quitclaim deed conveys all of the grantor's interest in the property to the grantee, if the grantor has any interest

Settlement Statement (HUD-1 form)

- By federal regulation, a HUD-1 closing statement must be used in every settlement involving a federally related mortgage loan in which there is a borrower and a seller
- The HUD-1 is a debit and credit type closing statement that shows the net amount to be received by the seller and the net amount to be paid by the borrower

- All funds to be received and disbursed as part of the transaction must appear on the HUD-1
- Borrowers, sellers, agents, and settlement agents should take care that a true and accurate picture of the transaction is contained on the HUD-1
- Borrowers, sellers, and the settlement agent must all sign the HUD-1, stating that the information contained on the statement is true and correct
- Knowingly making false statements on the HUD-1 is illegal and can lead to criminal penalties
- Real estate agents do not typically complete the HUD-1, but they should have the knowledge to review it for accuracy

Other Settlement Documents (e.g., deed, bill of sale, note, deed of trust)
- The seller is responsible for bringing the deed to the closing
- A deed conveys real property and is signed by the grantor
- Some states require that the grantee sign the deed, certifying that the consideration contained in the deed is true and correct
- Deeds should be reviewed by the settlement agent to ascertain that the information contained in the deed is accurate and that it conveys the right property
- A bill of sale transfers personal property and should be signed by the seller at the closing
- Bills of sale are filed in the public records to give notice of the holder's interest in the property
- Bills of sale are necessary when mobile homes are being transferred as part of a real estate transaction
- Promissory notes are signed at the closing
- A promissory note is the borrower's promise to repay the money borrowed
- Promissory notes are negotiable instruments and are not recorded in the public records
- Depending on state law, lenders either require a deed of trust or a mortgage to be signed at the closing to secure repayment of the money borrowed
- Both deeds of trust and mortgages are recorded in the public records to give constructive notice of the lender's interest in the real property

Real Estate Settlement Procedures Act
- A federal law that became effective in 1974
- It applies to one-to-four family residential transactions
- Purposes of the RESPA include:
  - requires effective advance disclosure to buyers and sellers of closing costs
  - eliminates kickback or referral fees by stating: "no person shall accept a fee, kickback or thing of value for referring business incident to the settlement services"
  - reduces the amount of money held by lenders for taxes and insurance in escrow accounts
  - reforms and modernizes local record keeping of land information

- Requires lenders to provide good faith estimates within three days of mortgage application
- Requires use of the HUD-1 Settlement Statement
- Imposes criminal penalties on those who violate RESPA

Transfer Tax

- States impose taxes on the privilege of transferring ownership to real estate,
- known as a transfer tax
- The tax is sometimes referred to as deed stamps
- Different states have different tax rates
- Transfer taxes are paid at the time of transfer and may be paid either by the seller or buyer as negotiated in the sales contract

Content Outline: Settlement/Transfer of Ownership

D. Completion of the Transaction

1. Negotiations between buyers and sellers leading to an agreement
2. Contract requirements and fulfillment of contingencies leading to closing
3. Federal statutory requirements
4. Rights of home ownership (e.g., homestead, rights of husband and wife)
5. Rights of others related to property (e.g., adverse possession, adjoining owners, encroachments)
6. Nature and types of common interest ownership (e.g., condominium, planned unit development, cooperative, townhouse)
7. Eminent domain proceedings
8. Legal proceedings against property (e.g., attachments and notice of pending legal action)
9. Securities law application and referral
10. Situations where experts are required (e.g., financial planning and legal advice)
11. Closing statements (e.g., calculate amount owed by buyer and net to seller)

Completion of the Transaction

Negotiations between Buyers and Sellers Leading to an Agreement

- In most real estate transactions, the offer is made by the buyer to the seller, although the seller may make an offer to the buyer
- The offer is made by the offeror and the other party is the offeree
- The offeree has several options when an offer is made:
  o accept the offer as presented
  o counter the offer with her own offer
  o reject the offer without a counteroffer
  o take no action at all which is, in essence, a rejection
- Although real estate agents use printed forms, all terms, including those printed may be countered by the offeree
- Once the offer is accepted by all parties, it becomes an executory contract

- An executory contract becomes an executed contract once all of the terms of the contract have been fulfilled

Contract Requirements and Fulfillment of Contingencies Leading to Closing

- To be valid and enforceable, contracts require certain essential elements to be created:
  - offer and acceptance, also known as meeting of the minds
  - consideration
  - reality of consent
  - legal competency of all parties
  - legal purpose
- If one of these essential elements is missing, the contract will be either void, voidable, or unenforceable
- All states have adopted the Statute of Frauds that requires all real estate contracts to be in writing
- Contracts may be unilateral, e.g., the option contract and open   listings, or bilateral, e.g., the exclusive right to sell listing contract and the sales/purchase contract
- Parties may enter into express or implied contracts; although real estate contracts are always express because they must be in writing
- Contracts may contain contingencies that must be removed before the party is required to perform the contract. Examples of contingencies are financing, home inspections, and buyer or seller relocation

Federal Statutory Requirements

- Real estate contracts are not governed by federal statutes
- Certain aspects of the settlement process are governed by federal statutes: Real Estate Settlement Procedure, Truth-in-Lending, Internal Revenue Service Code, the Patriot Act, fair housing laws, and the various federally funded, insured, and guaranteed mortgage programs

Rights of Home Ownership (e.g., homestead, rights of husband and wife)

- Homestead rights are used to protect the family home from creditors
- Some states prevent the creditor from foreclosing on the property to satisfy the debt, while others only give the homeowner a certain amount of equity that must be paid to him in the event the house is sold for the debt
- State laws protect the spousal interest in real estate in different ways. Some states give the wife a dower interest in her husband's property while giving the husband a curtesy interest in the wife's property
- Community property rights are used in some states to protect the spouse's interest
- Other states have changed their probate laws to give the surviving spouse a life estate interest in the property

Rights of Others Related to Property (e.g., adverse possession, adjoining owners, encroachments)

- Someone who has adversely possessed property for a period of time may file a legal action to obtain title to that property
- Adverse possession is regulated by state law, but generally requires that an adverse possessor use the property in an open, notorious, hostile, and continuous manner
- The statutory period of use to claim adverse possession is between five and thirty years, depending on state law
- Some states permit tacking of years to achieve the statutory period
- A property owner cannot use his property in a way that creates a nuisance to the adjacent property
- Landowners may not re-contour their land or build improvements on the land that creates run-off onto their neighbors' property
- Encroachments are improvements that cross boundary lines
- A neighbor who has not agreed to the encroachment may file legal action to either have it removed or to recover damages
- When an adjacent property owner benefits from the encroachment, she may file legal action to require the encroachment to stay on her property
- An encroachment creates a title defect and affects the marketability of the property

Nature and Types of Common Interest (e.g., condominium, planned unit development, cooperative, townhouse)

- Real estate may be owned in common with others
- In a condominium regime, the property owners own the interior of the units individually and share common ownership of the common areas
- Interior, individual ownership is sometimes referred to as paint-to-paint ownership
- Condominium owners have deeds to their individual units which include a percentage or fractional interest in the common areas
- Owners of property in a planned unit development, also known as a PUD, own their individual units, and the homeowner's association owns the common area
- Property owners in a PUD pay an association fee to have the common area maintained
- Cooperatives are owned by a corporation with shareholders
- Each owner owns a share in the corporation that gives them the right to use a unit in the cooperative
- A townhouse has two or more floors and shares a common wall with the other units
- Townhouse owners own the unit and the land under the unit individually, while sharing, as tenants in common, ownership of the common areas, such as the yards, sidewalks, and recreation area

Eminent Domain Proceedings

- The government, certain quasi-government entities, and some public companies have the power of eminent domain

- When exercising eminent domain, the process is first to condemn the property by filing a legal action
- In a condemnation actions there are two issues: (1) may the property be condemned; (2) what is the amount that must be paid the property owner
- The condemning party has to prove that "taking" the property is for the "common good" of the community, e.g., building or widening roads, installing sewers, expanding a hospital, or creating a public park
- Payment for the property is known as "just compensation"

Legal Proceedings Against Property (e.g., attachments and notice of pending legal action)

- If a creditor gets a judgment against a property owner that is not paid by the owner, the creditor may file an attachment against the property to satisfy the judgment
- State law must be followed when obtaining a writ of attachment
- A writ of attachment is a lien on the property, and the property may only be sold subject-to the lien
- When a legal action is filed that affects the title to real estate, a lis pendens must be filed
- A lis pendens gives constructive notice of the legal action, and anyone taking an interest in the property after that time takes subject-to the lawsuit
- Lis pendens should always be filed in a foreclosure action, notifying prospective buyers and lenders of the lawsuit

Securities Law Application and Referral

- A real estate license does not qualify an agent to give clients and customers advice on securities
- A group of people getting together to purchase real estate to make a profit may be subject to the securities laws
- Securities are regulated by the Securities and Exchange Commission (SEC) and by state laws

Situations Where Experts Are Required (e.g., financial planning and legal advice)

- Real estate agents should always give their clients and customers the option of seeking legal and/or accounting advice prior to signing a contract
- Some of the areas where legal and/or accounting advice may be helpful are:
  - taking and holding title to property
  - title issues
  - financing possibilities
  - contingencies
  - zoning designations and changes
  - tax treatment of certain investments
  - 1031 tax-deferred exchanges
  - environmental issues

Closing Statements (e.g., calculate amount owed by buyer and net to seller)

- A debit and credit closing statement should be used at settlement
- The HUD-1 statement is the closing statement most commonly used
- All of the buyer's expenses should appear as debits on the buyer's side of the closing statement
- Monies paid by the buyer before closing, and monies received from the lender (including the new mortgage), and money from the seller to offset money owed by the buyer at closing, are shown as buyer credits on the closing statement
- All of the seller's expenses, including his current mortgage, should be shown as debits on the seller's side of the closing statement
- Money received from the buyer should be shown as a credit on the seller's side of the closing statement
- Buyer credits are subtracted from the buyer's debits to determine the amount owed by the buyer at closing
- If the buyer's credits exceed his debits, the buyer will receive money at the settlement
- Seller debits are subtracted from seller credits to determine the amount of net proceeds to the seller
- If the seller's debits exceed her credits, the seller will owe money at the closing

Key Term Match: Settlement/Transfer of Ownership

Work on mastering real estate language by matching the following terms with the correct definition. For additional key term matching exercises, see Appendix A.

Terms

A. Mechanic and materialman's lien

B. Specific lien

C. Owner's title insurance

D. Leasehold title insurance

E. Judgment lien

F. Insurable title

G. Title examination

H. General lien

I. Lien priority

J. Contract buyer's title insurance

K. Foreclosure

L. Title abstract

M. Lender's title insurance

N. Declaratory judgment

Definitions

1. _____ The order in which liens will be paid in the event of a foreclosure action.

2. _____ Protects the new owner's interest in real property from defects in title that existed before conveyance to the new owner.

3. _____ Title insurance that protects a buyer who purchasers under an installment sales contract against defects in the seller's title prior to the contract.

4. _____ A lien that is filed against a certain parcel of real estate and does not attach to other property owned by the debtor.

5. _____ Protects the lessee against defects in the lessor's title that may interfere with the lessee's quiet enjoyment of the property.

6. _____ Insurance that protects only the mortgagee's interest in the mortgagor's property during the term of the mortgage.

7. _____ A statutory lien that may be filed by suppliers of material and labor when they are not paid for their services and supplies.

8. _____ A condensed chronological history of all recorded instruments in the chain of title which affect the title that is passed down from owner to owner.

9. _____ Title to real estate that is clear enough of defects to allow the owner to obtain title insurance.

10. _____ Lien that, once recorded, becomes a lien on all personal and real property owned by the lienee.

11. _____ The process used to enforce a mortgage when the mortgagor fails to repay the money as agreed.

12. _____ When the court enters a judgment based solely on the law, because the parties agree to the facts and the only issue is how the facts will be interpreted under the current law.

13. _____ A lien placed on real estate to secure repayment of a loan for the construction of an improvement upon the property.

14. _____ The process of reviewing all recorded documents relating to a specific parcel of property to locate the names of the current and prior owners, to determine if the property is subject to any liens other encumbrances, and to review all recorded documents

O. Construction lien

that may affect the marketability of the property.

15. _____ A statutory general lien that may be filed against a judgment debtor by the judgment creditor once the court enters its final decision.

Practice Questions: Settlement/Transfer of Ownership

1. At the closing the deed is signed by the

A. grantee.
B. grantor.
C. party of the second part.
D. purchaser.

2. The sales contract stated that the usual and customary fees would be paid by each party. That MOST likely means the transfer tax will be paid by the

A. purchaser.
B. settlement agent.
C. seller.
D. lender.

3. A buyer was trying to decide whether or not to purchase a home. His agent told him that a home was a good investment because it would save him money on his federal and state income tax. That information was

A. correct, because homeowners may deduct interest paid on their home mortgages on their federal and state income tax returns.
B. correct, as long as the mortgage on the house is not larger than $500,000.
C. incorrect, because homeowners can only deduct mortgage interest paid on their federal income tax return and not the state income tax return.
D. incorrect, because the interest cannot be deducted unless the homeowner lives in the house for two years.

4. Homeowners may deduct all of the following on their income tax returns EXCEPT

A. ad valorem taxes.
B. mortgage interest.
C. discount points.
D. homeowner's insurance.

5. Settlement agents must have the seller's social security number, because they must

A. ascertain if the seller is a US citizen.
B. report the sale to the IRS if the seller is selling investment property.
C. match the social security number as part of the title examination.
D. send the social security number to the lender.

6. A closing takes place on February 22nd. The taxes for the calendar year are $1,785, and they have not been paid by the seller. On the settlement statement, the buyer will get a

A. credit of $259.19.
B. debit of $259.19.
C. credit of $1,525.81.
D. debit of $1,525.81.

7. Before calculating depreciation on investment property, the owner MUST

A. determine the replacement cost of the improvement.
B. calculate the ad valorem taxes for the year.
C. subtract the land value.
D. decide if she will keep the property for another two years.

8. On an installment sale, the seller pays capital gains

A. in the year of the transfer of title.
B. when the last payment is received.
C. on the money received annually.
D. at the end of the first, third, and fifth years.

9. Fees charged by a municipality to add city sewers are known as

A. ad valorem taxes.
B. assessments.
C. liens.
D. transfer taxes.

10. A 1031 tax-deferred exchange may be used to defer taxes on

A. investment property.
B. residential property.
C. all real property regardless of its use.
D. residential property that has been owned at least two years.

11. A purchaser bought a house that had been recently constructed. The builder had placed a mechanic and materialman's lien on the property prior to the closing that was not paid off at the closing. Because the deed was signed after the lien was placed on the property and it was not paid at closing, the

A. lien merged into the deed
B. seller was required to pay the lien within 30 days
C. buyer took title to the property subject-to the lien
D. lender's mortgage had priority over the lien

12. Title insurance may be purchased to protect all of the following parties

EXCEPT

A. lessee
B. seller
C. buyer
D. lender

13. A title insurance premium must be paid

A. annually
B. monthly with the mortgage payment
C. once, at the time of purchase
D. at the closing and annually thereafter

14. A title defect arises when the

A. grantor's marital status is unknown.
B. buyer cannot obtain financing.
C. settlement agent gets incorrect information for the HUD-1.
D. square footage has been misrepresented by the real estate agent.

15. When more than one party is claiming an interest in the property, what type of action must be filed to have the court determine the true owner?

A. Foreclosure action
B. Declaratory judgment action
C. Bankruptcy action
D. Quiet title action

16. The MOST true statement about a foreclosure lawsuit is

A. the property always sells for a below market price at the judicial sale.
B. a lis pendens must be filed or the lawsuit is defective.
C. that the lawsuit terminates all interest in the property for the names parties.
D. the lawsuit may only be filed by a mortgage holder.

17. A chronological history of the title to real property is known as a title

A. examination.
B. abstract.
C. opinion.
D. recording.

18. After a closing, the lender failed to record the first mortgage until after a judgment lien and income tax lien were recorded. The bank's attorney informed the bank that it still had first lien priority, because the mortgage had an earlier date and the bank had given value in the form of a check delivered to the borrowers before the liens were recorded. This advice was

A. correct, because the date on the mortgage was earlier than the recording dates on the judgment lien and income tax lien.
B. correct, because the bank had delivered value to the borrower before the liens were recorded.
C. incorrect, because the judgment lien and income tax liens were recorded prior to the mortgage.
D. incorrect, because an income tax lien always has priority over all other liens.

19. Recorded notice is

A. actual notice.
B. legal notice.
C. constructive notice.
D. presumed notice.

20. A federal income tax lien is a

A. specific lien.
B. general lien.
C. judgment lien.
D. public lien.

21. All of the following statements are true about a settlement EXCEPT

A. title to property changes hands at the closing.
B. the settlement agent has an obligation to close the transaction according to the sales contract.
C. all states require either an attorney or escrow agent to act as settlement agent.
D. some states refer to the settlement as a closing.

22. The annual homeowner's association dues are $480, are paid for the year, and are to be pro-rated at settlement. The association runs on a fiscal year (July 1 – June 30) and the settlement is June 28th. At closing, prorated dues will be shown on the closing statement as

A. $2.63 credit to the buyer.
B. $2.63 credit to the seller.
C. $36.82 credit to the buyer.
D. $36.82 credit to the seller.

23. The BEST deed for a buyer to receive is a

A. special warranty deed.
B. quit claim deed.
C. warranty deed.
D. general warranty deed.

24. An owner wants to sell land she inherited from her great grandfather. The family knows generally where the boundaries are, but the land has not been surveyed. The BEST deed for Meredith to use when conveying title to the seller is a

A. special warranty deed.
B. grant, bargain, and sale deed.

C. warranty deed.
D. quitclaim deed.

25. The covenant of seisen assures the grantee that the grantor has the

A. title to both the surface and subsurface.
B. peaceful possession of the property being conveyed.
C. right, power, and authority to convey the title being conveyed.
D. exact quantity and quality of title being conveyed.

26. A HUD-1 settlement statement must be used in all transactions

A. with real estate agents.
B. involving federally related mortgages.
C. where the borrower is using secondary market money.
D. underwritten by mortgage brokers.

27. Title to personal property is transferred by

A. warranty deed.
B. bill of sale.
C. certificate of title.
D. deed of trust.

28. A borrower's personal promise to repay a debt is known as a

A. promissory note.
B. mortgage.
C. consideration certificate.
D. trust deed.

29. While meeting with a borrower, the mortgage broker informed the borrower of her closing costs and told her that she would receive a good faith estimate in the mail at her current home address within seven working days. If she receives the good faith estimate as promised, the mortgage broker is

A. in violation of RESPA.
B. complying with the requirements of RESPA.
C. following good business practices.
D. setting high ethical standards.

30. The Real Estate Settlement Procedures Act prohibits

A. high closing costs.
B. misleading advertising.
C. kickbacks for settlement services.
D. unlicensed mortgage activity.

31. When the listing agent presented the offer to the seller, the seller wanted to hold the offer for a few days and think about it. The listing agent told the seller that was illegal and insisted the seller respond to the offer immediately. The listing agent acted

A. appropriately, because she informed the seller of the law.
B. appropriately, because it is unfair for the buyer not to get an answer.
C. inappropriately, because the seller had until the expiration date on the offer to respond.
D. inappropriately, because the seller does not have to respond at all to an offer.

32. A sales contract that is not yet closed is known as an

A. executed contract.
B. executory contract.
C. contingent contract.
D. unilateral contract.

33. Essential elements of a contract include all of the following EXCEPT

A. offer and acceptance.
B. financing terms.
C. legal competency.
D. consideration.

34. At the time of the listing, the seller was not sure if he wanted to leave the window treatments. Later he personally told the buyer that he would leave the window treatments. However, the listing contract was not changed and the window treatments were not included in the sales contract. When the seller moved, he took the window treatments. The buyer's BEST option for getting window treatments is to

A. file a lawsuit against the seller for breach of contract.
B. call the seller and ask him to return t the window treatments.
C. go shopping for new window treatments.
D. ask the agent to buy new window treatments.

35. A sales contract is a

A. unilateral contract.
B. valid contract.
C. bilateral contract.
D. voidable contract.

36. Sal's buyer wanted to include a term in his offer that his mother-in-law must approve the condition of the house before he would be obligated to purchase it. This term is known as

A. a warranty.
B. an option.
C. an inspection.
D. a contingency.

37. All of the following are federal statutes regulating real estate transactions EXCEPT the

A. Internal Revenue Code.
B. Patriot Act.
C. Real Estate Settlement Procedures Act.
D. Homestead Act.

38. William and Mary have been married for 28 years and live in a state that recognizes dower and curtesy. Mary owned a service station prior to their marriage and the deed only has her name on it. The sales contract must be signed by both William and Mary, because William has a

A. dower interest in the property.
B. life estate interest in the property.
C. curtesy interest in the property.
D. community property interest in the property.

39. Harry built a fence on his farm. He has placed the fence on the right side over on his neighbor's property by about 25 feet to get around a large rock outcrop. Harry knows that after a period of time, he may be able to make a claim for the property because of the legal principle of

A. adverse possession.
B. prescriptive easement.
C. quiet title.
D. encroachment.

40. If an owner builds a rock quarry on his property, the neighbors may be able to bring a legal action to make the owner remove the quarry under the legal theory of

A. quiet possession.

B. adverse possession.
C. nuisance.
D. trespass.

41. A condominium deed gives the owner the right to use all of the following EXCEPT the

A. interior of his unit.
B. "handicapped" parking spaces.
C. roof.
D. common hallways.

42. The main difference in a condominium and a cooperative is

A. condominiums are all multi-level developments, while cooperatives are generally one-story structures.
B. cooperatives are only found in large cities, while condominiums may be in any size city.
C. cooperative owners own the land under their unit, while condominium owners only own air space.
D. condominium owners hold title to their units, while cooperative owners own a share in a corporation that owns the unit.

43. Eminent domain allows the government to take property for

A. business development.
B. the common good.
C. sewer installation.
D. large corporations.

44. "Just compensation" is

A. another phrase for fair market value
B. the amount of money required to be paid in a condemnation action.
C. a negotiated amount in an adverse possession action.
D. an average of three appraisals.

45. To prevent the transfer of property without notice while a foreclosure is in progress, the plaintiff should record a

A. notice of foreclosure.
B. caveat emptor.
C. lis pendens.
D. constructive notice.

46. Rolando has just received a call from several of his friends who are getting together to form a group to purchase small apartment buildings on a national level. Because he has a real estate license, they would like him to advise the group on the investment details and on their potential earnings. Rolando's should advise the group that

A. they should retain the services of an attorney to determine if they need a securities broker.
B. he will be happy to help and will get a prospectus together for them within the week.
C. they should retain the services of a CPA to advise them on their potential earnings.
D. he will immediately start looking for apartment buildings that are on the market.

47. When a client asks a questions about a 1031 tax-deferred exchange, the agent's BEST course of action is to

A. advise the client to speak to her attorney or CPA.
B. give the client information obtained from the broker.
C. suggest the client call the IRS.
D. explain the process and offer to act as the escrow agent.

48. The first year's homeowner's insurance premium that is paid at closing will appear on the HUD-1 closing statement as a

A. debit to the buyer.
B. credit to the buyer.
C. debit to the seller.
D. credit to the seller.

49. If the buyer pays for the termite inspection prior to the closing, it will be shown on the HUD-1 closing statement as

A. a credit to the buyer.
B. a debit to the buyer.
C. neither a debit or credit to the buyer.
D. part of the net proceeds to the seller.

50. A seller who has a mortgage balance of $122,873.42, a credit for property taxes of $897.52, a legal fee charge of $175, real estate commission of $2,500, and transfer tax of $350, will net how much at the closing if the property sells for $350,000?

A. $227,126.58
B. $223,379.06
C. $223,204.06
D. $224,999.10

Content Outline: Financing

A. Sources of Financing

1. Institutional (e.g., savings and loans, banks, mortgage brokers)
2. Seller financing (e.g., land contract, purchase money mortgage)
3. Assumption of financing
4. Other sources of financing

Key Point Review: Financing

Financing

- Because most purchasers of real property do not have cash to purchase property, they must obtain mortgage financing to make the purchase
- Although the final decision on financing must be between the purchaser and lender, real estate agents must have a good understanding of financing
- Agents must understand the types of available loans and their underwriting requirements, closing costs and prepaids, and down payment amounts and structures

Sources of Financing

Institutional (e.g., savings and loans, banks, mortgage brokers)

- Financing may be obtained from commercial sources, private sources, and individuals (including the seller)
- Savings and Loan Associations provide mortgage financing
- At one time, S&Ls provided more mortgage financing than any other type of entity and are still a large source for residential mortgages
- Savings and Loan Associations either have federal or state charters
- Mutual Savings Banks are depositor-owned entities that provide mortgage financing
- Commercial banks are a source of mortgage financing for construction, purchase, and home improvements
- Mortgage Bankers, commonly referred to as mortgage companies, make loans for both construction of new homes and purchases of existing properties
- Mortgage companies, in addition to conventional financing, provide FHA and VA financing
- Mortgage brokers are not mortgage bankers
- A mortgage broker brokers money in much the same way that a real estate broker brokers property

- Mortgage brokers find lenders who have money to lend and find buyers who want to borrow money, then gets the two together for a fee
- One mortgage broker may have access to funds from a number of different sources
- Life insurance companies, pension funds, credit unions, and real estate investment trusts also provide mortgage financing

Seller Financing (e.g., land contract, purchase money mortgage)
- Sellers may agree to carry the financing
  - for a buyer who cannot obtain financing from a commercial source
  - as an investment when other investment interest rates are lower than the mortgage rates
- Land contracts are one method of seller financing
  - Land contracts are also known as installment sales contracts, contract for deed, bond for title, land sales contract, and articles of agreement for warranty deed
  - The buyer and seller enter into a written contract that includes the terms of payment, including the interest rate charged by the seller
  - In addition to the principal and interest payments to the seller, the buyer pays the property taxes and insurance premiums
  - Although the buyer has possession of the property, the seller retains legal title to the property until the terms of the contract are met
- Purchase money mortgages may also be used by seller to carry the financing
  - With a purchase money mortgage, the buyer signs a mortgage and promissory note similar to one he would sign with a commercial lender
  - Title to the property passes to the buyer at the time of signing the mortgage and promissory note
- Sellers may use vendor's liens to extend seller financing
  - With a vendor's lien, the seller transfers title to the buyer and retains a lien in the deed
  - Unlike a land contract, the title passes to the buyer at the time of closing

Assumption of Financing
- Some sellers have mortgages that can be assumed by the buyer
- Mortgages are written to be either assumable or non-assumable.
- Assumable mortgages may require the new mortgagor to be qualified, while others permit anyone to assume them
- Loan assumptions were a more popular option in the past when the interest rates were higher
- When a loan is assumed the terms remain the same, including the interest rate
- With an assumption, the purchaser becomes personally liable for the debt
- Unless the lender specifically agrees to release the original mortgagor, the

- original mortgagor also remains liable on the promissory note, and in the event of a default, the original mortgagor is liable for any deficiency
- A release of liability is known as a novation, and has the effect of substituting the new mortgagor for the original mortgagor
- If the purchaser takes title "subject-to" the mortgage, the purchaser does not become liable for the debt; however, if the payments are not made, the purchaser will lose the property in a foreclosure action

Other Sources of Financing

- There are various government organizations that provide mortgage funding
  - The Rural Economic and Community Development division of the U.S. Department of Agriculture administers mortgage assistance programs
  - The Farm Service Agency, formerly the Farmers Home Administration
- Individuals may also provide mortgage financing in transactions in which they are not the seller, but simply to serve as an investment tool

Content Outline: Financing

B. Types of Loans

1. Security for loans (for example, trust deeds, land contracts, mortgages)
2. Repayment methods (for example, adjustable rate mortgage, fully/partially/ nonamortized renegotiated rate)
3. Forms of financing (such as FHA, VA, FmHA, conventional loan)
4. Secondary mortgage markets (for example, Fannie Mae, FHLMC, GNMA)
5. Other types of mortgage loans (for example, wraparound, blanket, package)
6. Down payment assistance programs

Types of Loans

- There are numerous types of loans, and agents should advise their clients to shop around before deciding which loan is best for them

Security for Loans (e.g., trust deeds, land contracts, mortgages)

- Lenders want to be assured that, once they extend a mortgage loan to a buyer, they will be repaid
- Because mortgages and trust deeds are contracts, all of the requirements of a contract must be met in order to create a valid mortgage or trust deed
- The Statute of Frauds requires that all documents creating security interests be in writing
- Borrowers must sign promissory notes in which they personally promise to repay the debt

- In addition to the promissory note, lenders want to keep a security interest in the real estate
- A security interest in property allows the lender to foreclose on the property in order to be repaid the money owed
- When a lender has a security interest, the property is known as collateral
- The process of pledging property as surety is known as hypothecating
- States are either lien theory states, title theory states, or intermediate theory states
- In lien theory states the security interest is a lien on the property in the form of a mortgage
- In title theory states the security interest is title to the property in the form of a trust deed or deed of trust
- In an intermediary theory state the security interest is created by a specific lien on the property and a trust deed
- States that use mortgages to secure the interest are lien theory states, while states that use deeds of trust or trust deeds to secure the interest are title theory states
- Trust deeds are used in some states to secure repayment of the mortgage debt
  - There are three parties to a trust deed – the trustor, the beneficiary, and the trustee
  - In the event of a borrower (trustor) default, the trustee sells the property following the proper legal procedure
  - State laws vary on the foreclosure procedures
  - The defeasance clause in the trust deed states that, when the debt is repaid, the trustee will prepare a deed of reconveyance (also referred to as a deed of release) conveying the title back to the trustor

Land contracts are used in all states to assure the seller that the purchase price of the property will be paid
  - The agreement between the seller and buyer outlines how the buyer will pay for the property and when legal title will pass to the buyer
  - At the time of executing the land contract, equitable title passes to the buyer
  - If the buyer defaults in payment, the seller may then follow the proper legal procedure to terminate the land contract and regain full title to the property
  - Laws relating to foreclosing a land contract have changed in recent years, and sellers should know the current law before taking action
  - Under the old law, that has changed in many states, the seller simply treated all payments as rent and evicted the buyer
  - Current laws, in many states, require the seller to proceed with a judicial foreclosure in the same manner as a commercial lender is required to follow
- Mortgages are liens placed on property to secure repayment of the mortgage debt
  - The parties to the mortgage are the owner (or purchaser), known as the mortgagor, and the lender, known as the mortgagee
  - When the mortgage is repaid, the lien is released by the lender by filing a deed of release (also referred to as a mortgage release)
  - Should the mortgagor default in repaying the debt, the mortgagee may file a foreclosure action to recover the amount owed

- A common misstatement when referring to a mortgage is to say "the bank gave the buyer a mortgage," when, in fact, the correct statement is to say "the buyer gave the bank a mortgage"

Repayment Methods (e.g., adjustable rate mortgage, fully/partially/nonamortized, renegotiated rate)

- When negotiating with a lender, the borrower should inquire about possible repayment methods
- Some mortgages have an adjustable interest rate that may change periodically over the life of the loan
  - These mortgages are also known as variable rate mortgages
  - Beginning interest rates are generally lower than fixed rate mortgages
  - ARMs contain interest rate caps (upper and lower), set time for change in the rate, the index that will be used to adjust the rate, and the margin
  - Monthly payments will change when the interest rate changes
  - There are some ARM products that keep the same monthly payment, which is not a good idea because of negative amortization
  - Adjustable rate mortgages are advantageous for people who plan on owning the property for a short period of time
- The periodic repayment of the mortgage loan is referred to as its amortization
- A payment that is being amortized will have a portion of the payment applied to principal reduction and a portion applied to accrued interest
- Loans may amortized in three ways: fully, partially, and nonamortized
  - A fully amortized loan payment contains the principal and interest necessary to pay the loan in full on the last payment
  - A partially amortized loan payment contains a principal and interest payment, but the payment is not enough to pay the balance in full on the last payment, resulting in a balloon payment
  - A nonamortized payment will include the accrued interest only
    - nonamortized loans are called term mortgages or straight mortgages
    - there is a balloon payment due upon maturity
    - construction loans and bridge loans are examples of nonamortized loans
- Some mortgages are renegotiable rate mortgagees
  - These mortgages are actually a series of short term loans
  - The Federal Home Loan Bank Board sets guidelines for the

lenders to follow
- o The interest rate may change every three to five years based on a national index set forth in the mortgage
- o There are interest rate caps set out in the mortgage to protect the mortgagor from higher than expected rates
- o As long as mortgagor is not in default, the mortgagee must comply with the terms of the mortgage and renew the mortgage at the end of each renewal period

Forms of Financing (such as FHA, VA, FmHA, conventional loan)

- There are numerous forms of mortgage financing, and buyers should investigate them before choosing the best loan product for them
- Each loan type has its own underwriting criteria, down payment and closing costs requirements, and mortgage terms
- Some of the financing is by the government, either as insured or guaranteed loans, while other forms are by private lenders
- Federal Housing Administration (FHA) loans
  - o These are government insured loans designed to help people purchase homes
  - o The program is administered by HUD
  - o Income-to-debt ratios are reduced when qualifying for an FHA loan
  - o Borrowers pay the insurance to protect the lender in the event of default
  - o A one-time mortgage insurance premium (MIP) is paid at closing with additional insurance premiums paid each month as part of the mortgage payment
  - o Higher loan-to-value ratios
  - o Lower down payments
  - o Interest rates are negotiated between the borrower and lender
  - o Discount points may be paid by the buyer or seller to reduce the interest rate
    - Discount points are prepaid interest
    - The rule of thumb is that paying one discount point reduces the interest rate by approximately 1/8%
  - o Lenders may only charge a one-percent origination fee and cannot charge a pre-payment penalty
  - o FHA loans are assumable, but the new buyer must qualify
  - o There are numerous FHA programs
- Veterans Administration (VA or GI) loans
  - o Qualified veterans and unremarried widows/widowers may obtain VA loans
  - o Income-to-debt ratios are lower with VA loans than with conventional financing

- These are guaranteed, not insured, loans
- The borrower does not pay insurance, but does pay a funding fee that may be financed as part of the mortgage
- To prove eligibility, the borrower must obtain a certificate of eligibility from the veterans administration
- The fair market value is determined by a VA approved appraiser who issues a certificate of reasonable value (CRV)
- VA loans have up to a 100% loan-to-value ratio
- The lender and borrower establish the amount of the loan, and VA will guarantee a certain portion against default
- Discount points may be paid by the seller or buyer to reduce the interest rate
- VA does not permit prepayment penalties to be included in the mortgage
- VA loans are assumable
  - if the buyer is not an eligible veteran, the selling veteran does not get her eligibility back until the loan is paid
  - if the buyer is an eligible veteran, the selling veteran can regain her eligibility for another VA guaranteed loan
- Farmer's Home Administration (FmHA) loans
  - An agency in the Department of Agriculture that provides mortgage lending to purchasers and owners in rural communities
  - There are two programs: direct loan program and guaranteed loan program
  - Loans are made to low and moderate income families
  - Discount points cannot be paid with this program to reduce the interest rate
- Conventional loans are loans without government participation and may be insured or uninsured
  - Loan amounts are based on the sales price or the appraised value, whichever is less
  - Uninsured loans are loans that the lender feels have enough security without requiring mortgage insurance
  - The loan-to-value ratio for uninsured loans is generally between 75-80%
  - Insured loans are loans in which the mortgagor is borrowing above 80% loan-to-value
  - Loans to borrowers who do not have at least 20% equity are considered high risk loans
  - Default insurance is referred to a private mortgage insurance (PMI) and is paid monthly along with the mortgage payment

- When an owner's equity position reaches 80%, the PMI may be canceled
- Generally, the underwriting requirements for conventional loans are more strict than those for FHA and VA loans in that the debt-to-income ratio must be lower

Secondary Mortgage Markets (e.g., Fannie Mae, FHLMC, GNMA)

- The secondary mortgage market was developed to increase available funds for mortgage lending
- Lending institutions are known as the primary mortgage market and they get their funding from the secondary mortgage market
- The secondary mortgage market buys and sell mortgages created by the primary market, thereby providing liquidity to mortgages
- Primary lenders originate and close loans directly to the borrowing public and then assign their rights in those loans to the secondary market in order to replenish their funds, enabling them to make more loans to the consuming public
- In order to sell mortgages in the secondary market, the lenders must conform to the secondary market guidelines and use their forms
- Mortgage liquidity reduces the impact of disintermediation to lenders
- Three of the secondary market lenders are: Federal National Mortgage Association (FNMA, pronounced Fannie Mae); Government National Mortgage Association (GNMA, pronounced Ginnie Mae); and Federal Home Loan Mortgage Corporation (FHLMC, pronounced Freddie Mac)
- FNMA – Fannie Mae
  - is the oldest and largest of the secondary market lenders
  - privately owned
  - purchases conventional, FHA and VA loans
  - traded on the New York Stock Exchange
- GNMA – Ginnie Mae
  - government agency of HUD
  - purchases FHA and VA mortgages
- FHLMC – Freddie Mac
  - purchases conventional mortgages from savings and loans, mutual savings banks, and commercial banks
  - FHLMC may also purchase VA and FHA mortgages
  - Freddie Mac refers to itself as The Mortgage Corporation

Other Types of Mortgage Loans (e.g., wraparound, blanket, package)

- Real estate agents should be aware of other mortgage types, but as a practical matter they do not deal with these mortgages on a day-to-day basis, and in fact, may never deal with them
- New types of mortgage loans come and go as the real estate market and the economy change
- Wraparound mortgage loans help buyers with first mortgages obtain mortgages on their property without paying off the first mortgage
  - the lender pays the owner's existing first mortgage and wraps a new mortgage around it
  - in order for this to work, the owner's first mortgage must be assumable
  - instead of paying a first and second mortgage payment, the owner pays one wraparound payment
  - used in times of extremely high mortgage interest rates.
- Blanket mortgage loans are used to finance several parcels of land at the same time, hence, the term blanket
  - used to finance subdivision developments
  - a partial release is filed each time a lot is sold and closed
- Package mortgage loans are used to finance purchases that include personal property, such as an apartment building with appliances
- Buydown mortgage loans allow the buyer to either temporarily or permanently reduce the mortgage rate by someone (buyer, seller, or lender) paying discount points
- Shared-appreciation mortgage loans allow the buyer to get a reduced interest rate while the lender shares in the appreciation
- Graduated payment mortgage loans have lower payments in the early months, and the rate, along with the payment, increases after a few months
  - helps the buyer get into a property when she can't qualify for the loan
  - used in time of high interest rates
  - these are high risk loans because there is large default rate when the payments increase
- Reverse annuity mortgage loans allow borrowers who qualify (based on age) to receive payments from the lender over a period of time, and the lender is repaid at the time the mortgagor dies
- Open-end mortgage loans allow the property owner to refinance without additional closing costs, because the additional moneys are secured by the original mortgage
- Participation mortgage loans are of two varieties: (1) more than one lender participates in making the loan, thereby reducing the

risk; (2) the lender participates in the profits generated by the property as an inducement to make the loan in the first place
- Growing equity mortgage loans have payments that increase over a period of time, with the additional amount being applied directly to principal to shorten the maturity date
- Construction mortgage loans are temporary financing while construction is continuing
  - the entire amount is not disbursed at one time, but rather disbursed in the form of draws as the work is completed
  - interest is charged only on the amount drawn
  - once the construction is completed, the owner obtains permanent financing
- Home equity mortgage loans allows the owner to borrow against the equity in the property
  - the amount borrowed may be taken at one time or treated as a line of credit and accessed as needed by writing a check
  - most often these are second mortgages
  - there may be income tax consequences with equity line mortgages that should be discussed with a tax accountant or attorney

Down Payment Assistance Programs
- There are private and government sources of down payment assistance programs
- Some programs are in the form of grants that are not repaid if the property owner meets certain conditions, and there are other programs that are in the form of second mortgages

Content Outline: Financing

C. Terms and Conditions

1. Compliance with provisions of federal regulations (e.g., Truth-In-Lending Act, Equal Credit Opportunity Act)
2. Loan origination costs (e.g., appraisal fee, credit reports, points)
3. Lender requirements (e.g., property insurance, escrow, deposits, underwriting criteria)
4. Conditional approval
5. Default
6. Foreclosure and redemption rights
7. Nonrecourse provision

Terms and Conditions
- Mortgages have different terms and conditions

- Although real estate agents are not experts on the terms and conditions in mortgages, they should caution their clients and customers to read and understand the documents before signing them

Compliance with Provisions of Federal Regulations (e.g., Truth-In-Lending Act, Equal Credit Opportunity Act)

- There are numerous federal regulations that must be followed by mortgage lenders
- Truth-in-Lending Act
  - part of the Federal Consumer Credit Protection Act
  - requires lenders to disclose: annual percentage rate (APR), finance charges, amount financed and total of payments
  - the law is enforced by the Federal Trade Commission (FTC)
  - Regulation Z was written pursuant to the Truth-in-Lending Act and requires
    - consumer must be fully informed of all finance charges and the true interest rate
    - finance charges include: loan fees, finder's fees, service charges and points, and interest
    - not included in finance charges are: title fees, legal fees, appraisal fees, credit report fees, survey fees, and closing expenses
    - lender must give borrower a disclosure statement within three days of loan application that discloses the APR and includes the amount of the loan fees, discount points, and interest
    - a three-day right of rescission is required when a borrower refinances or obtains a mortgage on property she currently owns – this does not apply to purchase money mortgages
    - advertising credit terms require specific information, when a trigger term is used
    - trigger terms are numbers: down payment, cash price of property, annual percentage rate, interest rate (if variable or adjustable, must be stated as variable or adjustable), amount of down payment, amount of each payment, date when each payment is due, and total number of payments
    - when one trigger term is used in an advertisement, all terms must be included
    - criminal and civil penalties, plus damages for the borrower, for violating Reg Z
- Equal Credit Opportunity Act prohibits discrimination in the lending process based on race, color, religion, national origin, sex, marital status, age, and dependence on public assistance
  - if loan is denied, borrower must be given reason, in writing, within 30 days
  - requires lender to give borrower a copy of the appraisal on the property, if the borrower paid for the appraisal

Loan Origination Costs (e.g., appraisal fee, credit reports, points)

- There are costs incurred by the borrower in mortgage loan transactions
- Although the costs are paid by the borrower, they are for the benefit of the lender
- Lenders generally want an independent appraisal of the property to inform them of the fair market value of the property and of its condition

- A credit report will be ordered by the lender to inform it of the past credit history of the borrower, as well as to give it an opportunity to verify credit information provided by the borrower
- Most of the time both the appraisal and credit report are paid for by the borrower at the time of the loan application
- An origination fee is typically paid to the lender by the borrower to compensate the lender for its work in processing the loan
- Origination fees are stated as a percentage of the loan amount
- Although origination fees are negotiable between the lender and borrower, some of the insured and guaranteed loan programs limit the origination fee to 1% of the loan amount

Lender Requirements (e.g., property insurance, escrow deposits, underwriting criteria)

- Lenders have specific requirements for different types of mortgages
- Because the lender would suffer a financial loss if the property is damaged or destroyed by fire or other casualty, the property owner is required to carry hazard insurance for at least the amount of the loan
    - the insurance must be in effect at the time of closing with proof of such insurance delivered to the lender
    - many lenders require the first year's premium to be paid in advance
    - certain types of loans require an escrow account in which the mortgagor deposits one month's insurance premium each month when paying the mortgage payment
    - policies must name the lender as either an additional insured or as a loss payee
    - the policies must contain a provision to notify the lender if the policy is canceled for any reason
- In addition to the lender requiring the borrower to place property insurance in escrow on a monthly basis, lenders may also require real property taxes and other governmental assessments be placed in escrow to assure the lender that the money will be available when the taxes and assessments become due
- Each type of mortgage has specific underwriting requirements
    - An underwriter assesses the risk for the lender by evaluating the borrower as a credit risk
    - A review of the borrower's loan application and supporting documentation help the underwriter determine if the borrower meets the requirements for a particular mortgage
    - Items reviewed by the underwriter include employment (current and past), income, available funds for closing, income-to-debt ratio, past history for repaying debts
    - Underwriters often ask for additional supporting documentation while making their evaluation
    - If the borrower does not meet the underwriting guidelines the loan will be denied
    - If the borrower meets the criteria the loan will be approved

Conditional Approval

- Once the loan is approved, the underwriter may require that certain criteria be met prior to the closing
- Some of the conditions relate to the borrower
  - must maintain the same income-to-debt ratio
  - must payoff a certain debt
  - provide proof that current property sold and closed
  - must obtain a hazard insurance policy
- Some of the conditions relate to the property and seller
  - the property must appraise for a certain amount
  - repairs required by the appraiser must be completed
  - the title must be clear
  - a survey must be performed

Default

- Mortgages and promissory notes contain default provisions
- These provisions spell out what constitutes a default and the procedure that will be followed in the event of a default
- Default can occur in more ways than not paying the mortgage payment, including failure to keep the property insured, failure to pay property taxes, and failure to maintain the property

Foreclosure and Redemption Rights

- In the event of default, the legal process for the lender to recover its money is called foreclosure
- This legal process is regulated by state law, which vary, but generally, the lender files a lawsuit to "foreclose" the borrowers interest and the interest of all other parties who may have liens on the property
- Once the foreclosure is complete, the only person with right, title, and interest in the property is the person who purchases the property at the foreclosure sale, unless a party with a lien has not been named in the lawsuit
- It is important for the successful purchaser at the foreclosure sale to immediately have a title examination to assure herself that all other parties with an interest in the property have been named
- If money is left over from the foreclosure sale after all liens are paid, the property owner will receive the equity
- Equity of redemption gives the property owner the right to reclaim the property after the foreclosure lawsuit has been filed, but before the foreclosure sale, and the process depends on state law that varies from state to state
- Statutory redemption is permitted in some states, and it allows the property owner to reclaim the property after the foreclosure sale
- Strict foreclosure is not permitted in many states; however, where it is permitted, the property owner loses all equity in the property
- An owner in default of a mortgage may surrender the title to the mortgage holder without the benefit of a foreclosure action by simply deeding the property to the mortgage holder by executing a "deed in lieu of foreclosure"

- If the foreclosure sale does not net enough money to the lender to pay the mortgage balance, plus costs of the foreclosure in full, the lender is entitled to a deficiency judgment under the terms of the promissory note
- A deficiency judgment may be collected by the lender by attaching other assets of the borrower, including bank accounts, wages, and automobiles

Nonrecourse Provision

- A recourse provision in a mortgage and promissory note states that the lender may not only foreclose on the mortgagor's property to collect the debt, but may also collect the amount owed from the borrower personally
- A nonrecourse provision in a mortgage and promissory note states that the lender will not look to the borrower personally for the debt.
  - o In the event the debt is not repaid, the lender agrees to collect what it can through a foreclosure
  - o In the event of a deficiency, the lender waives its right to pursue the borrower personally
  - o Nonrecourse notes are used in syndicates and limited partnerships to encourage participation
  - o Nonrecourse loans are also called "dry mortgages"

Common Clauses and Terms in Mortgage Instruments

- Most mortgages instruments have similar clauses and terms; however the mortgagor should read the mortgage prior to signing it because there are some provisions that definitely favor the mortgagee over the mortgagor
- Agents should not advise on terms in the mortgage, but rather should Suggest to their clients that they seek legal advice if they have a question about a term and its legal effect

Content Outline: Financing

D. Common Clauses and Terms in Mortgage Instruments

1. Clauses and terms in mortgage (e.g., prepayment, interest rates, release, due-on-sale, subordination)
2. Escalation
3. Acceleration

Clauses and Terms in Mortgage (e.g., prepayment, interest rates, release, due-on-sale, subordination)

- Prepayment clauses tell the mortgagor if he can prepay the principal balance prior to its maturity date

- unless the mortgage and promissory note allow prepayment, the mortgagor will penalized for paying the debt early
- prepayment penalties can run all the way from one month's interest to large amounts of interest
- when the debt can be paid earlier than its maturity, the mortgage and promissory note are said to have a "prepayment privilege"
- The interest rate charged may or may not be stated in the mortgage, but will always be included in the promissory note
  - if the interest is not stated in the mortgage, the mortgage will refer to the promissory note
  - the promissory note is signed by the maker and given to the holder
  - if the interest rate is adjustable or variable, or if there is a balloon payment, that must be stated in the note
  - the process to be used for adjusting the interest rate along with the caps and margin will be included in the note
- Release provisions are included that state when and how the lien on the property will be released
  - the mortgagor pays to have the lien released once the debt is paid
  - the mortgage prepares the lien release and either records it, or sends it to the mortgagor to be recorded
- Due-on-Sale clauses prohibit the mortgagor from selling the property while it is encumbered with a mortgage or deed of trust
  - if the mortgagee discovers that the property has been transferred, the entire loan balance will be due and payable
  - due-on-sale clauses are also referred to as alienation clauses
  - long term leases and land contracts may activate a due on sale clause
- Subordination clauses allow for the re-ordering of lien priorities
  - except for property tax liens and assessments, lien priority is established at the time of recording
  - a subordination clauses requires the junior lienholder to remain a junior lienholder, regardless of the recording time
  - an example of when subordination of priorities would be necessary is when a homeowner refinances and the current first mortgage is paid, leaving the second mortgage holder in the first lien position – unless the second mortgage holder subordinates, the homeowner will not be able to get another first mortgage

Escalation

- It is necessary to have an escalation clause in an adjustable or variable rate mortgage to provide for the possible increase in the interest rate
- Escalation clauses are also referred to as escalator clauses
- Escalation clauses are also found in leases and permit the landlord to raise the lease payments over a period of time

Acceleration

- The acceleration clause in a mortgage or promissory note allows the lender to accelerate the balance due when there has been a default
- Unless there is an acceleration clause, the lender cannot sue to foreclose or collect on the note until the payment is actually past due
- Acceleration clauses are also found in leases

Key Terms Matching Exercise: Financing

Work on mastering real estate language by matching the following terms with the correct
definition. For additional key term matching exercises, see Appendix A.

Terms	Definitions
A. Underwriting	1. _____ A company who brings borrowers and lenders together, makes loans, packages them, and sells the packages to both primary and secondary investors.
B. Vendor's lien	2. _____ A form of owner financing in which the seller retains title to the property and the buyer has possession of the property.
C. Subject-to	3. _____ A mortgage that can be assumed by a new mortgagor without changing its original terms.
D. Savings & Loan Association	4. _____ The borrower.
E. Purchase money mortgage	5. _____ A person who brokers money by bringing together a borrower and a lender for a fee.
F. Non-assumable mortgage	6. _____ A voluntary lien given by the mortgagor to the mortgagee to secure the repayment of a debt.
G. Mutual savings bank	7. _____ The lender.
H. Mortgagor	8. _____ A primary source of financing real estate for residences that are chartered and regulated by the state where they do business.
I. Mortgagee	9. _____ A person who works for a company that makes real estate loans and services them.
J. Mortgage company	10. _____ A mortgage that contains a due-on-sale clause.
K. Mortgage broker	11. _____ A loan to a buyer to cover all or part of the purchase price.
L. Mortgage banker	12. _____ A primary supplier of mortgages for new construction and the purchase of existing properties, primarily in the residential real estate market.
M. Mortgage	13. _____ A real estate transaction in which the grantee takes title to real estate that has existing liens, thereby agreeing that the property will be liable for those liens.
N. Installment sales contract	14. _____ A form of seller financing in which the seller conveys title to the buyer by deed, but retains a lien in the deed.
O. Assumable mortgage	15. _____ The process of assessing the risk to the lender when making a mortgage loan.

Practice Questions Financing

1. The MOST likely sources of mortgage financing include all of the following EXCEPT

A. mortgage bankers.
B. commercial banks.
C. savings and loan associations.
D. real estate brokerages.

2. Which of the following is TRUE about a mortgage broker?

A. The terms mortgage broker and mortgage banker are synonymous.
B. Mortgage brokers can get lower interest rates.
C. Mortgage brokers lend money from their depositors.
D. Mortgage brokers typically work with more than one lender.

3. Mortgage bankers are commonly referred to as

A. mortgage companies.
B. commercial lenders.
C. savings and loan associations.
D. mortgagors.

4. Cleo wants to sell her house quickly, but the market is slow because of rising interest rates. There is one woman who wants to buy the house, but has not worked at her job very long. To sell her house to this buyer, Cleo may want to

A. pay her closing costs.
B. sell the property to her on a land contract.

C. reduce the asking price.
D. rent it to her for a period of time.

5. A novation

A. releases the original mortgagor from liability.
B. releases the mortgagee from liability on the promissory note.
C. permits a loan assumption without increasing the interest rates.
D. removes the mortgage from the mortgagee's credit report.

6. Documents creating security interests must be in writing because of

A. contract law.
B. real estate settlement procedures act.
C. consumer protection act.
D. statute of frauds.

7. The document creating personal liability for a person who borrows money to purchase property is the

A. sales contract.
B. mortgage.
C. deed.
D. promissory note.

8. States that use only trust deeds to create security interests are known as

A. title theory states.
B. lien theory states.
C. collateral states.
D. intermediate states.

9. A seller sold his farm on a land contract. The buyer stopped making payments and disappeared. According to the seller's agent, he can move back onto the farm and treat all payments made by the buyer as rent. The agent's advice is

A. correct because once a buyer stops making payments under a land contract the property automatically reverts to the seller.
B. correct because the buyer has abandoned the property and the seller is not required to look for him.
C. incorrect because most states require the seller to file a judicial foreclosure to terminate the buyer's interest in the property.
D. incorrect because the buyer may have personal property on the farm and the seller cannot remove that property without a court order

10. The mortgage and promissory note for an adjustable rate loan must contain all of the following EXCEPT the

A. margin.
B. change date.
C. lifetime cap.
D. lifetime APR.

11. The borrower was informed that his monthly payment, including principal and interest, will be $978.22 for 360 payments. This information means that the loan will be

A. fully amortized.
B. nonamortized.
C. partially amortized.
D. a term loan.

12. A mortgage that is actually a series of short term loans is known as

A. a construction loan.
B. an adjustable rate loan.
C. a renegotiable loan.
D. a bridge loan.

13. The BEST loan type for a non-veteran borrower who wants a low down payment and low income-to-debt ratios would be

A. an FHA loan.
B. a FNMA loan.
C. a GI loan.
D. FmHA loan.

14. Meredith has applied for a loan that has an interest rate of 6.5%. She wants to reduce her rate to 6% by paying discount points. How many discount points would she need to pay to reduce the rate?

A. 2
B. 4
C. 6
D. 8

15. A veteran wants to buy a new house. She has saved $4,000 and the closing costs will be $3,200. Because she is qualified for a VA loan, her agent tells her she has enough money. Is the agent's advice correct?

A. Yes, because she can get a 100% loan.
B. Yes, because her down payment on a VA loan in only $1,000.
C. No, because she must pay the funding fee that will be about $2,000.
D. No, because she is not a first time home buyer.

16. To obtain an uninsured conventional loan on a property that has a purchase price of $185,000, the borrower must make a down payment of at least

A. $18,500.
B. $20,000.
C. $37,000.
D. $40,000.

17. Loans without government participation are known as

A. shared equity loans.
B. conventional loans.
C. primary loans.
D. amortized loans.

18. The main purpose of the secondary mortgage market is to provide

A. liquidity to mortgages.
B. short term equity line mortgages for homeowners.
C. an investment source for the stock market.
D. a stable environment for mortgage brokers.

19. All of the following are secondary market lenders EXCEPT

A. Federal National Mortgage Association.
B. Government National Mortgage Association.
C. Farmers Home National Mortgage Association.
D. Federal Home Loan Mortgage Corporation.

20. A lender has proposed lending Richard $150,000 by assuming his current mortgage of $80,000 and giving him the additional $70,000, less closing costs, in cash. This type of mortgage is called a

A. blanket mortgage.
B. wraparound mortgage.
C. shared equity mortgage.
D. discounted mortgage.

21. Roger has made an offer on an apartment complex. While discussing a mortgage with his banker, the banker mentioned a package mortgage. This would be a good mortgage for him, because

A. it will allow him to get a lower interest rate.
B. the banker can participate in the net profits from the investment.
C. he can finance the building and personal property with one mortgage.
D. it will enable him to borrow in the future without writing a new mortgage.

22. Lois is looking at a new house that is under construction. The builder is offering to buy down her mortgage interest rate for 24 months. This can be accomplished by the builder

A. paying discount points.
B. co-signing the mortgage for 24 months.
C. paying the loan origination fee at the time of closing.
D. giving her an amount of money equal to the additional interest.

23. An elderly couple need the equity out of their home for living expenses. They called a local real estate agent who suggested they look into a mortgage that would pay them instead of them paying the mortgage company. What is this type of mortgage called?

A. Shared equity mortgage
B. Participation mortgage
C. Reverse annuity mortgage
D. Growing equity mortgage

24. One of the main features of a construction mortgage is the

A. interest rate is typically lower than permanent financing.
B. money is disbursed as the project is completed.
C. only builders may obtain these mortgages.
D. they automatically convert to permanent mortgages.

25. Home equity mortgages

A. are often second mortgages.
B. have lower interest rates than first mortgages.
C. have higher closing costs than first mortgages.
D. must be disbursed completely within 30 days.

26. The Truth-in-Lending Act requires that all of the following be disclosed to the borrower EXCEPT

A. annual percentage rate.
B. finance charges.
C. total of payments.
D. loan origination fee.

27. A borrower received information about his annual percentage rate about a week after he applied for his loan. The lender was

A. in compliance with Regulation Z.
B. in compliance with RESPA.
C. not in compliance with Regulation Z.
D. not in compliance with RESPA.

28. Last Thursday, Barney closed the refinance on his home. Monday, Barney decided to sell the home instead of refinancing it. Barney delivered his rescission form to the lender's office who told him he could not rescind the refinance. Is that true?

A. Yes, because the rescission period expired on Sunday.
B. Yes, because the rescission period only applies for second mortgages.
C. No, because he is within his rescission period.
D. No, because he hand-delivered the form to the lender.

29. The Equal Credit Opportunity Act provides for all of the following EXCEPT

A. prohibits discrimination in the lending process based on dependence on public assistance.
B. prohibits discrimination in the lending process based on familial status.
C. requires lenders to give. borrowers a copy of the appraisal if they paid for it.
D. requires lenders to give written notice stating the reason for denial of loan approval within 30 days.

30. A buyer bought a house for $195,000 that appraised for $199,000. He obtained an 80% conventional loan with an origination fee of 1% and discount points of 2%. How much did he pay for the origination fee?

A. $1,560
B. $1,592
C. $1,950
D. $1,990

31. Who usually pays for the credit report when the buyer applies for a mortgage loan?

A. Buyer
B. Lender
C. Underwriter
D. Negotiable between the buyer and lender

32. At closing the lender required the buyer to pay the first year's hazard insurance premium. In addition, the buyer was required to place two month's insurance premium in the escrow account. The monthly insurance premium is $82. How much did the buyer pay at closing for insurance?

A. $164
B.. $984
C. $1,148
D. $1,230

33. The lender required 7 month's property taxes be placed in the escrow account at the closing on May 1st. The annual taxes were $1,800 and were prorated between the buyer and seller on a calendar year. How much did the buyer actually pay for taxes at closing?

A. $450
B. $750

C. $1,050
D. $1,800

34. The MOST complete description of an underwriter's job is that she

A. assesses risks for the lender.
B. approves mortgage loans.
C. reviews credit reports.
D. evaluates loan documentation.

35. Darren has been informed that his interest rate will be 6.5%. According to a chart his agent has shown him, his monthly payment per thousand for a 30-year mortgage will be $6.32. If he wants to keep his payment less than a $1,000 per month for principal and interest, he can only borrow approximately how much?

A. $63,200
B. $126,400
C. $158,227
D. $163,200

36. Conditional loan approval means

A. certain conditions must be met before the closing.
B. approval is conditioned upon money becoming available.
C. the seller must make certain repairs.
D. all contingencies in the contract must be met.

37. A mortgagor has failed to pay his property taxes. This constitutes

A. negligence.
B. disintermediation.
C. default under the mortgage.
D. breach of contract.

38. At the foreclosure auction, the house sold for $172,500. The costs of sale were $6,320, the pay-off of the first mortgage was $158,200, and the tax lien pay-off was $5,432. How much equity did the owner receive after everything was paid?

A. $2,548
B. $7,980
C. $8,868
D. $14,300

39. An owner may redeem her property prior to the foreclosure sale under the

A. statutory right of redemption.
B. equity of redemption.
C. mortgage redemption clause.
D. constitutional right of redemption.

40. When a property owner wants to transfer mortgage property to the bank without a lawsuit being filed, the deed that can be used is a

A. quit claim deed.
B. deed of surrender.
C. deed in lieu of foreclosure.
D. foreclosure deed.

41. A homeowner recently refinanced his home. About a month later he saw an advertisement that he could refinance his home again and reduce his rate by 2%. When he called the first lender, he was informed that he could not pay off his loan with them for another 23 months without paying $5,000. Could this be correct?

A. Yes, if the homeowner has a prepayment penalty clause in the mortgage and promissory note he signed.
B. Yes, the lender has a prepayment privilege that allows it to charge the additional interest.
C. No, it is illegal to charge more than the principal balance plus accrued interest.
D. No, because homeowner's have, by law, six months to pay off a mortgage without a penalty.

42. A mortgage written on May 1, 2006 for one-year has a maturity date of

A. May 1, 2006.
B. April 30, 2007.
C. April 1, 2007.
D. May 1, 2007.

43. Billie has paid off her mortgage loan. The lender has returned her promissory note marked "paid" to her and has given her a release of mortgage. What should she do with these documents?

A. She should record both documents in the public records.
B. She should keep the promissory note and return the release to the lender for recording.
C. She should keep the promissory note in a safe place and record the release in the public records.
D. She should keep both documents in a safe place.

44. Al wants to sell his house on a land contract. He has a current first mortgage on the property. He and his buyer have decided not to inform the lender of the sale. Why would they make that decision?

A. Because his mortgage has a subordination clause
B. Because his mortgage has a due-on-sale clause
C. Because his mortgage has an escalation clause
D. Because his mortgage has a subrogation clause

45. A homeowner paid off his first mortgage when he refinanced. The new lender has asked his second mortgage holder to sign a subordination agreement. What is the purpose of that agreement?

A. It assures the second mortgage lender that he still owns the property.
B. It reverses the priority of the new first mortgage and the second mortgage.
C. It allows the second mortgage to continue without being paid off.
D. It gives the first mortgage holder the right to foreclose if necessary.

46. An escalation clause is necessary in a/an

A. second mortgage.
B. reverse annuity mortgage.
C. FNMA mortgage.
D. adjustable rate mortgage.

47. The acceleration clause in a mortgage allows the lender to

A. collect the entire amount due when a default occurs.
B. increase the interest rate over a set period of time.
C. increase the monthly escrow deposit when taxes increase.
D. file a lawsuit when two or more payments are late.

48. A buyer is has purchased property for $210,000. He is obtaining a 97% FHA loan, with 2 discount points, and a 1% origination fee. How much does he need to bring to the closing as a down payment?

A. $2,100
B. $6,300
C. $8,400
D. $12,600

49. An underwriter must consider all of the following factors in evaluating a loan application EXCEPT

A. monthly housing expense.
B. credit history.
C. employment history.
D. number of family members living in household going to school.

50. The parties to a promissory note are the

A. maker and holder.
B. buyer and seller.
C. maker and guarantor.
D. guarantor and holder.

Content Outline: Professional Responsibilities/Fair Practice/Administrative

A. Professional Responsibilities/Fair Practice/Administrative
    (Topics in *Italics* appear on the Broker Examination Only)

1. *Terms of contract between salesperson and Broker (e.g., employee, independent contractor)*
2. *Trust accounts*
3. Complete and accurate records of business transactions
4. *Required notifications and reports to real estate regulatory agency*
5. *Company policies, procedures, and standards*
6. Market trends, availability of financing, rates and conditions of obtaining credit
7. Resolving misunderstandings among parties to real estate transactions
8. *Sales force training*
9. *Sales force supervision*
10. Commissions from sales of real estate
11. *Appropriate distribution of commissions*
12. *Accounting procedures in the office*

Key Point Review: Professional Responsibilities/Fair Practice/Administrative

Professional Responsibilities/Fair Practice/Administrative

*   Because different states have different titles for the supervising broker, trust accounts, and salespeople, in this section the following terms will be used:

    Broker = Supervising Broker, Principal Broker, and Sponsoring Broker
    Trust Account = trust account, escrow account, impound account, and earnest money account
    Salesperson or Salespeople = sales associate, affiliate, and salesperson

Terms of contract between salesperson and Broker (e.g., employee, independent contractor)

*   State licensing laws require a salesperson to work with a Broker
*   Each Salesperson must work with only one Broker, while a Broker may be associated with more than one Brokerage
*   The Broker has the duty to supervise the activities of the Salesperson

- Brokers must determine if the Salesperson will be an employee or an independent contractor
- The usual relationship of the Salesperson with the Broker is that of an independent contractor
- Because there is a contractual relationship between the Salesperson as independent contractor and the Broker, there should be a written contract between the parties
- Some state's licensing laws require a written agreement between the Broker and Salesperson, while other states do not
- Because of the income tax laws, it must be clear that an independent contractor is "independent"
- Brokers cannot treat their Salespeople as employees if they want to pass the IRS independent contractor test
- If a Broker treats an independent contractor like an employee the Broker may be liable to the Internal Revenue Service and the state revenue cabinets for uncollected income taxes, interest, and penalties
- Some of the things the Broker cannot require of an independent contractor that could be required of an employee are:
  - set office hours
  - specified working days
  - set vacation time
  - floor duty
  - dress codes
  - sales quotas
  - attendance at meetings and other functions
  - specific way to do a certain task
- Terms that should be included in the independent contractor agreement are:
  - compensation amount, when it is earned, when and how it will be paid
  - expenses that are to be paid by each party
  - office policies relating to licensing, professionalism, and ethics
  - agreement to adhere to laws on anti-trust, fair housing, sexual harassment
  - term of the contract and how it is terminated

Trust Accounts

- The Broker must maintain the Trust Account to deposit client's money for safekeeping
- State licensing laws regulate how and where Trust Accounts must be kept
- Brokers cannot commingle Trust Account funds with general Brokerage account funds
- Brokers cannot use Trust Account money for personal expenses (referred to as conversion)
- In addition to civil penalties for violating laws relating to Trust Accounts, there may also be criminal penalties
- Trust Accounts are non-interest bearing, unless the person depositing the money with the Broker agrees that the funds may be kept in an interest bearing account

- If the Trust Account is interest-bearing, the person who owns the money must agree on how the interest will be disbursed
- Each Broker must sign a consent form permitting the state licensing regulatory body the right to audit the trust account

Complete and Accurate Records of Business Transactions

- State regulatory agencies establish what records must be kept by a Brokerage and the length of time to keep the records. Examples of the records to be kept include: listing contracts; sales contracts; trust/escrow account information, including copies of checks and money orders; promissory notes; closing statements; disclosures, including agency, seller, wood-destroying insect, and lead-based paint; inspection information; and licensed affiliate information, including licenses and compensation records
- Federal and state tax laws require records of income and expenses be kept by the Brokerage

Required Notifications and Reports to Real Estate Regulatory Agency

- Each state regulatory agency requires the Broker to give certain notices and to file certain reports
- Brokers must know which notices are required because failure to comply may result in the Broker and salespeople being penalized by the regulatory agency. Examples of notices that are required include: change of company name and address; change of offices by salespeople; change of surname; information about errors and omissions insurance; conviction or guilty plea entered for felony and/or certain misdemeanors; and completion of education
- The regulatory agency is the state office that issues real estate licenses

Company Policies, Procedures, and Standards

- Each company Broker establishes the company policies, procedures, and standards
- A written manual should be provided by the Broker to each salesperson notifying him of the companies policies, procedures, and standards
- The written policy manual will protect both the Broker and Salesperson from misunderstandings while assisting the Salesperson in understanding what is expected of him
- Some of the state regulatory agencies require written policy manuals as part of the Broker's supervision of the Salespeople

Market Trends, Availability of Financing, Rates, and Conditions of Obtaining Credit

- One of the most valuable services an agent can provide a consumer is a knowledge of the real estate market
- Because financing is changing daily, it is important for salespeople to stay abreast of the changes
- Agents should have the ability to explain the financing process and assist the

buyers in understanding what will be necessary for them to obtain credit

- A successful agent will have sources to obtain financing and rate information for their clients and customers, including personal contacts, on-line resources, and printed material
- Brokers and their sales staff should also have an understanding of illegal practices, like flipping and predatory lending, to assist their clients in avoiding these problems

Resolving Misunderstandings Among Parties to Real Estate Transactions

- One of the most important jobs of a Broker is to resolve disputes and disagreements that arise in real estate transactions
- These disputes can involve the consumers, other Brokerages and their agents, as well as salespeople in the office
- The office policy manual is a valuable tool for resolving disputes
- A thorough knowledge of license law will be beneficial in resolving disputes relating to license law issues
- Real estate board and association rules and regulations may be helpful in resolving issues
- One of the most effective ways to resolve a misunderstanding is to return telephone calls
- Face-to-face meetings are effective because it shows the parties that the Broker has taken time to be of assistance
- Brokers should be responsive – do not wait for the problem to get better, because it won't
- Third party mediations have become a very good way to resolve problems

Sales Force Training

- Training is a never ending process
- New salespeople need basic training in how to perform their tasks as real estate agents
- Experienced agents need refresher courses to review things they may have forgotten and to keep up with changes in the industry
- Brokers should utilize various training methods from the classroom to hands-on field work

Sales Force Supervision

- State licensing laws require the Broker to adequately supervise her Salespeople
- Brokers may hire office managers and other staff to assist in supervising the sales force; however, the Broker still remains liable for the supervision
- A good Broker will be accessible to his Salespeople to answer questions and handle problems as they arise
- Supervision includes not only observing the actions of the Salespeople as they go about their day-to-day activities of meeting clients and customers, but also how their paperwork is completed and how they follow up on problems

Commissions From Sales of Real Estate

- The real estate commission to be charged by a Brokerage is established by the Broker, independent of input on what other Brokers may be charging
- Federal and state anti-trust laws, specifically the Sherman Anti-Trust Act, prohibit
  - price fixing, boycotting, tying agreements, and territorial allocations
  - Brokers conspiring to fix commission rates and/or commission splits
  - state regulatory agencies and trade associations from establishing set commissions
- Real estate commission may be a percentage of the sales price, a flat fee, or any other thing of value
- To receive a real estate commission, a person must have an active real estate license
- Referral fees may be paid, but the referring agent must have a real estate license, even if the license is in another state
- Salespeople can only receive commissions from their Broker

Appropriate Distribution of Commissions

- Because of federal and state anti-trust laws, there are no "appropriate" distributions of commissions
- Brokers must decide on the division and distribution of commissions in two instances: (1) between cooperating companies, and (2) to the Brokerage's salespeople
- Brokers are not required to cooperate with Brokers and Salespeople from other Brokerages
- If the Broker decides to cooperate, he must decide how much of the real estate commission will be paid to the cooperating Broker
- The employment agreement or independent contractor agreement should clearly state how the commission that comes into the office will be divided between the Broker and the salesperson
- Some Brokerages divide commissions with Salespeople, while other Brokerages allow the salespeople to keep 100% of the commission, while paying desk fees and other expenses to the Brokerage
- Brokerages that divide commissions with the Salespeople may have a graduated scale so that the more commission that is earned by the salesperson, the more commission the salesperson is paid

Accounting Procedures in the Office

- Brokers must maintain accurate records of all client monies as they are received and disbursed
- Unless the Broker has an understanding of bookkeeping and accounting principles, she should hire a bookkeeper and/or an accountant
- Separate accounts must be maintained for client funds and Brokerage funds – there must never be commingling of funds

- Each time money is received, either from or on behalf of a client, a receipt should be given
- Each time money is spent on behalf of a client, a receipt should be obtained
- Brokerage accounts should be maintained to show all monies received for commissions, as well as distribution of commissions, both to salespeople and cooperating Brokerages
- One of the main reasons a Brokerage fails and/or has serious legal problems is poor bookkeeping practices
- Serious tax problems can arise from poor bookkeeping and accounting practices
- Trust Accounts should be balanced every month
- Brokers should have accounting safeguards to prevent embezzlement of client funds

Key Term Match: Professional Responsibilities/Fair Practice/Administrative

Work on mastering real estate language by matching the following terms with the correct definition. For additional key term matching exercises, see Appendix A.

Terms

A. Tying agreements

B. Boycotting

C. Trust Account

D. Sherman Anti-Trust Act

E. Territorial allocations

F. Commingle
G. Brokerage accounts

H. Sponsoring Broker

I. Flipping

J. Cooperating broker

K. Regulatory agency

L. Predatory lending
M. Independent contractor

N. Referral fee

O. Price fixing

Definitions

1. _____ The illegal practice of requiring the consumer to purchase goods and services as a bundle in an effort to keep prices high and to prevent comparison shopping.
2. _____ The act of refusing to cooperate with another company in an effort to show disapproval of its policies and procedures.
3. _____ The practice of purchasing real estate for a low dollar amount with the intention of quickly transferring it to another buyer for a hefty profit.
4. _____ The person who is in charge of running the brokerage and supervising the licensed associates in the brokerage.
5. _____ A separate account used to hold client's money and money belonging to others.
6. _____ The operating bank account for the brokerage.
7. _____ The process of depositing client funds into the brokerage's account or into the broker's personal account.
8. _____ A federal statute prohibiting price-fixing, certain types of boycotts, tying arrangements and market allocation schemes.
9. _____ The broker bringing the buyer to the transaction when the property is listed with another broker.
10. _____ The illegal practice used by companies with a large market share to prevent other companies from coming into their area of town to do business.
11. _____ The governmental agency that licenses, regulates, educates, and disciplines real estate agents.
12. _____ A self-employed individual.
13. _____ A recent development in lending practices that includes deception and fraud by lenders.
14. _____ The fee received for recommending someone to a service provider.
15. _____ The illegal practice of conspiring to fix fees or prices for services rendered or goods sold in an effort to protect the service or goods provider.

Practice Exam: Professional Responsibilities/Fair Practice/Administrative

1. A sponsoring broker is required by the licensing law to

A. compensate the sales agents.
B. supervise the sales agents.
C. write a policy and procedures manual.
D. have adequate staff.

2. If a sales agent is an independent contractor, she must

A. keep regular office hours.
B. pay her own federal and state income tax.
C. attend office meetings once a month.
D. pay a portion of the office rent.

3. Earnest money deposits must be deposited into the broker's

A. brokerage account.
B. security deposit account.
C. trust account.
D. management account.

4. Broker Jim decided to open an interest-bearing escrow account to help defray the costs of maintaining the account. Under the license law this is permissible if

A. he uses the interest earned only to maintain the account.
B. the bank will agree to give him free checks.
C. he does not earn more than $600 interest each year.
D. the clients agree in writing that he may use the interest in this way.

5. In order to save storage space, Broker Mary Ann has decided to shred all files that are more than three years old. She should first

A. remove copies of the closing statement and commission check.
B. review the licensing law to find out how long she needs to keep her files.
C. ask her agents if they want to keep their files.
D. make a list of the files being shredded for future reference.

6. A Broker has decided to change his company name. He should

A. contact the post office.
B. ask his agents to make sure they do not object.
C. send notice to the regulatory agency.
D. verify that no other company is using the new name.

7. Written policy manuals are used to protect the

A. sales agents.
B. sponsoring broker.
C. clients.
D. all of the above.

8. Brian was on phone duty today and received a call from a prospect asking about the new first-time homeowners lending program that was advertised in today's local newspaper. Brian had not seen the newspaper. He told the prospect he did not know anything about the new program and suggested that he call the newspaper for information. Brian's advice was

A. appropriate, because an agent should never advise on anything he isn't sure about.

B. appropriate, because the newspaper would have all of the information and could refer the prospect to the right lender.

C. inappropriate, because the newspaper isn't going to know where to send him or that information would have been in the newspaper.

D. inappropriate, because agents on phone duty should know about financing programs that have appeared in the newspaper.

9. Broker Stewart has just received a call from a cooperating broker who is upset about how one of Stewart's agents acted at a closing. Stewart's FIRST action should be to

A. assure the cooperating broker that he would have a talk with the agent and make sure the agent acted better the next time.

B. assure the cooperating broker that he would talk to his agent and then call the broker back to discuss the situation further.

C. tell the broker that he did not appreciate complaints about his agents and ask the broker not to call again.

D. set up a meeting with the cooperating broker and agent to work out the problem.

10. Broker Beatrice has an office policy of only hiring agents who have been in the business for at least ten years. She has this policy to keep from having to hire someone to hold training sessions. This policy is

A. a good one to save money for the brokerage that can be used to upgrade the computer system and

web site.

B. a good one because agents with ten years experience do not need training and would only be bored if they were required to attend training sessions.

C. not a good one because the real estate business changes and everyone needs to be updated.

D. not a good one because there are lots of good agents with less than ten years experience that would be likely to join the brokerage.

11. A principal broker has just received a letter from the state regulatory agency. Apparently, someone has complained about an advertisement placed by one of his salespeople. The principal broker does not understand why he received the letter, because he has an office manager that handles all of the sales staff problems. What would you suggest he do?

A. Give the letter to the office manager and tell her to follow-up with the regulatory agency because that is her job

B. Speak to his salesperson to find out what happened and then respond to the letter

C. Set up a meeting with the office manager and salesperson to find out what happened and to plan a strategy for responding to the letter

D. Send the letter back to the agency and explain that it should be re-directed to his office manager

12. A referral fee may be paid to

A. anyone making a referral once the transaction closes.

B. on licensed brokers.

C. to the sales associate making the referral.

D. only out-of-state brokers.

13. The largest brokerage in town just raised its commission by 1% on properties listed for more than $400,000 because they required more advertising. Today at lunch three brokers from different companies were talking and decided they would follow suit and raise their commissions. Their decision is

A. a good one in light of the cost of advertising.
B. premature because they don't know for sure if the brokerage will lose listings with the new policy.
C. not a good one because they are violating anti-trust laws.
D. questionable until they have a chance to discuss it with their agents.

14. A group of brokers refusing to cooperate with another brokerage because they don't like that brokerage's commission policy is an example of

A. boycotting.
B. tying.
C. price fixing.
D. market allocating.

15. The commission paid to a sales associate by the broker is

A. established by the regulatory agency in each state.
B. negotiated between the broker and sales associate.
C. set by custom in the area.
D. determined by the local board of REALTORS®

16. If a brokerage has fewer than three sales agents, the broker may place all funds coming into the company in one account.

A. True, because with so few agents one account is all that is necessary
B. True, as long as there is a deposit ticket with the name of the buyer and seller next to the check being deposited
C. False, because it will be too confusing for the bookkeeper to track the general funds and escrow funds
D. False, because that would commingling funds and illegal

17. If the real estate commission is 5.75%, how much will the brokerage net on the commission if the house sells for $172,500 and the advertising cost was $895?

A. $9,023.75
B. $9,918.75
C. $10,813.75
D. $11,813.75

18. The sales associate earns 40% of the commission that comes into the brokerage as the selling agent. The house sells for $219,900 with a 6.25% real estate commission. How much will the sales associate receive from her broker if she is in the 28% tax bracket?

A. $3,958.20
B. $5,497.50
C. $9,895.50
D. $13,743.75

19. A farm sells for $547,000. The listing commission is based on 4.75% and the split with the cooperating broker is 50/50. Advertising cost $2,500 and the survey fees were $1,800. How much commission will the selling office receive?

A. $8,691.25

B. $10,491.25
C. $12,991.25
D. $25,982.50

20. An office building sold for $875,000. The real estate commission was a flat fee of $35,000. A referral fee of 10% was paid from the top and the balance was divided 50/50 between the listing office and selling office. The sales associate in the selling office received 60% of the commission paid to his company. How much did he receive?

A. $6,300
B. $9,450
C. $10,500
D. $21,000

Chapter One

Key Term Match

1. O
2. M
3. A
4. K
5. L
6. N
7. G
8. B
9. C
10. F
11. H
12. I
13. J
14. D
15. E

Practice Questions

1. B – The main element of the exclusive agency contract is that the seller retains the right to sell the property without paying the broker a real estate commission. If the seller signs an exclusive right to sell contract, the broker must be paid even if the seller sells the property. With an open listing, the seller lists with more than one broker and pays only the real estate broker who actually sells the property, while reserving the right to sell it himself. Open listing is not the best answer in this question, because the seller wants to hire "a" real estate broker. A net listing refers not to the type of relationship created, but to how the compensation will be paid. In most states, net listings are illegal.

2. D – This is the correct answer because all owners must sign the listing contract. Any owner who does not sign the listing cannot be forced to sell the property. An agent marketing property without all signatures takes the risk that the non-signing parties will not agree, and is likely violating licensing laws that require all owners' signatures before marketing the property. Response "A" is incorrect in that a spouse cannot legally obligate the other spouse to anything without a written power of attorney. If the broker advertises property without all signatures, as suggested by Response "B", he is probably violating his state's licensing laws. Response "C" is incorrect because the form of ownership is not relevant when discussing signing the listing – all owners, regardless of form of ownership, must sign.

3. C – Multiple listing services are designed for brokers to cooperate in marketing their listings. Member brokers have agreed on how the process will work and on the compensation that will be earned by the cooperating broker. The other three responses, although legal, would not likely be effective because they are awkward to use, and brokers may not consider showing the property because of the decreased likelihood of being compensated for their service.

4. D – Sally has a duty to verify information before passing it along as being true. Response "A" is a correct statement, in that she is not a surveyor or

appraiser; however, her action is not appropriate. Response "B" is correct in that her actions were inappropriate, but it is incorrect because state law does not require her to measure a lot. Response "C" is incorrect in that her actions are not appropriate, and it is debatable as to whether or not it is the sellers' responsibility to know this information.

5. C – All of the others are different types of legal descriptions. A "county clerk survey" is something that does not exist.

6. D – Correct number of square miles.

7. B – When stating a lot size, the footage along the road is stated first.

8. C – To answer the question you must first calculate the total square footage in the lot (100' x 200' = 20,000 sq. feet). Add 2,800 + 673 + 160 for a total square footage for the improvements. That total is 3,633. Subtract 3, 633 square feet from the total lot square footage of 20,000. The square footage without improvements is 16,367. It is irrelevant that the house has unlivable square feet because that part of the house still covers the lot.

9. C – A surveyor is a professional qualified to determine the size of a lot. Responses "A," "B," and "D" are all options; however, they are not the best option for a number of reasons. Sellers often forget lot sizes and confuse the numbers, deeds may not contain the actual size of the lot, and the property valuation records may or may not contain the needed information.

10. A – First calculate the size of the lot (200' x 550' = 110,000 square feet). Add the total square footage in the building and in the improvements (6,000 + 3,200 = 9,200 square feet). Subtract the total of the improvements from the total in the lot (110,000 – 9,200 = 100,800 square feet for the green space). Divide the total green space square footage by the number of square feet in an acre (100,800 ÷ 43,560 = 2.31). The last calculation shows you that there will be 2.31 acres for green space. Because the green space requirement is 2 acres, he will be able to meet the green space zoning requirement.

11. D – You should not use finished square footage below grade in stating the total gross living area regardless of how well the basement has been finished. Remember – a basement is a basement. Finished square footage below grade may be used for marketing the property, but agents should specifically point out that the area is below grade.

12. A – Language in the deed includes all appurtenances without naming them specifically. Deeds may exclude certain appurtenances, but unless they are excluded they are included. Response "B" is irrelevant, "C" and "D" are incorrect statements of real estate principles and law.

13. B – An appurtenant easement is one that requires two parcels of land. The parcel that is benefited by the easement is known as the dominant tract and the one that has the easement on it is known as the servient tract. Responses "A," "C," and "D" are other types of easements.

14. D – An easement in gross involves only one parcel of land and gives the easement holder a personal right to use the property. A utility company is the perfect example of a entity that would have an easement in gross to give it access to install and maintain utility service.

15. C – Riparian water rights are incidental to owning land that is adjacent to water and these rights give the owner the right to use the water. Responses "A" and "D" are other forms of water rights.

16. A – This is the term used to describe the process where land is added to the shoreline or riverbanks by alluvial deposits. When the passing water slows down because it hits the shoreline or riverbank, it drops the particles of soil and rock that it is carrying. Over a period to time, additional land is created.

17. D – Property is insurable whether or not it has utilities. The other items would be directly affected by either the presence or absence of utility service.

18. A – These are the four basic types of architectural roof styles. The other responses each contain incorrect items.

19. B – An encumbrance is a limitation on the owner's rights in her land, and a lien is one form of encumbrance. Response "A" refers to someone's rights to use land that belongs to another; and response "D" is a physical improvement on one person's land that crosses the boundary line onto another persons' land.

20. A – When one person sues another person and wins, he may place a lien on property owned by the person he sued. This is known as a general lien and it will attach to all property, real and personal, that is owned by the person who was sued and lost. These liens typically run with the land and would stay on the land regardless of who owns it. Some states have provisions for the lienholder to foreclose on the real estate even after the property transfer to an owner that was not involved in the lawsuit. Response "B" is incorrect, because a person suing you cannot take ownership of the property; rather they obtain a judgment that may lead to the sale of the property. Response "C" is incorrect – see explanation for response "A." Response "D" is incorrect, because filing an appeal will probably have no effect on the lien being placed on the real estate.

21. B – The purpose of building codes are to set minimum standards, not maximum or acceptable standards. If an area has building codes, the builders have no choice but to follow them.

22. D – A certificate of occupancy informs the new owner that inspections required by the building code have been completed and that the house is habitable. Response "A" is incorrect, because the deed is evidence of title. Response "B" is incorrect, because a building permit must be obtained prior to construction. Response "C" is incorrect because, although the certificate of occupancy means the construction is complete, that is not the proper name for the form.

23. C – Merely having a copy of the obituary is not enough to tell the listing agent who owns the property and who has the right to sign the listing.

Response "A" is incorrect because without more information, the listing agent cannot say the widow owns the property and has the right to administer the estate. Response "B" is incorrect, because the obituary is not "constructive" but "actual" notice of his death. Response "D" is incorrect, because a death certificate would be of no more help to the listing agent than the obituary when trying to determine who needs to sign the listing.

24. B – Recording the document does, by definition, give constructive notice. That is, once the document is recorded this fact is considered to be notice to the world of who owns the property. Response "A" is incorrect, because the title is conveyed once the deed is signed and delivered by the grantor, and is accepted by the grantee. Response "C" is irrelevant. Response "D" is incorrect, because "actual notice" means that someone has firsthand knowledge of a fact that may or may not come from recording a document.

25. C – Once a neighborhood association is established, all owners who own property in the area covered by the association must belong.

26. B – The bylaws set out the way the homeowner's association will be run and by whom. Response "A" is incorrect, because the master deed is used to create a condominium. Response "C" is incorrect, because articles of incorporations are used to create a corporation. Response "D" is incorrect, because restrictive covenants are limitations on how owners may use their land.

27. C – All real estate commissions are established by the brokerage and negotiated between the broker and seller when the listing is signed. It is illegal, under both federal and state anti-trust laws, for anyone to attempt to set real estate commissions for an area or particular group of brokers. Each broker must establish her own fees independently of other brokers.

28. C – Multiply $135,000 by 7%. The amount is $9,450. Because the commission is 7% or $7,500, whichever is less, the commission will be $7,500. Responses "B" and "D" factor in the $750 in advertising which is irrelevant information. Response "A" does not factor in the "whichever is less" term of the agreement.

29. C – This is the value used by property valuation administrators to value property for tax purposes.

30. D – Multiply $150,000 x .020 = $3,000. Then divide the $3,000 by 2 to get one payment of $1,500. One mill is one-tenth of 1¢ (.001); therefore 20 mills will be the decimal equivalent of .20. The question asked the amount for an equal installment in June and December; therefore, Response "A" was incorrect. Responses "B" and "C" used the fair market value and not the assessed value.

31. B – This is the title for someone who performs appraisals. Response "A" is incorrect, because that refers to someone who sets value for property tax purposes. However, the AMP test writers appear to use "assessor" when referring to an "appraiser." If there is a question on the test discussing either appraisers or assessors, read the question very carefully to determine which one

they mean. Response "C" is incorrect, because a surveyor measures land. Response "D" is incorrect, because, although real estate brokers prepare comparative market analyses, they are not generally hired for the purpose of giving the owner a fair market value for the property.

32. C – Location of property is said to be the main element in determining value of property. The old joke is: "What are the first three elements in determining property value?" The answer is: "location, location, and location." Response "A: is incorrect, because prior selling price is irrelevant for determining current fair market value. Amenities are included in determining the value, but is not generally considered one of the "most" most important. Response "D" is used only for determining value for property tax purposes.

33. D – Anticipation is the principle that value changes in expectation of a future change in the use of the land which may either increase or decrease the value. Response "A" is incorrect, because appreciation refers to the increase in value of a property over time. Response "B" is incorrect, because highest and best use value refers to the legal use of land that will generate the greatest net return. Response "C" is incorrect, because market value refers to the value of land that is negotiated between a willing seller and willing buyer with neither under duress.

34. D – Subtract $30,000 from $210,000 (purchase price minus land value) = $180,000. Then divide the $180,000 by 15 years for an annual depreciation of $12,000. With the straight line method,

each year has the same amount of depreciation. In this problem the asking price and mortgage amounts are irrelevant.

35. B – Deterioration from physical and/or cosmetic problems is referred to as physical deterioration. These problems may be either curable or incurable depending on whether or not it is economically feasible to make the repairs. Response "A" is incorrect, because functional obsolescence refers to the poor design of the improvement. Responses "C" and "D" are incorrect because they refer to environmental, social, and economic factors outside the property that lead to depreciation.

36. A – Accessing a bathroom through a bedroom is considered incurable functional obsolescence, because it would not be economically feasible to move the bathroom to another part of the house. Response "B" is not correct, because of the cost to move the bathroom. Response "C" is incorrect, because it is nonsensical. Response "D" is incorrect, because the bathroom arrangement is not physical deterioration, but functional obsolescence.

37. C – Some improvements to property, including swimming pools, cost more to add to the property than they increase the fair market value of the property. Response "A" is incorrect and is instructive for the test taker. Always be wary of questions that use "always" as part of the question or the answer. Responses "B" and "D" are incorrect, because it is impossible to tell if either event will occur, and if it does, how much the property value will increase or decrease in a given year.

38. A – Because the economic principle of supply and demand is important in determining property values, it is reasonable to assume that values in the community will decrease. When there are more sellers than buyers, values will decrease. When there are more buyers than sellers, values will increase.

39. B – Because the comparable does not have a garage, but does have a fence, subtract $1,500 from $9,500. The value of the comp would be reduced by $8,000.

40. B – The comparable sales approach compares properties that have recently sold that are similar in size, amenities, and location. It is assumed that properties that are the same size with the same amenities in nearby proximity would have the same value for a purchaser. Response "A" is incorrect, because the cost approach determines the value to replace the property with a new one. Response "C" is incorrect, because you use the income approach in valuing investment property. Response "D" is not an approach in appraising.

41. D – Listing agents should not become involved in the seller's homeowner's insurance, except to remind the seller that it is important to keep the property insured. The tasks in Responses "A," "B," and "C" are tasks that should be performed by the listing agent.

42. B – Subdivision plats have the lot dimensions listed; therefore this is the best option. In some locations, the property assessment records and the zoning maps include the lot dimensions, but not always; therefore Responses "A" and "D" are not the best answers.

Because most sellers do not obtain an independent appraisal prior to placing the property on the market, Response "C" is not the best answer.

43. B – Sellers should disclose latent defects, because these defects are not readily apparent to prospective purchasers. Response "A" is incorrect, because the crack is probably not a patent defect in that a patent defect would be readily apparent, and based on the location of the crack, it is unlikely a prospective purchaser would see it. Response "C" is incorrect, because the laws in most states require the seller to disclose a latent defect.

44. A – This is simply a statement of the law.

45. C – This is the best option for Barney. Whether or not mineral rights would be returned at some future date is a complicated legal issue. Because of the legal nature of the issue, it would be best for Barney to discuss this matter with his broker before proceeding. Response "A" would be correct after determining what should be included in the listing. Response "B" would not be a good option, because it would require Barney to draw a legal conclusion. Response "D" would always be incorrect, because important information should be included in listings.

46. D – Once the storage building was attached to the real estate it became a fixture that stays with the real estate. Response "A" may be true in some states, but most state laws require the building to stay because the concrete pad is permanent. Response "C" is a false statement, because the storage building has become an appurtenance.

47. B – Water rights are not tangible because you cannot touch the rights. You can touch the water, but you cannot "touch" the rights. All other responses are tangible personal property, because you can touch all of them.

48. B – Begin the problem with the sales price of $185,000. Subtract from that figure the current mortgage of $92,000, the real estate commission of $11,562.50 ($185,000 x 6.25%), subtract the legal fees of $250 and the prorated taxes of $832. That makes the net proceeds $80,355.50.

49. C – Because the seller wants to net $155,000, the listing agent must list the property for enough to pay the commission, taking into account the fact that the property will probably sell for only 95% of the listing price. Start by subtracting 5.75% from 100%. That number is 94.25%. Because you are want to increase the $155,000, divide the $155,000 by 94.25% and get $164,456.23. That would be the listing price, except for the fact that it will bring only 95% of the listing price. Therefore, you will need to increase the $164,456.23 by dividing it by 95%. The answer is $173,111.82. The answer must be "C," because the other options are not high enough to achieve the seller's net of $155,000. **Note**: If you forget how to do a math problem, many times you can go to each answer and work it backwards. For example, if you start with option "A." Calculate the probable sales price by multiplying $164,500 and 95% for a total of $156,275. Multiply that number by the commission of 5.75%. The total commission is $8,985.81. Subtract the commission of $8,985.81 from the $156,275. You see that amount is

$147,289.19. That means "A" is not correct, because the net would be too low.

50. D – Obviously, the sales price will not be in the listing, because it will not be known until the property sells.

51. D – The sign should not be placed in the yard until all sellers have signed the listing. Most states require written authorization from all of the sellers before the property can be advertised, and, of course, the yard sign is advertising. All of the other responses to this question can lead to legal problems for the listing agent.

52. A – Sellers should be educated on how the showing process works. They should be informed of the process for showing the property and whether or not the listing agent will need to make the arrangements and/or be present. Sellers should also be educated on hiding valuables and protecting pets.

53. A – This has always been the most effective (and cheapest) marketing tool.

54. A – An easy way to remember whether or not the ending is "or" or "ee" is to ask one question. Who owns the item? The owner will be the "or" ending. Who owns the offer? The "offeror."

55. A – For an offer to become a contract, the acceptance must be identical. Think about holding the offer up to a mirror. If the acceptance is identical to what is seen in the mirror, it becomes a contract; hence, the "mirror image rule." Response "B" is incorrect, because the offer is never

accepted by the agent, unless the agent has a written, signed, notarized, and recordable power of attorney for the client for whom he is signing. Response "C" is incorrect, because there is no time limit for delivering offers back to the buyer. The delivery should be as soon as possible, unless the offer stipulates otherwise. Response "D" is incorrect, because the offer must be signed by all owners to create a contract.

56. C – Unless the closing date is the last day of the tax year, the seller will either owe prorated taxes, which will decrease her net proceeds, or the seller will receive prorated taxes from the buyer, which will increase her net proceeds. Response "A" is incorrect, because this would only be correct if the closing was on the last day of the tax year and that information was not included in the question. An important point like that would be included in the question. Response "B" would only be correct if the seller had not paid the taxes in advance. Again, another fact that would have to be included in the question. Response "D" is incorrect, because
buyers would only in rare cases have "net proceeds."

57. C – Divide the amount of taxes ($2,874.76) by the number of days in the year (365). The amount of taxes for each day would be: $7.876. There are 31 days in August. Multiply $7.876 x 31 days. The amount of taxes for August would be $244.16.

58. D – Brokers must keep their records for the period of time set in their state by the licensing laws. States vary on their requirements. When taking the examination, students should be careful to pay attention to the part of the test they are taking. Do not give state specific answers on the national part of the test.

59. A – Once subdivision restrictions are recorded, they are usually enforceable by the homeowner's association.

60. B – Owners may add private restrictions on their land that controls how future owners use the land. Responses "A" and "D" are not correct, because deed restrictions are not placed on land by the government. Response "C" is not correct, because future owners are on notice of the restrictions prior to accepting title to the property. They have the option, if they do not want to adhere to the restrictions, of not accepting title.

61. B – In joint tenancy with right of survivorship, the survivor owns the property. In this question, when Bill died Elizabeth became the 100% owner of the property. When she married Alex, he may or may not (depending on state law) have had an interest during his lifetime. And, had he survived Elizabeth (depending on state law) his estate may or may not have had an interest in the property. However, because Alex died before Elizabeth, and she was the 100% owner at the time of her death, Alex's children inherited no interest in the property unless Elizabeth specifically left them an interest in her will. Because that is not a fact included in the question, you must assume she did not leave them an interest in the property in her will.

62. B – This was the first fair housing law and it was designed to prevent racial discrimination in housing.

63. A – Each person has the right to choose where he wants to live. The fair housing laws are designed to give each person that option and to prevent others from interfering with that choice.

64. D – Mortgage lenders have been accused of redlining, and, of course, that practice is illegal under the fair housing laws. Although appraisers, insurance agents, and real estate agents are governed by the fair housing laws, none of them, acting in those capacities, have been accused or redlining.

65. B – Sellers can use the CMA to decide on the best listing price. Responses "A" and "B" are legitimate uses of the information, but they are not the best use. Response "D" is clearly not appropriate and may be illegal in some situations.

66. D – This is a several step problem. First calculate the potential gross income by multiplying $850 x 24 x 12. The total potential gross income is $244,800. Next multiply the $244,800 by 95% (100% - 5% vacancy loss) to get a potential gross after vacancy of $232,560.
Subtract $24,480 (fixed expenses), $76,500 (operating expenses), and $5,000 (reserve) from the $232,560. That amount ($126,580) is net operating income for one year. The question asks for one month. Divide the $126,580 by 12. The monthly net operating income is $10,548.33.

67. D – To calculate the market value under the income approach the only numbers you need to use are the net operating income and the cap rate. In this problem the 7% and $180,000 were meant to distract you. When performing your math calculations on the exam, decide on what numbers you need, then ignore the surplus information. This problem is worked by dividing the net operating income of $81,000 by the cap rate of 8%. $81,000 ÷ 8% = $1,012,500.

68. D – This is a statement of the current law on appraisers being licensed and certified.

69. B – The standards for appraisers are known as the Uniform Standards of Professional Appraisal Practice. Response "A" is the acronym for the Federal National Mortgage Association which participates in the secondary mortgage market. Response "C" is the acronym for the Uniform Residential Appraisal Report. Response "D" is the acronym for the Real Estate Settlement Procedures Act.

70. C – Inspections by home inspectors are the norm in the industry now. Many real estate contracts have a contingency that the property must be inspected by a home inspector and may even give the buyer the right to terminate the contract based on information from the home inspector. Response "A" would not be the best because the sellers may fail to include information on the disclosure form, because they don't want to disclose a defect or because they are unaware of it. Response "C" would not be good for the buyer and would definitely not be good for the real estate agent. Most agents are not trained to inspect properties to the extent that a home inspector would inspect it. Response "D" would not be the best because appraisers give an opinion of value based on their observations, but do not actually inspect the property.

71. A – A life estate is an ownership interest that continues during a person's lifetime, but terminates at his death. The other responses are interests in real estate owned by others, but are not ownership interests for the holder of the easement, license, or lease.

72. A – Licenses are personal interests that can be revoked. Some states may have laws that prohibit revocation of a license if the licensee has spent money on the improvement, but that is not an issue in this question. Response "B" may be true, but it is not necessary to get to the nuisance issue because the permission is only a license. Response "C" and "D" are incorrect, because the radio station had neither an easement nor a lease.

73. B – The tenant has a leasehold interest known as a tenancy for years. It has a beginning date and an ending date. The other responses are not correct, because no notice is required. Because of the nature of a tenancy for years, the tenant may move at the end of the lease without a notice and the landlord can expect the tenant to move without a notice at the end of the term.

74. A – This is the purpose for a comprehensive plan. Response "B" is incorrect, because a plat merely shows how the area is to be developed. Response "C" relates to valuing property for property tax purposes. Response "D" would likely be an engineering evaluation of the property to determine whether or not the land can actually be developed.

75. B – By definition a PUD is the way to develop land for mixed uses. The development may include low density housing, high density housing, commercial, and retail all in the same area. Response "A" is incorrect, because a condominium is not a mixed use development. Responses "C" and "D" are not forms of zoning.

Chapter 2

Key Term Match

1. N
2. L
3. J
4. I
5. G
6. D
7. F
8. C
9. H
10. O
11. E
12. M
13. B
14. K
15. A

Practice Questions

1. A – Fiduciary duties include loyalty, confidentiality, disclosure, obedience, due care and diligence, and accounting. Honesty is obviously an important trait in a real estate agent, but it is not considered one of the fiduciary duties.

2. B – An agent cannot be a dual agent without the informed consent of both of his clients. Response "A" is correct in that, if an agent sells her own listings, she is likely a dual agent. However, if an in-house listing is sold, all of the agents in the office may be dual agents. Response "C" is not correct because a

disclosure does not create agency but, rather discloses it.

3. B – Under agency law, the unrepresented party is referred to as the customer. Response "A" is incorrect, because the represented party is the client. Response "C" is incorrect because at the prospect stage of the relationship it is unclear whether any relationship will occur. Response "D" is incorrect because offeree refers to the person receiving the offer and is irrelevant to the question.

4. B – Several ownership is ownership of property by one person. The other Responses refer to concurrent ownership of property..

5. D – In dower/curtesy states a married person, who owns property in his individual name, must still have his spouse sign the deed before title can transfer. A spouse signs the deed to release either his curtesy interest or her dower interest in the property. Response "A" is incorrect, because it is irrelevant when he purchased the property if he is going to sell it during the marriage. Response "B" is incorrect, because dower and curtesy interests are ownership of undivided interests in the whole, not in one-half shares. Response "C" is nonsensical.

6. C – Tenancy from year to year refers to a type of lease and not to a type of joint ownership.

7. D – The only unity for tenancy in common is unity of possession that gives each co-owner the right to use and possess the property equally with the other co-owners.

8. C – Divided uneven percentage ownerships must be as tenants in common. With tenants in common ownership, the only unity required is unity of possession. Responses "A" and "B" are not correct, because both require an undivided interest in the property. Response "D" is incorrect because severalty refers to individual ownership.

9. D – When a husband and wife own property as tenants by the entirety, one cannot leave his spouse's share to someone else in the will. Because ownership as tenants by the entirety requires a husband and wife, all of the other responses destroy that relationship.

10. C – A life estate gives the life tenant the right to live in the property during the life tenant's lifetime, not the lifetime of another person. The other Responses are a misstatement of the law relating to life estate.

11. C – Joint ventures are a form of partnership that terminate once the reason for forming the joint venture is accomplished. Response "A" is incorrect in that a corporation has shareholders and not partners, and it continues for an indefinite period of time. Response "B" could arguably be similar to a joint venture; however, a limited liability company has members and not partners, and it continues for an indefinite period of time. Response "D" is incorrect, because a sole proprietorship is ownership of property by one person.

12. A – A condominium, by definition, has units that are owned by individuals and common area that is jointly owned by all of the owners. All other responses may describe elements of

condominiums, but they also describe other forms of property.

13. C – This is the best answer, because people who have not purchased property in the past need to be educated about the process. All of the other Responses are actions an agent may want to take, but compared to Response "C" they are not the best answer.

14. A – When there are more houses for sale than buyers to buy them, it is said to be a "buyer's market" because the buyers have more of a selection and can negotiate a better purchase price. Response "B" is incorrect, because it implies that there are fewer houses on the market than buyers to purchase them. Responses "C" and "D" refer to the stock market trends and not real estate market trends.

15. D – Agents have a legal requirement to disclose material defects. Although an agent may believe the defect is so obvious everyone can see it, it is still the responsibility of the agent to point it out. Response "A" is incorrect because it is impossible to say "everyone" saw it. And, whether or not the home inspector will see it and include it in his report is speculative. Response "B" is incorrect, because agent disclosure of material defects is required regardless of whom the agent represents. Response "C" is true, but Response "D" is more complete.

16. A – When considering value characteristics, whether or not property is transferable from one owner to another owner is important. Property that cannot be transferred to a new owner has less value than one that is freely transferable. The other responses

are about selecting property, but none of them are economic value considerations.

17. C – Agents must be aware of how the buyer's intend to use property and whether or not such use is appropriate under the zoning ordinances. All of the other Responses are important, but if the property does not have proper zoning, the buyer will never reach the other issues.

18. C – Agents should not advise outside their area of expertise. Unless the agent was a qualified environmental engineer, she should not have made a statement about radon and certainly should not have discouraged a radon test. Response "A" is true in that an agent does want to advise her buyer in such a way as to save money in the buying process, her advice was not appropriate in this case. Response "B" is incorrect, because the agent likely breached her fiduciary duty by discouraging the test. Response "D" is a correct statement of fact, but not the best answer.

19. C – It is important for agents to know their state laws relating to stigmatized property. Some states require disclosure while others do not. Response "A" is incorrect unless state law requires such disclosure. Response "B" leaves it up to the agent to determine if it is a material fact, which may be a violation of state law. Response "D" may be correct in some states and not in others.

20. D – Giving a buyer tax advice was beyond the scope of marketing real estate. Unless the agent was also an accountant, it was inappropriate to give tax advice. Real estate agents must

know when to refer their clients to attorneys and accountants. The other Responses may be true, but the information, if incorrect, could lead to serious legal consequences.

21. C – Agents may distribute fair housing literature, but that literature is not normally referred to as a disclosure. The forms referred to in the other responses are all typically referred to as disclosure forms.

22. B – A buyer or seller's social security number should never be included on any form that will be seen by other parties. All of the other responses are items that should be included in a sales contract.

23. A – The entire agreement between the parties should be written in the sales contract. Response "B" is incorrect, because the issue of personal property should be resolved during contract negotiations. Response "C" raises the issue of fixtures, which is not responsive to the question. Response "D" would be a way to include personal property as part of the contract; however, if a separate form is used, steps must be taken so that the personal property becomes part of the contract. Such a form must be incorporated into the sales contract.

24. B – Parties to the contract should determine which party will carry the property insurance after the sales contract is signed and before the closing. Agents need to understand the state law, because some states require the buyer to obtain insurance when the sales contract is signed, in the event of a fire or other casualty loss. The other responses are not relevant to the term "risk of loss."

25. C – This response points out the importance of wording in the contingency. One word makes a huge difference. Response "D" states the house must "sell" and not "close." A property may sell many times before it actually closes and until it closes, the buyer would not have money to purchase the new property. This buyer's concern would not be the proper use of either of the terms used in Responses "A" and "B."

26. D – Unless a contract contains a term that it may be terminated in the event of death, death will not terminate a sales contract. Responses "A" and "B" are incorrect statements of contract law. Response "C" would place the agent in the position of practicing law without a license.

27. A – Basic contract law states that mistakes in the contract will be interpreted against the draft. Because Frank was the agent for the buyer, mistakes made in the contract will be interpreted against Frank's clients. Response "B" is incorrect because that party is the seller and not Frank's client. Response "C" is incorrect, because it is the selling agent and not the listing agent who is drafting the contract. Response "D" is incorrect, because Frank is not a party to the contract, and the contract cannot be interpreted against a non-party. Obviously, however, a mistake by Frank may well leave him liable to his client for breach of his agency duties.

28. A – The appropriate way to negotiate changes in the offer is by a counteroffer. Response "B" is not a good alternative, because there may not be another offer. Response "C" is not a good alternative because this would be

an inappropriate use of a contingency. Response "D" may leave the seller in position of breaching the contract.

29. B – Agents have a duty to present offers as soon as the seller wants to see the offer. Response "A" and "D" make the offer presentation at the convenience of the agent and does not serve the seller well. Response "C" is incorrect, because the listing agent should not call the buyer when he is representing the seller.

30. D – In this scenario, the seller keeps the counteroffer in place until he knows for sure he has sold the property to the second buyer. Because all offers may be withdrawn until accepted, the second offer may be withdrawn until the acceptance has been communicated to the second buyer. Response "A" is not a good alternative, because the first offeror may accept the counteroffer before it can be withdrawn and the seller will have sold the property twice. Response "B" is not a good alternative, because the second offeror may withdraw the offer pending the expiration of the counteroffer. Or, in the alternative, the counteroffer may not expire, but rather be accepted by the first offeror. Response "C" is not the best option, because the seller could withdraw the counter offer only to have the second offeror withdraw the second offer leaving the seller with no offers.

31. C – The zoning should be confirmed, because if the zoning does not allow the apartment, the other issues are irrelevant.

32. B – Many companies sell home warranties, and one of the items generally covered is the hot water heater. Response "A" will not alleviate the

concern, because it may be working during the inspection and stop afterwards. Response "C" would be an alternative, but would probably meet with resistance if it is actually working at the time of the contract. Response "D" is not a good choice, because the seller would probably object, and if the seller agreed, it would be difficult to enforce the agreement at a later date.

33. C – It is always important to look at the language of the contract for all issues in the transaction. Generally, contracts terms may vary state law; therefore, the other Responses would vary depending on the contract language.

34. B – Co-insurance is typically 80/20 insurance. The land value is 20% and land does not need to be insured under the homeowner's policy.

35. B – Because each person has the right to choose where he wants to live, the fair housing laws are designed to afford all of us that right. Response "A" is an incorrect statement of the reason for the fair housing laws. Response "C" is incorrect, because the fair housing laws do not prevent discrimination in other areas of our lives. Response "D" is arguably correct, but does not specifically state how fairness will be ensured.

36. B – Agents should provide service to clients that does not lead to additional liability for themselves. In the event the home inspector makes a mistake, the buyer would very likely blame the agent. The agent made it worse by choosing his friend, opening himself for claims of conflict of interest and conspiracy. And, in the event the buyer refused to pay the

inspector, the agent may have to pay for the service. Response "A" is incorrect because, although the statement is correct that it was not good to call a friend, it is still a problem if the inspector makes a mistake in the inspection that leads to damage for the buyer. Response "C" may appear to be correct, but it was not wise to hire the inspector. Response "D" is clearly incorrect for the reasons stated above.

37. B – This is the best answer, because the inspector is working for the buyer and should be the one to discuss the report. Response "A" places the agent in the position of discussing the report and reporting to the buyer. There can always be allegations that the agent either misunderstood or misreported the information. Response "C" is not the best answer because the home inspector is not part of the discussion. Response "D" is not correct because the listing agent should not be reviewing the report that was prepared for the buyer.

38. D – A survey is the procedure for determining boundary lines. Response "A" is incorrect, because an appraiser determines an estimate of value. Response "B" would be appropriate if the seller knew the exact boundaries. Response D" is incorrect, because the listing agent only knows what has been told him by the seller.

39. C – An appraisal by an independent appraiser is the best way to get information about the fair market value of the property. Response "A" would be an option, but agents are typically not trained as appraisers. Response "B" would give her the tax assessment, which is generally not the current fair market value, but rather the taxable

value. Response "D" is incorrect, because until the lender sees the appraisal report, she will not know the information.

40. D – This response is the best one, because it gives the buyer the option of voiding the contract and not purchasing the house if lead based paint is discovered prior to closing. Response "A" is incorrect, because, first of all, the date is 1978 and, secondly, not all houses built prior to 1978 have lead based paint. Response "B" is not the best, because the language would give her the right to have the test, but not the right to void the contract. Response "C" is not the best, because the sellers are already required to disclose their knowledge of lead based paint if the house was built prior to 1978.

Chapter 3

Key Term Match

1.	M
2.	L
3.	I
4.	A
5.	O
6.	H
7.	F
8.	C
9.	N
10.	E
11.	J
12.	G
13.	D
14.	K
15.	B

Practice Questions

1. B – State laws require a written property management agreement

between the property owner and the property manager. Response "A" is incorrect, because property managers may be employees of the owner, in which case even they are not required to have a real estate license. Response "C" is incorrect, because property managers may be employees and not independent contractors. Response "D" is a good idea, but not required.

2. B – Leases by definition are contracts between the lessor and lessee. Response "A" is incorrect, because leases for a year or less may be oral. Response "C" is incorrect, because leases are bi-lateral contracts and as such cannot be terminated unilaterally by one party. Response "D" is incorrect because, unless the lease states otherwise, the new owner must comply with the lease.

3. B – Property managers should always advise tenants that they have the right to have their attorney and/or accountant review the lease before signing it.

4. B – A triple net lease is one in which the lessee agrees to pay the base rent plus the insurance, property taxes, and maintenance costs. The debt service is the mortgage payment, and that is the responsibility of the owner to pay.

5. B – A rental application will allow the property to manager to get needed financial information in a uniform and non-discriminatory way.

6. B – The first step is to determine the prorated rent. Divide the rent of $1,150 by 30 days to get $38.33 per day. Determine how many days from June 18th to June 30. The number of days is 13 not 12. Do not forget to count the

18th, because rent is due the day the lease begins. Multiply 38.33 x 13 to get $498.33. The deposit of $1,000 is irrelevant to this question, because it was paid when the lease was signed.

7. C – By definition you do not include variable expenses in an operating budget, because the amounts are unknown at the time of budgeting.

8. A – Trust accounts are designed to hold other people's money until it is returned to them or forfeited by them for some legal reason. This is the only one of the responses in which the money is held.

9. A – By definition the ROI measures profitability.

10. D – Because an important function of the property manager is to keep the property safe, the property manager should always be alert to something that doesn't "seem right." A light fixture that keeps blowing bulbs may be defective and lead to more serious problems. The other three responses may be correct but they may lead to a serious problem being undetected.

11. A – Part of ADA is the requirement that the owner make reasonably achievable modifications.

12. A – Under the fair housing laws, the protected classes are race, religion, color, national origin, sex, familial status, and handicap/disability. Some areas have the additional protected class of sexual orientation. Marital status is not one of the protected classes.

13. D – The four types of maintenance are construction, corrective, preventative

and routine.

14. D – The lead-based paint law requires the landlord to disclose the known presence of lead-based paint. Owners are neither required to inspect for lead-based paint nor are they required to remove it, paint over it, or take other action. Not only did the manager misstate the law, but appears to have obligated the owner to do something without authority to do so. All of the other responses are a misstatement of the law.

15. C – Eviction proceeding are regulated by state law. Property managers must follow the law or place the owners and themselves in legal jeopardy. Response "B" is a true statement, but the response is not appropriate behavior. The eviction process probably requires a written notice to the tenant, but not for the reason stated in response "D."

Chapter 4

Key Term Match

1.	I
2.	C
3.	J
4.	B
5.	D
6.	M
7.	A
8.	L
9.	F
10.	H
11.	K
12	N.
13.	O
14.	G
15.	E

Practice Questions

1. B – The grantor is the party conveying title to the grantee. The other responses are different names for the person receiving title to real estate.

2. C – Although payment of costs can be varied by the terms of the sales contract, most of the time, the seller will pay the state transfer tax. Response "A" would be correct if the parties had agreed for the purchaser to pay the transfer tax. It is highly unlikely that either Response "B" or "D" would ever be correct.

3. A – One of the advantages of home ownership is the tax deductibility of the mortgage interest on both state and federal income tax returns. Both Response "B" and "D" may mislead the answerer, because both statements may "sound" correct because of the capital gains tax laws. Response "C" is incorrect, because the deduction is for both tax returns. Applicants taking the examination should take care not to be misled, because an answer "sounds" correct.

4. D – Homeowner's insurance is not a tax deduction for the owner's primary residence. All of the other Responses are deductible for primary residences.

5. B – Settlement agents are required to prepare a 1099 (or substitute 1099) when closing real estate. This form requires the seller's social security number and is used to inform the IRS of possible capital gains tax. Response "A" is incorrect, because a social security number does not guarantee that someone is a US citizen. Response "C" is

incorrect, because social security numbers should not be recorded, and if they are, they play no part in the title examination process unless a lien is discovered. In that event, the title examiner can contact the party to ascertain the social security number for cross reference purposes. Response "D" is incorrect because the buyer's lender does not need the seller's social security number.

6. A – Taxes are prorated on a calendar year basis. Because the seller has not paid taxes for the year, she will owe taxes from January 1st through the closing date, February 22nd. There are 31 days in January and 22 in February that are owed by the seller. Divide $1,785 by 365 to get a daily tax amount of $4.8904. Multiply $4.89 x 53 for a total of $259.19. This is the amount that the seller will "owe" at the closing. Amounts "owed" by the seller are debits to the seller and credits to the buyer. Response B is incorrect, because it says "debit" and not "credit." Responses "C" and "D" are incorrect, because to use $1,525.81 would mean that the seller had already paid the taxes for the year.

7. C – When depreciating investment property, you must first subtract the land value. Improvements, not land, are depreciated. The other Responses have no bearing on depreciating investment property, although each may sound familiar because the principles are used in other aspects of real estate.

8. C – One of the advantages of a seller carrying the financing for the buyer as in an installment sale, is that capital gains taxes are not paid on the full sales price; but, rather, on the amounts as they are collected. This delays payment of capital gains taxes until the money is actually received. All of the other Responses are simply misstatements of the tax laws.

9. B – Assessments are actually another form of taxes that are levied by governmental entities for a special project. Assessing property for a specific purpose allows the government to add the "tax" for a specific purpose for a specific period of time. Response "A" is incorrect, because ad valorem a/k/a property taxes, are always on real property and are not added for a specific purpose. Response "C" is partly correct in that governments use liens on property to collect the assessments. It is incorrect for this question, because the lien is a result of the assessment and not the assessment. Examination takers should be careful to make these distinctions, because the test may include partially correct answers. Response "D" is incorrect, because transfer taxes are paid when the owner is transferring title to the property and are paid prior to recording the deed.

10. A – The 1031 tax deferred exchange is a vehicle for deferring the payment of capital gains tax. "Response "B" is incorrect, because the exchange cannot be used to defer capital gains on the primary residence. Responses "C" and "D" are simply incorrect.

11. C – Liens generally take their priority from the time of filing. If a lien is recorded before the deed is recorded, the lien will remain on the property even though it has changed owners. The new owner takes title subject-to the lien and may have to pay it in the future if the lienholder files a collection lawsuit against the property. Response "A" is

incorrect because liens do not merge into the deed. Representations, agreements, and contract merge into the deed and disappear, but liens do not. Responses "B" and "D" are incorrect statements of the law.

12. B – Title insurance may be purchased to protect lessees, buyers, and lenders. Sellers title insurance does not exist, although the seller can pay for the buyer's or lender's insurance if that is part of the contract. However, even if the seller purchases the insurance, it is not for the benefit of the seller.

13. C – A title insurance premium is a one-time premium that is generally paid at the closing.

14. A – When a deed does not contain a grantor's marital status a defect is created. Without the marital status, there is always the possibility that a spouse has not released his/her marital interest. Although the other Responses would all have an effect on the real estate transaction, none of them would create a title defect.

15. D – The purpose of a quiet title action is to determine who has the right, title and interest to the property. Response "A" is the action filed when a lienholder wants to collect money owned by the property owner. Response "B" is a legal action filed when there is a dispute and the parties both agree on the facts, but not on the applicable law. The parties ask the Judge to decide the case by applying the facts to the correct law. Response "C" refers to an action filed when a party cannot pay its debts.

16. C – The purpose of a foreclosure action is to terminate all interests in the property of the named parties. If a foreclosure action does not name all of the people with an interest in the property, the unnamed party's interest is not extinguished. Response "A" is not correct, because there may be occasions when the property sold at foreclosure actually sells for more than the market value. Response "B" is not correct in that a lis pendens should be filed, but failure to file one does not create a defective lawsuit. Failure of the plaintiff in the lawsuit to file a lis pendens will not keep the owner from further encumbering, or even selling, the property during the lawsuit. Response "D" is incorrect, because parties other than mortgage holders have a legal right to file a foreclosure action.

17. B – This is the definition of a title abstract. Response "A" is the process for reviewing the recorded records to determine the condition of the title. Response "C" is the attorney's response to the condition of the title after the title examination is performed. Response "D" is the process of filing certain documents in the public record.

18. C – Recording of documents establishes the lien priority. Response "A" is incorrect, because the date appearing on the document is irrelevant for establishing lien priority. Response "B" is irrelevant for establishing lien priority. Delivering value may be important in other legal actions relating to the transaction, but not for issues of lien priority. Response "D" is an incorrect statement of the law.

19. C – The purpose of recording documents in the public records is to give notice to the world of the party's interest in the property. This public

notice is known as constructive notice. Someone taking an interest in the property has a duty to review the public records to protect their own interests. Response "A" refers to a situation in which a party has first-hand knowledge of certain information. Response "B" refers to notice that is required to be given pursuant to a certain law or statute. Response "D" is nonsensical.

20. B – The law provides that certain liens attach to all property owned by someone, not just a specific parcel of land he may own. These blanket liens are known as general liens and the federal income tax lien is an example.

21. C – Some states require attorneys to perform closings while others do not. All of the other Responses are correct.

22. B – The annual dues are $480 per year and the year runs from July 1 – June 30th (fiscal year). Because the fees are paid, the seller should receive a refund of 2 days (the seller pays the day of closing). Divide 480 by 365 and multiply by 2 to get 2 days dues in the amount of $2.63. The seller has paid the dues; therefore will receive a credit of $2.63 on the closing statement. Response "A" is incorrect because it says "credit" to the buyer when it is actually a debit to the buyer, because the buyer is paying the money not receiving the money. Responses "C" and "D" are incorrect because it treats the amounts as though 28 days and not 2 days should be used in the problem. And, or course, Response "C" is incorrect because it is a credit to the buyer and not a debit. On the examination, because of rounding, your numbers may be off a little on the decimal points.

23. D – The general warranty deed contains the greatest number of warranties from the grantor and it is not limited by time of the grantor's ownership. Response "A" is not the best, because the warranties are limited by the time of the grantor's ownership. Response "B" is incorrect, because there are no warranties with a quit claim deed. Response "C" is incorrect, because the type of warranty deed is unclear.

24. D – When a grantor conveys land by a quit claim deed there are no warranties. The grantor is not even warranting that she owns the land she is conveying. All of the other Responses are incorrect, because they contain some warranties. In this question, because of the uncertain boundaries, the grantor would be taking a chance she is selling land she may not own.

25. D – This is the definition of covenant of seisen. Seisen is also spelled seizen. Response "A" refers to conveyance of land in which the surface and subsurface have not been divided. Response "B" refers to the covenant of quiet possession. Response "C" refers to the covenant of right to convey.

26. B – One of the provisions in the Real Estate Settlement Procedures Act is that the HUD-1 settlement statement must be used in all closings involving federally-related mortgages. Although the other Responses contain instances where it is likely a HUD-1 settlement statement will be used, the law does not contain specific language requiring the form.

27. B – Personal property is transferred by a bill of sale. Response "A" is for transferring real estate. Response "C" is

the document that shows who owns personal property. Response "D" is a way to secure payment of a debt using real estate as the collateral.

28. A – When borrowing money, the borrower must personally promise to repay the debt, and the legal instrument for that promise is the promissory note. Responses "B" and "C" are documents that secure the repayment of the debt on the property. Response "D" is a certificate used in some deeds that certifies that the consideration stated in the deed is true and correct.

29. A – The Real Estate Settlement Procedures Act requires the good faith estimate be sent to the buyer within three business days. Response "B" is incorrect because of the number of days. Responses "C" and "D" are not true because violating the law is neither a good business practice nor ethical.

30. C – RESPA contains a provision that service providers cannot pay kickbacks for performing settlement services. Response "A" is incorrect, because under RESPA lenders may charge high costs as long as they disclose them. Response "B" is incorrect, because Regulation Z, not RESPA deals with advertising issues. Response "D" is incorrect, because state agencies regulate unlicensed mortgage activity.

31. D – When presented with an offer, the seller may accept it, reject it, counter it, or do nothing now or later. Responses "A" and "B" are incorrect, in that the agent not only misstated the law, but she also forgot whom she was representing. Response "C" is incorrect because offers should be presented before the expiration date, but the sellers are not required to answer by that date.

32. B – This is the definition of a sales contract that has been signed by everyone, but not yet closed. Response "A" is a sales contract that has been closed. Response "C" refers to a contract that is conditioned upon an event or event occurring before one or both parties are obligation to perform. Response "D" is a contract that has one party that is obligated to perform. An open listing contract and an option contract are examples of unilateral contracts.

33. B – Contacts are not required to have financing terms. Most buyers ask for them, but sales contracts are enforceable without the financing clause if it is enforceable in all other respects. All of the other Responses are essential elements to form a contract.

34. C – Under the Statute of Frauds, the window treatments must be included in the sales contract or the seller is not required to leave them. Response "A" is incorrect, because there was no writing stating that the window treatments were included in the transaction. Response "B" would be a waste of time. If the seller had wanted to leave the window treatments, he would have left them. Response "D" would be incorrect, because from the facts in the question, the agent was not aware of the seller's statement. If, however, the agent had been aware and failed to prepare an amendment for the contract, Response "D" may be an option for the buyer.

35. C – A sales contract is a bilateral contract because there are two parties, and both parties must perform.

Response "A" is a contract in which one party only has to perform. Response "C" is a contract that contains all of the essential elements of a contract. Response "D" is a contract that may be voided by one of the parties, because one of the essential elements is defective.

36. D – A term in a contract that must be met before one party is required to perform the contract is known as a contingency.

37. D – Homestead laws are state statutes. All of the other Responses are federal statutes.

38. C – Some states have dower and curtesy laws that give one spouse interest in the other spouse' s property. Because the state in the question is a dower and curtesy state, the husband has to sign the contract agreeing to release his curtesy interest in the property. Response "A" is incorrect, because dower refers to the wife's interest. Response "B" is incorrect, because the husband's interest in his wife's property in this situation is more than a life estate interest. Response "D" is incorrect, because the state in the question is not a community property state.

39. A – Claiming ownership to someone else's property after a period of use is known as adverse possession. Response "B" refers to claiming an easement on someone else's property after a period of use. Response "C" refers to a legal action to determine which party actually has an interest in property. Response "D" does not refer to an ownership interest, but rather an improvement that crosses a boundary line.

40. C – Using your property in a way that disturbs the neighbor's use of their property may lead to a nuisance action. One owner cannot use his property in such a way as to keep the neighboring property owners from using their property. A rock quarry with both dust, noise, and heavy equipment moving on the roads may qualify as a nuisance in some neighborhoods. Response "A" refers to quieting the title to real estate, not actually stopping noise. Response "B" refers to making a claim to the owner's title. Response "D" refers to actually coming onto someone else's land.

41. B – The fair housing laws and local ordinances on handicapped parking gives the condominium owner the right to use the parking spaces designated for handicapped parking. All of the other responses refer to rights granted the owner under a condominium deed.

42. D – A cooperative is a corporation that owns real estate. Individual owners own shares of the corporation that give them the right to use one of the units owned by the cooperative. Condominium owners have deeds that convey their individual units to them while granting them an undivided interest in the common area. The remaining responses are untrue.

43. B – When the government condemns land in a eminent domain action, it must prove to the courts that the taking is for the "common good" of all of the citizens. Although responses "A" and "C" may be partially true, neither response gives the most complete response. Response "D" is incorrect.

44. B – According to the eminent domain laws, the government must pay "just compensation" for property taken. Generally, the property owner believes this number is larger than what the government believes. When the parties cannot agree, appraisals are made by both sides, and the Court has to determine what "just compensation." is. The other responses are incorrect.

45. C – State laws require that a lis pendens notice be recorded to alert those who may take an interest in the property during a foreclosure action that the lawsuit which involves the title to the real estate is occurring. Response "A" is incorrect, because, although that is the purpose of the lis pendens, the answer is not the correct term. Response "B" has nothing to do with a lawsuit, but rather the buyer's obligation to inspect the property prior to purchase. Response "D" is the term for the type of notice given by a lis pendens.

46. A – It is likely that a securities broker, not a real estate broker would be required to give advice in this situation. Response "B" is incorrect unless he has a securities license. Response "C" is incorrect, because a CPA would not be qualified unless she had a securities license. Response "D" shows that Rolando does not understand the situation.

47. A – Real estate licensees, unless they are CPAs or attorneys, should not be giving advice to clients about a 1031 tax-deferred exchange. Response "B" is incorrect unless the agents broker is a CPA or attorney. Response "C" would not be a good option, because either the client would never get through to the proper person, and if she does get them,

the information will not likely be understandable and/or correct. Response "D" is incorrect, because the agent is placing himself in the position of practicing law and/or accounting without a license to do so.

48. A – Because the homeowner's insurance is a charge to the buyer, it will be a debit. Response "B" is incorrect because it says credit. Response "C" and "D" are incorrect, because the seller's column will not include buyer's insurance information.

49. C – Items paid for outside of closing should appear on the HUD-1 as POC items and should not be in either the debit or credit column. Response "D" is incorrect, because the buyer's insurance has nothing to do with the seller's net proceeds.

50. D – To calculate the net proceeds for the seller, subtract all of the costs, except the credit for property taxes, from $350,000. Add the credit for the property taxes to the balance after subtracting all charges to reach the net proceeds (350,000 minus 122,873.42 minus 175 minus 2,500 minus 350 plus 897.52). The other Responses either subtracted the prorated taxes instead of adding them, or failed to subtract the other items.

Chapter 5

Key Term Match

1. J
2. N
3. O
4. H
5. K
6. M

7.   I
8.   G
9.   L
10.   F
11.   E
12.   D
13.   C
14.   B
15.   A

Practice Questions

1. D – Although some real estate brokerages own mortgage companies, it is not the real estate brokerage itself that is lending money, but rather a company owned by the brokerage. The other Responses are all sources of mortgage financing.

2. D – Mortgage brokers are often approved to work with several lenders, a fact they promote, promising to obtain the best terms and rates for borrowers because they are not tied in to one lender. Response "A" is incorrect, because mortgage brokers and mortgage bankers are completely different ways of doing business and the terms are not synonymous. Response "B" may or may not be true. Response "C" is incorrect, because mortgage brokers do not have "depositors."

3. A – This is a true statement. All other responses are incorrect.

4. B – Often sellers will carry financing for buyers who are unable to obtain financing for one reason or another. One method of seller financing is the land contract. Responses "A" and "C" may encourage the buyer to purchase the property, but will not help her obtain financing. Response "D" is not responsive to the question because the seller wants to sell the house, not rent it

5. A – This is the purpose of the document. Response "B" is incorrect, because the mortgagee is the lender, not the borrower. Responses "C" and "D" are irrelevant to the question, as well as being untrue.

6. D – All states have adopted the Statute of Frauds. The Statute of Frauds require certain documents, including security interests, to be in writing. Response "A" may also be correct in some states, but not all. Response "B" regulates real estate lending practices, but not security interests. Response "C" does not, in most states, relate to real estate transactions.

7. D – The promissory note is the document that creates personal liability. Response "A" is the document entered into between the buyer and seller setting forth their agreement. Response "B" is the document signed by the borrower that creates a security interest in the real estate for the lender. Response "C" is the document that conveys title from the grantor to the grantee.

8. A – By definition, states that use trust deeds instead of mortgages are known as title theory states. Response "B" refers to states that use mortgages as security. Response "C" is nonsensical. Response "D" refers to states that use a specific lien and a trust deed to create the security interest.

9. C – First, agents should not be giving legal advice as the agent did in this scenario His advice was incorrect because most states require that a land contract be foreclosed by judicial sale in the same manner as a mortgage.

Responses "A" and "B" are incorrect statements of the law. Response "D" may be a correct statement of law, but it does not apply in this situation.

10. D – It would be impossible for a mortgage and promissory note for an adjustable rate loan to have the lifetime APR. Because the interest rate may change from period to period, there would be no way to calculate the lifetime APR. In closing loans, an APR is provided to the borrower based on the assumption that the rate will change at the first change date and not again. All of the other Responses are terms that must be included.

11. A – A fully amortized loan is one that will be paid off at a specified time without a balloon payment, because the payments include both principal and interest sufficient to pay the full amount by maturity. Responses "B" and "C" are for loans that have interest-only payments that will leave a balloon payment of the entire principal at maturity. Response "D" refers to payments that include both principal and interest, but the principal reduction is not enough to pay the loan in full at maturity thereby leaving a balloon payment.

12. C – This is the definition of a renegotiable loan. Response "A" refers to a loan obtain to construct an improvement on property. Response "B" refers to a loan that has an interest rate that may change from time to time based on the agreement set forth in the promissory note between the lender and borrower. Response "D" refers to a short term loan used to "bridge" the time until permanent financing can be obtained.

13. A – This is the best answer, because FHA loans are available to most buyers. Response "B" is nonsensical in that the Federal National Mortgage Association does not make loans. FNMA is part of the secondary market that buys loans from the primary lenders after they are closed. Response "C" is another term for a VA loan that is only available to veterans or widows of veterans. Response "D" meets the criteria in the question, but not all areas offer FmHA loans.

14. B – The rule of thumb is that eight (8) discount points equal one (1%) percent interest. Therefore, to reduce the interest by ½% it would take ½ of 8 or 4 points.

15. A – This answer is correct, because the buyer could not purchase property with only $4,000 if she had to pay a down payment. It the closing costs are $3,200, she would only have $800 for a down payment. This would not be enough for a down payment under most mortgage programs. Response "B" is an incorrect statement of the parameters of VA loan. Response "C" is incorrect, because the funding fee can be borrowed in a VA loan. Response "D" is incorrect, because there is no requirement for a VA loan that the borrower be a first time home buyer.

16. C – Because mortgage insurance is required for loans with greater than an 80% loan-to-value, the borrower must make a down payment of at least 20%. In this case, 20% of $185,000 is 37,000.

17. B – This is the definition of a conventional loan. Response "A" is incorrect, because a shared equity

mortgage is one in which the lender shares in the equity as it increases. Response "C" is incorrect, because a primary loan is one obtained from a lender that works directly with the consuming public instead of in the secondary market. Response "D" is incorrect, because amortizing refers to how loans are repaid.

18. Response "A" is the reason the secondary market was born. Secondary mortgage lenders purchase mortgages from primary lenders. This enables the primary lender to replenish funds to make loans to consumers. Hence, the secondary market makes the primary market "liquid." Response "B" is confusing secondary lenders with second mortgage lenders. Response "C" may be correct, but an investment source is not the main purpose of the secondary lenders. Response "D" is nonsensical.

19. C – There is no such entity. All other Responses refer to lenders in the secondary market.

20. B – The scenario describes how a wraparound mortgage works. Response "A" refers to a mortgage covering several parcels of property. Response "C" refers to a mortgage in which the lender shares in the equity of the property in order to give the owner more favorable mortgage terms. Response "D" is nonsensical.

21. C – The facts in the question describe a package mortgage in that it allows the borrower to have one mortgage for both personal and real property. Response "A" may or may not be true, but a lower interest is not the usual reason for obtaining a

blanket mortgage. Response "B" describes a shared equity mortgage, not a package mortgage. Response "D" refers to an open-end mortgage that may or may not be a component of a package mortgage.

22. A – One of the ways to reduce a mortgage interest rate is to pay discount points upfront at the time of closing. Typically, discount points may be paid by anyone. Response "B" is not likely to happen, and if it does, it will not reduce the interest rate. Response "C" refers to the loan origination fee paid to the lender, and that does not typically affect the interest rate. Response "D" will not accomplish the goal of reducing the interest rate, because the amount of interest will not equal the amount to buy-down the loan. The buy-down sum will be significantly lower than the actual interest that would be paid over the life of the loan.

23. C – This scenario describes when a reverse annuity mortgage would be used. This mortgage allows the owner to keep the property and receive a payment from the mortgage payment. Response "A" refers to a mortgage in which the lender shares in the equity in return for giving the borrower a lower interest rate. Response "B" refers to a mortgage in which more than one lender shares in the loan, thereby reducing the risk for all of them. Response "D" refers to a mortgage in which the mortgagor pays more than a fully amortized payment in order to build up additional principal.

24. B – One of the features of a construction mortgage is that the money is disbursed by the use of "draws" as the project progresses. This keeps the borrower from paying interest on the

money until the money is actually needed for the building project. Response "A" is generally not true in that construction financing may carry a higher interest rate than permanent financing. Response "C" is incorrect, because property owners often obtain these mortgages to pay the builder. Response "D" is incorrect, because construction loans may or may not convert to permanent financing, depending on the lender and the type of construction loan obtained.

25. A – This is a true statement, because most of the time homeowners have first mortgages when they obtain an equity line mortgage. Because the first mortgage is recorded first, the equity line will become a second mortgage. Response "B" may or may not be true, but generally it is untrue. As a second mortgage, the equity line is a higher risk mortgage and, therefore, carries a higher interest rate. Response "C" is incorrect because, generally, lenders offer lower closing costs to entice homeowners to borrow the money. Response "D" is an incorrect statement.

26. D – The loan origination fee must be disclosed under the Real Estate Settlement Procedures Act, not the Truth-in-Lending Act. All other Reponses are required under TIL.

27. C – The lender has three days, not a week, to provide the APR; therefore, the lender was not in compliance with Regulation Z. Response "A" is not correct, because of the delay in sending the information. Response "B" and "D" are incorrect because it is Regulation Z not RESA that requires the disclosure.

28. C – This response is correct, because the borrower has three business days to rescind the transaction. If the transaction closed on Thursday, the first day to be counted was Friday. Because the lender is closed on Saturday and Sunday, the rescission period did not end until midnight on Tuesday. Response "A" is incorrect, because the rescission expired on Tuesday, not Sunday. Response "B" is incorrect because the rescission period applies anytime the property owner is borrowing money on his primary residence. Response "D" is incorrect, because the notice may be hand-delivered as well as mailed.

29. B – Response "B" refers to a protected class under the fair housing laws, not under the Equal Credit Opportunity Act. All other Responses are correct statements under the ECOA.

30. A – The key to this question is to determine how much was borrowed. The 80% is based on the appraised value or the sales price, whichever is less. In this question, $195,000 is less; therefore, the amount borrowed is 80% of $195,000, or $156,000. The origination fee is 1% of the 159,200 or $1,560. Discounts points are irrelevant to answering this question.

31. A – The buyer usually pays for the credit report, although it is for the benefit of the lender. Responses "B" and "D" may be true when a lender has a promotion as an inducement for the buyer to use the lender. Response "C" would never be true.

32. C – Because the lender requires 14 months of hazard insurance premium to

be paid at closing (1st year plus 2 months), multiply the monthly premium of $82 per month by 14 months.

33. A – The lender required 7 month's taxes to be placed in escrow. However, because the taxes were prorated between the seller and buyer on a calendar basis, the seller was reimbursing the buyer for 4 months. Therefore, the borrower was actually only paying 3 month's of taxes, or $450, at closing. ($1,800 ÷ 12 x 3 = $450)

34. A – Underwriters assess risk for the lender. As part of that assessment, she must perform all of the tasks outlined in the other responses.

35. C – To determine how much he can borrow and keep his payment for principal and interest under $1,000, start by dividing $1,000 by $6.32. That number, ($158.227) is how money can be borrowed for each $6.32 paid. Then multiply $158.227 by 1,000 for a total loan of $158,227.

36. A – Underwriters often approve loans subject to certain conditions being met before closing. The phrase used to describe that approval is "conditional loan approval." All of the other Responses may be true of some of the items in the conditional approval, but they are not responsive to the question.

37. C – Because property taxes are liens prior to a first mortgage, lenders typically include failure to pay taxes as a default under the mortgage. Response "A" may be a correct description of the property owner's behavior, but it is not responsive to the question. Response "B" refers to depositors withdrawing

money from their bank accounts, which has nothing to do with property taxes. Response "D" is technically correct, because a mortgage is a contract, however, Response "C" is the better answer.

38. A – To find this answer, simply subtract the costs of sale, the mortgage pay-off, and the lien pay-off from the sales price. Equity is the amount left, and that money will be returned to the property owners.

39. B – This Response states the law. Response "A" refers to redeeming property after the foreclosure sale. Response "C" and "D" are nonsensical.

40. C – The deed used in this situation is a deed in lieu of foreclosure. Response "A" is the type of deed used to transfer the grantor's interest in property, if any, without any warranties. Response "B" is a deed used by a life tenant to relinquish her interest in the property. Response "D" is a deed used after a foreclosure sale.

41. A – A prepayment penalty clause requires a penalty be paid to pay off the loan balance unless certain conditions are met. Response "B" is incorrect, because a prepayment privilege would favor the borrower, not the lender. Responses "C" and "D" are incorrect statements of the law.

42. C – The maturity date ends one month before the month in which the mortgage was written. For example, a mortgage that is written in May would have a maturity of April, a mortgage that was written in December would have a maturity of November, and a mortgage written in September would have a

maturity date in August.

43. C – The canceled promissory note should be kept to show it was paid, and the mortgage should be recorded in the public records to give constructive notice that there is no longer a lien on the property. Response "A" is incorrect, because a promissory note cannot be recorded. Response "B" is incorrect, because the mortgage may call for the mortgagor to record the release. And, in the event the mortgage calls for the mortgagee to record the release, it may well be lost and never recorded if it is returned. Response "D" is not correct, because the release should be recorded.

44. B – It is likely that the mortgage has a due-on-sale clause that would accelerate the balance, requiring the balance of the loan to be paid in full. Response "A" does not apply because the lender would have to agree to take a less than first lien priority before the subordination clause would be relevant. Response "C" refers to increasing the payments on the loan, which is not responsive to the question. Response "D" is irrelevant in this situation.

45. B – Because the first mortgage is being paid and released, the second mortgage will move into the first lien position. Unless the second mortgage holder will agree to reverse priorities, the first mortgage lender would be in second lien position and would not likely agree to the mortgage. Response "A" is nonsensical. Response "C" and "D" are true, but irrelevant to the question.

46. D – Because an adjustable rate mortgage's rate and payment may change, it is necessary to have a clause that allows for an increase in the monthly payment. The other responses are incorrect.

47. A – Correctly states the reason for an acceleration clause. The other responses are incorrect.

48. B – The only math to be performed is to multiply $210,000 x 3% (100% - 97%). This gives the down payment amount of $6,300. The other information in the question is irrelevant to answering the question about the down payment because those items are part of the closing costs.

49. D – The underwriter does not consider the number of family members under 18 years old and to do so may be a violation of the fair housing laws that prohibit discrimination on the basis of familial status. All of the other Responses are appropriate considerations.

50. A – A note is signed by a maker and delivered to the holder. Response "B" is incorrect, unless the seller is carrying owner financing, and that information was not part of the question. Responses "C" and "D" are incorrect, because the question does not state that the promissory note has a guarantee.

Chapter 6

Key Term Match

1.   A
2.   B
3.   I
4.   H
5.   C

6. G
7. F
8. D
9. J
10. E
11. K
12. M
13. L
14. N
15. O

Practice Questions

1. B – State licensing law require the sponsoring broker, sometimes referred to as the principal broker or supervising broker, to supervise the activities of the salespeople. Response "A" will be expected by the associates, but not required by the licensing law. Response "C" will be true in some states, but not all. Response "D" is not responsive to the question.

2. B – One of the features of independent contractor status is the obligation of the sales associate, not the broker, to pay federal and state income tax. The associate will receive his share of the real estate commission as it is earned, and a tax form 1099 at the end of the year. Responses "A" and "C" are incorrect, because the broker cannot require an independent contractor to keep office hours or attend sales meetings. Response "D" may or may not be true, depending on the contract between the broker and sales agent.

3. C – Brokers must maintain a trust account to be used for holding client money that comes into the brokerage for any reason. Response "A" refers to the operating account of the brokerage. Response "B" is a special account used by property managers to hold only security deposits and not other money belonging to the client. Response "D" would likely be an operating account used in a property management business.

4. D – Interest earned on a trust account can only be used as directed by the owner of the money, i.e. the client. The other Responses are incorrect and would be a misuse of the trust account.

5. B – Each state licensing law states the number of years a broker must keep files. Response "C" is an option to save space, but may be a violation of license law. Response "D" would be a good idea, but not the best response to this question. Response "A" is an option to save space and retain part of the file, but is not the best response to the question.

6. C – Regulatory agencies have certain notice requirements for licensees, and those requirements would likely include notice of a change of company name. The other Responses would be appropriate actions, but are not the best responses for this question.

7. D – All of the parties are protected when a written policy manual exists.

8. D – Agents who are answering the phone at the office should always stay abreast of developments in real estate. If an agent is asked a question she doesn't know, she should attempt to find out. Response "A" is a true statement, but the agent should make an attempt to find the correct information. Responses "B" or "C" may or may not be true, but they are not an appropriate response for an agent.

9. B – This action lets the cooperating broker know that Broker Stewart is

concerned that there may have been a problem while giving the agent the opportunity to give his side of the story. Response "A" presumes the agent acted inappropriately, without giving him a chance to explain what happened. Response "C" is not appropriate because Brokers need to be made aware of problems that may be occurring with the sales staff because Brokers are required to adequately supervise the agents. Response "D" is the second step after speaking with the agent. A face-to-face meeting is always a positive way to work out issues.

10. C – Agents need to review continually what is happening in the industry, and it doesn't matter how long they've been in the business. All of the other responses are inappropriate.

11. C – The Broker needs to meet with this office manager and agent to get the facts behind the advertisement and to work together to respond to the regulatory agency. All of the other responses are inappropriate, because the "buck stops" on the Broker's desk, and he is ultimately responsible for everything that happens.

12. B – Real estate commission may only be paid to the Broker of the firm who then pays the salesperson. Response "A" is incorrect unless the referring agent has a real estate license. Response "C" is incorrect, because the money is paid to the Broker not the sales associate. Response "D" is incorrect, because out-of-state brokers may make referrals as can in-state brokers.

13. C – This is a perfect example of a price-fixing arrangement and is illegal. Brokers must set their own rates based

on their own expenses and profit margins. All of the other answers are inappropriate responses to the facts in the question.

14. A – This is an example of boycotting, and it violates the anti-trust laws. The other Responses are all examples of activity that also violate the anti-trust laws, specifically the Sherman Anti-Trust Act.

15. B – Brokers and their salespeople negotiate the fees that will be paid to them. Responses "A" and "D" are incorrect, because it is a violation of the anti-trust laws for either group to have any input in both the amount of commissions charged and how they are divided. Response "C" is also incorrect, and if practiced, could also lead to allegations of anti-trust.

16. D – Brokers must keep their trust accounts separate from all others. All of the other Reponses are incorrect.

17. A – First determine the amount of commission and then reduce that amount because of the advertising. (172500 x .0575 = 9,918.75 – 895 = 9023.75) The question must be read carefully. It does not ask for "gross" commission, but rather asks for "net" commission.

18. B – This question gives you unnecessary information. Because the Broker pays the sales associate the entire amount due, without withholding income taxes, it is not necessary to consider the tax percentage. Determine the full commission by multiplying the sales price by the commission rate to get the total commission, (219,900 x .0625 = 13,743.75) then multiply the total

commission by 40% (13,743.75 x .40 = 5,497.50).

19. C – The information on the advertising and survey are irrelevant to the question. Multiply the sales price by the commission and divide by 2 . (547,000 x .0475 ÷ 2 = 12,991.25)

20. B – All information in the question is needed. Determine how much is left after the referral fee is paid (35,000 x . 90 = 31,500). Then divide that number by 2 (31,500 ÷ 2 – 15,750). Then multiply that number by 60% (15,750 x .60 = 9,450).

Sales Exam One

1. A grantor who wants to sell property without any warranties may use a

A. special warranty deed.
B. limited warranty deed.
C. quit claim deed.
D. general warranty deed.

2. How much are the annual taxes if the ad valorem taxes are based on 50% of the assessed value, the assessed value is $225,000, and the tax rate is 3.9876?

A. $4,486.05
B. $2,243.03
C. $8,972.10
D. $2,243.03

3. A listing contract is

A. a real estate contract.
B. a personal services contract.
C. voidable at will by either party.
D. required to be in writing only in a few states.

4. Growing crops are known as

A. appurtenances.
B. emblements.
C. fixtures.
D. encumbrances.

5. A seller's agent should do all of the following EXCEPT

A. place a sign on the property.
B. explain the listing contract to the seller.
C. advise the seller on terms in the sales Contract.
D. review the closing/settlement statement with the seller.

6. While driving through a subdivision with clients, Sue saw a new "for sale" sign. Her clients wanted to see the house, but she was unable to reach the listing agent by phone. Because she was already in the neighborhood and her clients were in the car, her BEST action would be to

A. knock on the door, apologize for the inconvenience, and ask to show the house.
B. continue to try to reach the listing agent to get an appointment.
C. call the sellers and ask them if she could show the house.
D. walk around in the yard hoping the sellers would see her and ask her in to see the house.

7. A house that has at least three levels on the inside is known as a

A. multi-level house.
B. split level.
C. two and one-half story.
D. split foyer.

8. Last year Sandy built a new garage near her back property line. She has recently discovered that the overhang on the roof actually goes over her property line about 1 ½ feet. The part of the garage that goes over the property line is known as

A. an encumbrance.
B. a fixture.
C. an encroachment.
D. a building code violation.

9. When an offer was presented to the sellers, they agreed to everything but the time for possession. They asked their agent to change the time for possession. The change to the offer created a/an

A. contingency.
B. counteroffer.
C. acceptance with a condition.
D. executory contract.

10. Rental property has been depreciated $25,000 for income tax purposes. Because of that depreciation, the fair market value has

A. depreciated $25,000.
B. appreciated $25,000.
C. not changed because of the depreciation.
D. decreased in value $25,000.

11. In a state that has dower and curtesy laws, a single woman who purchases a property in her individual name then gets married

A. will need her husband to sign the deed if she sells the property.

B. will need her husband to sign the mortgage only if the money goes into a joint bank account.
C. will not need her husband to sign the deed if she sells the property.
D. will not need her husband to sign the mortgage because she owns the property in her individual name.

12. When Marvin closes his convenience store, can he remove the built-in refrigeration units?

A. Yes, because they are trade fixtures.
B. Yes, because health regulations do not allow a new owner to use old refrigeration units.
C. No, because once they are attached to the building they must stay.
D. No, because the owner has leased the building to a new convenience store.

13. Property that has been re-zoned from agricultural use to commercial use would MOST likely

A. increase in fair market value.
B. decrease in fair market value.
C. have no change in fair market value.
D. increase only if there was no other commercial property nearby.

14. Combination forms of real property ownership found in resort communities include all of the following EXCEPT

A. interval ownership.
B. timeshares.
C. condominiums.
D. cooperatives.

15. A legal description that reads: "Being all of Lot 14, of Block C, in the Hometown Subdivision, as shown on plat of record in Plat Cabinet 48, Slide

78, in the office of the Snyder County Court Clerk" is an example of a

A. government survey system description.
B. metes and bounds legal description.
C. lot and block legal description.
D. monument legal description.

16. Protected classes include all of the following EXCEPT

A. marital status.
B. handicap.
C. religion.
D. familial status.

17. The income approach to appraising is used to appraise

A. residential property.
B. investment property.
C. condemned property.
D. estate property.

18. Just prior to closing, a buyer should make a

A. final walk through inspection.
B. checklist of everything the seller has repaired.
C. list of items that will stay with the property when the seller moves out.
D. list of the neighbors with their phone numbers.

19. A leasehold interest in property is

A. personal property.
B. real property.
C. both personal and real.
D. neither personal nor real.

20. An easement that is written and recorded

A. runs with the land.
B. terminates in 25 years.
C. may not be terminated by either party.
D. terminates when it is no longer necessary.

21. When the sellers discussed listing their property with Roberto, they informed him they wanted to net at least $223,000 after paying his 7% listing commission. What should be their minimum listing price?

A. $207,390
B. $239,785
C. $239,758
D. $238,610

22. Zoning designations include all of the following EXCEPT

A. single family.
B. commercial.
C. professional.
D. farm.

23. Real estate licensees may work as all of the following EXCEPT

A. dual agent.
B. seller's agent.
C. principal agent.
D. buyer's agent.

24. Mr. Abraham gave the American Birdwatching Society permission to use his land in August to watch birds. When Mr. Abraham died, his widow decided she did not want the Society on her property. Mr. Abraham had given the Society a/an

A. easement.
B. license.
C. lease.

D. encroachment.

25. The term used to describe all of the owner's rights in the property is

A. bundle of rights.
B. package of rights.
C. warranty of rights.
D. value of rights.

26. Tenancy by the entirety requires the tenants to be

A. husband and wife.
B. willing to sign a one-year lease.
C. equal owners in all of the property.
D. in a community property state.

27. A house with a fair market value of $245,000 is heavily damaged by fire. It will cost the owners about $100,000 to repair the damage. This is an example of

A. curable physical deterioration.
B. incurable physical deterioration.
C. curable functional obsolescence.
D. incurable functional obsolescence.

28. Language in a deed that states "To Bobby for the life of Sarah" sets up a

A. limited life estate.
B. life estate *pur autre vie.*
C. remainder interest to Bobby's estate.
D. legal life estate.

29. Clarice is negotiating a lease on behalf of the property owner. The owner wants the tenant to pay the property insurance and the taxes. This type of lease is known as a

A. percentage lease.
B. double net lease.
C. base lease.

D. shared cost lease.

30. Two people want to own property jointly and neither of them wants to be personally liable in the event someone is hurt on the property. The BEST way to achieve this goal is to

A. take property in their joint names so neither one can be sued individually.
B. form a limited liability company to take title to the property.
C. take title by land contract that specifically states neither owner is liable.
D. form a general partnership with an agreement of no liability.

31. A seller's agent informed the buyer that the seller was getting a divorce. This was a breach of the fiduciary duty of

A. disclosure.
B. accounting.
C. confidentiality.
D. loyalty.

32. If three people own property as joint tenants with right of survivorship and one of them dies, the two surviving owners

A. own the property as joint tenants with right of survivorship with the deceased owners' heirs.
B. own the property as tenants in common with the heirs of the deceased owner.
C. continue to own the property as joint tenants with right of survivorship, and the deceased owner's heirs have no ownership interest.
D. continue to own the property as joint tenants with right of survivorship, and the heirs of the deceased owner

have a life estate interest.

33. The first step for an agent to take when starting to work with a buyer is to

A. tell the buyer to list everything they want in a house.
B. send the buyer to a lender to be pre-qualified.
C. ask the buyer to drive through different areas of town.
D. discuss the buying process with the buyer.

34. Generally speaking, what is the most important feature of a property for a buyer

A. size of lot.
B. school district.
C. location.
D. number of bedrooms.

35. One of the economic value factors of a property is its

A. neighborhood.
B. transferability.
C. size.
D. affordability.

36. Sales Associate Mark has just listed a house for a flat fee commission of $3,500. Flat fee commissions are

A. appropriate, if authorized by the principal broker.
B. appropriate, if the sales associate agrees to accept the fee.
C. inappropriate, because this the same things as a net listing.
D. inappropriate, because commissions must be stated as percentages.

37. A seller sells his property on a land contract for $100,000 and his basis was

$0. He collects $20,000 at the time of closing, and the buyer agrees to pay $20,000 per year for the next four years. If the buyer pays the $20,000 each year, how much capital gains will the seller report in the second year?

A. $20,000
B. $40,000
C. $60,000
D. $80,000

38. A huge crack in the foundation wall is a

A. material fact.
B. relevant fact.
C. discoverable fact.
D. provable fact.

39. A property manager has been asked by the owner to give him a list of modifications that need to be made to bring his office building into conformity with ADA requirements. The property manager makes a list and all of the following modifications would need to be made EXCEPT

A. adding braille letter and markings to the elevator buttons.
B. reversing the direction in which the doors open.
C. adding a dog walk area for guide dogs.
D. adding grab bars to public restroom Stalls.

40. Because it was obvious that the roof needed to be replaced, when Valerie showed buyers the property on Main Street she did not go into detail about the roof. Were Valerie's actions appropriate?

A. Yes, because everyone saw the roof

and there was no need to talk about it.
B. Yes, because it would have embarrassed the sellers to mention the roof.
C. No, because the buyers may not have noticed the roof.
D. No, because she should have had bids on the replacement cost.

41. Harrell is purchasing a $250,000 property. How much will the down payment be for a 80/20 loan with closing costs of 6% and discount points of $2,000?

A. $50,000
B. $52,000
C. $67,000
D. $76,000

42. Property management agreements must be

A. recorded.
B. written.
C. no longer than 3 pages.
D. signed by the owner and tenant.

43. The seller disclosure of property condition form should be completed by the

A. seller.
B. home inspector.
C. listing agent.
D. selling agent.

44. Parties to the sales contract are

A. buyer and seller.
B. buyer, seller, and listing agent.
C. buyer, seller, and listing broker.
D. buyer, seller, listing broker, and l listing agent.

45. If a buyer must obtain financing before she can purchase property, her agent should include what type of clause in the purchase contract?

A. A financing contingency clause
B. A limited liability clause
C. An appraisal contingency clause
D. A covenant to obtain financing clause

46. If a buyer obtains a new loan to buy a car, his credit score is LIKELY to

A. go down.
B. go up.
C. remain unchanged.
D. not enough information to know.

47. A buyer was nervous about signing the offer, because she wasn't sure she understood everything. The agent's BEST action was to

A. suggest the buyer seek legal counsel.
B. explain the offer over and over until the buyer understands.
C. take the buyer to her broker and let the broker explain the terms.
D. recommend the buyer talk to her family before signing the offer.

48. Property taxes are paid on a fiscal year basis and are to be prorated at closing. If the closing takes place on September 15th, the seller will owe the buyer how many days of taxes at closing?

A. 77 days
B. 303 days
C. 15 days
D. 257 days

49. When the offer was presented to the seller, the seller made a couple of changes. The offer is now known as a

A. contract.
B. seller's offer.
C. counteroffer.
D. negotiated offer.

50. How many years must an unmarried homeowner live in a property as her primary residence before she can sell it without paying capital gains tax on the first $250,000?

A. Two of the last five years
B. Three of the last five years
C. Two of the last seven years
D. Five of the last seven years

51. Once the buyer signs the offer, it must be

A. hand-delivered to the seller.
B. negotiated by the buyer's agent.
C. presented to the seller.
D. considered by the seller.

52. Duties for property manager include all of the following EXCEPT

A. financial management.
B. fiduciary management.
C. physical management.
D. administrative management.

53. If there are few apartments available to rent and many tenants who want to rent them, the rents are likely to be higher because of the economic principle of

A. diminishing returns.
B. return on investment.
C. caveat emptor.
D. supply and demand.

54. Cassandra listed a house built in 1977. One of the forms she needs to ask the seller to complete is the

A. seller's disclosure of property condition.
B. lead-based paint disclosure.
C. septic inspection and certification.
D. mortgage information letter.

55. Another name for a nonamortized loan is a

A. term loan.
B. mature loan.
C. negative interest loan.
D. secured loan.

56. Ralph purchased an undeveloped tract of land. ABC retail store has asked him to sell it the property before he closes the transaction. The store's owner is offering to pay him more than he paid the seller. Can Ralph do this?

A. Yes, as long as the seller agrees and the extra money is paid to the seller.
B. Yes, as long as the sales contract is assignable.
C. No, because it will be tax fraud if he sells the property before closing.
D. No, he must close it first to keep the chain of title clear.

57. A lease is being signed on August 14th. It begins on September 1st. The rental amount is $895 per month. What will be the prorated rent if a calendar year is the basis for the pro-ration?

A. $0
B. $404.19
C. $477.33
D. $895.00

58. When there is a dispute over the ownership of real property, the legal

mechanism for resolving the issue is a/an

A. foreclosure action.
B. settlement action.
C. adverse possession Action.
D. quiet title action.

59. Broker Louise was preparing a monthly profit and loss statement for the owner of three duplexes that she has been managing for several years. The total rent receipts for the month are $6,000, the monthly operating expenses are $1,325, the mortgage payments total $2,898 for the month, and the total principal reduction $648. What is the amount of the monthly net profit she will show on the statement?

A. $1,873
B. $2,425
C. $3,087
D. $6,000

60. When Beth called the listing agent to inform him she had an offer on one of his listings, he told her he was on his way to an out-of-town basketball game and would be gone for two days. He asked her to call his sellers and ask them when she could present the offer. She was to call him back and let him know the time so he could possibly be on the phone with them while she was at the house with the offer. The listing agents actions were

A. Appropriate, because he had a plan for getting the offer presented.
B. Appropriate, because he was going to try to be on the phone to answer questions for the sellers.
C. Inappropriate, because Beth might talk the sellers into taking less money than they wanted for the

property.
D. Inappropriate, because he has a duty to represent his clients' best interest and to be available to them when they need assistance.

61. An example of a combination form of property ownership is a

A. condominium.
B. life estate.
C. corporation.
D. limited liability company.

62. States that secure repayment of a mortgage debt by having a mortgage executed is known as a

A. lien theory state.
B. title theory state.
C. intermediary theory state.
D. collateral theory state.

63. Hannah is managing several single family residences for one client. She had a call today about one of the houses that had been rented recently by a man who had AIDS and died. The neighbor on the right has told Hannah that she will inform anyone who looks at the house about the man who died. Hannah has decided she will mention what happened to rental prospects before the neighbor says anything. Hannah's actions are

A. correct, because prospects have a right to know and disclosure is a very important aspect of leasing property.
B. correct, because she can make it sound better and not scare off prospects.
C. incorrect, because she should wait until they ask to tell them.
D. incorrect, because disclosing this

information violates fair housing laws.

64. Jason has just purchased a small convenience store. He is concerned that someone may fall and hurt themselves on the property. The type of insurance he needs to buy is

A. casualty.
B. personal injury.
C. liability.
D. extended coverage.

65. The transfer tax rate is $1.00 per thousand rounded to the nearest $500. The sales price is $158,592. How much is the transfer tax?

A. $158.00
B. $158.50
C. $158.59
D. $159.00

66. Happy Valley subdivision has recorded restrictive covenants that prohibit detached garages and outbuildings. Over the past 20 years several homeowners have built detached garages and outbuildings. If a new owner moves into the neighborhood, in all likelihood, she will

A. be able to make them remove the garages and outbuildings because the restrictions are recorded.
B. be able to make them remove the garages and outbuildings only if they are less than ten years old.
C. not be able to make them remove the garages and outbuildings because the restrictions have occurred over time with no objection from the owners.
D. not be able to make them remove the

garages and outbuildings because she is only one owner.

67. The closing occurs on July 14th and the taxes are paid on a calendar year, with the taxes being due and payable on December 31st. Taxes for the year of closing are $1,878 and are prorated between the buyer and seller. How much will be credited to the buyer on the closing statement?

A. $0
B. $874.69
C. $1,003.32
D. $1,878.00

68. Loan discount points are

A. considered an origination fee.
B. part of the down payment.
C. pre-paid interest.
D. used to reduce the real estate Commission.

69. April wants to pay off her mortgage. She has just learned that if she pays it off before the end of the year, she will owe an additional $2,000. This additional money is likely a

A. prepayment privilege.
B. accrued interest.
C. prepayment penalty.
D. short payment.

70. Roscoe was having problems obtaining a mortgage loan because of bad credit. What would be the BEST option for Roscoe to obtain mortgage financing

A. ask the real estate agent to co-sign a mortgage with him.
B. ask the seller to carry the financing.
C. take out a loan on his life insurance

policy.

D. wait for a couple of years until his credit is better.

71. Prior to occupancy, a builder must provide the purchaser a

A. certificate of completion.
B. building permit.
C. plumbing permit.
D. certificate of occupancy.

72. The city government decided to install street lights in one of the inter-city neighborhoods. To pay for the street lights, the city required each property owner to pay $1,000. This payment is known as

A. ad valorem tax.
B. a special assessment.
C. a one-time property taxes.
D. a home improvement tax.

73. Licensees must do all of the following EXCEPT

A. stay abreast of trends in the industry to better advise clients.
B. advise buyers on the best type of mortgage financing for them.
C. understand the forms required by the state regulatory agency.
D. read and understand the office policy manual.

74. The property manager has received a phone message that the tenants are moving and that she should keep their security deposit for the last month's rent. They've asked for her to call them back to let them know if this is OK. Is it?

A. No, because at this point the property manager does not know if there is any damage to the property.

B. No, because security deposits may not be used for rent.
C. Yes, it's better to use the money for rent than to return it to the tenants.
D. Yes, because under the law security deposits may be used for rent or to repair damages to the property.

75. A property owner is in default on her mortgage. She owes $162,432 on the first mortgage, $15,472 on her second mortgage, and her unpaid property taxes total $3,316. At the foreclosure sale, the property sells for $177,000. The costs of sale are $4,200. How much money will the second mortgage holder receive?

A. $7,052
B. $10,368
C. $14,568
D. $15,472

76. A roofing contractor was not paid for repairing the roof on an office building. He may file what type of legal document against the property?

A. Judgment lien
B. Mechanic and materialman's lien
C. Lis pendens
D. Mortgage

77. The basic rule for trust accounts is that funds are
A. held until instructions are received from the property owners.
B. never commingled.
C. disbursed according to the license Law.
D. kept until a signed release from all parties is received.

78. A lot that measures 198' x 248' contains how many acres?

A. 1.31
B. 2.10
C. 1.73
D. 1.13

79. Valerie has just been informed that the legal description on her deed is incorrect. This is an example of a/an

A. encumbrance.
B. title defect.
C. clerical error.
D. acknowledgement.

80. Costs paid by the buyer and seller prior to closing should appear on the closing statement marked

A. POC.
B. POA.
C. PAID.
D. POD.

81. A buyer's agent has just learned that a house her buyer likes was the scene of a murder about two years ago. The agent should

A. immediately disclose that fact to her buyer.
B. not mention the fact because the seller has the right to her privacy.
C. determine whether or not disclosure is required under state law.
D. suggest to her buyer that she look for another property.

82. Oral leases for less than one year are generally

A. legal.
B. illegal.
C. unenforceable.
D. invalid.

83. Federal regulation requires what type of closing statement for federally related mortgage loans?

A. HUD-1
B. RESPA
C. TIL
D. REG Z

84. If a seller decides to sell property using a 1031 exchange, he is

A. increasing the property value.
B. lowering the capital gains tax.
C. decreasing depreciation.
D. deferring capital gains tax.

85. Which of the following statements is TRUE about a mortgage broker

A. closing costs are higher than through a mortgage banker.
B. only people with bad credit use mortgage brokers.
C. mortgage brokers have access to funds from a number of sources.
D. mortgage broker is just another name for a mortgage banker.

86. A mortgage rate that has equal payments and pays off fully over a period of time is known as a

A. partially amortized loan.
B. fully amortized loan.
C. non-amortized loan.
D. monthly amortized loan.

87. A sales associate who states: "the standard real estate commission is 7%" is making a/an

A. correct statement because the industry is required to have a standard fee.
B. correct statement because the real

estate board sets the commission.
C. incorrect statement that violates the federal anti-trust laws.
D. incorrect statement because the standard fee is actually 6%.

88. Felix, a qualified veteran, wants to purchase a home using his VA eligibility. He wants to ask the seller to pay discount points to reduce his rate. According to his agent this is permissible under the VA guidelines. Is it?

A. Yes, as long as the seller agrees and the property appraises for enough.
B. Yes, as long as the discount points do not reduce the rate more than 2 %.
C. No, because the rates are already reduced compared to other loan types.
D. No, because adding discount points to the sales price is inflationary.

89. A conventional insured loan

A. has a loan-to-value ratio greater than 80%.
B. has a requirement of full-coverage hazard insurance.
C. may only be obtained by first time home buyers.
D. is only available to borrowers with a credit score higher than 800.

90. Fences, barns, easements, and flowers are all examples of

A. improvements.
B. fixtures.
C. encroachments.
D. emblements.

91. Which of the following is not considered a capital improvement?
A. new roof.

B. maintenance.
C. swimming pool.
D. storage building.

92. A mortgage underwriter would be MOST concerned about which of the following situations?

A. A borrower who works for a factory that has just announced it has filed for federal bankruptcy protection.
B. A borrower who is a registered nurse who has decided to change from working in a hospital to working in a doctor's office.
C. A borrower who has recently graduated with a master's degree in teaching, but has not yet signed a contract with the school system.
D. A borrower who is a retired firefighter on a fixed income.

93. Lenders are required to adjust the escrow account deposits at the closing to avoid having the borrower have too much in his escrow account at the end of the year. This adjustment is known as the

A. buyer's credit.
B. escrow deposits.
C. aggregate adjustment.
D. yield spread premium.

94. A buyer purchased property at a foreclosure auction. Because the attorney filing the foreclosure lawsuit performed a title search, the buyer decided not to have another one performed. The buyer believed having another title search was a waste of money. Was his reasoning sound?

A. Yes, courts can not sell property at foreclosure auctions unless the title is clear.

B. Yes, the attorney would be liable to the buyer for any defects in the title.
C. No, it is the responsibility of the buyer at a foreclosure auction to protect his interest by having a title search.
D. No, because the attorney who filed the foreclosure action would have done the title search again for a very small fee.

95. Latitia has had an exclusive agency listing on an office building for about three months. Two weeks ago she received a telephone call from the seller telling her he had changed his mind about selling. She let him withdraw the listing with the understanding that, were he to decide to sell it later, he would call her. She has just learned that he sold the building. Can she sue him for her commission?

A. Yes, because he clearly terminated the listing to avoid her commission.
B. Yes, because he failed to call her when he decided to sell the property as he had agreed.
C. No, because he had the right to sell the building himself.
D. No, because he was not legally bound to call her if he decided to sell the building.

96. In order to conform to the licensing laws real estate agents must

A. have an escrow account for holding client's money.
B. keep accurate records of transactions in which they are involved.
C. provide the sponsoring broker with the names and addresses of all clients.
D. report all illegal behavior of other licensees.

97. The buyer wanted his home inspector to attend the closing to discuss problems with the property, and the seller refused. Was the seller being unreasonable?

A. Yes, because the home inspector always attends the closing to answer questions.
B. Yes, because this is one of the few times in the transaction when all parties are together.
C. No, because the home inspector should have met with the sellers before the closing.
D. No, the settlement is not the time to discuss problems with the house discovered by the home inspector.

98. At the foreclosure sale, the property sold for enough to pay the costs of sale and all liens with money left over. The property owner is bankrupt. Who will receive that money?

A. The court
B. The property owner
C. The bankruptcy trustee
D. The property owner's other creditors

99. If the seller is aware of lead based paint in the house, he must disclose its presence and complete the federally mandated lead based paint form. Once the disclosure has been made the

A. buyer must have an EPA inspection within ten days.
B. seller has no further obligations.
C. seller must paint over all surfaces that contain lead based paint.
D. buyer cannot obtain an FHA loan.

100. How does a brokerage establish the amount of real estate commission to be charged?

A. Because most brokerages charge the same commission, the brokers generally go along with the market rate.
B. The sponsoring broker determines the commission to be charged by the associates based on an analysis of expenses and profit margin.
C. The local board of Realtors® sets the rate for the community.
D. Each state's regulatory agency suggests a commission to be charged throughout the state.

Sales Exam Two

1. The real estate commission for leasing a retail store is 7.25% of the 1st three year's gross rents. According to the lease, the monthly rental is $2,300, and the common area maintenance fees are $200 per month. How much is the commission?

A. $2,001
B. $6,003
C. $6,525
D. $6,255

2. In areas that suffer from a scarcity of water, the right to use water is determined by the doctrine of

A. caveat emptor.
B. merger.
C. beneficial use.
D. prior appropriation.

3. To reduce the selling agent's risk a home inspection should be ordered by the

A. buyer's agent.
B. seller's agent.
C. seller.
D. buyer.

4. Square footage of an improvement that is located below ground level at any point is said to be

A. substandard.
B. below value.
C. below grade.
D. subsurface.

5. In a community property state, upon the death of the husband, his interest in jointly owned property passes

A. to his heirs.
B. to his wife.
C. one-half to his wife and one-half to the heirs.
D. to the wife unless he has children, then it passes to the children.

6. Pablo has recently listed a house for $135,000 with a commission of $6.5%. When he listed the property, he asked the sellers how much they owed on their current first mortgage. They told him their first mortgage was around $115,000. When he asked for an exact amount, Ms. Seller became upset with him and told him it was none of his business. Should Pablo continue to market the property without that information?

A. Yes, because he really doesn't need to know the amount until the time for the closing and then the settlement agent will get the information.
B. Yes, because they will have enough money to pay off the mortgage and pay his commission.
C. No, because they could owe more

than the $135,000 and be unable to close the transaction.

D. No, because they don't sound like they will be very cooperative throughout the listing.

7. If a buyer is concerned about a landfill, he should order a/an

A. environmental inspection.
B. appraisal.
C. property inspection.
D. health department evaluation.

8. Accepting an offer creates an

A. executed offer.
B. executed contract.
C. executory offer.
D. executory contract.

9. Listing Agent Marilyn has sellers who want to list and sell 250 acres of their land that they have named "Paradise Acres Subdivision." They want her to market it in 10-acre tracts that are outlined on a drawing prepared by the sellers' son who is an architect. Their goal is to have all of the tracts sold by December. The sellers will pay to have surveys on each tract as they sell them. Marilyn's BEST course of action is to

A. get the listing signed as soon as possible because it will be hard to sell the property by December unless she starts advertising it now.
B. ask them to survey the land prior to her listing it.
C. ask them to place colored markers along the front boundary of each tract so prospective buyers can visualize where the tracts lie.
D. ask them to subdivide the land prior to her listing it.

10. A hog farm is moving next door to a hospital. The value of the hospital will likely depreciate because of

A. curable functional obsolescence.
B. incurable functional obsolescence.
C. incurable external obsolescence.
D. curable external obsolescence.

11. Flood insurance is purchased from

A. FEMA.
B. private insurance companies.
C. government run insurance companies.
D. homeowner's associations.

12. The Sellers want to sell two lots. One has dimensions of 180' x 331' and the other lot has dimensions of 192' x 300' x 218' x 350'. How many acres will the Seller be selling?

A. 76
B. 3.0
C. 3.2
D. 2.8

13. When the buyers looked at the house, they noticed that the front door deadbolt lock was missing. This is an example of a

A. patent defect.
B. latent defect.
C. hidden defect.
D. safety defect.

14. The HUD-1 settlement statement is typically completed by the

A. real estate agent.
B. buyer.
C. closing agent.
D. underwriter.

15. Buyers should be informed that lenders

A. have certain income-to-debt ratios for different types of loans.
B. will not make a loan to someone who has ever filed bankruptcy.
C. will not make loans unless the buyer has a good down payment.
D. have certain criteria for appraisers and will only hire good ones.

16. When the county government adds sewers to an area, it may increase the ad valorem taxes to pay for the sewers, or it may choose to ask each property owner to pay a share by levying a/an

A. fixture tax.
B. easement in gross.
C. special assessment.
D. government bond.

17. Miranda owns a condominium. She has just learned from the plumber that she has a plumbing leak in the wall between her unit and the one next door. According to the property manager, Miranda will be responsible for repairing the leak. Is this information correct?

A. Yes, because Miranda must have created the problem because it leaked into her unit first.
B. Yes, because one of the property manager's duties is to decide issues like this one.
C. No, because the plumbing in the wall is part of the common area and must be repaired by the condominium association.
D. No, because there is no proof that Miranda created the plumbing problem.

18. If a couple owns property as tenants by the entirety and they get a divorce, the property will be owned by them as

A. severalty owners.
B. tenants in common.
C. joint tenants with right of survivorship.
D. joint tenants without the right of survivorship.

19. Formal complaints alleging violation of fair housing laws can be filed by

A. HUD.
B. FHA.
C. FNMA.
D. EPA.

20. The Seller informed the listing broker that he had paid $210,000 when he purchased the property three years ago, and that he believed the property had appreciated 4% per year. If the seller is correct, how much would the property be valued at this time?

A. $236,212
B. $236,221
C. $219.085
D. $210,000

21. A commercial lender's interest in real estate may be secured by which of the following?

A. Deed of trust and mortgage
B. Mortgage and promissory note
C. Vendor's lien and promissory note
D. Promissory note and guarantee

22. Items that are paid into an escrow account on a monthly basis include all of the following EXCEPT

A. property taxes.
B. homeowner's insurance.
C. flood insurance.
D. homeowner's association dues.

23. There are 18 units in a condominium group with a total of 26 owners. There are 15 tenants. If the bylaws call for a vote of 75% to increase the dues, how many votes will it take to increase the condominium fees?

A. 14
B. 20
C. 15
D. 31

24. Two neighbors have shared a driveway for a number of years. Both have use of the driveway and share in its maintenance and upkeep. This is an example of an

A. appurtenant easement.
B. easement by necessity.
C. easement in gross.
D. easement by prescription.

25. Listing agent Carol has been authorized by her broker to accept listings at a flat fee of $5,000. Carol is giving a listing presentation to a seller who wants to pay $4,000. What is the BEST thing for Carol to do? Explain to the seller that

A. everyone in the area charges a flat fee of $5,000 for listings under $200,000.
B. she is authorized by her broker to accept $5,000 and suggest the seller speak to the broker.
C. only the brokers who advertise sporadically charge less commission.

D. her time is more valuable than $4,000 and suggest the seller call someone else.

26. A property manager has just learned that a tenant is not going to pay rent for the month and that he is moving as soon as he finds a new apartment. The property manager's first legal step is to

A. file a forcible entry and detainer action.
B. deliver the tenant a notice that his rent is past due and must be paid.
C. change the locks.
D. contact the owner with the information.

27. Owners of a 100 acre farm want to subdivide their land into 5 acre tracts. The zoning restrictions require that they dedicate 8% of the land to the county for roads. How many tracts will they have to sell after they dedicate the land to the county?

A. 21
B. 20
C. 19
D. 18

28. n the typical transaction with mortgage financing, the appraiser is representing the

A. lender.
B. real estate agent.
C. buyer.
D. seller.

29. Flowers planted in a home garden should stay with the property when it transfers to the new owners, because

A. they are emblements.
B. they are improvements.

C. it would damage the yard to remove them.

D. their value was included in the purchase price.

30. The most important consideration in appraising real estate is its

A. square footage.
B. location.
C. current assessment.
D. condition.

31. A counter offer is a/an

A. acceptance of the offer.
B. rejection of the offer.
C. modification of the offer.
D. improvement on the offer.

32. Broker Joy listed a seller's property on Sunday evening using an Exclusive Right to Sell Listing Contract. On Wednesday afternoon, Mr. Seller called and asked her to cancel it because he was going to sell the property to his mother. By the time he called, Joy had paid the MLS fee, prepared color data brochures, and had three people seriously interested in the property. She refused to cancel the listing unless he paid her the full commission. Did Broker Joy have a legal right to take that position?

A. Yes, once an Exclusive Right to Sell Listing Contract is signed, the broker should be paid regardless of who sells the property.
B. Yes, Broker Joy has spent money and time on the listing and should be paid her commission.
C. No, because of the short period of time from the listing until the request to cancel, Broker Joy must cancel the listing without payment.

D. No, because Broker Joy is entitled to be reimbursed for her out of pocket expenses, but she must cancel the listing.

33. Facts that would make a difference in the tenant's decision to rent property are known as

A.   material
B.   latent
C.   required
D.   patent

34. For variable rate expenses, the operating budget should include a/an

A. cash reserve fund.
B. income stream.
C. cash before taxes estimate.
D. fixed income analysis.

35. If the risk of loss passes to the buyer at the time the sales contract is signed, the buyer should obtain property insurance

A. immediately.
B. at the time of closing.
C. within 30 days after closing.
D. when the seller cancels her policy.

36. Fred was visiting his friend when he fell down the steps. The insurance that is MOST likely to pay for Fred's injury is his friend's

A. homeowner's.
B. liability.
C. hazard.
D. extended coverage.

37. If the buyer's credits total more than the buyer's debits, the buyer will

A. receive money at the closing.

B. pay money at the closing to the lender.
C. owe the seller money at the closing.
D. receive money from the seller at the closing.

38. A listing contract creates an agency relationship between the

A. seller and the company's broker.
B. seller and sales associate working the listing.
C. seller, buyer, company broker, and sales associate.
D. seller and buyer.

39. If the rental amount for the year is $10,800 and the security deposit is $1,000, and if the property manager must collect two month's rent and the security deposit when the lease is signed, how much will be collected if the tenant signs the lease on the 15th of the month?

A. $3,250
B. $1,800
C. $2,800
D. $1,000

40. A buyer who wants to know where the property boundaries are located should order a/an

A. appraisal.
B. home inspection.
C. pinned and staked survey.
D. subdivision plat.

41. Broker Sam has just listed an apartment complex for $3,000,000 with a commission rate of 7%. If Broker Sam sells the property for 90% of its listing price, the seller will pay Broker Sam at the closing

A. $210,000, because Broker Sam is an

independent contractor and will be responsible for reporting his own federal and state income taxes.
B. $210,000 less federal and state income tax, because Broker Sam is an employee and the Seller is required to the taxes.
C. $189,000, because Broker Sam is an independent contractor and will be responsible for reporting his own federal and state income taxes.
D. $189,000 less federal and state income taxes, because Broker Sam is an employee and the Seller is required to deduct the taxes.

42. What is the maximum loan-to-value ratio for a VA loan?

A. 75%
B. 80%
C. 90%
D. 100%

43. Buyers believe they were not represented well by their agent. In fact, they believe that any other agent would have done a better job. If they file a lawsuit, they will likely allege a breach of which of the fiduciary duties?

A. Loyalty
B. Due care and diligence
C. Disclosure
D. Accounting

44. All of the following terms should be included in a lease EXCEPT

A. default clause.
B. names of the parties.
C. amount of the rent.
D. option clause.

45. Pamela, a buyer's agent, explained to the buyers that they must pay her for

her services. She informed them that she could not represent them if she was paid by the seller. Was her information correct?

A. Yes, because an agent always represents the party who pays them.
B. Yes, because a seller can never pay a buyer's agent.
C. No, because the seller can pay a buyer's agent if both parties agree.
D. No, because the seller always pays the buyer's agent.

46. Building codes are designed to

A. set maximum standards for builders in the area.
B. protect the health, safety and welfare of the public.
C. assure lenders of the quality of construction.
D. give consumers confidence that their investments will be protected.

47. Tim has heard that Carlos sold his farm, but Carlos denies it. Tim wants to find out if this is true. What is the BEST way for Tim to find out if the property has been sold?

A. Look in the public records to see if a deed has been recorded
B. Call the closing attorney and ask her
C. Look in the public records to see if a mortgage has been recorded
D. Call the real estate agent that had the property listed

48. Which of the following is the BEST first step when measuring the square footage of a house?

A. Measure the outside of the house
B. Look at the plat of the lot
C. Draw a diagram of the house

D. Discuss the size with the seller

49. A husband and wife owned property as joint tenants with right of survivorship. When the husband died, the wife owned the property

A. in severalty.
B. as surviving tenant in common.
C. by devise.
D. under her husband's last will and testament.

50. A valid and enforceable contract must contain which of the following elements

A. date, signatures of the parties, legal description of the property, and closing date.
B. offer and acceptance, consideration, reality of consent, legal competency of the parties.
C. earnest money, legal competency of the parties, reality of consent, and signatures.
D. purchase price, earnest money, names and signatures of the parties, and closing date.

51. All of the following are characteristics of tenants in common EXCEPT that

A. each co-owner has an undivided interest.
B. a co-owner may lease his share without the consent of the other co-owner.
C. a co-owner may use the entire property without the consent of the other co-owners.
D. a co-owner cannot sell his interest in the property without the consent of the other co-owners.

52. Building codes cover all of the following EXCEPT

A. building design.
B. building construction.
C. building completion schedule.
D. building location.

53. Aletha and Alex were on the beach one day. A real estate agent came up to them and asked if they would like to look at nearby property in exchange for dinner at a local restaurant. The agent explained that they could purchase the property, in fee simple, for a week each year. This form of ownership is known as

A. cooperative ownership.
B. multiple ownership.
C. condominium ownership.
D. interval ownership.

54. The inspection made just prior to closing is known as the

A. final inspection.
B. full house inspection.
C. limited purpose inspection.
D. 30-day inspection.

55. When a corporation sells real property, the deed must be signed by the

A. president or vice-president, depending on who can attend the closing.
B. shareholders named in the books of the company.
C. person designated by the corporate Resolution.
D. secretary who signed the minutes authorizing the purchase.

56. Jessica built a large storage building on the back of her property. Her neighbor has just had his land surveyed and discovered that the storage building is about 5 feet over onto his property. The storage building is BEST described as

A. a legal nuisance.
B. an encroachment.
C. common property.
D. jointly owned.

57. An agent's fiduciary duties to his buyer includes

A. finding the right loan for the buyer.
B. protecting the buyer's confidential information.
C. ordering the home inspection and reviewing the written report.
D. assisting the appraiser to obtain the full appraised value.

58. If a condominium group has 22 units, 38 owners, 2 laundry rooms, 1 swimming pool, and 44 parking spaces, how much of the common area is in each deed?

A. $1/22^{nd}$
B. $1/38^{th}$
C. $1/24^{th}$
D. $1/44^{th}$

59. Home warranties are designed to

A. make money for real estate agents.
B. replace or repair items that may break for a period of time after closing.
C. keep the seller from replacing items in the property after closing.
D. give the buyers confidence that nothing is wrong with the property.

60. Property management agreements create an

A. employer/employee relationship between the tenant and owner.
B. agent/principal relationship between the owner and property manager.
C. agent/principal relationship between the owner, property manager, and tenant.
D. employer/employee relationship between the owner and property manager.

61. A judgment lien on real property title may be referred to by all of the following terms EXCEPT a/an

A. cloud.
B. encumbrance.
C. general lien.
D. specific lien.

62. A buyer wants to purchase a new home and obtain an FHA loan. The maximum origination fee she can be required to pay is

A. 1/8 %
B. 1/2 %
C. 1 %
D. there is no maximum because the borrower and lender negotiate the fee.

63. When the mortgage is paid in full, the

A. mortgagor should release the lien on the property.
B. mortgagee should release the lien on the property.
C. the promissor should release the lien on the property.
D. the maker should release the lien on the property.

64. Lucian, a property manager for a duplex, has just had a call from the tenant in Unit A. Apparently, the tenants are disputing over who has to mow the grass. The lease for Unit A says the Unit B tenant is to mow the grass and the Unit B lease does not address the issue. The BEST action for Lucian is to

A. tell the tenant that they need to work it out.
B. call the owner to get his opinion on who he thinks should mow the grass.
C. talk to both tenants and help them resolve the problem.
D. call the tenant in Unit B and tell her to mow the grass.

65. A Broker has just listed property for sellers who were being relocated by Ms. Seller's employer. Ms. Seller has informed him that her employer will pay the real estate commission. This is

A. acceptable, as long as the employer agrees in writing to pay the commission.
B. acceptable, because Broker has dealt with the employer lots of time before and that they have always paid the commission.
C. not acceptable, because Brokers cannot be paid by third parties who do not own the property.
D. not acceptable, because there is no agent-principal relationship between the company and Broker.

66. In order to comply with the Americans with Disabilities Act, the owner of an 8-unit apartment building MUST

A. remodel 25% of the units to include larger doors and hallways

B. make reasonably achievable accommodations to provide access to the facilities and services.
C. make reasonable accommodations for handicapped individuals who want to rent one of his apartments
D. do nothing, because his apartment building is too small to be affected by the Act.

67. The owner's right to mortgage real estate is

A. not applicable when the owner only has a life estate interest.
B. a fundamental right of all owners.
C. an owner's constitutional right.
D. one of the rights in the owner's bundle of rights.

68. Roger has just purchased an office building. He should talk to his insurance agent about which type of insurance?

A. Fire and hazard
B. Use and occupancy
C. Multi-peril
D. Liability

69. A seller was going to give a buyer $1,000 for repairs to the property. Because the mortgage broker did not want the FHA underwriter to know about the $1,000, the amount was left off the closing statement. After the closing, the seller gave the buyer a $1,000 check. This action was

A. illegal and may lead to criminal charges.
B. a good way to handle a difficult underwriter.
C. the proper way to handle the situation.
D. handled properly as long as the seller's check clears the bank.

70. A legal description that reads in part "the NE ¼ of the NE ¼ of Section 12," is an example of a

A. metes and bounds legal description.
B. monument legal description.
C. a government survey legal description.
D. a lot and block legal description.

71. A deed in lieu of foreclosure
A. releases all liens on the property.
B. avoids a foreclosure sale.
C. releases the mortgagee from a deficiency judgment.
D. protects the mortgagor's equity.

72. All of the following would likely influence the fair market value of property in an area EXCEPT

A. a factory closing.
B. interest rates decreasing.
C. builders increasing production.
D. increase in number of real estate agents.

73. A mortgage broker has decided to increase business by giving real estate agents who refer him business a $100 gift certificate. Is this is a good plan to increase business?

A. Yes, because none of the other mortgage brokers are making this offer.
B. Yes, because it will encourage new agents to refer him business.
C. No, because it violates the Real Estate Settlement Procedures Act.
D. No, because not all referrals result in business and he will lose money.

74. If the assessed value of a property is $165,000 and the annual tax bill is

$1,545. What is the tax rate expressed per $100?

A. .936
B. .639
C. 2.54
D. 6.39

75. The seller is considering an offer just presented to her. She does not have the option to

A. counter the offer.
B. hold the offer and do nothing.
C. accept the offer.
D. ask her agent to accept on her behalf.

76. Mediation is the process of having the

A. mediator suggest how the dispute should be resolved.
B. mediator make a decision on the issues in dispute.
C. parties resolve their dispute through discussion.
D. parties make a motion to the court for the judge to decide.

77. Lenders typically require an escrow account because

A. unpaid property taxes are a lien superior to the first mortgage.
B. the federal government requires an escrow account.
C. it makes it easier to determine the tax assessment.
D. it keeps the lender from sending a separate bill each year for taxes.

78. The Statute of Frauds requires that

A. a lawsuit alleging fraud be filed within five years of the closing.
B. real estate contracts be in writing.

C. deeds, mortgages, and deeds of trust be recorded.
D. complaints before the real estate commission be filed within two years.

79. Molly went to her closing and accepted delivery of the deed from the seller. The settlement agent said he would record the deed and send it to her within a week or so. Now, three days later, the seller says he has changed his mind and doesn't want to sell the property to Molly. He wants to give her money back and cancel the deed because it has not been recorded. Can the seller do this?

A. Yes, if the deed was not recorded, he still owns the property.
B. Yes, as long as he cancels the deed within three days after the closing.
C. No, title passed to Molly at the time of closing and she owns the property.
D. No, because Molly has three days after the closing to record the deed.

80. Raymond has been claiming part of his neighbor's farm for a number of years. He has been mowing the weeds, mending the fences, and paying the taxes. At some point, Raymond may make a claim of ownership under

A. quiet title.
B. adverse possession.
C. probate.
D. constructive notice.

81. A townhouse owner owns his individual unit and owns a share of the common area as

A. a joint tenant with right of survivorship with the other owners.
B. a tenant in common with the other

owners.
C. community property with the other owners.
D. a tenant by the entirety.

82. When a property owner's land fronts on a river and additional land is added because of the gradual accumulation of rock, sand, and soil, this process is called

A. accretion.
B. avulsion.
C. annexation.
D. reliction.

83. The road in front of Max's property is being widened. He has just learned that the government wants to use some of his property for the new road, but he doesn't want to sell it. If Max refuses to sell, the action that will be filed by the government against Max is known as

A. condemnation.
B. eminent domain.
C. police power.
D. governmental authority.

84. A property owner failed to pay his credit card debt. The credit card company filed suit and obtained a judgment against the property owner. If the property owner does not pay the judgment, the credit card company may file a

A. writ of attachment.
B. lis pendens.
C. mortgage.
D. foreclosure.

85. Cleaning the gutters in an example of which type of maintenance

A. preventative.
B. corrective.

C. routine.
D. construction.

86. Mutual Savings Banks are

A. depositor-owned entities that provide mortgage financing.
B. limited to making purchase money mortgages.
C. not permitted, by law, to provide second mortgages.
D. have higher interest rates than other mortgage lenders.

87. Which of the following is NOT a good reason for a seller to carry the mortgage financing for a buyer?

A. Seller can defer paying taxes on some of the capital gains
B. Seller can earn a higher interest rate on the mortgage than other forms of investment
C. Seller can sell house faster
D. Seller can assist a buyer with poor credit

88. A defeasance clause in a trust deed requires the

A. trustee to reconvey the property when the debt is paid.
B. lender to file a foreclosure action when there has been a default.
C. trustee and lender to give notice to the borrower in default.
D. borrower to give notice if the payment is going to be late.

89. Nora has been managing property for Mr. Elias for several years. He had rented the property at 123 Broadway to the current tenants before she started managing his properties. The tenants moved last week and Nora has just walked through the house. She was

appalled at the condition of the property. When she called them to tell them he was not returning their security deposit, they threatened to sue Mr. Elias for their deposit. Although it was required by law in order to collect damages, Mr. Elias did not do a walk-through inspection with them prior to occupancy. If they sue, it is

A. likely they will win, because there is no proof as to the condition of the house prior to their occupancy.
B. likely they will win, because Mr. Elias violated the law by not doing a walk-through inspection.
C. unlikely they will win, because it will be clear the damage occurred during their occupancy.
D. unlikely they will win, because they have no proof of the condition of the property.

90. Morgan sold his farm on an installment sales contract last year. The buyer has been late several times with the payment and has now disappeared. Morgan's BEST course of action is to

A. treat all payments as rent and cancel the contract.
B. refund the buyer the down payment before canceling the contract.
C. foreclose on the property to regain full title to it.
D. wait thirty days, then remove the buyer's personal property.

91. What legal document transfers the title to a mobile home that is permanently affixed to real estate?

A. Bill of sale
B. Deed
C. Chattel mortgage
D. Release

92. Fair housing laws apply to

A. all residential dwellings.
B. all rental property marketed by a real estate agent.
C. only single family residential Dwellings.
D. only properties built since 1978.

93. Homeowner's associations have the right to do all of the following EXCEPT

A. collect dues and assessments.
B. enforce the restrictive covenants.
C. place a lien on property for unpaid Assessments.
D. change the master deed without the property owners' approval.

94. An uninsured loan is

A. an FHA loan.
B. a loan with a loan-to-value ratio higher than 90%.
C. available to borrowers with credit scores of over 750.
D. a low risk loan.

95. How much will Vicki need for a down payment on a 90% loan if she purchases a house for $159,000 and it appraises for $158,000? Her closing costs are 4% and the discount points are 1 ½%.

A. $15,900
B. $16,800
C. $22,488
D. $25,860

96. Once the offer is signed by the buyer and seller, it is known as a/an

A. executory contract.
B. accepted offer.

C. executed contract.
D. completed contract.

97. If a man owns property while he is married, in some states the wife has a

A. homestead interest.
B. dower interest.
C. curtesy interest.
D. estate interest.

98. Property sold in a foreclosure sale. It did not sell for enough to pay the costs of sale and all of the first mortgage. At this point, the lender's BEST option is to

A. write off the balance of the mortgage.
B. place a lien on the property.
C. pursue the borrower for a deficiency Judgment.
D. hold another foreclosure sale.

99. Two agents were having a dispute in the office over floor time. The BEST way to resolve the dispute is to

A. review the office policy manual.
B. mediate the dispute.
C. ask the principal broker to settle the matter.
D. discuss it at an office meeting and let the agents decide.

100. The Sherman Anti-Trust Act prohibits all of the following acts EXCEPT

A. territorial allocations.
B. price fixing.
C. kickbacks to suppliers.
D. boycotting.

Sales Exam Three

1. When measuring square footage of a house, the agent should include all property that is

A. completely finished.
B. above grade.
C. enclosed.
D. below grade.

2. Federal anti-trust laws are designed to prevent all of the following EXCEPT

A. price fixing.
B. steering.
C. monopolies.
D. boycotting.

3. Maryann purchased property about six miles out of town. When she called the electric company to have electricity brought to her property, she discovered it would be necessary to grant the company an

A. appurtenant easement.
B. easement by necessity.
C. easement by prescription
D. easement in gross.

4. A drawing of a subdivision that shows the lots, easements, lot numbers, and subdivision name is known as a

A. building plan.
B. plat.
C. plot plan.
D. zoning map.

5. Julia, a licensed appraiser, was retained to do an appraisal for purchasers. One of the values she placed on the property was the amount of money it would cost to replace it. That approach to value is known as the

A. cost approach.
B. reproduction approach.
C. market data approach.
D. income approach.

6. Roberta was called to meet with the President of ABC Corporation for the purpose of listing one of its farms. After completing the listing, Roberta asked the President to sign the listing on behalf of the corporation and he did so. Her actions were

A. appropriate, because the president always has the authority to sign the listing.
B. appropriate, because it would be too long until the next board of directors meeting and valuable marketing time would be lost.
C. inappropriate, unless the president presented her with a corporate resolution stating he had the authority to sign the listing.
D. inappropriate, unless the president agreed to ask the board of directors to also sign the listing at the next board meeting.

7. The business model where the broker offers unbundled services is known by all of the following names EXCEPT

A. fee for service brokerage.
B. discount brokerage.
C. multiple service brokerage.
D. limited services brokerage.

8. If a residential dwelling was built before 1978, the listing agent must ask the seller to

A. complete a seller's disclosure of property condition.
B. sign a lead-based paint disclosure form.

C. sign a fair housing agreement.
D. disclose all FEMA information.

9. The constitutional right of the government to adopt and enforce laws that promote the public health, safety and welfare is known as

A. condemnation.
B. police power.
C. eminent domain.
D. due process.

10. When listing commercial property, the listing agent should ask the seller which items in the property are considered

A. trade fixtures.
B. collateral.
C. appurtenances.
D. fixtures.

11. When there are more houses on the market than there are buyers, which of the following is FALSE

A. houses will sell for close to the asking price.
B. houses will be on the market longer.
C. lower priced houses will sell faster than higher priced houses.
D. sellers will need to offer more concessions to buyers.

12. It is BEST for agents showing property to

A. allow the prospective purchasers to walk around by themselves so they do not feel pressured.
B. ask prospective purchasers if they prefer to look around the house by themselves or have the agent walk with them.
C. stay with the prospective purchasers

as they look at the house.

D. ask the sellers to be present to answer questions that the buyers may have.

13. If the buyer talks about adding a swimming pool in the backyard, the agent should

A. encourage him to do so by pointing out the extra value that will be added to the property.
B. recommend the buyer determine whether or not the zoning regulations and subdivision restrictions allow pools in the area.
C. assist the buyer is obtaining bids prior to making the offer to make sure the pool will not cost more than the buyer anticipates.
D. supply the buyer with names and phone numbers of at least three pool installers in the area.

14. A property's water supply is a well. The buyer's agent should

A. have the seller sign an affidavit that the water is drinkable.
B. suggest to the buyer that the water be tested by the health department.
C. get a statement from the health department that the water is OK to drink.
D. ask the seller if they've ever had problems with the water.

15. The party making the offer is known as the

A. offeror.
B. offeree.
C. buyer.
D. seller.

16. Two days after the buyer moved

into the property, the air conditioner stopped working. They called the home warranty company who refused to pay to have it repaired. The MOST LIKELY reason for their refusal was because the

A. defect in the air conditioner was a pre-existing condition.
B. buyers did not make a timely claim.
C. air conditioner was excluded under the policy.
D. real estate agent failed to send in the warranty premium.

17. A buyer asks the agent to locate the best area of town for him to buy his dream home. The agent should

A. find the area that will have the highest appreciation rate in the next 3 years in the event the buyer needs a quick sale.
B. explain to the buyer that the buyer needs to choose where he wants to live.
C. ask the buyer questions about his family size, religious preference, and opinions on living in a diverse neighborhood.
D. financially qualify the buyer first, then look for an area that suits the buyer's needs.

18. If the property value is $237,000, the amount of insurance coverage required under the coinsurance provision is

A. $47,400
B. $189,600
C. $198,600
D. $237,000

19. The property inspection that would MOST LIKELY inform the purchaser of the presence of termites would be the

A. full house inspection.
B. wood destroying insects inspection.
C. environmental inspection.
D. pest inspection.

20. Unity of time means all owners

A. have the right to use the property at the same time.
B. took title at the same time in the same conveying instrument.
C. must agree to hold the property for a certain period of time.
D. have a right to use it for a set amount of time each year.

21. After closing, if the buyer discovers a title defect, he may make a claim against his

A. homeowner's insurance policy.
B. lender's title insurance policy.
C. agent's errors and omissions insurance policy.
D. owner's title insurance policy.

22. Simultaneous ownership of property by two or more people is known as

A. severalty ownership.
B. trust ownership.
C. concurrent ownership.
D. unity ownership.

23. Albert has been asked to sell a house owned by Mr. and Mrs. Alvarez. When he went to the property to get the listing signed, he met Mr. Alvarez' 95-year old mother, Sarah, who has a life estate in the property. Albert should

A. make sure Sarah will agree to move when the house sells.
B. assure Sarah that he will not disturb her when showing the house.
C. explain to Sarah that she may be

entitled to some of the proceeds of sale.
D. get Mr. Alvarez' mother to sign the listing contract.

24. A marketing plan would be helpful in

A. convincing the owner to hire you as property manager
B. getting a reduction in advertising rates from the local newspaper
C. obtaining tenants for the property
D. keeping current tenants

25. Rent for the condo is $675 per month. A tenant moving in on the 22nd of May would pay how much in pro-rated rent for the month of May?

A. $195.97
B. $217.74
C. $457.26
D. $479.03

26. At closing the buyer will be required to pay interim interest at the rate of $42.38 per day. The closing takes place on May 17th and the first payment is due July 1st. How much mortgage interest will the buyer pay at closing?

A. $593.32
B. $635.70
C. $1,864.72
D. $1,907.10

27. In order to place a billboard along a highway, the sign company must obtain from the landowner a/an

A. easement.
B. license.
C. appurtenance.
D. right-of-way.

28. Sand, mud, and rocks carried by a river that are deposited onto the bank when the river slows down is known as

A. alluvion.
B. fructus naturals.
C. appurtenance.
D. emblement.

29. Smalltown USA has decided to add about 800 acres of county property to the city in order to increase its tax basis. This process is known as

A. prior appropriation.
B. platting.
C. annexation.
D. transferability.

30. The local government requires that a front porch with more than four steps must have a handrail. This requirement is an example of a/an

A. encroachment.
B. appurtenance.
C. building code.
D. license.

31. How much would it cost to carpet a house that has 1,850 square feet? The kitchen which is ceramic tile is 12 x 15, the bathroom which is 8 x 9 has vinyl, and the screened porch which is 12 x 16 has indoor/outdoor carpeting. The carpet cost $22.00 per square yard installed.

A. $3,436.89
B. $3,609.22
C. $3,906.22
D. $4,522.22

32. When listing the property, the sellers informed the listing agent that they had not paid their real property taxes for three years. The listing agent informed the sellers that they must pay the property taxes prior to conveying title to the purchasers, because the purchasers would expect to receive

A. marketable title to the property.
B. clear title to the property.
C. cloudless title to the property.
D. recordable title to the property.

33. When a developer is required to plant trees between a commercial development and a residential development, this is called

A. blockbusting.
B. buffer zoning.
C. bulk zoning.
D. aesthetic zoning.

34. A husband's right in his wife's property is known as his

A. dower interest.
B. curtesy interest.
C. life interest.
D. estate interest.

35. Personal property that changes character when affixed to real estate is known as

A. fixture.
B. easement.
C. emblement.
D. chattel.

36. Operating expenses

A. vary from month to month.
B. include the mortgage debt service.
C. are used when completing a CMA.
D. are never shown on the P & L statement.

37. Henry's lot had a setback of 50'. He wanted to build the house 37' from the road. In order to do so, Henry would need to obtain a/an

A. non-conforming use permit from the county government.
B. variance from the zoning board.
C. amended plat from the county court clerk.
D. spot zoning designation.

38. Information about real property related to zoning, building codes, land use restrictions, and property taxes are all considered

A. material facts.
B. appraisal facts.
C. subjective facts.
D. objective facts.

39. All of the following should be included in a sales contract EXCEPT

A. property description.
B. seller's social security number.
C. date of closing.
D. sales price.

40. In order to purchase property insurance, a person must have

A. the deed to the property.
B. an insurable interest.
C. a recorded mortgage.
D. clear title to the property.

41. If a buyer is concerned about the presence of mold in the property, the BEST inspection to have is a/an

A. full house inspection.
B. health department inspection.
C. environmental inspection.

D. wood destroying organisms inspection.

42. When making a bid to obtain a management agreement with an owner, a licensee wants to prepare a/an

A. budget for the property.
B. rate of return analysis.
C. management proposal.
D. advertising plan.

43. The neighbor on the right side of the property has just called Max, the property manager. According to the neighbor, Max's tenant is playing loud music until 1:00 a.m. every night. Max's BEST action is to

A. call the tenant, tell him the neighbor has complained, and ask him to talk to the neighbor.
B. look at the lease to see if the tenant has agreed not to disturb the neighbor, and if it does, send an eviction notice to the tenant.
C. call the tenant, tell him about the complaint, and ask him to turn his music down so it does not disturb the neighbor.

D. tell the neighbor that he cannot call the tenant because the tenant has a right to play the music in his home.

44. The purpose of a profit and loss statement is to determine

A. net profit.
B. gross profit.
C. loss factor.
D. operating expenses.

45. An owner of an existing commercial building must make reasonably

achievable accommodations because of
the

A. Americans with Disabilities Act.
B. Federal Fair Housing Act of 1968.
C. Equal Employment Opportunity Act.
D. Equal Housing Opportunity Act of
1988.

46. A tenant has called stating that there
is a leak in the bedroom ceiling. Fixing
the leak in the ceiling is what type of
maintenance?

A. corrective.
B. routine.
C. construction.
D. preventative.

47. A married taxpayer that sells his
jointly owned home after occupying it
for two of the last five years may
exclude

A. up to $500,000 from capital gains.
B. up to $250,000 from capital gains.
C. all of his capital gains if this is not
the first house he has sold.
D. interest paid for the past five years
from capital gains.

48. When listing property, agents should
ask the seller about special assessments
on the property. This is TRUE because
a special assessment

A. a lien on the property that runs with
the land.
B. limits the marketability of the
property.
C. discloses potential problems with the
property.
D. makes it more difficult to obtain a
mortgage loan.

49. Lender's title insurance

A. protects the buyer from defects in
title.
B. decreases as the mortgage balance is
reduced.
C. remains with the property for ten
years.
D. increases if the buyer obtains a
second mortgage.

50. The borrower has an escrow account
for his taxes, insurance, and sewer
assessment. His taxes are $1,823
annually, the homeowner's insurance is
$632 annually, and the sewer assessment
is $1,200 annually. He paid the first
year's homeowner's insurance at
closing. How much will he pay into
escrow each month?

A. $151.17
B. $251.92
C. $304.59
D. $403.58

51. All of the following are TRUE
about a promissory note EXCEPT it

A. is the borrower's personal promise to
repay the debt.
B. must be recorded in the county where
the real estate is located.
C. contains the terms for repayment of
the money borrowed
D. is a negotiable instrument

52. Real estate contracts are always

A. implied contracts.
B. executed contracts.
C. express contracts.
D. unilateral contracts.

53. Mortgages and deeds of trust must be in writing because of the

A. banking regulations.
B. statute of frauds.
C. statute of limitations.
D. recording statutes.

54. Mr. Abrams needed to use his neighbor's driveway to access the pond on the back of his property. After several discussions, Mr. Gray, the neighbor, agreed to grant Mr. Abrams an easement to use the driveway. After the easement is established

A. Mr. Abram's property will be known as the servient estate.
B. Mr. Gray's property will be known as the servient estate.
C. Mr. Abram's property will be known as the appurtenant estate.
D. Mr. Gray's property will be known as the appurtenant estate.

55. If a lot's dimensions are 132' x 101' x 97' x 117', the footage running along the road is

A. 132'
B. 101'
C. 97'
D. 117'

56. The clause that a real estate broker can include in the listing contract to protect the broker in the event the seller tries to deal around the broker known by all of the following names EXCEPT

A. default clause.
B. carryover clause.
C. extender clause.
D. protection clause.

57. All of the following are protected classes under the fair housing laws EXCEPT

A. handicap.
B. religion.
C. marital.
D. sex.

58. Joshua is excited about his first closing. The property was listed with another company that splits 50/50, the commission rate is 6.25%, the property sold for $217,000, he splits 60/40 with his broker, the referral fee for the listing company is 20%, the advertising cost was $450, and his income tax will be based on his tax bracket of 23%. How much will Joshua receive from his broker.

A. $3,618.75
B. $4,068.75
C. $7,312.50
D. $10,850.00

59. Property sold for $293,000 with a real estate commission of 5.75% that is divided between two brokerages. The seller's first mortgage balance is $128,563.42, the deed preparation is $125, the prorated taxes are $728.00 credited to the seller, the advertising cost was $426, and the origination fee is $2,093.00. What is the seller's net?

A. $148,192.08
B. $146,736.08
C. $146,310.08
D. $144,217.08

60. All of the following will appear on a pinned and staked survey EXCEPT the

A. house.
B. setback lines.

C. easements.

D. unattached storage building.

61. Marvin has just entered into a property management agreement with Mr. Elliott. Mr. Elliott owns only three rental properties, all of which are single family dwellings. Because he has recently remodeled the properties, he has instructed Marvin that he will not rent to people with children and pets. Marvin explained to Mr. Elliott that he will not be able to advertise "no children and pets" in the newspaper. Mr. Elliott said that was OK and that Marvin could just place a sign in the front yard. Marvin

A. may follow Mr. Elliott's instructions, because he owns only three properties and is exempt under the fair housing laws.

B. may follow Mr. Elliott's instructions as long as they do not advertise in the newspaper and only place a sign in the yard.

C. may not follow Mr. Elliott's instructions, because the exemption does not apply when a licensee is involved in the transaction.

D. may not follow Mr. Elliott's instructions, because that will reduce the number of potential renters and breach Marvin's fiduciary duty to Mr. Elliott.

62. At closing the real estate agent should

A. review the closing statement for accuracy.

B. ask for a copy of all documents signed by his client.

C. review the loan documents for accuracy.

D. review the deed for accuracy.

63. Louise owned property in her individual name when she married Larry. Louise died and her two children wanted Larry to move immediately, because he did not have any interest in the property. If the state law provides for Larry to have a curtesy interest in the property, he now owns

A. all of the property.

B. one-half interest in the property.

C. one-third interest in the property.

D. none of the property.

64. When the seller sells property on a land contract, the seller

A. has legal title and the buyer has equitable title to the property.

B. pays all taxes owed because of capital gains at the time of the closing.

C. passes the deed to the buyer and the buyer agrees not to record it.

D. can evict the buyer if the buyer fails to make payments as agreed.

65. A borrower has just obtained a new mortgage with a mortgage payment of $1,000 for the first year, $1,050 for the second year, and $1,100 for the remaining years. All payments will be applied first to interest then to principal. This is known as a

A. growing equity mortgage.

B. participation mortgage.

C. graduated mortgage.

D. buy-down mortgage.

66. Lola, a new agent, has decided to increase her listings by offering a $250 referral fee to her church friends, sorority sisters, and garden club members who send her listings. This plan

A. should increase her listings dramatically.
B. violates the licensing laws unless the referring agent is licensed.
C. will be a nice surprise for her sponsoring broker.
D. may not have any effect on business because the market is slow.

67. The difference in the amount owed on the property and the fair market value is known as the

A. loan to value ratio.
B. equity.
C. discounted value.
D. spread.

68. A borrower wants a low interest rate for the first few months because he does not know how long he will be living in the property. A good type of interest rate for him would be a/an

A. fixed rate.
B. renegotiable rate.
C. adjustable rate.
D. amortized rate.

69. Nancy wants to sell her house, but the interest rates are high and buyers don't seem to be interested in buying at this time. She has an assumable mortgage. Would there be a problem with her allowing a buyer to assume her mortgage?

A. Yes, because she might want to keep her low interest rate to be used in purchasing her next property.
B. Yes, unless the lender would agree to give her a novation.
C. No, this would be a good idea because it will make the property more marketable.
D. No, once the transaction is closed,

the buyer is liable for the mortgage debt.

70. The seller's current mortgage is shown on the closing statement as a

A. debit to the seller.
B. credit to the seller.
C. credit to the seller and debit to the buyer.
D. credit to the buyer and debit to the seller.

71. The covenant of further assurances in a deed means the

A. grantor will defend the title to the real estate during the grantee's ownership.
B. grantor will perform necessary acts to correct defects in the deed.
C. grantor has the exact quantity and quality of title conveyed.
D. grantor has the right to convey the title.

72. A son is purchasing for cash property owned by his parents who have owned it for 35 years. They have told him the mortgage was paid off years ago and they do not have any other liens on the property. The son does not need a title examination or title abstract. This is

A. true, because the property has been in the family more than 30 years and the mortgage has been paid in full.
B. true, because the son is paying cash and not obtaining a mortgage to buy the property.
C. false, there may be liens, or other defects on the title, that his parents are not aware exist.
D. false, because the law requires a title search for every transaction.

73. A homeowner paid $2,200 in property taxes last year. This amount is

A. deductible on his federal and state income tax return.
B. deductible only if his income exceeds $100,000 per year.
C. not deductible unless the property has been used for investment purposes.
D. not deductible unless the amount is at least 3% of his gross income.

74. When a tenant does not pay rent, the appropriate court proceeding to remove the tenant is known as a

A. quiet title action.
B. forcible entry and detainer action.
C. lawsuit for removal from property.
D. foreclosure.

75. A buyer's agent advised her buyer that, because of the age of the property, there was no need to have a pinned and staked survey. Was this good advice?

A. Yes, agents are supposed to help their clients save money and not having the survey saves money.
B. Yes, the agent was correct in that the property was old and had not moved since it was built.
C. No, because there can be a boundary problem regardless of the age of the property.
D. No, because agents are not supposed to discuss surveys with their clients.

76. If the seller rejects the buyer's offer and makes a counteroffer that is not acceptable to the buyer, the seller can always accept the original offer.

A. True, unless the buyer withdraws the original offer.
B. True, until the expiration date on the offer.
C. False, once a counteroffer is made the original offer is terminated.
D. False, the original offer has expired.

77. Darren was looking for a new career when he noticed an advertisement placed in the local newspaper by XZY Realty for new agents. He phoned the company and made an appointment to meet with Ms. Clary. At the meeting, he learned that if he obtained a real estate license and went to work for the company, he MOST LIKELY would be working as a/an

A. employee.
B. assistant to the sponsoring broker.
C. independent contractor.
D. principal broker.

78. Lending that is designed to get buyers into property regardless of whether or not they are qualified is known as

A. special.
B. innovative.
C. predatory.
D. accelerated.

79. The primary purpose of the secondary mortgage market is to

A. provide money for home improvements.
B. provide mortgage liquidity and reduce the impact of disintermediation.
C. give mortgage brokers a source of funding.
D. bail out the savings and loans that went bankrupt in the 1980s.

80. The parties to a deed of trust are

A. seller, beneficiary, and trustee.
B. attorney, lender, and beneficiary.
C. trustee, seller, and buyer.
D. trustor, beneficiary, and trustee.

81. If the government takes property from an owner, the government must pay the owner

A. the fair market value.
B. just compensation.
C. the assessed value.
D. the appraised value.

82. A deed that is signed by a mentally incompetent grantor is

A. voidable.
B. void.
C. unenforceable.
D. invalid.

83. Ray, the leasing agent, met with potential tenants for a shopping center. He showed them the property three times. Yesterday, he received a call from Shanta who introduced herself at the tenants' agent. Ray informed Shanta that she could not represent the tenants and could not participate in the negotiations. He was

A. correct, because he was representing the owner and tenants as a dual agent.
B. correct, because the tenants cannot retain their own agent after he shows them the property.
C. incorrect, because he did not get a written buyer broker agreement from the tenants.
D. incorrect, because the tenants can retain an agent if they choose to do so at any point in the transaction.

84. If a buyer wants to have an environmental assessment before closing, her real estate agent should

A. help her arrange for the assessment.
B. include a clause in the sales contract providing for the assessment.
C. give her a list of three names of environmental engineers.
D. ask the seller to pay for the assessment.

85. Mr. and Mrs. Seller want to remove their beautiful dining room light fixture before they move. The BEST advice for the listing agent to give them is to

A. state in the listing that the light fixture does not stay with the house.
B. state in the sales contract that the light fixture does not stay with the

house.
C. remove the light fixture before the house is listed and replace it with another fixture.
D. offer an allowance to the buyer for them to purchase a light fixture of their choice.

86. While Oscar was making a listing presentation, the seller mentioned in passing during the conversation that a FEMA representative had been out to the property last summer. Oscar should have followed up on that comment because he will need to know

A. the seller's current loan to calculate their net sheet.
B. how much crime is in the area so he can inform prospective purchasers.
C. if there was a disaster in the area that affected the property.
D. if the loan on the property is assumable.

87. When listing property owned by tenants in common, the listing agent must get the signatures of all of the people

A. who must sign the deed at closing.
B. who agree to list the property.
C. named in the current deed.
D. people who have at least at 50% ownership.

88. The earnest money deposit should be

A. given to the seller.
B. given to the broker for deposit into the broker's escrow account.
C. held by the agent until all contingencies have been met.
D. held by the broker until closing.

89. Charles has a practice of taking rental applications and asking for a non-refundable application fee at that time. The fee is used to pay for a credit check and other administrative work. He has just shown the property to a woman who has accused Charles of violating the law by asking for an application fee. Her accusations are

A. true, because processing the application is the cost of doing business.
B. true, because it is discriminatory to charge an application fee.
C. false, because the law does not prohibit the owner from charging an application fee.
D. false, because the landlord tenant laws require property managers to charge an application fee.

90. RESPA applies to

A. one-to-four family residential

transactions.
B. all real estate transactions.
C. single family residential transactions.
D. properties with a federally related mortgage.

91. The rule of thumb is that paying one discount point reduces the interest rate by approximately

A. 1/8 %.
B. 1/4 %.
C. 1/2 %.
D. 1 %.

92. Tax deductions for investment properties include all of the following EXCEPT

A. lost rent.
B. legal fees.
C. advertising.
D. wages for management.

93. Insurance that pays in the event of an act of God is known as

A. hazard insurance.
B. homeowner's insurance.
C. extended coverage insurance.
D. liability insurance.

94. Barbara's buyers did not want to use the standard form purchase contract. They asked her to prepare a contract for them from a book they purchased at a local bookstore. Barbara prepared the contract. Should she have prepared the contract?

A. Yes, as part of her fiduciary duties to her clients she had to follow their instructions.
B. Yes, because the book provided by the buyers gave her the information she needed.

C. No, because preparing a form is the practice of law and she is not licensed to practice law.

D. No, because she may forget to add something important to protect the buyers.

95. Everyone is tired of the newspaper raising its advertising rates. Several brokers and agents got together today at lunch and decided to boycott the newspaper for three months. Hopefully, after three months the newspaper will realize how valuable the real estate ads are and reduce their rates. The meeting today

A. was a smart move.
B. violated the Sherman anti-trust law.
C. should help reduce advertising costs in the future.
D. violated Regulation Z and the truth-in-advertising laws.

96. Sam and Rosie own property as joint tenants with right of survivorship. They have three children and two grandchildren. If Sam dies, Rosie will

A. become the sole owner of the property.
B. have a life estate in the property until her death at which time the property their children in equal shares.
C. own the property if Sam had a will
D. own one-half and the children will each own one-sixth.

97. The goal of an operating budget is to determine the

A. net operating income.
B. gross operating income.
C. potential gross income.
D. estimated vacancy loss.

98. Contract law is

A. federal law.
B. state law.
C. case law.
D. administrative law.

99. In the past what type of lender has been the largest source of mortgage financing

A. mutual savings banks.
B. savings and loan associations.
C. credit unions.
D. commercial banks.

100. Farmer's Home Administration loans

A. are provided by the Department of Housing and Urban Development.
B. can not be made directly and must be obtained through mortgage brokers.
C. are for properties in urban areas for low to moderate income families
D. do not allow discount points to be paid to reduce the interest rate.

Broker candidates may wish to take the three sales exams for additional practice.

Broker Exam

1. Trust accounts should be

A. non interest-bearing accounts.
B. balanced each month.
C. in a different bank from the general account.
D. closed and re-opened each year.

2. When opening a brokerage, the sponsoring broker must

A. sign an agreement that the licensing

agency may audit her trust account.
B. inform the licensing agency of the number of agents she expects to have associated with the brokerage.
C. notify the licensing agency when the office address changes.
D. provide the licensing agency with the annual gross revenues.

3. Which of the following cannot be included in the written office policy manual

A. how compensation is calculated
B. expenses that are paid by each party
C. minimum number of hours for floor Time.
D. agreement to follow the fair housing laws.

4. A loan that prohibits the lender from seeking a deficiency judgment is a/an

A. guaranteed loan.
B. insured loan.
C. nonrecourse loan.
D. subordinated loan.

5. All of the following statements are true about FHA loans EXCEPT

A. they are government guaranteed loans to help people purchase homes.
B. the program is administered by HUD.
C. buyers may pay a lower down payment than with conventional loans.
D. interest rates are negotiated between the borrower and lender.

6. Writing contingencies in a contract

A. is the practice of law.
B. is permissible for real estate brokers, but not associates.

C. may be necessary to protect the buyer and seller.
D. is permitted under the Statute of Frauds.

7. Deborah has just learned that the city wants to take her property to re-route a road. She does not want to sell the house, but knows the city will take it by force. The city's right to take the property is known as

A. condemnation.
B. eminent domain.
C. common good.
D. police power.

8. An offer was presented over the phone to the seller. The seller accepted the offer and asked the agent to drop by his offer the next day to sign it. When the agent went to the seller's office, the seller informed the agent that he had sold the property to someone else. Can the seller sell the property to someone else after accepting the first offer over the phone?

A. Yes, because of the Statute of Frauds; until the seller signs the offer a contract is not created.
B. Yes, because of the Statute of Limitations; until the seller signs the offer a contract is not created.
C. No, because when he accepted the offer while talking to his agent on the phone a contract was created.
D. No, because of the Parol Evidence Rule; a contract was created during the phone conversation.

9. Rent paid in advance that is to be prorated at closing is shown on the closing statement as a

A. credit to the seller and debit to the

buyer.

B. credit to the buyer and debit to the seller.
C. debit to the seller and debit to the buyer.
D. credit to the seller and credit to the buyer.

10. The seller is trying to avoid paying capital gains tax all at one time. According to his real estate broker, he can sell the property on an installment sales contract and only pay capital gains tax on the amount collected each year. Is this true?

A. Yes, capital gains taxes will only be paid on the amounts collected.
B. Yes, as long as the seller has a promissory note signed by the buyer.
C. No, the capital gains tax must be paid at the time of sale.
D. No, not unless the annual payments are less than 20% of the total.

11. One of the best ways for a property manager to avoid allegations of discrimination in violation of the fair housing laws is to

A. always have a witness when showing property.
B. have a standard application form that all prospects complete.
C. qualify prospects over the phone so their race is not obvious.
D. show the property to all prospects at the same time.

12. The rent on the retail storefront has been quoted at $22.50 per square foot. It has 1,485 square feet. What is the monthly rent?

A. $2,784.38
B. $2,874.38

C. $3,341.25
D. $3,431.25

13. Broker Ed has just signed a property management agreement to manage six multi-unit apartment buildings for one owner. The owner has asked him to inspect the property for compliance with ADA. Broker Ed should explain to the owner that he

A. should call an attorney for such an evaluation, because that evaluation is practicing law.
B. should call the local human rights commission for that evaluation.
C. will be required to make reasonably achievable accommodations.
D. will not be required to make any changes, because the buildings were built before 1978.

14. Mildred is moving into a new apartment on February 13th. On the 13th, she will be required to pay the security deposit of $850, the prorated rent for February, the prorated clubhouse dues for February and the last month's rent. The monthly rental is $1,350 per month and the clubhouse fees are $50 per month. How much will she pay on the 13th if a calendar year is used for the pro-rations?

A. $2,191.99
B. $2,951.78
C. $2,999.99
D. $3,021.42

15. When drafting the property management agreement, Broker Eliza should include all of the following except

A. names and addresses of the property owner and broker.

B. property location and description.
C. how the Broker's compensation will be calculated and paid.
D. names and addresses of the current tenants.

16. A written offer that is presented over the telephone and accepted by the seller becomes a contract. Is this a true statement?

A. Yes, as long as the agent writes "accepted per telephone conversation."
B. Yes, once the seller verbally accepts a written offer a contract is formed.
C. No, until the offer is actually signed by the seller a contract is not formed.
D. No, the oral acceptance has to be communicated to the buyer.

17. One of Barney's agents has just listed a rural property. During the conversation with the seller, they told the listing agent that there had been an EPA superfund clean-up down the road. The listing agent told the seller that was "good news" and didn't say anything further. Did the agent act appropriately?

A. Yes, the EPA had taken care of the problem.
B. Yes, the clean-up was not on the property being listed.
C. No, the property he listed may be stigmatized by the other property and he needed more information.
D. No, the agent should have declined the listing because environmental concerns may make the property unmarketable.

18. Houses in the area are staying on the market an average of 28 days. This is an indication that

A. this is a seller's market.
B. this is a buyer's market.
C. agents are under-pricing the properties.
D. agents are doing a good job of marketing.

19. If a husband and wife owns their home as joint tenants with right of survivorship and the wife prepares a will leaving her one-half of the property to her sister, who owns her one-half when she dies?

A. Her one-half passes to her husband under the survivorship clause.
B. Her one-half of the property passes to the sister under the will.
C. The sister and husband share the one-half.
D. The Court must decide who receives the one-half.

20. If a principal broker hires an office manager to assist his agents, the principal broker

A. has met his responsibilities under the licensing law of adequately supervising the agents.
B. will still be liable for adequately supervising the agents.
C. should have a hold harmless agreement with the office manager.
D. will not be liable to the licensing agency for mistakes made by his agents.

21. A sponsoring broker may have an office policy of only representing sellers.

A. True, because the sponsoring broker determines policy for his company.
B. True, because it is impossible to represent both buyers and sellers in the same company.

C. False, because that would be discriminating against buyers.
D. False, because sponsoring brokers must offer services to both buyers and sellers.

22. If a purchase/sales contract calls for prorating of taxes, the taxes paid in advance by the seller for the current tax year will appear on the closing statement as a

A. credit to the seller and a debit to the buyer.
B. credit to the buyer and a debit to the seller.
C. credit only to the buyer.
D. debit only to the seller.

23. Two sellers have listed their properties with the same broker. They have each signed an exclusive right to sell listing contract with a commission of 4.5%. The sellers decide to trade houses and place a value of $155,000 on each house. What is the total commission due the broker?

A. $ 0
B. $6,975.00
C. $10,462.50
D. $13,950.00

24. Before using a plat to market property, the listing agent should look for what kind of data on a plat?

A. Name of the developer
B. Recording data
C. Clearly written numbers showing the lot dimensions
D. Signature of the owner

25. Barry listed a property that was part of Ms. White's estate. Ms. White's oldest son was appointed by the family to handle the sale of the property. He signed the listing and answered all of Barry's questions. It was

A. appropriate to have the son sign the listing, because he was appointed by the family to handle the sale.
B. appropriate to have the son sign the listing, because he was the executor of the estate by virtue of being the oldest son.
C. inappropriate to have the son sign the listing until Barry had proof that the son had legal authority to sign the listing contract.
D. inappropriate because only the executor can sign a listing contract.

26. When Angela measured a two-story house with a nicely finished basement, she included the finished area in the walk-out basement as part of the gross living area. She decided to include that area because it was professionally finished with the best materials. Angela's decision was

A. correct, because you always look to quality of finish materials when deciding whether or not to include the basement in the gross living area.
B. correct, because the buyers will want to know the total livable area.
C. incorrect, because you do not include below grade area in the gross living area regardless of the finish.
D. incorrect, because basement footage is never finished nicely enough to be considered gross living area.

27. The seller has sold her property for $210,000 with a closing date of May 13th. Real estate commission is 6% or $10,000, whichever is less. It will cost the seller $75 to have the deed prepared and her first mortgage pay-off is $113,000. What amount will be credited to the seller on the closing statement?

A. $210,000
B. $113,000
C. $97,000
D. $86,925

28. Jim used the builder's plans when listing property for the second owners. Jim's actions were

A. appropriate, because it is important to always have accurate measurements, and the builder's plans are the best way to ensure accuracy.
B. appropriate, because the builder's plan showed the below grade square footage that could be deducted from the total.
C. inappropriate, because the builder's plans may not be accurate.
D. inappropriate, because the builder did not sell the house to the current owners and his plans cannot be used by any owner after the first owner.

29. When a junkyard relocated near a residential area, it is likely that the residential area suffered what type of obsolescence?

A. Functional
B. Physical
C. External
D. Straight line

30. The seller wants to net $176,000 and the real estate commission is 6.5%.

Houses generally sell for about 98% of their listed price, and this seller says he will not negotiate the price. Based on this information, which of the following listing prices would meet the seller's goal?

A. $195,500
B. $188,500
C. $187,500
D. $184,500

31. The buyer wanted to make an offer. He informed the agent that he liked the house because of the long driveway which would allow him to park his RV in it during the summer months. What is the BEST next step for the agent?

A. Ask the buyer the exact length of the RV so he can measure the driveway to make sure it is long enough.
B. Ask the sellers if they have any information about parking an RV in the driveway.
C. Get a copy of the subdivision restrictions to ascertain whether or not it is permissible to park a RV in the driveway.
D. Write the offer before the buyer changes his mind.

32. If an agent receives an offer on one of his listings that is not very good, he must inform the seller that it is not a good offer even if it means he will not be able to sell the property and receive a commission. This is an example of the duty of

A. confidentiality.
B. accounting.
C. due care and diligence.
D. loyalty.

33. A deed states: "To Bob for the life of Emily then to Carlos." Carlos is known as the

A. reverter.
B. remainderman.
C. grantor.
D. grantee.

34. The seller purchased property at an absolute auction. When he completed the seller disclosure, he indicated that he knew nothing about the property. Before turning the form into his broker, the listing agent felt this was unfair to prospective buyers and completed the form based on his own observations. Were the agent's actions appropriate?

A. Yes, under the fiduciary duty to disclose the agent had no other choice.
B. Yes, a listing agent should have enough property condition knowledge to see what is wrong with the property.
C. No, the agent should have refused the listing unless the seller completed the form.
D. No, the agent should have left the form as it was as a notice to prospective buyers that the seller did not want to complete the form.

35. This afternoon, the Principal Broker has learned that one of his agents drafted a lease for an owner about six months ago. He used an old lease from another client. The owner has now become involved in a lawsuit over the way the lease was drafted. It appears that the Principal Broker and his company may become involved in the lawsuit. According to the Principal Broker's attorney, they will be immediately dismissed from the lawsuit.

This advice is

A. correct, because all the agent did was draft the lease using an old one from another client.
B. correct, because an agent cannot be liable in a dispute between the owner and tenant.
C. incorrect, because the agent drafted the lease using an old lease in his files.
D. incorrect, because the agent may be liable for practicing law without a license and drafting the lease.

36. If a sponsoring broker meets monthly with other brokers to discuss issues in the industry, including commission rates, advertising policies, and innovative business models, the sponsoring broker is

A. staying up with the industry and should be commended.
B. violating the state and federal anti-trust laws.
C. hurting his company by giving other companies his good ideas.
D. wasting time that could be spent on more beneficial endeavors.

37. A real estate broker that closes a transaction must obtain the seller's social security number. Is this a true statement?

A. Yes, the broker must report the sale to the IRS for capital gains purposes.
B. Yes, the broker must ascertain that the seller is a US citizen.
C. No, it is illegal to ask for someone's social security number.
D. No, a real estate broker is not responsible for filing any forms.

38. Who is responsible for the correctness of settlement documents

A. buyer.
B. mortgage broker.
C. settlement agent.
D. real estate agent.

39. Principal brokers may require their agents to do all of the following EXCEPT

A. complete all forms accurately and completely.
B. attend a monthly sales meeting.
C. deliver client deposits to the office immediately for deposit.
D. complete all continuing education requirements.

40. A lot in the shape of a triangle with a base of 250' with a height of 665' has an area of how many acres

A. 5.7
B. 3.8
C. 2.7
D. 1.9

41. All of the following are types of easements EXCEPT

A. appurtenant.
B. in gross.
C. prescriptive.
D. encroachment.

42. When a lead based paint disclosure form is required, the agent's first duty relating to the lead based paint form is to

A. write the address and seller's name on the form to make sure there is no confusion in the files.

B. ask the seller to complete and sign the form.
C. ask the seller whether or not the house has lead based paint to determine whether or not the form is necessary.
D. ask the seller if he is willing to remove the lead based paint before closing.

43. It is good practice to include all of the following in the listing contract EXCEPT

A. extender clause.
B. automatic continuation clause.
C. fair housing clause.
D. lock box clause.

44. If the gross annual income for an 8-unit apartment building is $144,000, its annual net income is $58,000, it is being depreciated over 39 years, and the fair fair market value of the building is $750,000, the capitalization rate is

A.   1.92%.
B.   7.73%.
C.   8.23%.
D.   19.2%.

45. A broker listed investment property that had a tenant with a lease for two more years. Once the property sells, the tenant may remain on the property

A. for thirty days rent free.
B. until the end of the lease if he will agree to increase the rent to the market rate.
C. under the terms of the lease.
D. under the terms of the lease if the new owner agrees.

46. The unrepresented party in a real estate transaction is the

A. client.
B. customer.
C. buyer.
D. seller.

47. A Planned Unit Development is known as a

A. combination form of ownership.
B. condominium form of ownership.
C. cooperative form of ownership.
D. common form of ownership.

48. Buyers are moving to the area for a brief period. Because of her job they will be moving again in anywhere from 3-12 months. The MOST important value aspects of the property they purchase is its

A. transferability.
B. utility.
C. appreciation.
D. marketability.

49. A property is insured for $190,000 (replacement cost). It is completely destroyed by fire and it will take $245,000 to replace the house and $32,000 to replace the contents. The insurance company will pay how much to the property owner.

A. $32,000
B. $190,000
C. $213,000
D. $245,000

50. If the owner wants to keep his rents lower without having a lot of cost, what is the best type of commercial lease to use?

A. Triple net lease
B. Percentage lease
C. Gross lease
D. Base lease

51. Carolyn has signed a three-year office lease. Her total rent is $31,500. What is her monthly rent?

A. $785.00
B. $875.00
C. $2,265.00
D. $2,625.00

52. Government deeds are typically

A. special warranty deeds.
B. general warranty deeds.
C. quit claim deeds.
D. strawmen deeds.

53. An option to purchase contract is an example of a/an

A. unilateral contract.
B. bilateral contract.
C. executed contract.
D. open-ended contract.

54. Which of the following is the LEAST likely entity to furnish mortgage financing?

A. Seller
B. Commercial bank
C. Real estate agent
D. Savings and loan associations

55. When a veteran allows his VA loan to be assumed, if he wants to use his eligibility in the future to buy another home, he must require the buyer to

A. have a good credit score.
B. be an eligible veteran.
C. sell the house within three years.
D. agree to take the house subject-to the mortgage.

56. In order to have an adjustable rate loan, the promissory note and mortgage must have a/an

A. acceleration clause.
B. prepayment clause.
C. escalation clause.
D. subordination clause.

57. One of the MOST useful things a sponsoring broker can do for his agents is to

A. increase the commission split in favor of the agents.
B. provide continuing education.
C. pay for attendance at national meetings.
D. be available to assist them when they need help.

58. Barry has just hired a new bookkeeper. Her job is to write checks on the general account and the trust account. If he isn't available, she is authorized to use a signature stamp for his signature. She is to balance the accounts once a month and give him a written report. To be safe, the company has purchased a bond for her. Are there any problems with this arrangement?

A. Yes, the same person should not be writing the checks, signing the checks, and balancing the accounts.
B. Yes, there must always be two signatures on the trust account checks.
C. No, not as long as she gives him a written report each month and he looks at it carefully.
D. No, as long as she is bonded there is nothing that can wrong that won't be covered by the bonding company.

59. When a lender has a security interest in real property, the property is known as

A. an appurtenance.
B. chattel.
C. collateral.
D. personalty.

60. If a real estate broker is advising a group of people about pooling their money to invest in a parcel of real estate, she must have a

A. license to practice law.
B. securities license.
C. principal broker's license.
D. banking license.

61. HUD-1 closing statements are signed by

A. buyers, sellers, real estate agents, and settlement agents.
B. mortgage brokers, real estate brokers, buyers, and sellers.
C. buyers, sellers, and settlement agents.
D. buyers and sellers.

62. An income producing property will be depreciated over 39 years. The total value is $975,000 with a land value of $175,000. What is the annual amount of depreciation?

A. $4,487.18
B. $20,512.82
C. $25,000.00
D. $29,487.18

63. Pat had a written and signed open listing for a lot with a warehouse. The listing commission was 7.25% of the sales price. He marketed the property for several months and had a couple of offers, but nothing the seller would accept. Pat received word from the seller today that the seller had sold the property for $623,000 and that he wanted the listing contract terminated. Pat is

A. entitled to a commission of $45,167.50, because the seller sold the property while it was listed with him.
B. entitled to the commission, but only to $22,583.75 because the seller sold the property.
C. not entitled to the commission because the seller sold the property to the buyer.
D. not entitled to the full commission because the seller is entitled to a portion which must now be negotiated between them.

64. While Manual was completing the listing contract he asked the sellers for an approximate balance on their first and second mortgages. They told him they owed about $96,000 on their first mortgage, $32,000 on their second mortgage, plus 4 months mortgage payments on their first mortgage in the amount of $900 per month. The CMA he prepared showed him the house had a range of fair market value between $135,000 and $143,000. The company listing commission is 5.75%. What is Manual's BEST course of action?

A. He should start marketing the property immediately and try to get a quick sale.
B. He should suggest a higher listing price to make sure they get enough money to pay his commission at the time of closing.
C. He should discuss the listing with his broker before committing the company to list the property.
D. He should ask them to give him the name of the mortgage companies so he can try to negotiate lower pay-offs for them.

65. An encumbrance on title will

A. affect the property's marketability.
B. be removed once the property changes hands to the new owner.
C. expire at the end of 15 years.
D. continue on the property with no affect on its title.

66. The MOST professional way to obtain a listing is to

A. provide the seller a marketing plan.
B. explain to the seller that your company is best in the area.
C. suggest a higher than market listing price to the seller.
D. make sure your commission rate is lower than your competitors.

67. An appraiser called the selling agent and asked for a copy of the sales contract for the commercial building he had been hired to appraise. This surprised the selling agent, but he gave him the copy anyway. The appraiser's actions were

A. appropriate, because the appraisal standards require him to have a copy of the contract.
B. appropriate, because it saves him time if he knows the sales price before beginning his appraisal.
C. inappropriate, because he should never see the contract before beginning work on the appraisal.
D. inappropriate, because the appraisal standards specifically state that the appraiser should not see the sales contract.

68. Carla has 20 minutes to show property before her son's soccer game. She explains the timetable to the prospective buyers and they agree to hurry. However, once they get there they want to stay longer and agree to lock up the house when they leave. The prospects are well-known physicians. Is there a problem?

A. Yes, they may want to write an offer and Carla is not there.
B. Yes, prospects should never be left in a property alone.
C. No, the prospects are professional people and can be trusted.
D. No, when a seller lists property they know people will be in the house.

69. The sponsoring broker had an attorney draft new sales contract forms. She sent them out with a memo to all of the agents that they must use the forms, because using any other form was illegal. Is it true that using any other form is illegal?

A. Yes, the broker can adopt forms that must be used in her office.
B. Yes, an agent cannot prepare a contract and must use a form.
C. No, using another form would be against office policy but not illegal.
D. No, not as long as the other form was approved by an attorney.

70. Bradley is preparing an operating budget for one of the apartment communities he manages. There are 60 units, and each unit rents for $985 per month. The vacancy runs about 5% per month, the vending machine income is $600 per month, and the fixed expenses are $30,141 per month. What is the projected net operating income for the year?

A. $312,048
B. $319,248
C. $673,740
D. $709,200

71. Barbara was managing a large apartment complex with a clubhouse and swimming pool. Today a single father with three small children completed a rental application. He wants to rent a unit that is located very near the pool. She checks his credit and calls him back to tell him he is approved to rent. However, she told him that he cannot rent a unit near the pool. She suggests one that is larger with the same rent and away from the pool. Her actions are

A. appropriate, because with three children he can not watch them at all times and she does not want one of them to fall into the pool.
B. appropriate, because he really needs a larger unit and it was good of her

to find a larger one for him.

C. inappropriate, because it was rude of her to insinuate he could not watch his children

D. inappropriate, because he has a right to choose where he wants to live.

72. A second mortgage is recorded on June 23, 2006 at 1:30 p.m. At 2:45 p.m. on June 23, 2006, the first mortgage is recorded. The next day a federal tax lien is recorded at 9:30 a.m., and later that day a state tax lien is recorded at 1:13 p.m. What are the lien priorities?

A. second mortgage, first mortgage, federal tax lien, state tax lien

B. federal tax lien, state tax lien, first mortgage, second mortgage

C. first mortgage, second mortgage, federal tax lien, state tax lien

D. state tax lien, federal tax lien, first mortgage, second mortgage

73. A seller may carry owner financing for the buyer by including the terms of the lending agreement in the deed. This is known as

A. contract for deed.
B. vendor's lien.
C. purchase money mortgage.
D. bond for deed.

74. The sponsoring brokers MAIN duty is to

A. train the associates.
B. supervise the associates.
C. help the associates succeed.
D. resolve disputes among associates.

75. Possible compensation arrangements between the sponsoring broker and her agents include all of the following EXCEPT

A. a division of the commission coming into the office for each transaction.

B. a salary paid to the agents on a specified time table.

C. commission paid directly to the agent by the seller.

D. a flat fee paid to the agent by the broker.

76. Derrick wants to sell his property on a land contract, but his mortgage has a due-on-sale clause in it. This means

A. he cannot sell the property without giving the down payment to the mortgage company.

B. he cannot sell the property until the maturity date of the mortgage.

C. he cannot sell the property on a land \ contract without paying the balance of the mortgage.

D. he cannot sell the property unless the buyer assumes the mortgage.

77. Before someone can purchase property insurance, he must have

A. title to the property.
B. a contract to purchase the property.
C. a financial interest in the property.
D. an insurable interest.

78. While showing rental property to prospects from a neighboring city, the prospective tenant asked the property manager where the nearest subway entrance was located. The property manager said he did not know, but that he would find out. This is information that the property manager should

A. have anticipated and found out before showing the property.

B. let the tenant find out for himself.

C. be careful in disclosing the location because of fair housing laws.

D. not disclose unless the prospective tenant gives him a written waiver.

79. The sponsoring broker has just signed a contract with a home warranty company. When an agent sells a warranty the company will receive $85. The fee information

A. should be disclosed to the buyers and sellers.
B. does not need to be disclosed to the buyers and sellers.
C. should be disclosed only to the party being represented.
D. should be disclosed only to the party paying for the warranty.

80. A sponsoring broker asked a CPA to explain to his agents how to calculate income tax savings for homeowners. After the presentation, the broker recommended to his agents that they use the information from the CPA with every buyer prospect and calculate their tax savings for them. Was the broker's recommendation a good one?

A. Yes, once a buyer prospect can see how much money they are saving they will be more likely to purchase the property.
B. Yes, calculating the tax savings falls under the fiduciary duty of accounting.
C. No, because he was asking his agents to practice accounting without a license.
D. No, because they may make a mistake in their calculations which would be considered a material misrepresentation.

81. The principal broker has just been informed of a problem. Apparently, last month his agent, Jim, sold a property

that belongs to an estate. The sales contract was signed by the son of the deceased. Now, they learn that there is an executor who is refusing to close the transaction. Does Jim have a valid sales contract?

A. Yes, because the contract was signed by the only heir.
B. Yes, because an executor cannot renege on a contract once it is signed.
C. No, because the contract was not signed by the competent party.
D. No, because the contract was not approved by the court.

82. If one owner owns a 50% interest in the property and the other two owners each own 25% of the property, the owners must hold title as

A. tenants in common.
B. joint tenants.
C. tenants by the entirety.
D. joint tenants with right of survivorship.

83. Building code violations may result in

A. criminal and civil penalties for the builder.
B. criminal penalties for the homeowner.
C. civil penalties for the real estate agent.
D. fines for the real estate agent, appraiser, and first owner.

84. A metes and bounds legal description must have a

A. beginning point and an ending point that closes.
B. lot and block number along with the

name of the subdivision.
C. principal meridian.
D. mailing address including the county, city and state.

85. Broker Barnes was discussing listing property for Mr. and Mrs. Strauss. They told him they wanted to net $178,000 and that he could charge any amount he wanted as long as they received that amount. Broker Barnes decided to list the property for $210,000. His listing price was

A. appropriate, because he could at least earn his standard 6% commission.
B. appropriate, because he had could possibly make much more than 6% commission if he found a strong buyer.
C. inappropriate, because it was going to be on the multiple listing and agents would be confused.
D. inappropriate, because it was a net listing.

86. Chuck has a listing to lease a convenience store with gasoline pumps. The store has shelving, counters, refrigeration and freezer units, and underground storage tanks. According to the owner, everything stays for the use of the new tenant. Should Chuck have any concerns over what stays with the store?

A. Yes, Chuck needs to do a chattel search, because there is a possibility that the owner does not own some of the things being left.
B. Yes, Chuck should obtain proof from the owner that there are no negative environmental issues about the underground storage tanks.
C. No, the owner obviously knows what he owns and what will stay.

D. No, trade fixtures always stay with the rental property and these items are all trade fixtures.

87. When the sellers tell the listing broker that they want to sell part of their farm, the BEST advice for the broker to give the seller is for the seller to

A. order an appraisal of the farm before placing it on the market to make sure they don't list it below the market price.
B. have the part of the farm they want to sell surveyed and marked to make it clear to buyers which land is being sold.
C. check with the zoning board about possible development in the area.
D. consider an absolute auction because farms sell faster at auctions.

88. Sam has just received a letter from an attorney about the property he closed last week. When Sam measured the house at the time of listing, he determined that the property had 2,147 square feet. The attorney's letter says the house actually has 1,847 square feet. According to the letter, the buyer is demanding to be compensated for the difference in value because the house is smaller than represented. If the buyer sues

A. both Sam and his broker may be liable to the buyer for the misrepresentation.
B. Sam may be liable, but his broker will not be because the broker did not make the misrepresentation.
C. Sam's broker may be liable for not training Sam to measure property accurately.
D. neither Sam nor his broker will be liable because the buyer had the

opportunity to measure the house.

89. Rosemary was a single mother with three small children, one of whom was in a wheelchair. She looked at a second-floor condominium being marketed by XYZ Realty. The agent told Rosemary that the association did not want owners with small children in the upstairs units because the units have balconies and children could easily fall off. According to the agent, the association had even amended the condominium bylaws to prohibit children under the age of six from living in units above ground level. And, of course, the agent reminded Rosemary there was no elevator for her handicapped child to use. The agent's actions were

A. appropriate, because she was the agent for the condominium association and needed to protect them from potential lawsuits.
B. appropriate, because the prospect needed to be on notice of the bylaws before purchasing the property.
C. inappropriate, because the association cannot pass bylaws that discriminate against prospective buyers.
D. inappropriate, because the association should have added special fencing around the balcony to protect the children.

90. May a real estate agent draft a sales/purchase contract?

A. Yes, as long as one of her clients is a party to the contract.
B. Yes, as long as no one pays her a fee specifically for that service.
C. No, she may complete a sales/purchase contract form.
D. No, not unless the client's attorney approves her drafting the contract.

91. An offer is presented to the seller. The seller counters the offer with a 48-hour expiration for the counteroffer. Two hours after the counteroffer is made, a second offer is made to the seller which the seller wants to accept. The seller

A. must wait until the 48-hour period expires before accepting the second offer.
B. may withdraw the counteroffer and accept the second offer.
C. may accept the second offer only if the terms are better than the counteroffer.
D. must reduce the time period from 48-hours to 12-hours for the counteroffer to be accepted.

92. If a buyer wants to buy a timeshare, but does not want his name on the deed, the BEST way to do this is to

A. form a corporation and hold title in the corporation's name.
B. ask his real estate agent to buy it for him in the agent's name.
C. take title in his minor child's name.
D. create a revocable trust.

93. When training his agents, a sponsoring broker should train his agents to do what when they first meet a buyer?

A. Pre-qualify them for financing
B. Explain the buying process
C. Check their identification
D. Ask them what area of town they like

94. Buyer Rex is considering purchasing a single family residential property for $165,000. Rex will need to invest cash of $22,000 and get a mortgage for the difference. He asks his Buyer Broker, who will act as the property manager, to calculate a rate of return for him before income taxes. The house will rent for $1,125 per month and has a historical vacancy rate of less than 1%. Expenses have been 8% per year. If he buys the property, his debt service will be $750 per month. What is his projected ROI?

A. 8%
B. 11.7%
C. 17.5%
D. 22.5%

95. A broker has just been contacted by sellers who bought a large house from him last year. The house has appreciated about 10%, but they are unhappy with the neighborhood and size of the house. They want to buy a smaller house closer to town. What is one of the MAIN things he should tell them?

A. That they will probably feel crowded in a smaller house
B. That they should consult a tax professional
C. That they should stay in the house because 10% appreciation is great
D. That they may not like living closer to town because of noise

96. At a closing, the settlement agent asked the buyer if he wanted to purchase owner's title insurance along with the required purchase of lender's title insurance. The buyer asked the agent if he should buy owner's title insurance. According to the agent, the owner's insurance was not necessary because the attorney had performed a title examination and the buyer had to buy lender's title insurance. Was the agent's advice correct?

A. Yes, because the attorney would be liable for defects in the title.
B. Yes, because the buyer would only be wasting money on owner's title insurance because he was purchasing lender's title insurance.
C. No, because the lender's title insurance is for the lender's protection against defects in title and does not protect the buyer.
D. No, because the attorney may not have performed a title examination.

97. A deed that contains a covenant of warranty forever means that the grantor is agreeing to pay

A. legal expenses if anyone establishes a claim superior to the grantee.
B. all legal fees in defending a claim against the title.
C. legal fees that arise during the grantee's ownership.
D. only legal fees relating to the claims during the grantor's ownership.

98. The seller listed 100 acres with three mobile homes. After the contract was signed, the seller removed the largest and best mobile home. When the buyer noticed it was missing, he called the seller who informed him the mobile home was not attached to the real estate and was not part of the deal. Is it possible the buyer could terminate the contract?

A. Yes, the buyer would have a claim that there had been no offer and acceptance.
B. Yes, the buyer would have a claim

that the contract lacked
consideration.
C. No, once the contract is signed the
buyer is bound to perform.
D. No, the buyer had a duty to ask if all
of the mobile homes were attached to
the property.

99. A partially amortized loan will
result in

A. additional principal.
B. lower interest.
C. shorter pay out period.
D. a balloon payment.

100. A buyer is going to obtain a 75%
loan with closing costs of 5% on a house
that costs $185,000. The buyer has paid
an earnest money deposit of $2,000 and
is getting a repair credit of $1,500. How
much money will he need to bring to
closing?

A. $35,812.50
B. $46,250.00
C. $49,687.50
D. $53,187.50

Sales Exam One

1. C – By definition a quit claim deed is one use to convey title when the grantor wants to make no warranties. Quit claim deeds do warrant that the grantor actually owns the property. Response "A" is a deed used to warrant title for a limited period of time – the period of time the property is actually owned by the grantor. Response "B" is nonsensical, because there is no such deed. Response "D" is the deed that contains the greatest number of warranties.

2. A – The first step is to determine 50% of the assessed value: $225,000 x .50 = $112,500. Then apply the tax rate: $112,500 x 3.9876% = $4,486.05.

3. B – A listing contract is a contract for a real estate broker to personally perform a service. Obviously, the broker often uses the assistance of associates to perform the service. Response "A" is incorrect, because a listing contract is not a real estate contract. Response "C" is incorrect, because as long as all of the elements necessary for a contract are included in the contract, the listing contract is not voidable by either party. Response "D" is incorrect, because listing contracts must be in writing if the agents are going to enforce their right to collect the commission under of the Statute of Frauds.

4. A – Emblements are growing crops. Response "A," appurtenances, are rights, privileges, and improvements that pass with the land. Response "C," fixtures, are items of personal property that have become affixed to real property in such a way that they have become part of the real property. Response "D," encumbrances, are liens, claims, and liabilities that are attached to the property that reduce its value.

5. C – The seller's agent should explain the terms of the sales contract, but should not "advise the seller" because "advising" is the unauthorized practice of law. All of the other responses are appropriate activities for the seller's agent.

6. B – Although an agent is anxious to show a property, it is never appropriate, without the listing agent's permission, for the buyer's agent to make contact with the seller. Responses "A" and "B" are incorrect, because each action would have the buyer's agent making direct contract with the sellers. Response "D" is incorrect, because although the seller may or may not see the buyer's agent, it is improper to walk around on a seller's property without permission.

7. B – By definition a split level has three inside levels. The other responses describe property with only two interior levels.

8. C – An encroachment is an improvement to land that crosses a boundary line. In this scenario, the overhand actually crosses the boundary although it is in the airspace and not on the ground. Response "A" would be a lien, claim, or liability that is attached to the property and that reduces its value.

Response "B" describes personal property that has become affixed to real property in such a way that it becomes part of the real property. Response "D" may or may not be correct, but it is not the correct term to describe the roof's overhang.

9. B – When the offeree makes any change to the offer and tenders it back to the offeror with the change, it is known as a counteroffer. Response "A" indicates a term has been included in a contract that has to be met before the contract must be performed. This answer is not responsive to the question, because a contingency has not been created unless the counteroffer is accepted. Response "C" indicates the offer has been accepted, but it contains a term that must be met before the party who inserted the condition must perform the contract. Again, this answer is not responsive, because, until the offeror accepts the condition, there is no contract. Response "D" is incorrect, because an executory contract is one that has been accepted and is in the process of being performed. In this question, the contract is not yet created.

10. C – Depreciation for tax or accounting purposes is a change in the book value, but not an actual change in the fair market value of the property. Responses "A" and "D" are incorrect, because the value of the property has not decreased. Response "B" is incorrect, because depreciation for tax purposes does not increase the value of the property.

11. A – In states with dower and curtesy laws, neither spouse can transfer real estate without the other spouse signing the deed. Response "B" is irrelevant to the question. Response "C" is the opposite of the correct answer. Response "D" is incorrect, because in dower and curtesy states, the spouse must sign the mortgage in order to relinquish his or her rights in the event the spouse borrowing the money defaults in repayment.

12. A – Trade fixtures may be removed by the tenant at the end of the lease unless the lease agreement states otherwise. Response "B" is incorrect, because the health laws do not address trade fixtures. Response "C" states the general rule for fixtures, but not trade fixtures. Response "D" is incorrect, because the owner's new lease is irrelevant as to whether or not the current tenant may take his trade fixtures.

13. A – Changing a property's zoning will change its fair market value. A property rezoned from anything to commercial will increase its fair market value. Responses "B" and "C" are incorrect, because commercial property has a higher fair market value than agricultural property. Response "D" is incorrect, because the proximity of other commercial property is irrelevant in most cases.

14. D – A cooperative is not a combination form of ownership. All of the other responses are examples of combination forms of ownership.

15. C – This is how a lot and block legal description is written. Response "A would use terms like township, sections, ranges, and meridians. Response "B" would read like an engineer had written it, using feet, degrees, minutes, and seconds. Response "D" is incorrect, because the term "monument legal description" doesn't exist. Monuments are often used in metes and bounds descriptions.

16. A – Under the fair housing laws, martial status is not a protected class. The protected classes include race, national origin, color, religion, sex, familial status, and handicap/disability. Some areas have added sexual orientation as a protected class.

17. B – Because investment property is purchased for the purpose of producing income, the income approach is used to find a fair market value for that property. Its value is directly related to the amount of income it will produce. Response "A" is incorrect, because purchasers of residential property are generally not concerned about its value for income

purposes as it will be used for a residence and not income. Response "C" is not correct, because of one of two reasons. If by using the term "condemned" you are referring to property that is in disrepair and needs to be demolished, an appraisal will not be performed at all. If by using the term "condemned" you are referring to property taken in a condemnation action, the income approach may be one of the appraisal methods to determine the value, but the comparative market approach is also used. Response "D" is incorrect, because, unless the property is income producing, the property would be valued using the comparative market approach.

18. A – Buyers should make a walk-through prior to closing to ascertain that the property is in the same or better condition than it was when the contract was written. Responses "B" and "D" are actions buyers may want to take. Response "C" should have been done at the time the contract was written.

19. A – A lease is personal property and not real property. Responses "B" and "C" are incorrect by definition. Response "D" is nonsensical, because everything in the world must be either personal or real property.

20. A – Easements that are written and recorded will stay with the land regardless of who owns the land and regardless of how many times the land changes owners. Response "B" may be correct if the written easement specifically states a termination period. Response "C" is incorrect, because an easement may be terminated if both the dominant and servient tenant agree to the termination. Response "D" may be

correct in some states when certain conditions are met.

21. B – To determine the listing price when the seller wants to net a certain amount, first subtract the commission percentage from 100%, then divide the net amount by that percentage. (1) 100% - 7% = 93%. (2) $223,000 ÷ .93 = $239,784.94 (3) round to the nearest number that would net the amount in step (2). Check your answer: If you aren't sure you remember how to do these math problems, it is simple to check your answer. Take each answer and multiply it by 7%. Subtract that number from the answer. Example: $239,758 x 7% = $16,783.06. Subtract $16,783.06 from $239,758 = $222,974.94. Obviously, this one is not correct because the seller will not net the $223,000.

22. D – Zoning for farms is known as "agricultural zoning." All of the other responses are terms used for zoning designations.

23. C – This term is non-existent in agency law. All of the other responses are terms that define agency relationships.

24. B – A license is a personal right to use someone else's property that may be terminated. Response "A" is incorrect, because easements run with the land and cannot be terminated by one party. Response "C" is incorrect, because a lease cannot be terminated without notice and there is no information in the question that notice was given. Response "D" is incorrect, because an encroachment is an improvement that crosses a boundary line and is not permission to use property.

25. A – This is a phrase frequently used to describe the owner's rights in his property. The other responses may not exist and, if they do, do not apply to owner's rights in property.

26. A – The main requirement to hold title to property as tenants by the entirety is that the owners must be married to each other. Response "B" is incorrect because tenancy by the entirety refers to holding title, not leasing property. Response "C" is correct in that the parties are equal owners, but that does not answer the question. Response "D" is incorrect, because being a "whether or not the state is a community property state" is irrelevant.

27. A – Curable physical deterioration means it is economically feasible to make repairs. One would assume that it is economically feasible to spend $100,000 to make repairs on a $245,000 property. Response "B" is incorrect, because the deterioration is not incurable in this example. If it cost more than $245,000 to make the repairs, it would be incurable. That is, it is not longer economically feasible to repair the damage. Responses "C" and "D" are incorrect, because this question is not about functional obsolescence.

28. B – A deed that includes life estate language creating a life estate for one person based on the life of another person is a life estate *pur autre vie*. In this question, Bobby has the life estate that is measured on the life of Sarah. Response "A" is a non-existent term. Response "C" is incorrect, because the remainder interest is the grantor or the grantor's estate. Response "D" is incorrect, because in a legal life estate the life tenant and the measuring life are

the same person.

29. B – In commercial leases the landlord requires the lessee to pay all, or some combination, of the real property taxes, hazard insurance, and property maintenance. These are referred to as net leases. Because this landlord wants the tenant to pay two of the three, the lease is a double net lease. Response "A" is incorrect, because percentage leases base the lease payment on the income of the tenant's business. Response "C" is incorrect, because a base lease refers to the amount of the lease before there are any add-ons. Response "D" is not a term relating to types of leases.

30. B – Limited liability companies are formed to limit the liability of the company's owners. If the company owns the real estate, the company would likely be liable to someone hurt on the property, and not to the owners personally. Response "A" is not correct, because both owners could be held personally liable. Responses "C" and "D" are incorrect, because each is an attempt for the two owners to enter into contracts that would affect a third party without the third party agreeing to the terms of the contracts.

31. C – One of the fiduciary duties of real estate agents is confidentiality. The fact that the sellers were getting a divorce was confidential information. Response "A" is a fiduciary duty, but it relates to disclosing material information about the transaction or the property. Response "B" is a fiduciary duty relating to the agent giving an accounting of all funds received by the agent that belong to the principal. Response "D" is a fiduciary duty that requires the agent to

hold the principal's best interest above all others, including the agent's interest.

32. C – Upon the death of one joint tenant, property owned by joint tenants with right of survivorship remains the property of the surviving joint tenants. As joint tenants die, their share passes to the other joint tenants equally. The decedent's share does not pass to his estate. The other responses are incorrect, because the deceased owner's heirs do not become owners of any interest.

33. D – Although all of the responses are good advice for the agent to give the buyer, the best answer is to discuss the home buying process with the buyer. Buyers are not generally familiar with the process, and a discussion up front may save both the agent and buyer a lot of time.

34. C – Location is generally thought of as being the most important feature of property for a buyer. The other responses are important, but not as important as the location. An old adage is that the top three most important features for a buyer are: "location, location, and location."

35. B – Whether or not a property is transferable has a direct economic bearing on the property. If an owner has property that is not readily transferable, its value will be substantially less. Property that is easily transferable will have a higher value. Although important to a buyer, neither of the other responses are categorized as "economic value factors."

36. A – The principal broker decides what the commission for the brokerage

will be and how it will be calculated. Response "B" in incorrect, because whether or not the sales associate agrees to accept the fee is an issue to be decided with the broker prior to listing property. Responses "C" in incorrect, because this is not a definition of a net listing. Response "D" is incorrect, because commissions can be stated either as flat fee, as a percentages, or combination of both. Commissions may not be money, but rather something else of value negotiated between the broker and seller.

37. A – The capital gains for the seller in this scenario would be $100,000. The seller will pay capital gains tax on the amount he collects each year. Therefore, if the buyer only pays the seller $20,000 per year, each year the seller will report a capital gain of $20,000.

38. A – A material fact is an important fact that would make a difference in whether or not the buyer would purchase the property. One would assume that a huge crack is an important fact to the buyer. Response "B" is correct, but real estate jargon does not refer to important facts relating to property as relevant. Response "C" and "D" are correct statements, but are not responsive to the question.

39. C – This is not a requirement under ADA. All other responses are ADA requirements.

40. C – Material facts should be pointed out to buyers even if they are obvious. Response "A" is incorrect, because there is no way to know if the buyer actually notices a problem with the property. Response "B" is incorrect, because the seller's embarrassment is irrelevant when it comes to informing the buyer of a material fact about the property. Response "D" is irrelevant, because if the agent had bids on replacement cost the buyer must still be informed.

41. A – In this problem, you must calculate the down payment. This is a tricky question, because it appears to be asking how much will Harrell have to pay at closing. That is not what it is asking. The closing costs and discount points are irrelevant information. To calculate the answer: $250,000 (purchase price) x 20% (the difference in the 80% loan and the total cost) = $50,000. The other responses are answers if you use different combination of the irrelevant information.

42. B – States that require property management agreements require them to be in writing. Responses "A" and "C" are simply incorrect. Response "D" is one you might choose if you don't ready carefully. True, the agreements should be signed, but by the owner and manager, not the owner and tenant. Reading carefully is very important in taking the licensing examination.

43. A – Most states require the form to be completed by the seller, or at least the seller be given the form.. However, as suggested by Response "C," some states permit the listing agent, at the request of the seller, to complete the form. The better practice is that the agents never complete the form. Responses "B" and "C" are nonsensical.

44. A – A sales contract is a bilateral contract between the buyer and seller. The brokers and agents are not parties to the contract as suggested by the other responses.

45. A – Contingency clauses should be included in contracts if one or more conditions must be met before one or both of the parties must perform. In this question, the buyer's ability to close is based on her obtaining financing. Response "B" is irrelevant to this question. Response "C" is a contingency clause that is often used, but it is not responsive to this question. Response "D" could appear correct if the question is not read carefully. A "covenant" is a promise to obtain financing, which is the exact opposite of a "contingency" to obtain financing.

46. A – Generally speaking, the more debt someone has the lower her credit score. Responses "B" and "C" are incorrect. Response "D" is a way to weasel out if you don't know the answer (of course, it's incorrect). Don't fall for this response, because there will always be enough information to answer the question.

47. A – Agents should always inform buyers that they have a right to seek legal advice. In this scenario, not only should the agent have informed the buyer about the right to legal counsel, the agent should have advised the buyer to seek legal counsel. All of the other responses may work, but none of them are better than suggesting the buyer seek legal advice.

48. B – When calculating the dates, remember that the seller pays the day of closing and the question says fiscal (not calendar year). Add 31 days for July, 31 days for August, and 15 days for September, for a total of 77 days.

49. C – Regardless of the seller agreeing over the phone to the changes and regardless of the agent writing on the offer, the offer is now a counteroffer. Agents should never write a note on the offer suggesting the seller has accepted the offer (this is a statute of frauds problem). Response "A" is incorrect, because until the buyer signs the seller's counteroffer, there is no contract. Response "B" is actually correct, but in real estate language you refer to the seller's offer as a counteroffer in this situation. Response "D" is a nonsensical term.

50. A – The current tax rule is two of the last five years. The other response are incorrect.

51. C – Once the offer is written it must be presented for consideration by the seller. Response "A" is incorrect, because there is no requirement to hand-deliver the offer to the seller, and in many cases hand delivery would not be possible. Response "B" is incorrect, because it would not be negotiated by the buyer's agent, it would be negotiated with the seller by the seller's agent. Response "D" is correct, but it has to be presented before it can be considered.

52. B – This answer is nonsensical. The other responses are all areas that property managers must manage.

53. D – Supply and demand is a basic economic principle that plays a role in our whole economy. Anytime there is an excess supply of an item without much of a demand the prices will go down. When there is a short supply and lots of demand, the prices will increase. Response "A" refers to the accounting principle that at some point the return on an investment begins to diminish. Response "B" refers to the

earnings on a particular investment based on how much money has been invested. Response "C" has nothing to do with economic principles. Caveat emptor means "buyer beware."

54. B – Because so many houses built before 1978 were painted with paint that had lead in it, the federal government requires the seller to sign a statement acknowledging whether or not the seller is aware of any lead based paint in the property. When real estate agents are involved in these transactions, they are required to provide the seller with the form. Response "A" refers to a form many states require agents deliver to the seller when listing the property regardless of the age of the property. Response "C" is incorrect, although many areas of the country do require sellers to disclose information about their septic systems. Response "D" is incorrect, because this form is not required by law, but many agents use it to help them obtain information for the seller.

55. A – Payments on a term loan are not amortized. Often there are no payments required at all for a period of time. Some term loans permit the borrowers to make payments as they choose. At some point, the entire loan balance is due. Response "B" is nonsensical. Response "C" refers to loans that have regular payments, but because the payment is not large enough to cover the interest due the interest begins to accrue interest. Basically, the borrower pays a payment and owes more after the payment than before. Response "D" refers to all loans that are secured by a mortgage or trust deed.

56. B – Contracts are generally assignable unless they state otherwise. The assignor can receive more money from the assignee for the property than the assignor has agreed to pay the seller for the property. One way to look at is, that the assignor is selling his right to purchase the property. Response "A" is incorrect, because the seller does not have to agree to the assignment. Response "C" is incorrect, because this situation does not deal with taxes. Response "D" is incorrect, because there is no legal requirement that the property must be closed by the purchaser before the contract is assigned.

57. A – There is no rent proration. Although the contract is signed on the 14th of the month, it does not begin until September 1st. This is an example of a question that can be easily misread.

58. D – When more than one claim is made to the title of property, a quiet title action should be filed to determine the true owner of the property. Response "A" is incorrect, because a foreclosure is an action in which a lien holder files a lawsuit to have the property sold in order to collect the amount due on the lien. Response "B" is nonsensical. Response "C" appears to be correct, but is not. The action that is filed in an adverse possession dispute is a quiet title action.

59. B – The key to this problem is to know that the principal reduction is not an expense and that it should be added back after expenses are deducted. When making an amortized mortgage payment, part of the payment is principal and part is interest. The payment reduces the principal; and, therefore, becomes part of the owner's equity (the owner pays

the payment, but actually keeps the money). The problem is solved as follows: $6,000 (total rent) - $1,325 (operating expenses) - $2,898 (mortgage payments) + $648 (principal reduction) = $2,425 (net profit).

60. D – An agent has a duty to represent her client's best interests and assist them as needed. The agent should have asked either his broker or someone else in the office to assist in the presentation of the offer. Response "A" is correct in that he needed a plan. However, the plan fell short of appropriate representation of one's client. Response "B" shows that the agent was aware of his duties, but failed to act in the best interest of his client. "Trying" to be available by phone is not enough. Response "C" is probably true, but not the best answer for this question.

61. A – A condominium is a combination form of ownership, because part of the property is owned individually and part of it is owned in common with other property owners. Response "B" is not a combination form of ownership, because the life tenant owns the property for his lifetime only and the remainder interest passes to someone else. Responses "C" and "D" are entities that may be owned by more than one person and that entity owns the real estate.

62. A – Lien theory states use mortgages to secure debt. Response "B" is incorrect, because a title theory state uses a deed of trust to secure the debt. Response "C" is incorrect, because intermediary is not the correct word. Intermediate theory states use mortgages to secure the debt. Response "D" is nonsensical.

63. D – Agents may not disclose information about a member of a protected class who has occupied property even if a direct question is asked. The agent's response to such a question is to inform the questioner that an illegal question has been asked and that it will not be answered. Response "A" is incorrect, because the prospect does not have a right to know and does not have a right to ask an illegal question. Response "B" is incorrect, because making an illegal question "sound better" is certainly not the right thing to do. Response "C" is incorrect, because she should not answer the question at all.

64. C – Liability insurance is the proper insurance to purchase when trying to protect against personal injury claims. Response "A" is insurance that may include personal injury damages, but also includes property damage. Response "B" is not the correct term. Response "D" is insurance that extends the coverage under certain types of policies.

65. D – This question takes careful reading. The tax rate is $1.00 per thousand, not $1.00 per thousand in $.50 increments. The sales price is $158.592; therefore, the tax at $1.00 per thousand rounded to the nearest $500 is $159.00. Response "B" is incorrect, because the rounding would be down and not up. Response "B" is incorrect, because the tax is not in $.50 increments. Response "C" is incorrect, because the question states $1.00 per thousand and the cent amount would never be $.59.

66. C – Generally, when subdivision restrictions are not enforced by the homeowners, over time they are waived.

Response "A" is incorrect for the reason response "C" is correct. Response "B" is irrelevant. Response "D" is incorrect, because one property owner can enforce the subdivision restrictions without the assistance or agreement of the other property owners.

67. C – There are a few key points to solving this problem. First, remember that it is a calendar year (January – December). If the taxes are not due until December 31st, the seller will not have paid them by July 14th when the property closes. If the question asks for a credit to the buyer, that is asking how much will the seller pay the buyer. To solve the problem: January 1 – July 14 = 195 days (seller pays the day of closing) $1,878 (annual taxes) ÷ 365 (days in year) = $5.145 per day for taxes $5.145 (per day) x 195 (1/1 to 7/14) = $1,003.32 (credit to buyer). Response "B" is the amount if you debit the buyer the amount at closing.

68. C – By definition, loan discount points are prepaid interest. Because the borrower pay the discount points, her interest rate is less over the term of the loan. Response "A" is incorrect, because an origination fee is the fee paid to the mortgage lender for services performed. Response "B" is incorrect, because the down payment is the amount of money paid out-of-pocket by the buyer and not financed. Response "D" is incorrect, because discount points have nothing to do with the real estate agent.

69. C – Mortgage loans may have a clause that requires the mortgagor to pay a fee if the loan balance, or any part of it, is paid prior to its due date. Response "A" is the opposite of a penalty in that a privilege clause permits the mortgagor to pay in advance of the due date. Response "B" is the term for interest that is due on the mortgage balance since the last mortgage payment was paid. Response "D" is nonsensical.

70. C – This is best answer for the buyer. Sellers typically do not require the same underwriting requirements as a commercial lender. Response "A" would not be the best answer, because although it may get the buyer the mortgage, it may not be in the best interest of the real estate agent. Response "C" may be possible, but it is unlikely that a life insurance policy would have a loan value sufficient to purchase real estate. Response "D" is one option, but not the best option for someone wanting to purchase a property now.

71. D – Municipalities with building codes typically require a builder to obtain a certificate stating that the construction is complete and that the property is habitable. Response "A" is not the proper title of the form. Response "B" refers to the permit needed prior to beginning of construction. Response "C" refers only to a permit to install the plumbing.

72. B – Local governments may assess property owners for improvements that benefit all property owners. Examples of these special assessments include sidewalks, sewers, and street lights. Response "A" is incorrect, because this is the term used for property taxes. Response "C" is a term that describes a special assessment, but it is not the proper term. Response "D" is nonsensical.

73. B – Although licensees need to know about financing, they should direct buyers to mortgage lenders for advice on what type of financing is best for them. All of the other responses are activities which licensees should do.

74. A – An owner asks for a security deposit to insure that the property is returned in good condition, ordinary wear and tear excepted. If the tenant uses the deposit as the last month's rent, the owner will have no "security" that the property will be returned in good condition. And, if in fact, it is not in good condition, the owner may have to pay for repairs himself. Response "B" is incorrect, in that security deposits may be used as rent when the tenant and landlord agree. Response "C" is nonsensical. Response "D" may be correct in some states, but it still doesn't address the fact that the property may be damaged and the owner will not have the deposit to make repairs.

75. A – In solving this problem, you must first determine the lien priorities. Once the priorities are established, then start with the sales price and deduct each expense until your reach the second mortgage priority. The second mortgage holder will receive the money available at that point. $177,000 (sales price) – $4,200 (cost of sale and lst priority) = $172,800. $172,800 (after cost of sale) – $3,316 (property taxes) = $169,484. $169,484 (after taxes paid) - $162,432 (lst mortgage) = $7,052. Although the second mortgage is not paid in full, the second mortgage holder is only entitled to the amount left after the higher priority liens are paid.

76. B – If the property owner does not pay for work performed, or materials supplied, to improve his real estate, the contractor or supplier may file a mechanic or materialman's lien. These liens are statutory, which means the law must be followed exactly when the lien is filed to make it enforceable. Response "A" is the type of lien that can be filed once a judgment in obtained in a lawsuit. Response "C" refers to the legal document that is recorded in the public records once a lawsuit is instituted that may affect the title to the real estate. Response "D" is a voluntary lien that is placed on property to secure the repayment of a debt.

77. B – The most basic and important rule of trust accounts is that the funds in trust accounts belong to someone else and they should never be commingled. Responses "A" and "C" are true, but they statement are not most basic and important rule. Response "D" is true in some situations, but again is not the most basic and important rule.

78. D – The first step is to determine how many square feet are in the property, then divide by the number of square feet in an acre (43,560). 198' x 238' = 47,124 square feet ÷ 43,560(square feet in one acre) = 1.1272 acres (rounded to 1.13 acres)

79. B – If the legal description is incorrect in a deed that is a serious title defect in that the owner may not actually own the land. The title should not be transferred until the matter is resolved. Response A" in incorrect, because it is not an encumbrance on the title. Response "C" may be the reason the deed is incorrect, but that answer is not responsive to the question. Response "D" is incorrect, because an acknowledgment is a declaration before

an authorized official that he is the person signing the document and that he is signing it voluntarily.

80. A – POC is an acronym for paid outside of closing. Response "B" is an acronym for power of attorney. Response "C" could be used on the closing statement, but is not the generally accepted practice. Response "D" is an acronym for payable on death and not applicable on the closing statement.

81. C – This type of property is referred to as stigmatized property. State laws vary on disclosure requirements. Response "A" is incorrect, unless disclosure is required by state law. Response "B" is incorrect, because, although the seller has a right to privacy, state law still must be consulted. Response "D" is incorrect, because this may be the property that meets the buyer's needs.

82. A – Generally, leases for a year or less are not required to be in writing. Responses "B" and "D" are incorrect, because oral leases are legal and valid in some situations. Response "C" is the incorrect answer, although as a practical matter, oral leases may not be enforceable because of the problems encountered in proving an oral agreement.

83. A – a HUD-1 Settlement Statement is required under the Real Estate Settlement Procedures Act for all transactions involving federally-related transactions. Response "B" is incorrect, because it is the acronym for the Real Estate Settlement Procedures Act, the law that requires use of the HUD-1. Response "C" is incorrect, because it is

the acronym for the federal Truth-In-Lending law. Response "D" is incorrect, because it the abbreviation for the federal law regulating mortgage lending advertising.

84. D – The federal income tax provisions that provide a method for deferring the payment of capital gains when property is sold is known as a "1031 exchange." All of the other responses are irrelevant for a 1031 exchange.

85. C – One of the advantages claimed by mortgage brokers is their ability to shop around for the best deal for the borrower. Mortgage brokers have relationships with a number of mortgage money sources. Responses "A" and "B" are comments often heard about mortgage brokers, but they may or may not be true and the question asks for what is a "true" answer. Response "D" is incorrect, because a mortgage banker is not the same as a mortgage broker. This question reminds you to read the question carefully and pay attention to what the question is asking. If you use "opinion" instead of "fact" you can easily miss this one and answer either "A" or "B".

86. B – With a fully amortized loan each payment is made up of accrued interest and principal. At the maturity date of the loan, if paid as agreed, a fully amortized loan should be paid in full. Response "A" is incorrect, because a partially amortized loan is designed to have a balloon payment at the maturity date. Response "C" is incorrect, because a non-amortized loan is one in which only interest payments are made, leaving the full amount of the principal due upon maturity. Response "D" is nonsensical.

87. C – All real estate commissions are negotiable between the seller and broker. There is no "standard" real estate commission and making that statement violates the federal and state anti-trust laws. Responses "A" and "D" violate the anti-trust laws. Response "B" is incorrect, because real estate boards and associations are very careful not to set, or even suggest, a real estate commission that should be charged. A board or association can be found liable for violating anti-trust laws.

88. A – VA guidelines permit the seller to pay discount points for the buyer if the buyer and seller agree. The buyer cannot force the seller to pay discount points simply because he is obtaining a VA loan. Response "B" is incorrect, because the seller may pay as many discount points as the seller and buyer agree for the seller to pay. Responses "C" and "D" are debated in real estate seminars and discussions, but neither are responsive to the question. When taking the test, do not get off on a tangent that does not answer the question.

89. A – Mortgage insurance (PMI or MIP) is required for mortgages that have a greater loan-to-value than 80%. If the borrower does not have at least a 20% equity position in the property, the lender views the loan as one that has a higher risk of not being repaid. Because of that risk, the lender requires the borrower to purchase mortgage insurance that protects the lender in the event of default. Response "B" is incorrect, because the hazard insurance coverage requirement is not based on the loan-to-value ratio. Although some first-time home buyers may choose to obtain a conventional insured loan, being a first-time home buyer is not a requirement as suggested in Response "C." Response "D" is not correct, because, although credit scores are used, higher loan-to-value loans require higher credit scores. For example, it would take a higher credit score to get a 95% loan than a 60% loan.

90. A – An improvement to real estate is something that has become affixed to the land, as is the case with fences, barns, and flowers. Response "B" is incorrect, because a fixture is personal property that has become affixed to real estate in such a way that it becomes part of the real estate. An argument could be made that this is also the correct answer to the question. It is not, because there is no question that these items are improvements, while they may not be fixtures depending on whether or not they meet the fixture test for intent and annexation. Response "C" is incorrect, because, while an encroachment is something that is attached to the real estate, it must cross a boundary line. This question does not imply in anyway that the fence, barn and flowers cross a boundary line. Response "D" is incorrect, because it relates to growing crops.

91. B – Maintenance is not a capital improvement, because a capital improvement increases the useful life or the value of the improvement. All of the other responses would increase the useful life or the value of the property.

92. A – Although all of the situations in the question would concern an underwriter, this one would be of the most concern. A factory in bankruptcy may close or take other steps to reduce its expenses which could include lay-offs or reductions in salaries. Either

option would affect the borrower's ability to repay the debt. Responses "B" and "C" would be less of a concern, because in both situations, the borrower is either employed or employable. Response "D" has a borrower who not only knows his income, but the underwriter knows that it will continue.

93. C – The aggregate adjustment requires lenders to adjust the initial deposit into the escrow account at the closing to avoid a large surplus in the account at the end of the escrow year. Response "A" may be correct, because some adjustment result in a credit to the buyer, but this is not always true. Response "B" is incorrect, because this term refers to the deposits that are made on a monthly basis with the mortgage payment. Response "D" is incorrect, because this is the term that is used to show on the closing statement the amount of the commissions made by the mortgage broker.

94. C – A buyer should protect her own interest by having a title examination prior to closing. The attorney performing the title examination for the foreclosure was not representing the buyer's interests. Responses "A" and "B" are incorrect statements. Response "D" may or may not be true.

95. C – Because the seller had the right to sell the building himself once the listing was released. The agent could have protected herself by having the seller sign an agreement that were to decide to sell the property in the future (or at some specified time), he would list it with her. Response "A" is probably true, but it is an incorrect answer for this question. Response "B" is incorrect,

because he had no legal obligation to call her. Response "D" is incorrect, because the timing was unimportant since she would have had no basis for filing a broker's lien.

96. B – Record keeping is extremely important for agents, and each state has requirements for what need to be kept and for how long. Response "A" is incorrect, because it is the sponsoring broker that is required to have an escrow account, not the agent. Response "C" may or may not be a requirement of a sponsoring broker; however, it is not a license law requirement. Response "D" is a personal choice of real estate agents, but is not a license law requirement.

97. D – Questions relating to the home inspection should be addressed much earlier in the transaction that at the closing. By the time the parties reach the closing table all issues between the parties should be resolved. Responses "A" is an incorrect statement. Response "B" may be correct as it relates to the parties being together, but it is still not the appropriate time to discuss the inspection results. Response "C" is incorrect, because most home inspectors never meet the sellers.

98. C – The money from the bankruptcy sale will be held by the bankruptcy trustee pending a court order disbursing the money. Federal law determines to whom the money will be paid. Response "A" is incorrect. Responses "B" and "C" may be true at some future point, but not at the time of sale.

99. B – The federal lead based paint law is a disclosure law. The seller is required to disclose what she knows about lead based paint in the property by

completing the disclosure form.
Response "A" is incorrect, because the buyer is not required to notify anyone of anything relating to the lead based paint disclosure provided by the seller.
Response "C" is incorrect, because the seller is only required to disclose what she knows about the presence of lead based paint and after that she is not required to do anything further.
Response "D" is incorrect, because FHA has insured many mortgages on houses containing lead based paint.

100. B – Each sponsoring broker determines the commission to be charged in his brokerage. All of the other responses are a violation of the federal and state anti-trust laws.

Sales Exam Two

1. B – As in all math questions, determine which information is relevant to answering the questions. Many math questions include information you do not need to find the answer. That is the case here. You do not need to use the common area maintenance figure. Calculate the gross rent by multiplying $2,300 (monthly rent) by 36 months (lst three years of lease) for a total of $82,800. Then multiply $82,800 (gross rent) x .0725 (commission of 7 .25%) for a total commission of $6,003.00 or Response "B." $2,300 x 36 = $82,800 x .0725 = $6,003.00. Response "A" is the commission for one year, not three years. Response "C" is the answer if you consider the common area maintenance fees are rent (they are not). Response "D" is a transposition of numbers in Response "C." Always double check your answers to make sure you have not transposed numbers.

2. D – The prior appropriation doctrine is used in dryer areas to provide water that will benefit a few instead of being inefficiently used by many. Response "A" means "buyer beware" and not applicable to water distribution. Response "B" is a word used to indicate that two or more interests in land are being combined. Response "C" is a term used when discussing water usage under the doctrine of prior appropriation. A party wishing to use a certain amount of water must submit a plan for the beneficial use of the water.

3. D – If a buyer orders the home inspection, then it is buyer and not the real estate agent who has entered into the contract with the home inspector. In the event of inspector negligence, it is more likely that the liability for the negligence and resulting damages would fall on the inspector and not either of the agents.

4. C – This is the term used when discussing square footage located below the ground level. Response "A" is not correct, because the area below grade may not be substandard. Response "B" is not correct, because the term is nonsensical. Response "D" is correct in that the square footage is below the surface, but this is not the term used in real estate to describe such square footage.

5. A – This is a correct statement of the law. The other Responses are incorrect statements of the law in community property states.

6. C – Unless the seller cooperates with the listing agent in providing complete and accurate information, the agent may use his efforts to find a buyer and the seller will not be able to close the transaction. This can lead to the agent losing earned real estate commission, and may also lead to the agent being liable to the buyer who has relied on the agent's representations that the seller can close. Response "A" is incorrect, because the closing is not the time to learn that the seller does not have enough money to close the transaction. Response "B" is incorrect, because the agent does not know for a fact that there will be enough money to pay both the mortgage lien and the commission. Response "D" is correct, but not the best reason to walk away from the listing.

7. A – A landfill is an environmental issue and an environmental inspection could answer the buyer's questions. Response "B" is incorrect, because it relates to the fair market value of the property which would be affected by the landfill, but it would not answer the buyer's questions. Response "C" is incorrect, because a property inspection would reveal the landfill, but not answer questions about it. Response "D" may be

correct in some instances if the health department does such evaluations.

8. D – By definition, an executory contract is an offer that has been agreed upon and signed by all of the parties. An executory contract is one that is in the process of being performed. Response "A" and "C" are nonsensical terms. Response "B" is a contract that has been fully performed.

9. D – Because of the many governmental laws and regulations relating to subdividing land, not to mention the length of time often involved, the best course of action would be to have the land subdivided before it is listed. Response A" may be the best answer for some agents, but that is an action that often leads to legal problems. Don't list property until it is ready to be listed. Response "B" is the second best answer, because buyers would at least see where the tracts lie. However, surveying is not the only consideration when subdividing land. Response "C" is a lawsuit waiting to happen. Who knows if the markers will be placed in the correct locations and who is to say they may not be moved?

10. C – Generally, a hog farm next door does not enhance the value of property. The proper term to use in this situation is incurable external obsolescence. It is incurable, because the farm will not likely be moved. It is external, because it is outside the property boundaries. It is obsolescence, because it depreciates the value of the neighboring property. Response "A" is incorrect, because the farm is not functional obsolescence and it is not curable. Response "B" is incorrect, because although it is incurable, it is not functional obsolescence. Response "D" is incorrect, because it is not curable, although it is external.

11. B – Flood insurance required under the National Flood Insurance Act is purchased through private insurance companies and not the government. Response "A" is the Federal Emergency Management Agency that administers the flood program, but does not sell insurance. Response "C" is incorrect, because the government does not run insurance companies. Response "D" is incorrect, because homeowner's associations may purchase flood insurance but they do not sell flood insurance.

12. D – To calculate the answer, first determine how many square feet are in each lot, add the totals for each lot, and divide by the number of square feet in an acre. The second lot is more difficult to calculate. Draw the outline of the lot and divide I into a rectangle and a triangle. The rectangle will 192' x by 300'. The triangle will be 26' x 350'. The 26' is found by subtracting the front footage from the back footage (the back property line is longer). Lot #1: 180' x 331' = 59,580 square feet. Lot #2: 192' x 300' = 57,600 square feet. 218' – 192' = 26' (difference in front and back of lot). 26' x 350' = 9,100 square feet. 9,100 ÷ 2 = 4,550 square feet. 59,580 + 57,600 + 4550 = 121,730 square feet total in both lots. 121,730 ÷ 43,560 (square feet in acre) = 2.7945 rounded to 2.8 acres

13. A – A defect in the property that can be seen is a patent defect. Response "B" is incorrect, because a latent defect is one that is hidden and not obvious from looking at the property. Response "C" is incorrect, because it is a different way of saying latent defect. Response "D" may be correct, but is not responsive to the question.

14. C – The closing or settlement agent is typically the person to complete the HUD-1 settlement statement. There is no law or rule prohibiting someone else from

completing the form, but that is not typical This question is an example of a question that requires close reading. The work "typical" is important in this question.

15. A – Because buyers often have no knowledge of the mortgage lending requirements, the real estate agent should educate their clients about the income requirements for different types of loans. The other responses are not true.

16. C – Local governments may charge property owners a special assessment for public improvements when the property taxes being charged are insufficient to pay for the improvement. A special assessment is another form of property tax. Response "A" is nonsensical. Response "B" refers to an easement that the government must obtain from the property owner before using the property to install public improvements like sewers, sidewalks, and street lights. Response "D" may be a financing method used to pay for an improvement that will result in a special assessment.

17. C – Condominium owners are responsible for interior repairs of their units, often referred to as from paint-to-paint. A repair in the wall is not from paint-to-paint, but rather "behind" the paint; therefore, the association would be responsible for the repair. Response "A" is incorrect, because the leak may have let water run into her unit, but it originated behind the "paint." Response "B" is incorrect, because it is the association's bylaws, and not the property manager, that make these decisions. Response "D" is irrelevant.

18. B – Because marriage is required for tenancy by the entirety to exist, divorce will destroy the tenancy, leaving the owners as tenants in common. Each of them will have a one-half interest, but that interest will not descend to the surviving owner in the event of death. Response "A" is incorrect, because severalty ownership means that one of them would own the entire interest. Response "C" is not correct, because the divorce destroyed the right of survivorship aspect of the ownership. Response "D" is incorrect, because they are no longer joint tenants.

19. A – Fair housing law violations should be reported to Housing and Urban Development. Response "B" is incorrect, because that is the acronym for the Federal Housing Administration, which is an agency for insuring mortgage loans not accepting complaints on fair housing. Response "C" is incorrect, because it is the acronym for Federal National Mortgage Association, one of the sources for lending in the secondary mortgage market. Response "D" is incorrect, because it is the acronym for the Environmental Protection Agency that administers environmental concerns.

20. B – To calculate this answer, you will need to calculate the appreciation for each year and total it. $210,000 x .04 = $8,400 (appreciation lst year). $210,000 + 8,400 = $218,400 (value at end of lst year). $218,400 x .04 = $8,736 (appreciation 2nd year). $218,400 + $8,736 = 227,136 (value at end of 2nd year). $227,136 x .04 = 9,085.44 (appreciate at end of 3rd year). $227,136 + 9,084.44 = 236,221.44 (value at end of 3rd year).

21. A – Depending on the state, a lender may secure repayment of the mortgage debt by using either a deed of trust or a mortgage. Response "B" is incorrect, because a promissory note is the debt, not the security for the debt. Response "C" is incorrect, because a vendor's lien secures the debt, but the promissory note is not security, but rather the debt. Response "D" is incorrect,

because although the guarantee is security for repayment of the debt, the promissory note is not.

22. D – Although homeowner's association dues may in rare instances be paid into the escrow account, it is very unusual. The other Responses are all items that are typically paid into the escrow account.

23. A – The owners of each unit have one vote. If there are 18 units, then 75% of the 18 units will be necessary. 18 x 75% = 13.5, which would be rounded to 14. Response "B" is incorrect, because that would give each owner (26) a vote. The number of tenants is irrelevant, because tenants do not have a vote.

24. A – An appurtenant easement is a voluntary easement existing on adjoining properties, such as a shared driveway. Response "B" is incorrect, because an easement by necessity is an involuntary easement that is forced upon one property owner by another property owner out of necessity. Response "C" is incorrect, because, although voluntary, the easement requires only one property and is used for utility easements, railroad sidings, and similar purposes. Response "D" is an involuntary easement in which one property owner forces an easement on another's property because of prior use.

25. B – Sales associates must charge the real estate commission authorized by their principal (sponsoring) broker. If a seller wants to negotiate beyond the authority of the associate, the seller should speak to the broker. Response "A" is incorrect, because such a statement is a violation of the anti-trust laws. Response "C" is another anti-trust statement and should not be made. Response "D" may be correct for some associates, and if that is how they feel, they may walk away from the listing.

26. B – The first step for a property manager is to give the tenant notice making a demand for the rest. Response "A" is incorrect, because this is probably the second step taken by the property manager. Response "C" is incorrect, and in many states violates the law. Response "D" may be a correct answer if the property management agreement requires notice prior to giving the tenant notice, but this would be a rare occurrence. Most owners want the property managers to take care of problems without calling them.

27. D – The first step in solving this problem is to determine how much of the land will be dedicated for roads. 100 acres x .08 = 8 acres. Then subtract 8 acres from 100 acres to find the amount left to develop into 5 acre tracts. 100 acres – 8 acres (dedicated) = 92 acres. Then divide the 92 acres by 5 acres to find that there are 18.4 5-acre tracts. Because .4 is less than 5 acres, the largest number of tracts will be 18.

28. A – In most transactions involving mortgage financing, appraisers are hired by and represent the lender, although they are usually paid by the buyer. Response "B" is incorrect, although many times the real estate agent inappropriately pressures the appraiser into appraising the property for at least the sales price. Response "C" may be correct in situations where the buyer is either paying cash for the property or wants to make sure he is not paying more than the appraised value. Response "D" is correct in some situations if the seller wants an independent appraisal prior to either placing the property on the market or accepting an offer.

29. B – Flowers are considered improvements to the property. Response

"A" is incorrect, because emblements are growing crops that are harvested. Response "C" may be correct in some instances, but the statement is not always true. Response "D" is incorrect, because flowers add marketability, but not value to property.

30. B – The most important consideration in appraising property is its location. The phrase "location, location, location" is often used when determining the top three considerations in valuing property. Response "A" is important, but not the most important characteristic. Response "C" may be used to get a ball-park idea of value, but many times the assessment is much lower than the fair market value. Response "D" is an important characteristic, but not the most important.

31. B – When a counteroffer is made, the initial offer is rejected. This is important, because after a counteroffer is made the initial offer cannot be accepted. Response "A" is incorrect. Response "C" is incorrect, because, although the terms in the counteroffer may modify terms in the original offer, the original offer is rejected, not modified. Response "D" may or may not be true, but it is not responsive to the question.

32. A – One an exclusive right to sell listing contract is signed, the broker is entitled to be paid regardless of who sells the property. This is the reason brokers use this type of listing. Otherwise, sellers could use the services of a broker to bring prospective buyers to the property and then go around the broker to sell the property directly to the prospect without paying the commission. Response "B" may be correct, but it is not the reason she would be entitled to be paid. Response "C" is incorrect, because there is no length of time required before the broker is entitled to the commission. Response "D"

is incorrect, because the law does not necessarily entitle her to out of pocket expenses if she agrees to cancel the listing. And, the law does not require the listing agent to cancel a listing simply because the seller requests the agent to do so.

33. A – Material facts are facts important to a party in making a decision relative to the transaction. Response "B" is incorrect, because latent refers to hidden defects in the property and is not responsive to this question. Response "C" is nonsensical. Response "D" refers to obvious defects in a property and is not responsive to this question.

34. A – One of the purposes of an operating budget is to provide a way to pay variable rate expenses. A cash reserve fund provides that mechanism. Responses "B" and "C" are part of the operating budget. Response "D" is not part of the operating budget.

35. A – Risk of loss refers to do which party has to carry hazard insurance. In states that have laws that the risk of loss passes to the buyer when a sales/purchase contract is signed, the buyer should immediately purchase the insurance. Because, in the event the property is damaged or destroyed prior to the closing, the buyer would be expected to purchase it regardless of its condition.

36. B – Liability insurance pays for personal injury claims. The other Responses may be correct if the specific policy contains liability coverage, although most of this type of coverage is for damage or destruction to the improvements to the property.

37. A – Credits refer to the money that a party receives at the closing and debits refer to the money that a party pays at the closing. If the buyer has more credits than debits, the

buyer will receive money. Response "B" is a correct statement, but not responsive to the question. Response "C" is incorrect, because that would mean the buyer's debits exceeded the credits. Response "D" may or may not be correct, because the question does not state who is to pay the credits. In fact, the credit may come from money overpaid at some point by the buyer.

38. A – The agency relationship created when a property is listed is between the property owner and the principal (sponsoring) broker. Response "B" is incorrect, because, although the associate may be the only person in the brokerage that the owner knows, the associate is not a party to the listing contract. The associate's relationship is created with the owner through the owner's relationship with the broker. Responses "C" and "D" are nonsensical.

39. C – The first step is to determine the monthly rent. $10,800 ÷ 12 = $900 per month. Then multiply the monthly rent by 2 and add the security deposit. $900 x 2 + 1,000 = $2,800. The trick to this question is to use the 15 days. It doesn't matter when the lease is signed.

40. C – A survey is the process that locates the property boundaries. Response "A" is incorrect, because an appraisal deals with value, not boundaries. Response "B" is incorrect, because a home inspection is an inspection of the improvements on the property, not the boundaries of the property. Response "D" is incorrect, because a plat is a drawing of the lots that cannot be used to find the exact boundaries without a survey.

41. C – As an independent contractor, the agent is paid the entire commission and then must pay his federal and state income taxes

directly. To calculate the amount of commission, start by determining the sales price: $3,000,000 (listing price) x .90 (list to sale percentage) = $2,700,000 (sales price). $2,700,000 (sales price) x .07 (commission rate) = $189,000. Responses "A" and "B" are incorrect, because the commission is calculated on the listing price and not the sales price. Response "D" is incorrect, because the agent is an independent contractor and not an employee.

42. D – VA loans have a maximum loan-to-value of 100%.

43. B – The fiduciary duty of due care and diligence requires the agent to exercise the same level of expertise when representing a client as any other agent would use. Response "A" is the fiduciary duty that requires the agent to protect the client's interest above all others, including the interest of the agent. Response "C" is the fiduciary duty that requires the agent to disclose all material facts to the client. Response "D" is the fiduciary duty that requires the agent to hold and disburse client's money as the client instructs.

44. D – An option clause is a term that may or may not be included in a lease, depending on the agreement between the lessor and lessee. Response "A" should be included, because it is the clause that sets out what happens in the event one party does not perform under the terms of the lease. Response "C" should be included, because it is important to know the names of the lessor and lessee. Response "D" should be included, because the amount of the rent is an integral part of the lease.

45. C – The party that pays the agent is not necessarily the party that is being represented. As in most legal relationships,

one party can pay for another party to be represented. This is the reason it is important for agents to know not only who is paying them, but also whom they are representing. The other Responses are incorrect statements of the law.

46. B – Areas that have building codes do so to protect the public. Response "A" is incorrect, because building codes set the minimum and not the maximum standards of construction. Response "C" is incorrect, because the building codes are not written to help the lenders in any way. Response "D" is probably what the consumers think, but is not the reason for building codes.

47. A – Once the deed is recorded, the information is available to the public. Response "B" is incorrect, because the closing attorney will not likely divulge the information. Response "C" is incorrect, because there may not be a mortgage on the property. Response "D" is incorrect, because the real estate agent should not divulge client information.

48. C – The best way to start the measuring process is by drawing a diagram of the house. That way, it will be difficult to miss measuring part of the structure. Response "A" is not the best way to start, because, without a drawing, it is easy to miss a section of the house. Response "B" is incorrect, because the plat will probably not have the house shown on it. Response "D" is incorrect, because the longer a seller owns the property, the larger it seems to become in the seller's mind.

49. A – Individual ownership of property is known as several or severalty ownership. When the husband, died the wife was the sole or individual owner of the property they had owned jointly with survivorship. Response "B" is incorrect, because a

tenancy in common is not created when a joint owner with survivorship dies. Responses "C" and "D" are incorrect, because a deed controls the disposition of property when the deed and last will and testament are in conflict.

50. B – To create a contract, all of these elements must be included. Response "A" is incorrect, because the date, legal description and closing date are not necessary to create a contract. Response "C" is incorrect, because earnest money is not required to create a contract. Response "D" is incorrect, because the purchase price, earnest money, names and closing date are not required to create a contract.

51. D – One of the main characteristics of a tenants in common ownership interest is that each co-tenant may sell, or in some other way, transfer her interest in the property without the agreement of the other co-owners. All of the other Responses are incorrect answers to this question, because each response describes a characteristic of tenancy in common.

52. C – The building codes do not regulate the schedule for completing the project. Some subdivisions have time limits for finishing construction once it is started, but that is regulated by the subdivision restrictions or zoning regulations, not the building code. All of the other response include items that are regulated by the building codes.

53. D – An interval ownership interest is one that gives the owner a fee simple interest in the property for a set period of time each year. Generally, the actual time period is stated in the deed. An example may be for the 14th week of the year. The rest of the periods are owned by other owners. Response "A" is incorrect,

because a cooperative ownership is an ownership interest in a corporation that owns the real estate. Response "B" is incorrect, because it refers to ownership of property by an entity that is made up of multiple owners. Each owner owns a part of the entity: for example, a limited liability company that owns the real estate. Response "C" is incorrect, because condominium ownership is a form of ownership in which the owner owns her unit individually and a percentage share of the common area.

54. A – The final inspection is the inspection that should be made by the buyer immediately prior to closing to ascertain whether or not the improvement is in at least the same condition than it was a the time of the purchase contract. Response "B" is incorrect, because this term refers to the inspection performed by a home inspector soon after the purchase contract is written. Response "C" is incorrect, because the limited purpose inspection is performed to ascertain the condition of certain elements of the structure, i.e. roof, heating and air conditioning, and plumbing. Response "D" is incorrect, because this refers to an inspection that must be made within thirty days of signing the purchase contract.

55. C – A corporation must designate the person authorized to sign on its behalf. The other Responses may be correct if the corporation designates any of these people to sign on its behalf. However, simply being the president, vice-president, shareholder, or secretary is not legally proper authorization to sign on behalf of the corporation.

56. B – An encroachment is defined as an improvement that crosses a boundary line, and in this scenario the storage building crosses the boundary between the properties. Response "A" is incorrect, because the

storage building is not legally a "nuisance" as that term is generally used. A nuisance is something on another's property that adversely affects the neighbor. Response "C" is nonsensical. Response "D" may be correct depending on state law. Some states say that the encroaching portion belongs to the landowner on which it encroaches.

57. B – The duty of confidentiality is one of the fiduciary duties owed a principal by the agent. The other Responses are neither correct, nor are they a good idea because of liability issues.

58. A – Each unit owner owns a fractional share of the common area equal to the number of units in the condominium group.

59. B – Many brokerages sell home owner warranties that are designed to either replace or repair certain items after the closing. Response "A" is incorrect, because, although agents are generally paid a small sum for selling the warranties, that is not the purpose of the warranties. Response "C" is incorrect, because it is not the seller who replaces items after the closing, but rather the buyer. Response "D" is incorrect, because the warranties give the buyer the confidence that certain items will be replaced or repaired, not that there is nothing wrong with the property.

60. B – The written property management agreement creates the agent/principal relationship between the owner and the property manager. Response "A" is incorrect, because the agreement does not creates an employer/employee relationship between any of the parties, and the parties are the tenant and owner. Response "C" is incorrect, because the agreement does not create a relationship involving the tenant. Response "D" is incorrect, because the relationship between the owner and property

manager is typically as an independent contractor and not as an employer/employee.

61. D – A specific lien is a lien on a specific parcel of real estate: for example, a mortgage lien. Response "A" is an incorrect answer, because a judgment lien is a cloud on the title, i.e. the title is not clear. Response "B" is an incorrect answer, because a judgment lien is an encumbrance on the title that prevents the property from having a clear title. Response "C" is an incorrect response, because a judgment lien is a general lien, in that the lien attaches not to a specific piece of property but to everything owned by the judgment debtor.

62. C – FHA lending guidelines prohibit the lender from charging more than a 1% origination fee. Response "A" and "B" are origination fees that may be charged, because they are less than the 1% maximum. Response "D" is incorrect, and is trying to confuse the reader. There is no maximum or minimum interest rate that can be charged. The lender and borrower may negotiate the interest rate and may adjust it through the use of discount points. Read the questions carefully.

63. B – The mortgagee is the lender and is the one who must release the mortgage lien. Response "A" is incorrect, because the mortgagor is the borrower, not the lender. Responses "C" and "D" are incorrect, because the promissor and maker are the names for the person signing the promissory note, and the promissory note is not a lien on the property that must be released.

64. C – One of the duties of the property manager is to help the tenants resolve disputes that may arise. In this case there appears to be a problem with the leases that will take expertise on part of the property manager to resolve the problem. Response

"A" is not correct, because it isn't up to the tenants to determine what the landlord meant with the conflicting terms. Response "B" is not correct, because the owner is looking to the property manager to manage the problem and not to call with each problem. Response "D" is not correct, because the property manager cannot change the terms of someone's lease without their agreement.

65. A – The real estate commission may be paid by anyone who agrees to do so, but the agreement should be in writing. Response "B" is incorrect, because simply paying the real estate commission in the past does not obligate someone to pay it this time. Response "C" is an incorrect statement. Response "D" is incorrect, because the payment of real estate commission does not necessarily establish the agent-principal relationship. The agent should establish that relationship by an agency agreement.

66. B – One of the requirements of ADA is for owners to make "reasonably achievable accommodations" that will provide access to the facilities and services. Response "A" is an incorrect statement of the law. Response "C" is incorrect, but someone not reading carefully while taking the test could mistake this for the correct answer. The law requires the owner to allow the tenant to make changes that are reasonable to accommodate the tenant's needs. The question reads that the owner must make the changes, and that is not correct. Response "D" is incorrect, because the law does not change according to size of the property.

67. D – The owner's "bundle of rights" includes all of the rights the owner has relative to the property. An owner's right to mortgage the property is one of those rights, as it the right to sell it, give it away, grant an easement, use it, and lease it. Response "A"

is incorrect, because a life estate owner may mortgage the property. However, the mortgagee's interest in the property dies with the life tenant. Responses "B" and "C" are incorrect, because the right to mortgage real estate is neither a fundamental nor constitutional right.

68. C – A multi-peril insurance policy is the best one for a commercial building, because it offers coverage for fire, flood, earthquake, other natural hazards, casualty and liability. The other Responses are incorrect, because they do not afford as much protection as the multi-peril policy.

69. A – All monies that exchange hands relative to the transaction should appear on the closing statement. To purposely fail to include that information may lead to criminal charges. All of the other Responses are incorrect and are completely inappropriate.

70. C – This is a sample of a government survey description. An example of a metes and bounds legal description (Response "A") would begin: "A parcel of land located in Jefferson County, Louisville, Kentucky, described as follows" Beginning at the northeast corner of Harold's Crossing, thence east 25° for 200 feet…" An example of a monument legal description (Response "B") would begin: "A tract of land located in Lexington, Fayette County, Kentucky, described as follows: Beginning at the west line of Smith, running 400 feet to an intersection with Crimson Creek, north along the creek bed 257 feet…" An example of a lot and block legal description (Response "D") would begin: "All of Lot 3, Block H, in the Holly Farm Subdivision, as shown on plat of record in plat book C, page 72,…."

71. B – The purpose of a deed in lieu of

foreclosure is to transfer the property to the lien holder without the necessity of filing a foreclosure lawsuit and conducting a judicial sale of the property. Response "A" is incorrect and is one of the reasons there are only a few deeds in lieu of foreclosure executed. Because all liens remain on the property conveyed by a deed in lieu of foreclosure, lienholders are hesitant to accept such deeds. Response "C" is incorrect, because it is the mortgagor, and not the mortgagee, that is released from the deficiency judgment. Response "D" is incorrect, because the mortgagor loses all of the equity in the property in this situation.

72. D – Increasing the number of real estate agents is not likely to change the fair market value of property. Response "A" would probably decrease the fair market value of property, because there would likely be an increased number of houses on the market for sale and people may be hesitant to purchase with their job security unknown. Response "B" would likely increase the fair market value, because with lower rates more people want to purchase property. When there is a larger demand, the values are likely to increase. Response "C" may reduce the fair market value, because there will be more properties on the market. All of the responses, except D, are important when considering the effect of supply and demand in the real estate market.

73. C – The Real Estate Settlement Procedures Act prohibits kick-backs by service providers, including mortgage lenders. The gift certificate would be considered a kick-back. The other Responses may be true, but are irrelevant because the kick-back is illegal.

74. A – Work the problem as follows: $165,000 ÷ 100 = 1,650$ (there are 1,650 100s in 165,000)

$1,545 (tax bill) ÷ 1,650 = .9363 rounded to .936 (tax rate). With this type of problem, be sure to check your answers. It doesn't take long and will assure you that you have the correct answer. Check "A" – 165,000 x .9363 ÷ 100 = $1,544.89 (rounded to 1,545) – you know this is correct. Check "B" – 165,000 x .639 ÷ 100 = $1,054.35 – you know this is incorrect, because the problem gave you the tax amount of $1,545. Check "C" – 165,000 x 2.54 ÷ 100 = $4,194 – you know this is incorrect, because the tax amount is $1,545 not $4,191. Check "D" – 165,000 x 9.39 ÷ 100 = $15,493.50 – you know this is incorrect, because the tax amount is $1,545 not $15,493.50

75. D – When an offer is presented to a seller, the seller may counter the offer, hold the offer and do nothing, or accept the offer (all of the Responses except "D"). Although the seller may authorize her agent to accept the offer, this is unusual and is risky for the real estate agent.

76. C – Mediation is the process in which The parties discuss their dispute with the assistance of a mediator, but the mediator does not decide how the dispute will be resolved. The parties either come to an agreement on how the dispute will be settled or they proceed through the legal process. Response "A" is incorrect, because the mediator does not suggest a resolution. Response "B" is incorrect, because the mediator does not make a decision on the resolution of the dispute. Response "D" is incorrect, because the judge is not involved in the mediation.

77. A – Lenders want the escrow account to make sure the property taxes are paid. If property taxes are not paid, they become a lien superior to the first mortgage. When there are unpaid taxes, the first mortgage has second lien priority. Response "B" is

incorrect, because the federal government does not require an escrow account. Response "C" is nonsensical. Response "D" is true, but irrelevant to answering this question.

78. B – This is the most basic rule of real estate law, and the most often ignored by real estate agents. Real estate contracts must be in writing to be enforceable under the Statute of Frauds. Responses "B" and "D" are referring to the statute of limitations, not the Statute of Frauds. Response "C" is incorrect, because recording is not an element of the Statute of Frauds.

79. C – Once the property closed, and the deed was delivered by the seller and accepted by the buyer, title transferred from the seller to the buyer. Response "A" is incorrect, because recording is designed to give notice, not to pass title. Response "B" is incorrect, because it is referring to the lending laws that allow mortgagors to rescind mortgages within three days in certain situations. Response "D" is an incorrect statement, because a buyer may or may not record a deed, and there is no time limit for recording.

80. B – Adverse possession is the process of taking someone's property after certain legal requirements are met. Those legal requirements include using the property for a period of time in an open, hostile, notorious, and continuous manner. Response "A" is incorrect, because quiet title refers to the legal process of removing clouds on the real estate title. Response "C" is incorrect, because it refers to settling someone's estate after death. Response "D" is incorrect, because it refers to the type of notice given once a document is recorded in the public records.

81. B – In a townhouse community, the property owners own their individual units in fee simple and own the common areas as tenants in common, with each owning a fractional share, depending on how many townhouse units are in the townhouse community. The other Responses are an incorrect statement of the law.

82. A – The process of adding land along the river bank is known as accretion. Response "B" is incorrect, because avulsion refers to the washing away of land along moving water. Response "C" is incorrect, because the term is used to two ways in real estate: (1) refers to attaching real estate in such a way it becomes a fixture under the annexation test; and (2) refers to cities adding adjacent land to the city limits. Response "D" is incorrect, because it is a term used to describe running water receding from the banks to expose additional land.

83. A – The legal process for a government to take land is known as condemnation. Response "B" is incorrect, because eminent domain is the power that gives government entities the right to initiate a condemnation process. Response "C" is incorrect, because is the term used to describe the powers of the government to adopt and enforce laws that promote public health, safety, and welfare. Response "D" is incorrect, because it is not responsive to the question. This question is an example of how a question can be asked in which all of the answer choices are terms that are related to the topic of the question. You must analyze the question to get the right term, because all of the terms are involved in the particular process. These questions are easy to miss. Read carefully and think through the question and each response.

84. A – One of the ways to collect a judgment against a debtor is to attach the debtor's property. The legal way to attach the property is with a writ of attachment authorized by the court. Response "B" is incorrect, because this term refers to the notice filed in the public records when a legal proceeding is filed that affects the title to the real estate. Response "C" is incorrect, because a mortgage is voluntary lien on the property and has nothing to do with a judgment lien. Response "D" is incorrect, because a foreclosure is a legal proceeding filed to collect a debt against a certain parcel of real estate.

85. C – Cleaning gutters is a routine maintenance item, because it has to be done on a regular (or routine) basis to maintain the property. Response "A" refers to maintenance that is performed to prevent a component of the property from being damaged. An example would be cleaning the furnace before there is a problem. Response "B" is incorrect, because it refers to correcting a problem after is has occurred, i.e. patching a hole in the roof. Response "D" is incorrect, because it refers to tenant requested changes and modifications that may be made to the improvement for other reasons.

86. A – Mutual Savings Banks are deposit-owned entities that provide mortgage financing. The other Responses are incorrect statements about Mutual Savings Banks.

87. D – A seller who carries the mortgage financing for a person with poor credit is taking a risk that a commercial lender is not willing to take. Helping someone with poor credit is not a good reason for the seller to carry the financing, because of the risk. Response "A" is a good reason, because it helps the seller defer paying capital gains taxes on the sale of the property. Response

"B" is a good reason, because typically sellers can charge buyers higher interest rates than they would earn on other investments. Response "C" is a good reason, and it is true that the house may sell faster with seller financing.

88. A – The purpose of a defeasance clause in a trust deed is to require the trustee to reconvey the property when the debt is paid. The other Responses are not correct relative to defeasance clauses.

89. B – When landlord-tenant law requires the landlord to perform certain tasks or complete certain paperwork, if the landlord fails to follow the law this generally imposes a penalty against the landlord. That penalty is usually the inability to collect from the tenant for damages. Response "A" is a true answer, but not responsive to the question. Without proof of the condition prior to occupancy, courts are reluctant to award damages to the landlord. Response "C" is incorrect and an untrue assumption. Response "D" is incorrect, and probably not true, because courts, in the absence of proof by the landlord, are unlikely to give the landlord damages.

90. C – Just like a commercial lender, a seller must proceed with a foreclosure action to recover the property when the buyer defaults. Response "A" is incorrect in that sellers, in most states, must file a judicial foreclosure action to recover the property. Response "B" is an incorrect statement of the law. Response "D" is incorrect, and sellers should never remove a buyer's personal property without having court permission to do so.

91. A – A bill of sale is used to transfer title to personal property. Response "B" is incorrect, because a deed is used to transfer title to real estate. Response "C" is incorrect, because a chattel mortgage is used to place a lien on personal property. Response "D" is incorrect, because a release is used to remove an interest in real estate.

92. A – Fair housing laws are designed to protect buyers and tenants of residential real estate. Response "B" is incorrect, because "all" real estate is not covered by the fair housing laws. Test takers should be alert when they see the word "all" in a response – because there are numerous exceptions to every rule, the use of the word "all" may indicate an incorrect response. Response "C" is incorrect, because fair housing laws apply to all forms of residential real estate, not just single family residential real estate. Response "D" is incorrect, because the fair housing laws apply, regardless of the age of the property. This response could mislead someone who is thinking about the federal law relating to lead-based paint.

93. D – Master deeds may only be changed by a vote of certain number of property owners. That number is set out in the master deed and usually ranges anywhere from 40% to 100%. The other Responses all list tasks that are the duties of the homeowner's association.

94. D – A low risk loan is one that will likely be repaid by the borrower. Because the borrower is likely to repay, the lender does not require the borrower to purchase mortgage insurance. Likelihood of repayment is determined by the borrower's equity in the property and the borrower's credit score. Response "A" is incorrect, because all FHA loans are insured loans. Response "B" is incorrect, because a loan in which the borrower borrows 90% or more is a high risk loan that would require mortgage insurance. Response "C" is incorrect, because the credit score is an important factor, but not the only factor in determining

whether or not the borrower will likely repay the debt.

95. B – The borrower will need to pay down 10% of the purchase price plus $1,000, for a total of $16,800. First, remember the rule for mortgage loans: the loan is based on the appraised value or the sales price, whichever is less. In this case, the loan will be based on the $158,000 (the appraised value, because it is less than the sales price). Although the loan is based on the appraised value, the buyer still must pay the sales price of $159,000. Then remember the second rule: closing costs and prepaids (discount points) are not the same thing. Therefore, the closing costs and discount points are irrelevant for working this problem. Work the problem as follows:
(1) $158,000 (appraised value) x
(2) 10% (the down payment for a 90% loan) = $15,800 (amount over loan amount that must be paid out of pocket)
(3) $159,000 (sales price) - $158,000 (appraised value) = $1,000 (paid by borrower)
(4) $15,800 (amount over loan) + $1,000 (difference in sales price and appraisal) = $16,800 (amount to be paid out of pocket by buyer at closing

96. A – An executory contract is one that has been created, but not yet performed. Response "B" is incorrect, because, once an offer is accepted, it is referred to as a contract. Response "C" is incorrect, because an executed contract is one that has been completely performed. Response "D" is incorrect, because the contract is not completed at the time of signing.

97. B – In states that have dower and curtesy laws, the wife's interest in her husband's property that is owned during their marriage is known as dower. Response "A" is incorrect, because it refers to the equity in the property that can be protected from creditors. Response "C" is incorrect, because it refers to the husband's interest in the wife's property that she owns during their marriage. Response "D" is incorrect, because it refers to property that is part of a decedent's property.

98. C – If a lender does not receive enough money at the foreclosure sale to pay the debt, the lender may take the promissory note and pursue a deficiency judgment. While a foreclosure is against a specific parcel of property, a deficiency judgment can be collected against all assets of the debtor. Response "A" is an option for the lender, but probably not the best one if the debtor has other assets. Response "B" is not an option, because, once the foreclosure proceeding is finalized, the lender cannot place a lien on the property, even if it is still owed money. Response "D" is nonsensical.

99. A – All brokers should have a written office policy manual to set out the policies and practices followed in the brokerage. One of the items included in the policy manual should be the handling of floor time. Response "B" would be a good option if there is no written policy. Response "C" would be a possibility, although likely to alienate one of the agents. Response "D" would be a poor management choice and likely to create dissension in the office.

100. C – The law against kickbacks to suppliers is not the Sherman Anti-Trust Act, but the Real Estate Settlement Procedures Act. All of the other Responses are violations under the Sherman Anti-Trust Act.

Sales Exam Three

1.   B – The standard for measuring square footage is to use above grade (above ground) finished area only. Even if the basement level is finished as well as the above grade, it should not be included in the square footage calculation. Response "A" is too vague to be correct. Response "C" is nonsensical. Response "D" is incorrect, because any square footage below the ground level should not be included in the square footage.

2.   B – Steering is a fair housing concept and illegal for agents to do, but it is not part of the anti-trust laws. All of the other responses are included in the anti-trust laws.

3.   D – An easement in gross is a voluntary easement that attaches to the servient estate and grants a limited right to a person or company to the servient estate. A utility easement is the perfect example in that the easement grants the utility company the right to come onto the land to install and maintain a utility service. Response "A" is incorrect, because an appurtenant easement is a voluntary easement involving two parcels of land, the servient and dominant estates. In an easement appurtenant, the owner of the dominant estate has a right to use part of the servient estate for a designated purpose. Response "B" is incorrect, because this is an involuntary easement that is given to the dominant estate over the objections of the servient estate since it is necessary for the dominant estate landowner to have access to his property. Response "C" is incorrect, because this is an involuntary easement that is forced on the servient estate because of prior use by the owner of the dominant estate.

4.   B – This is the description of a plat. Response "A" is incorrect, because a building plan shows where the buildings will be built on the land. Response "C" is incorrect, because a plot plan shows where all of the improvements will be placed on the land. Response "D" is incorrect, because a zoning map shows the zoning designation for each area.

5.   A – The cost approach to appraising shows how much it would cost to reproduce or replace the property. Response "B" is incorrect, because the cost approach includes finding the reproduction cost. This is the type of question that can be easily missed if not read carefully. It would be easy to confuse reproduction approach with reproduction cost. Response "C" is incorrect, because the market data approach compares other properties with the subject property to arrive at a value. Response "D" is incorrect, because the income approach is used with investment property and uses the expected income to arrive at a value.

6.   C – Agents should ask for proof that someone signing any legal document on behalf of a corporation (or any non-individual entity) provide proof that he has the authority to sign. Response "A" is incorrect, because the president does not always have the right to sign the listing and agents should not assume someone has authority without proof. Response "B" is incorrect, because unless the listing is signed by the proper authority for the corporation the listing would be invalid and the agent would be marketing unlisted property. Response "D" is incorrect and nonsensical. Either the president has the authority to sign the listing or he does not have the authority. Getting someone else to sign later does not fix the problem.

7.   C – This term is nonsensical, because the term is not typically used in the real estate industry. The other Responses are all terms

used to describe the business model that allows the broker to unbundled services and charge for specific services.

8. B – The Lead-Based Paint Hazard Reduction Act requires listing agents to ask the seller to complete and sign a lead-based paint disclosure form when listing properties built before 1978. Response "A" is incorrect, because the seller's disclosure form may or may not be required when listing a property, depending on state law. If it is required, the age of the residential dwelling is irrelevant to its completion. Response "C" is incorrect, and the fair housing brochure is delivered by the listing agent to the seller informing the seller of the agent's commitment to fair housing. Response "D" is incorrect, although a prudent listing agent will ask a seller if there is anything about the house that involves FEMA.

9. B – This is the definition of police power. When taking the test, you should read this type of question carefully. Because Response "A" is the process for enforcing Response "C," and both "A" and "C" relate to the government's police power, it is easy to answer the question incorrectly. Remember that the police power (Response "B") gives the government the power of eminent domain (Response "C") that is enforced by the use of condemnation (Response "A). Response "D" is the constitutional right to defend yourself in court, which is, of course, important when the government uses its police power.

10. A – Trade fixtures are treated differently under the law than regular fixtures, and it is important for a listing agent to know what items the seller considers trade fixtures in a commercial transaction. Response "B" is incorrect, because collateral is a term used to describe

property that has been pledged as security to repay a debt. Response "C" is incorrect, because appurtenances is a term used to describe the rights, interests, and improvements that are attached to and pass with the real estate. Response "D" is incorrect, because the term applies to any personal property that has become attached to real estate in such a way that it becomes part of the real estate. It is important in reading this question not to miss the fact that it is "commercial property" that is being listed. If this question is not read carefully, Responses "C" and "D" could also be the answer.

11. A – This question revolves around the economic principle of supply and demand. Because the question states there are more houses on the market than buyers, you know that supply is up and demand is down. When the supply is up and the demand is down, a buyer will generally want to pay less for the house she buys; therefore, this response is false. Responses "B" and "D" are true, because houses will sell at a slower pace and the sellers will have to induce the buyers to buy. Response "C" is generally true regardless of supply and demand.

12. C – This is the best way to show the property, because it allows the agent to present the property in its best light and it allows the agent to protect the property from buyers who want to pocket the seller's personal property. Responses "A" and "B" are incorrect for the reasons given above. Response "D" is incorrect, for a number of reasons. First, it is not usually a good idea to get the sellers and prospective buyers together. Secondly, the seller has hired an agent to present the property and answer questions. Agents should look at the property, anticipate questions, and get the answers from the seller before the prospective buyers asks the question.

13. B – Anytime a buyer talks about changing the property in any way, the agent should immediately consider the zoning regulations and subdivision restrictions. These are two things that can make the difference in a buyer's decision to buy the property, and two things than cannot be easily changed. Response "A" is incorrect, because a swimming pool may or may not add value to property. Response "C" is incorrect, because the agent is taking on unnecessary liability in the event the bids turn out to be incorrect. Response "D" is an option for the agent, but Response "B" is a much more important action.

14. B – This is the best step for the agent to take, because of the importance of having potable water. Responses "A" and "D" may solicit remarks from the sellers that may or may be true. Response "C" would be the action the buyer's, not the agent, should take after the water is tested.

15. A – An offeror is the person making an offer. Response "B" is incorrect, because offeree is the person receiving the offer. Responses "C" and "D" are incorrect, because in any offer situation, the buyer or seller could be the offeror or offeree.

16. A – Most of the warranties have a pre-existing condition clause. Because the air conditioner was working so soon after the closing, this is the most likely reason for the denial. Response "B" is not correct, because they contacted the warranty company immediately. Response "C" is unlikely because air conditioners are generally covered under the warranty. Response "D" is not correct, because the agent must have sent in the premium or the claim would not have been denied; it would have been rejected.

17. B – Buyers, not agents, choose where they want to live. Agents who suggest areas for buyers can be liable for unlawful steering under the fair housing laws. Response "A" is not correct, because an agent would not know about future appreciation. Response "C" is incorrect because asking these questions violate the fair housing laws. Response "D" is incorrect, because, although the agent should qualify the buyer for price range, the agent should not then look for an area that suits the buyer's needs – again a fair housing issue.

18. B – Co-insurance is based on an 80/20 ratio. Take the property value and multiply by 80% to find the amount of coverage required. Insurance carriers assume that 20% of the value is in the land that will remain regardless of what happens to the improvement. Find the amount of insurance coverage required by:
$237,000 (value) x .80 (co-insurance) = $189.600 (amount of insurance required)

19. B – Termites and other wood destroying insects would be found by a wood destroying insects inspections. Response "A" may be correct in some areas and with some home inspectors, but generally home inspectors specifically exclude termites from their inspection reports. Response "C" is incorrect, because an environmental inspector does not look for termite infestation. Response "D" is incorrect, because "pest" inspection is too general and could mean an inspection for ants or roaches.

20. B – When unity of time is required, all owners must obtain their interest in the property in the same deed or last will and testament. Response "A" refers to the unity of possession. Response "C" is nonsensical.

Response "D" is referring to time shares or interval ownership arrangements.

21. D – An owner, who has purchased owner's title insurance policy, would make a claim against that policy if a defect was discovered in the title after closing. The problem often arises when the buyer does not purchase the owner's title insurance, which is optional. Response "A" is incorrect, because homeowner's insurance protects the property and its improvements, not the title to property. Response "B" is incorrect, because lender's title insurance only protects the lender against defects that affect the lender's interest in the property. Response "C" is incorrect, because the agent's insurance protects the agent against negligence claims that may be filed by a buyer or seller.

22. C – Concurrent ownership is the simultaneous ownership of property by two or more people. Response "A" is incorrect, because severalty or several ownership means that only one person owns the property. Response "B" is incorrect, because a trust ownership means that a trust actually owns the property. The trust have more than one beneficiary, but that is not the same as simultaneous ownership. Response "D" is nonsensical.

23. D -- Before a property can be sold, all parties with an interest must sign the deed. Because the mother has a life estate, she has an interest in the property. Unless she signs the listing contract, she cannot be forced to sign the deed. A prudent listing agent will always get all owners to sign the listing contract that must sign the deed. Response "A" is incorrect, because, although it is important that she move, it is more important that she sign the deed. Response "B" is the polite thing to do, but not responsive to the legal issue. Response "C"

is incorrect, because it places the agent in the position of practicing law without a license.

24. A – A marketing plan would not only show the owner how his property is going to be marketed, but would also show him that the agent is professional and well-prepared. All of the other Responses are irrelevant to the purpose of a marketing plan.

25. B – The number of days should be prorated from May 22nd through May 31st. Rent is paid for the day the tenant gets possession of the property. There are 10 days between the 22nd and 31st. Don't forget to count the first day. Calculate the proration by:
$675 (monthly rent) ÷ 31 (days in May) x 10 (days rent due) = $217.74
Response "A" is incorrect, because it uses 9 days in May for the rent and not 10. This is an easy mistake – don't forget to charge rent for the day of possession. Response "C" is incorrect, because it is for the first 20 days of May. Response "D" is incorrect, because it is for the first 21 days in May.

26. B – To calculate the amount of prepaid interest, you must determine the number of days from May 17th through May 31st. Interest is paid for the day of closing, regardless of how late in the day the transaction closes. The buyer will owe 15 days of interest at closing.

May 17th – May 31st = 15 days
$42.38 (per day) x 15 days = 635.70

Response A is incorrect, because it uses 14 days instead of 15 days. Responses "C" and "D" are incorrect, because they calculate the interest through the month of July. Prepaid interest is only collected from the date of closing through the end of that month. The next month's interest is paid as part of the lst mortgage payment.

27. B – A license is a revocable personal right to use someone else's property. Response "A" may, in some cases be correct, but it is unusual to have an easement for something as temporary as a billboard. Response "C" is incorrect, because an appurtenance is something attached to the land, not the permission to attach it. Response "D" is incorrect, because a right-of-way gives permission to use the land, not the right to attach something to the land.

28. A – This the definition of alluvion. Response "B" is incorrect, because fructus naturales refers to uncultivated crops such as trees and bushes. Response "C" is incorrect, because appurtenance refers to rights, privileges, and improvements attached to real estate. Response "C" is incorrect, because emblements refers to growing crops such as corn and tobacco.

29. C – This is the process of a municipality adding land to it boundaries to increase its tax basis. Response "A" is incorrect and refers to apportioning water in dryer areas. Response "B" is incorrect and refers to the process used in subdividing land to show how the lots, streets, and easements are placed. Response "D" is incorrect and refers to the principle of conveying land.

30. C – Buildings codes set the minimum construction standards, including standards for the health, safety and welfare of the building occupants. Response "A" is incorrect, because an encroachment is an improvement to land that crosses a boundary line. Response "B" is incorrect, because an appurtenance is a right, privilege or improvement that is attached to the real estate. Response "D" is incorrect, because a

license is a personal right to use the land of another.

31. A – The first step in calculating the cost of the carpet is to determine the areas that will be carpeted and subtract those square footages from the total. The bathroom, kitchen, and screened porch will not be carpeted. After subtracting the non-carpeted square footage, calculate how many square feet are left and convert to square yards. Them multiply the square yard by the price per yard.

> total square footage
> 1,850 square feet
> bathroom (8 x 9 = 72)
> -   72 square feet
> kitchen (12 x 15)
> -   180 square feet
> screened porch (12 x 16)
> -   192 square feet
> total to be carpeted
> 1,406 square feet
> 1,406 ÷ 9 (sq. ft in one yard)
> = 156.22 square feet to be carpeted
> 156.22 x $22.00 (per square yard) = $3,436.89

32. A – Buyers are entitled to receive marketable title to property. Marketable title is "clear enough" that a court would require the buyer to accept the title, i.e. title that has acceptable encumbrances. Response "B" is incorrect, because most title is not clear, rather it is marketable. A clear title would have no encumbrances. In developed areas it is difficult to have "clear" title, because of utility easements, zoning regulations, and subdivision restrictions. Response "C" is a nonsensical response. Response "D" may be correct in most instances, but not always.

33. B – This is the definition of a buffer zone. Response "A" is incorrect and refers

to the fair housing violation of trying to get people to leave the neighborhood because certain other people are moving into it. Response "C" is incorrect and refers to zoning designations that control density of development. Response "D" is incorrect and refers to zoning to control architectural design.

34. B – Curtesy refers to the husband's interest in property owned by his wife during their marriage. Response "A" is incorrect and refers to the wife's interest in property owned by her husband during their marriage. Response "C" is incorrect and refers to the interest of a life tenant in a life estate. Response "D" is incorrect and refers to an owner's interest in property.

35. A – Fixtures are personal property that become real estate when attached to the real estate. Response "B" is incorrect and refers to the right to use someone else's property. Response "C" is incorrect and refers to growing crops that are harvested. Response "D" is incorrect and is another name for personal property.

36. A – Operating expenses vary from month to month depending on the needs of the business. Response "B" is incorrect, because operating expenses do not include the mortgage debt service. Response "C" is incorrect, because operating expenses are not use in preparing a comparative market analysis. Response "D" is incorrect, because operating expenses are shown on the profit and loss statement.

37. B – A variance is required when an owner wants to "vary" from the requirements set forth by the zoning board. Response "A" is incorrect, because a nonconforming use permit allows the owner to use the property in a way that does not conform to the zoning designation.

Response "C" is incorrect, because amending a plat will not change the zoning requirements. Response "D" is incorrect, because spot zoning refers to changing the zoning for a small area that is inconsistent with the surrounding area.

38. A – Material facts are important facts that affect a buyer's, seller's, or owner's decisions on matters relating to the real estate. Response "B" is nonsensical. Response "C" is incorrect, because these items are not subjective. Response "D" is a correct statement, but is not responsive to the question.

39. B – Social security numbers should not be used on any forms gathered by the real estate agent. All of the other Responses are appropriate to include in the sales contract.

40. B – Insurance cannot be obtained by someone who would not suffer a monetary loss if the property were damaged or destroyed. That interest is known as an insurable interest. Response "A" is incorrect, because you can have an insurable interest in property even if you don't have the deed, such as in the case of a tenant. Responses "C" and "D" are incorrect, because a recorded mortgage and clear title are irrelevant for insuring real estate.

41. C – Mold is an environmental concern, and the appropriate inspection would be an environmental inspection. Response "A" may be correct in some situations if the home inspector is qualified to inspect for mold. Response "B" may be correct if the health department has a person qualified as a mold inspector. Response "D" may be correct if the inspector is qualified. This is a question where all Responses are correct some of the time, but the BEST one is Response "C". Read the questions very carefully.

42. C – A management proposal should be prepared by the property manager who is trying to obtain a contract to manage property. All of the other Responses are items that may be included in a management proposal.

43. C – This is the BEST response for the property manager. Response "A" is not a good method for handling the complaint and will likely lead to problems between the neighbors. Response "B" is not a good action, because the tenant may move and the owner will lose rent. Response "D" is not a good solution, because each tenant has a right to quiet enjoyment of the property leased.

44. A – Net profit is shown on the profit and loss statement. Response "B" is incorrect, because the gross profit does not take into consideration the expenses. Response "C" is incorrect, because loss factor relates to percentage of rentable space in a building compared to the usable space. Response "D" is incorrect, because operating expenses refers to the day-to-day cost to operate the business.

45. A – The Americans with Disabilities Act requires the owner to make reasonably achievable accommodations for a disabled tenants and visitors. Response "B" is incorrect, in that the Federal Fair Housing Act of 1968 requires all people be treated equally in housing decisions. Response "C" is incorrect, in that the Equal Employment Opportunity Act requires equal employment opportunities for all people. Response "D" is incorrect, because it refers to a non-existent law.

46. A – Corrective maintenance is repairing a problem that exists. Response "B" refers to maintenance that is performed on a regular basis to keep the property in good condition to avoid the need for corrective maintenance. Response "C" refers to maintenance during the time an improvement is being constructed or modified. Response "D" refers to maintenance performed to prevent a problem from occurring.

47. A – This is the current tax rule for excluding capital gains earned when selling a primary residence. All of the other responses are incorrect statements of the tax rules.

48. A – Special assessments have equal priority with property tax liens (first priority), and they run with the land. If the property is conveyed without the assessment being paid, the unpaid assessment remains attached to the property. The other responses may be true in some situations, but they are not the best answer for the question.

49. B – Lender's title insurance is a decreasing term policy. As the mortgage balance is reduced, so is the face amount of the policy. Response "A" is incorrect and it describes owner's title insurance. Responses "C" and "D" are incorrect statements about title insurance.

50. C – To solve this problem, you need to add the taxes, insurance premium and sewer assessment together. Then, divide by twelve. It is irrelevant that the first year's homeowner's insurance policy was paid at closing.

$1,823 (taxes) + $632 (insurance) + $1,200 (sewer assessment) = $3,655
$3,655 (annual amount needed) ÷ 12 = $304.59

51. B -- Promissory notes are not recorded in the public records. All of the other

responses are characteristics of promissory notes.

52. C – Real estate contracts must be in writing and must contain the agreement between the parties, which makes them an express contract. Response "A" is incorrect, because an implied contract is not in writing and does not necessarily contain all of the terms between the parties. Response "B" is correct when the parties have performed under the contract; however, real estate contracts are not "always" executed. If one or both parties fail to perform, the real estate contract never becomes executed. Response "D" is not correct, because real estate contracts are bilateral (two parties must agree) and not unilateral (one party agrees).

53. B – The statute of frauds is the law that requires all real estate contracts to be in writing. Because mortgages and deeds are real estate contracts they must be in writing. Response "A" may or may not be a true statement of banking regulations, but those regulations are not the reason mortgages and deeds must be in writing. Response "C" is incorrect, because the statute of limitations relates to the timing for filing legal actions. Response "D" is incorrect, because the recording statutes regulate recording mortgages and deeds. Obviously, these documents must be in writing to be recorded, but the writing is not a requirement of the recording statutes.

54. B – Property that has an easement running across it is known as the servient estate. Response "A" is incorrect, because the land that has the use of the easement is known as the dominant estate. Responses "C" and "D" are incorrect, because appurtenant is the type of easement created, not the type of estate.

55. A – To read this lot's dimensions you start with 132' (road frontage), then 101' (rear property line), then 97' (left property line), and then 117' (right property line).

56. A – The default clause in a contract states what will happen in the event one of the parties breaches the contract. All of the other Responses are terms used by brokers to protect themselves from sellers trying to deal directly with the buyers after the property is listed with the broker.

57. C – Marital status is not a protected class under the fair housing laws. All of the other Responses are protected classes under the fair housing laws. The other protected classes are race, color, national origin, and familial status. Some areas include sexual orientation as a protected class.

58. B – This question gives several irrelevant facts. To determine how much commission the agent will earn, you need the sales price, the commission rate, the division between companies (if two companies involved), and the split between the agent and broker. Referral fees are usually paid by the listing company, advertising is paid by the listing company, and the broker does not deduct income taxes from the commission before paying the agent. To calculate the commission:

$217,000 (sales price) x 6.25 (commission rate) = $13,562.50 (total commission)
$13,562.50 (total commission) ÷2 = $6,781.35 (commission to selling office)
$6,781.35 (commission to selling office) x .60 (agent's percentage) = $4,068.75

59. A – This is a math question that includes lots of irrelevant information. First, you must determine what is irrelevant. Unless the problem tells you otherwise, you can assume that it doesn't matter to the

seller how the commission is divided between the listing and selling companies, how much the advertising costs, and the amount of the buyer's origination fee. Then you must determine if a credit is something the seller receives or pays at the closing. A credit is received, not paid. Remember, that in most cases the seller will pay for the deed to transfer title.

$293,000 (sales price) x 5.75% (commission) = $16,847.50 (total commission)
$293,000 - $16,847.50 - $128,563.42 (mortgage payoff) - $125 (deed preparation) + $728 (prorated taxes received by seller) = $148,192.08 (net to seller)

60. D – Pinned and staked surveys include all permanent improvements, easements, and zoning requirements such as building lines and setback lines. Unattached improvements are not included on the survey, because their locations may change on the property or they may be removed altogether. All of the other responses are items that do appear on surveys.

61. C – Although there are certain exemptions to the fair housing laws that permit an owner to discriminate, those exemptions are lost once a licensee becomes involved in the transaction. Licensees should not take part in an owner's attempts to discriminate. Response "A" is incorrect, because a licensee is involved and the exemption is lost. Response "B" is incorrect, for the same reason as Response "A," but also because placing a sign in the yard is advertising. Response "D" is incorrect, because an agent must always follow his client's legal instructions, regardless of the marketing results. However, in this case, the instruction was illegal and should not be followed.

62. A – The agent should review the closing statement to protect her client's interest. Most buyers and sellers will not be able to read the closing statement. Response "B" is incorrect, because the agent does not need the copies and also because the client may not want his confidential information given to the agent. Response "C" is incorrect, because it is the lender, not the agent, who is responsible for having the loan documents prepared correctly. Response "D" is incorrect, because reviewing the deed is the practice of law.

63. B – In states that have dower/curtesy laws, the surviving spouse receives a one-half interest in the deceased spouse's property.

64. A – Under a land contract, the seller retains the legal title (the deed) and the buyer receives the equitable title (ownership rights) to the property. Response "B" is incorrect, because the seller only pays capital gains taxes on the amount of money received, not what is owed in the future. Response "C" is an incorrect statement. Response "D" is incorrect, because in most states, the seller under a land contract must foreclose on the buyer and cannot evict the buyer until the foreclosure is completed.

65. C – A graduated mortgage is one that has set increases in the payment over a period of time. The payments are applied first to principal then to interest. In the early years the payments may not pay all of the interest, in which event the interest is added to the amount of principal remaining. Response "A" is incorrect, because a growing equity mortgage is one that has increased payments over a period of time, and the additional payment is applied directly to the principal. Response "B" is incorrect, because a participation mortgage is one in which the mortgagee receives

repayment of the loan, but also receives a certain percentage of the cash flow that is produced by the property. Response "D" is incorrect, because a buy-down mortgage has the interest rate reduced, or bought down, in the beginning. The payment may change over a period of time if the buy-down of the interest rate is for a set amount of time, but this is not always the case.

66. B – Referral fees should be paid only to licensed brokers. Paying someone who is not licensed a referral fee violates the licensing laws in most states. Response "A" may be true, but the payment is illegal. Response "C" is not correct, because the surprise to her broker would not be nice when the licensing agent filed a complaint. Response "D" may or may not be true, but the payment is still illegal.

67. B – This is the definition of equity. Response "A" refers to the ratio of the mortgage loan to the property's appraised value or sales price, whichever is less. Response "C" refers to the process of buying mortgages for less than the balance due. Response "D" refers to the amount earned by a mortgage broker who obtains money at one rate and lends it at a higher rate.

68. C – The rate on an adjustable rate mortgage may increase over time, but most of them start out with a much lower rate than a fixed rate mortgage. If someone is not going to keep the mortgage for a long period, they could benefit from the lower upfront interest rate. Response "A" is incorrect, because the rate does not change and it doesn't benefit someone who is only keeping the loan for a short period. Response "B" is incorrect, because with a renegotiable rate loan the interest rate changes to the fixed rate at certain intervals. Response "D" is nonsensical.

69. B – When an owner allows his current mortgage to be assumed, he remains liable on the promissory note unless the lender agrees to give him a novation. A novation releases the owner from liability and accepts the new owner as the debtor. Response "A" is irrelevant to the question. Response "C" is correct in that it may make the property more marketable, but it still leave the problem of liability for the seller. Response "D" is an incorrect statement unless a novation is received from the lender for the seller.

70. A – The seller's mortgage that must be paid is a debit. A debit means that the seller has to pay the money at closing. Response "B" is incorrect, because a credit is something the party receives. Responses "C" and "D" are incorrect, because the seller's mortgage is neither a debit or credit to the buyer.

71. B – This is the definition of covenant of further assurances. Response "A" is incorrect, because this described the warranty of title. Response "C" is incorrect, because this described the warranty of seizin (also spelled seisin). Response "D" is incorrect, because this described the warranty of right to convey.

72. C – Anyone who takes title to property should have a title examination. There may be liens or other defects in the title that the current owner may not know about. Response "A" is incorrect, because it doesn't matter how long a person owns the property. A lien or other defect may last forever. Response "B" is incorrect, because having a title examination to make sure the title is marketable has nothing to do with the mortgage. The title examination is to protect the buyer. Response "D" is an incorrect statement of the law.

73.   A – This is a correct statement of the tax laws. The other responses are all incorrect statements of the law.

74.   B – This is the proper legal proceeding to remove a tenant. Response "A" is incorrect, because this refers to either a deed or lease in which the grantor or lessor guarantees the grantee or lessee the right to use the property without interference from a third party. Response "C" is a nonsensical term. Response "D" refers to the legal process filed by a lienholder to collect a debt from proceeds received from a foreclosure sale.

75.   C – Boundary problems can occur with a property, regardless of its age. Response "A" is correct in that agents may advise their clients on ways to avoid unnecessary expenditures, but a survey is not an unnecessary expenditure. Such advice may leave the agent liable to the client if the client suffers damage because of not getting a survey. Response "B" is correct in that the property may not have moved, but improvements on the property may have been added or re-positioned. Response "D" is incorrect, because agents should give clients needed information.

76.   C – A counteroffer is a rejection of an offer. Once a counteroffer is made, the original offer cannot be revived. Response "A" is incorrect, because once the counter occurs there is no offer for the original offeror to withdraw. Responses "B" and "C" are incorrect, because the expiration is irrelevant on a countered offer as the offer no longer exists.

77.   C – Most licensees associated with brokerages act as independent contractors. Response "A" is incorrect, because most licensees do not work as employees (they may do so, but it is the sponsoring broker's

choice). Response "B" may be correct in some situations, but the question asks for "most likely" and this is not a usual situation. Response "D" is incorrect, because a new licensee would not be a principal broker.

78.   C – Predatory lending is the type of lending engaged in by unscrupulous mortgage lenders whose main goals are to get the mortgage transaction closed regardless of the qualifications of the borrowers. This type of lending is designed to make money for the loan originator regardless of what happens to the mortgage in the future. Response "A" is incorrect, in that this is a term often used when lenders have a "special" program for first time homebuyers, senior citizens, and other underserved groups. Response "B" is the term often used by predatory lenders when they defend themselves. Response "C" is a term that lenders may use when advertising their ability to close transactions quickly.

79.   B – This is the stated primary purpose of the secondary mortgage market. Responses "A" and "D" are incorrect statements. Response "C" may be correct in some situations, but it is not the primary purpose.

80.   D – These are the parties to a deed of trust. The other responses are incorrect.

81.   B – The money paid to a landowner who has her property taken in a condemnation action is referred to as "just compensation." Response "A" is incorrect, in that the fair market value is defined as the price that a willing buyer would pay and a willing seller would accept with neither under duress. In a condemnation action, the landowner is not usually a willing seller and is likely under duress. Response "C" is incorrect, because it refers to the property

tax value of the property. Response "D" is incorrect, because, although the condemning authority has an appraisal, the appraisal is for condemnation purposes and not a transaction where the seller is a willing participant.

82. B – A deed or other legal document that is signed by someone who is mentally incompetent will not actually exist; therefore, it is said to be void. Mental competency is one of the required elements to form a contract. Response "A" refers to documents that may be voided by one of the parties. An example would be a contract that may be voided by a minor once the minor reaches majority age. Response "C" refers to a contract that a court will not enforce. A contract that does not have one of the required elements is void; therefore, there is nothing to enforce. Response "D" refers to a contract that is non-binding.

83. D – A person may choose her own agent. However, simply because someone has chosen an agent, they cannot force someone else to pay the agent. In this situation, the leasing agent would not be obligated to pay the tenant's agent. Response "A" is incorrect, because an agent cannot force representation on another person. Agency is a consensual relationship. Response "B" is incorrect. See explanation for Response "D." Response "C" is incorrect, because a written buyer broker agreement is not required in most states.

84. B – Inspections that a buyer wishes to make must be agreed upon by the seller. The time and place to get that agreement is in the sales contract. Response "A" may be correct in certain situations, but the agent should assess his risk in helping. Response "C" is incorrect in answering the question, but is a method often used by agents who want to assist clients. Response "D" may be

correct in certain situations, but this is a matter that should be negotiated as part of the sales contract.

85. C – Removing the light fixture before the listing is the best way to handle this situation. Otherwise, buyers are going to want to keep it and the seller may feel pressured to leave it. The other responses are ways to handle the situation, but not the best way.

86. C – Agents should listen to comments made by sellers and then follow-up. If FEMA was in the area, that would be a good indication of an federal emergency in the area. The other responses do not involve FEMA matters.

87. A – It is important for the agent to get all parties who must sign the deed at closing to sign the listing contract. Otherwise, once there is an offer or closing, the party who did not sign may refuse to sell the property. Response "B" is incorrect, because parties who don't want to list the property probably don't want to sell it. Response "C" is incorrect, because many times the parties named in the deed are not all of the current owners. Response "D" is incorrect for the above reasons.

88. B – Earnest money deposits must be held by the principal (sponsoring) broker. State laws regulate where and when the deposits must occur. Response "A" may be true in certain situations; however, if the money goes to the seller it must be clear in the contract that the seller, and not the broker, is holding the earnest money deposit. Responses "C" and "D" are incorrect in that the money should not be "held;" it should be deposited into the broker's trust (escrow) account.

89. C – Landlords may charge application fees, but should make sure the prospective tenant understands the purpose of the fee and understands that it is not refundable. Responses "A" and "D" are incorrect statements. Response "B" is incorrect, because charging the fee is not discriminatory. It may become discriminatory if the application fee is only charged to members of the protected classes.

90. A – This is a statement of RESPA's applicability. All of the other responses are incorrect statements.

91. A – As stated, the rule of thumb is that one discount point reduces the interest rate by approximately 1/8%. The other responses are incorrect.

92. A – Lost rent cannot be deducted on income tax returns. All of the other responses include items that are deductible on investment property.

93. C – By definition, extended coverage insurance covers events that are classified as acts of God. Responses "A" and "B" are the same type of insurance with different names. These policies may cover acts of Got, but not all of these policies have this coverage. Response "D" is insurance that covers injuries to person or property.

94. C – Barbara isn't licensed to practice law and therefore should not have prepared the form.

95. B – This is a clear example of illegal boycotting in violation of the Sherman anti-trust law. Brokers may decide on their own with whom to advertise, but getting together with one or more other brokers to make that decision violates the anti-trust laws. Response "A" is incorrect. Response "C"

may or may not be correct, but the action is illegal. Response "D" is incorrect because boycotting is not regulated by Regulation Z and the truth-in-advertising laws.

96. A – Property owned in survivorship belongs to the survivor(s) upon the death of one of the co-owners. The other responses are incorrect statements of the law.

97. A – Determining the net operating income is the goal when completing an operating budget. All of the other responses are used in preparing the operating budget.

98. B – Contract law is determined by state statutory and case law. Response "A" is incorrect in that federal law deals very little with contract law. Response "C" is partially correct in that state case law forms some contract law, but this is not the complete answer. Response "D" is incorrect, because administrative law only deals with contract to the extent real estate licensees are regulated. Again a partial answer. This question illustrates the necessity of reading the question carefully. Your answer should be the response that gives a complete, not a partial, answer.

99. B – Historically, savings and loan associations have been the largest source of mortgage financing. This trend has changed over the years. The other responses are all institutions that make mortgage loans.

100. D – This is a statement of the Farmer's Home Administration policy on discount points. Response "A" is incorrect, because the Farmer's Home Administration is not part of HUD. Response "B" is incorrect, because FmHA loans may be obtained directly. Response "C" is incorrect, because these are loans for rural properties.

Broker's Exam

1. B – Trust accounts hold money that belongs to clients and it is important that the funds in the account be protected. Good accounting practices require the account be balanced monthly. Response "A" is incorrect, because, by law, some trust accounts may be interest bearing accounts. Responses "C" and "D" are incorrect, because there no legal requirements for the broker to use a different bank or to close and re-open the account annually.

2. A – Licensing agencies require the sponsoring broker sign an agreement that the agency may audit the broker's trust accounts without notice to the broker. Responses "B" and "D" are incorrect, because there is no requirement that the sponsoring broker inform the agency of either the number of agents he expects to have affiliated with the brokerage or the amount of annual gross revenue. Response "C" is an example of a tricky question. You must read the question and the answer carefully. It is true that the broker must notify the licensing agency when the office address changes, but the question refers to "opening" a brokerage. This response indicates the brokerage is already open.

3. C – Most agents work as independent contractors. And, as independent contractors, they cannot be required to work a certain number of hours doing anything. If the policy manual requires affiliates to work a set number of hours for floor time, the IRS could challenge whether or not the agents were independent contractors or employees.

Responses "A" and "B" should be included in the policy manual to have a clear understanding of compensation and expenses. Response "D" should be included in the manual, because it not only confirms the brokerages commitment to fair housing laws, but also helps protect the broker from liability if an agent goes outside his scope of authority and violates the fair housing laws.

4. C – A nonrecourse loan is by definition a loan that prevents the lender from attempting to collect the debt personally from the borrower in the event the property is sold in foreclosure and does not bring enough to cover the debt. Response "A" refers to a veterans administration loan that guarantees the lender that any deficiency will be paid by the government's guaranty program. Response "B" refers to a loan that is either insured by FHA or a private mortgage insurer with an insurance premium that is paid by the mortgagor. In the event of a deficiency after a foreclosure, the insurer pays the lender and attempts to collect he deficiency from the borrower. Response "D" does not refer to a deficiency judgment, but to the re-ordering of mortgage priorities.

5. A – FHA loans are insured loans, not guaranteed loans. All of the other responses are true about FHA insured loans.

6. A – Writing anything in a contract is the practice of law. Most states allow licensed agents to complete form contracts that have been prepared and approved by attorneys. However, if the agent writes anything more than what is necessary to complete the blanks in the

form, she is practicing law without a license and could be held liable by a court or licensing agency. All other Responses are incorrect.

7. B – The right of the government to take personally owned property is known as the power of eminent domain. Response "A" is incorrect, because condemnation is the government's process, not the government's right. Response "C" refers to the legal standard for taking the property. That is, the government must prove it is for the common good of the community to take the property. Response "D" is incorrect because, although the governmental police powers include eminent domain, the phrase refers to much broader constitutional powers of the government. This is an example of a question that uses all of the rights terms to refer to a real estate principle, but you must read the question carefully to get the correct term to answer the specific question.

8. A – The Statute of Frauds requires that all real estate contracts be in writing and signed by the person to be charged. That is, if a person is selling or purchasing real estate, until he actually signs the contract, he cannot be required to buy or sell the property even if he verbally agreed to do so. Response "B" refers to the time someone has to bring a lawsuit against another person. This response shows that you must read carefully before answering the question. Response "C" is not correct because a real estate agent is not authorized to enter into a contract for the principal, and in the unlikely event the agent would be authorized to do so, the agent would need to sign the contract. A verbal acceptance by anyone is not binding. Response "D" refers to a legal

principle that is used to define terms in an ambiguous contract.

9. B – A credit on a closing statement is something the party receives and a debit on the closing statement is something the party pays. Because the seller has already received the money from the tenant and the buyer will own the property while the tenant is occupying the property, the buyer is entitled to have the money paid by the tenant. Therefore, the prorated rent would be received by the buyer, i.e. a credit, and would be paid by the seller, i.e. a debit. Don't forget that rent is paid in advance. Response "A" is incorrect, because it would give the money to the seller who already has the money. Response "C" is incorrect, because it would require both the seller and buyer pay the money to the other party, resulting in a non-proration of funds. Response "D" is incorrect, because both the seller and buyer would be receiving the money with neither one paying the money. These type questions are very confusing. If you have one on the test, think through it very carefully before answering.

10. A – This is a correct statement of the tax law. Response "B" is irrelevant as it relates to payment of taxes. However, a promissory note does secure the repayment of the debt and is very important to the seller in the event of a buyer's default. Response "C" and "D" are incorrect statements of the law. One overall point of this question is that the broker should NOT be giving tax advice. Clients who need tax advice should be referred to a tax professional.

11. B – One of the most important things for an agent to do is to treat all

parties the same. A good way to insure that every prospective tenant is treated the same is to ask each person the same questions, and a good way to make sure the same questions are asked is to have a standard application form. The other responses are incorrect, and actually may lead to allegations of discrimination.

12. A – Commercial property rental amounts are quoted annually based on a per square foot number. When the rent is quoted as $22.50 per square foot it means that it is based on an annual rental amount of $22.50 per square foot. That is important, because the first calculation you will make is the annual rent. However, because the questions asks for the monthly rent, you must divide by 12. You work this problem as follows: 1,485 (square footage) x $22.50 (amount per square foot) = 33,412.50 (annual rent) ÷12 (months in year) = $2,784.38. Response "B" is incorrect because the 8 and 7 are transposed. Be careful not to transpose numbers with math problems.

13. C – Under the fair housing laws, Landlords are required to make "reasonably achievable accommodations" for tenants. The phrase "reasonable accommodations" may also be used. A broker representing a client should be knowledgeable about the requirements of ADA, because compliance with the law is important for the both the owner and broker. Response "A" is incorrect, because making such an inspection is not the practice of law. Response "B" is incorrect, because although the local human rights commission may make such an evaluation, a property manager should be knowledgeable on ADA requirements. Response "D" is an

incorrect statement of the law. This response is informative for taking the test. Watch for questions that confuse two different laws. Obviously, the 1978 date refers to the lead-based paint disclosure law.

14. C – This type of math question calls for careful reading and application of several principles. First, the number of days to be used for the month is 28 (the actual number of days in February, because the question says to use a calendar year). Second, the number of days that will be owed by the tenant is not 15, but rather 16. The tenant pays for the day they take occupancy of the property. Once you determine the number of days, you should then prorate the two items that need to be prorated. Proration of rent: $1,350 (monthly rent) ÷ 28 (number of days in February) = $48.214 (per day – at this point round to three places). Then $48.214 (amount per day) x 16 (days) = $771. 42 (prorated rent). Proration of clubhouse fees: $50 (monthly fee) ÷ 28 (number of days) = $1.786 (per day). Then $1.786 (amount per day) x 16 (days) = $28.58 (prorated fees). Add: $771.42 (prorated rent) + $28.58 (prorated fee) + $850 (security deposit) + $1,350 (last month's rent) = $3,000.00. At this point, you do not see $3,000.00, but you do see $2,999.99 which is the correct answer. Because of rounding, your answer may be a few pennies off from the answer choices. Don't panic, choose the nearest number. If you use 15 days instead of 16 days, you will get Response "B." The easiest way to get the number of days correct is to count on your fingers. I know this is simplistic, but if you start with the occupancy date and count you will not miss the question.

15. D – Because state statutes have different requirements for what should be included in property management agreements, these agreements do not always contain the same information. However, it is clear that Responses "A," "B," and "C" are all basicly contract terms that would likely be included in the state statute. Response "D" is the correct answer, because not only are the names and addresses of current tenants irrelevant to an agreement between the owner and the broker, they are also confidential.

16. C – The Statute of Frauds requires that real estate contracts be in writing. An offer presented and accepted over the phone is not in writing as required. The offer may be in writing, but there are no written signatures. Response "A" is incorrect, and although a common practice among agents, it is a practice that can lead the agent to serious legal problems and should never be done. Responses "B" and "C" are incorrect statements of the law.

17. C – This is a good example of an agent who did not listen and did not ask enough questions. If the seller gives you any information about the property that is out of the ordinary, the agent must follow-up on that information. Response "A" is incorrect, because the listing agent did not have enough facts to form that opinion. Response "B" is incorrect, because the agent assumed facts that he didn't specifically confirm. Response "D" is incorrect, because if handled properly, the environmental concern may not impede the marketability of the property.

18. A – Because properties are staying on the market such a short period of time, it can be assumed that there are more buyers than sellers. Response "B" is incorrect, because a buyer's market would mean that properties were staying on the market for an unusually long period of time. A buyer's market is one in which there are more houses on the market than buyers who want them. Response "C" is incorrect, because it is unlikely that all agents would be under-pricing properties. Response "D" may be correct, but would not always be the reason properties are moving quickly.

19. A – Properties owned in joint tenancy with right of survivorship pass to the survivor regardless of what the deceased owner's will specifies. Ownership provisions in a deed cannot be changed by a last will and testament. The other responses are misstatements of the law.

20. B – State licensing laws require principal brokers (sometimes referred to as sponsoring brokers) to adequately supervise their agents. Simply hiring a manager to assist in those duties does not absolve the broker from those responsibilities. Responses "A" and "D" are incorrect statements of the law. Although not responsive to this question, Response "C" would be a prudent step for the broker to take when hiring a manager.

21. A – Sponsoring brokers set policy for their offices in all areas. Response "B" may be practically true, but the law in most states permit dual agency if that is the policy set by the broker. Response "C" is incorrect, because such a policy would have nothing to do with the fair housing laws. Response "D" is an incorrect statement.

22. A – Because the seller has paid the taxes in advance and will not own the property for the entire tax year, the buyer must refund the seller the amount owed for taxes while the property is owned by the buyer. In other words, the seller will receive a refund of the taxes paid when he will not own the property. If the seller receives the money, it will be paid by the buyer. On the closing statement, money received is a debit and money paid is a credit. Therefore, the prorated amount will be a credit to the seller and debit to the buyer. Response "B" is incorrect, because it has the buyer receiving money for taxes already paid by the seller. Responses "C" and "D" are not correct, because on a closing statement, when prorating taxes, there must be a debit and a credit shown.

23. C – When buyers and sellers trade houses the transaction is treated as two sales. Therefore, the total commission would be paid on both property. First, multiply $155,000 by 2 for a total gross sales price of $310,000. Then multiply $310,000 by 4.5% for a total commission of $13,950.00. Response "A" is incorrect, because there were two transactions and there would be some amount of commission due. Response "B" is incorrect, because that is the amount of commission for one transaction ($155,000 x 4.5% = $6,975.00). Response "C" is simply incorrect.

24. B – Plats must be recorded before they are enforceable. Unless the plat is recorded, there is no assurance that the property is subdivided as shown on the plat. All of the other Responses contain important information, but not the most important.

25. C – The personal representative (executor or administrator) of an estate must be appointed by a court of competent jurisdiction before she can act for the estate. Agents must ask for proof that the court has appointed the personal representative before allowing that person to sign the listing or sales contract. Response "A" is incorrect, because it is the court and not the family that makes the appointment. Responses "B" and "C" are incorrect statements of the law.

26. C – When measuring a house you can not include any square footage in a level that has any part of that level below grade. Response "A" is incorrect, because the quality of finish does not change the fact that the level is below grade. Response "B" is incorrect, because the question is about gross living area, not total livable area. Response "D" is incorrect, because it is a misstatement of the real estate principle that below grade square footage is not included in gross living area.

27. A – This is a trick question. You must read it closely. The amount to be credited (received) by the seller is $210,000. The other numbers will appear as debits (paid) on the closing statement. The closing date is also irrelevant. The other Responses are numbers reached by subtracting the seller's expenses to reach the seller's net proceeds. That is not the question. Read carefully.

28. C – Agents should never use someone else's work to make representations. In this case the builder may have deviated from the plans, resulting in incorrect square footage. Responses "A," and "B" are incorrect,

because one would assume the builder's plans contain accurate information, but an agent should not assume this when making representations about the property. Response "D" is incorrect, because whether or not the plans could be used by any owner after the first owner is a matter of state law and not a judgment call the agent should make.

29. C – This is a classic example of external obsolescence (sometimes referred to as locational obsolescence). With this form of obsolescence something is happening outside the property boundary that affects the property negatively. Response "A" and "B" refer to two other types of obsolescence. Response "D" refers to the method for calculating depreciation of investment property.

30. B – To answer this question, you must have a listing price that will net the seller $176,000, plus pay the real estate commission. First subtract 6.5% from 100% to get 93.5%. Remember when you are trying to calculate the net to the seller after your commission, you must subtract the amount of commission from 100%. Next, divide $176,000 by 93.5% = $189,247.31. The house must be listed for at least $189,247.31 and the nearest amount that is more than the amount needed is $188,500. In this question it is irrelevant that houses generally sell for 98% of their listed price. The seller has said he will negotiate; therefore, he is looking for 100% of the list price.

31. C – Because many subdivisions have restrictions prohibiting certain uses of the property, agents should help the buyer ascertain whether or not the buyer's intended use violates any of

those restrictions. Response "A" sounds logical, but does not address the problem of whether or not the RV can be parked on the property. Response "B" would be a good idea, but many times sellers are not aware of specific restrictive covenants on their properties. Response "D" is a bit of comic relief and wrong.

32. D – Loyalty is the fiduciary duty that requires an agent to look out for the best interest of his client above all others, including his own. Response "A" is the fiduciary duty confidentiality which requires the agent to guard a client's confidential information forever, even when the transaction is complete. Response "C" is the fiduciary duty that requires the agent to work as hard and do as good of a job for the client as any other agent would do.

33. B – A remainderman is the person who receives title to property when the life tenant dies. Response "A" refers to title that reverts back to the grantor or the grantor's heirs for some reason. Response "C" is the person who transfer's title and Response "D" is the person that receives title to property.

34. D – The seller disclosure forms used in several states are designed to have the seller give the buyer information known to the seller about the property. In addition to giving the buyer information, the forms are also designed to protect the agent from liability. In this question, when the agent completed the form, the buyer did not receive notice that the seller had not completed the form and the agent did not receive liability protection. Response "A" is incorrect, because there is no fiduciary duty for the agent to disclose information she does not have. Response "B" is incorrect,

because, although agents should make a visual inspection of the property for defects they can see, an agent is not required to be knowledgeable enough about property condition to see everything that may be wrong with the property.

35. D – The facts of this question indicate that the agent was practicing law without a license, and practicing it badly. If an agent gives wrong advice that damages a client, both the agent and his sponsoring broker may be liable. Responses "A," and "C" are incorrect, because, once again, the agent is practicing law. Using a form from another transaction does not make the agent's actions appropriate. Response "B" is an incorrect statement of the law.

36. B – Sponsoring brokers must make all business decisions for his firm independently. When a broker consults, discusses, or conspires with other brokers to set commissions, advertising policies, and other business practices, he is violating anti-trust laws.

37. A – This question should be read carefully. It specifically states that the broker is closing the transaction. In this scenario it is appropriate for the agent to get the seller's social security number, because she must report the sale to the IRS for capital gains purposes. Brokers should not collect anyone's social security number unless they are absolutely positive they need it. Response "B" is incorrect, because brokers are not required to determine if someone is a US citizen. However, in states that have escheat statutes for foreign nationals, agents should be aware of those statutes and should advise non-citizen buyers to seek legal advice before purchasing real estate. Response "C" is not correct; however, once collected for a legitimate purpose, it should be used only for that purpose and should be kept confidential. Response "D" is incorrect, because, in fact, brokers who perform real estate closings have certain IRS reporting requirements.

38. C – The settlement agent is the party ultimately responsible for having correct information on the settlement statement. Response "A" is not a legal requirement, but a prudent buyer would review the statement. Response "B" is not correct for the answer to this question, but professional mortgage brokers will review the closing statements prior to closing. Response "D" is incorrect; however, many courts are requiring that real estate agents review the statements for correctness and are holding the agents liable for mistakes.

39. B – Because agents are independent contractors, the principal broker cannot exercise much control over their activities. As independent contractors they are "independent" and decide when to work, what meetings to attend, and how to do their work. The other Responses are activities the principal broker can require, because they are mandated by license law.

40. D – The formula for determining the area of a triangle is ½ bh (1/2 base times height). To work this problem: .50 (½ in decimal form) x 250 (base) x 665 (height) = 83,125 (square feet) ÷ 43560 (number of square feet in one acre) = 1.9 acres.

41. D – An encroachment is an improvement that crosses a boundary line which makes it an encumbrance not

268

an easement. The other Responses are all types of easements.

42. B – The agent is legally responsible for asking the seller to complete the form if the house was constructed before 1978. Response "A" is a good idea, but not legally required. Response "C" is incorrect, but seller knowledge does not determine when the form is required. Response "D" is incorrect, because whether or not the seller is willing to remove the paint is irrelevant under the federal law.

43. B – Not only is it not a good practice to include an automatic continuation clause in the listing contract, in most states it is illegal to include such a clause. Response "A" is good clause to include, because it protects the agent from the seller selling the property to someone, after the listing expires, who was introduced to the property during the term of the listing. A fair housing clause as stated in Response "C" is not required by law, but is certainly a good clause to include to show the seller that the agent supports fair housing. It is good practice to include a lock box clause in the listing contract as stated in Response "D," because it is important for the seller to agree that the lock box can be placed on the property.

44. B – To find the capitalization rate, divide the annual net income by the fair market value of the property. $58,000 (annual net income) ÷ $750,000 (fair market value) = 7.73%. The gross annual income and the depreciation information are irrelevant.

45. C – Investment property that is sold under a lease must be sold with "landlord's possession." That means that the lease must be honored by the new owner and the tenant continues under the same terms. The exception would be if the tenant's lease contains a clause that terminates with the new owner (a most unusual clause). The other Responses are misstatements of the law.

46. B – The party without representation is the customer of the agent. Response "A" is incorrect, because the client is represented. Responses "C" and "D" may or may not be correct, depending on the relationship between the agent and the buyer or seller.

47. A – By definition a PUD is a combination form of ownership, because the lots are owned by individuals and the common area is owned by the development's association. Response "B" is incorrect, because PUD ownership and condominium ownership are different. In a PUD, the association owns the common area, while in a condominium the unit owners own a percentage share of the common area. Response "C" is incorrect, because in a cooperative form of ownership, a corporation owns the real estate and the owners own a share of the corporation. Response "D" is nonsensical.

48. A – The economic principle of transferability is important to an owner who may need to sell the property in a short period of time. A property that is not easily transferable would not be a good investment for someone who may need to sell quickly. Response "B" is incorrect, because, although utility is one of the value principles of real estate, any house suitable for them to live in will meet that criteria. Response "C" is

irrelevant, because it is unlikely a property will appreciate much in that short time period. Response "D" is important, but it is not considered a value aspect.

49. B – By definition, when a property is insured for replacement cost, if it is completely destroyed the insurance carrier will pay the full face amount of the insurance, not the cost to replace the property. Responses "A" and "D" are incorrect, because the cost to replace to the house and contents is irrelevant to the insurance company. If a property is underinsured, which is the problem here, the insurance company will not pay more than the face amount of the policy. Response "C" is the replacement cost of the house minus the contents – an irrelevant number for this problem. The response does show how the test writers arrive at certain responses. A test taker that does not understand the principle may select the wrong answer, because it seems "logical." Don't be tricked.

50. A – A triple net lease means that the tenant pays the property taxes, the property insurance, and the maintenance costs. This type of lease increases the net income to the owner. Response "B" is incorrect, because a percentage lease increases the base rent paid by the tenant and does not affect the cost to the owner. This is an example of a Response that may seem reasonable (more rent for the owner), if you have not read the question carefully. The question asks about costs, not about income. Responses "C" and "D" are both irrelevant to the owner's costs and are not responsive to the question.

51. B – This is a simple math question, as long as you don't misread it. The total rent quoted is for a 3-year lease not a 1-year lease. Divide $31,500 by 36 for a monthly rent of $875.00. Response "A" is a transposition of the numbers in the correct answer. Response "C" is a transposition of the correct answer if you use one year and not three years. Response "D" is the answer if you use one year and not three years. Because test writers know where you will make a mistake on math question, they will include those wrong answers as selections. You will see your answer and think you are correct.

52. A – A special warranty deed limits the time period for the warranties in the deed. Because the government only wants to warrant the title for the time period it owns the property, a special warranty deed is used. Response "B" is incorrect, because the government would not want to use a general warranty deed that contains warranty prior to the government taking title to the property. It is unlikely that the government would use a quit claim deed as stated in Response "C," because a buyer would be hesitant to take a quit claim deed with no warranties. The straw man deed Response "D" is used to either conceal the true parties or to change the form of ownership, neither of which would be appropriate when the government is conveying the property.

53. A – An option to purchase contract is a unilateral contract, because only one party, the seller, is obligated to perform. Response "B" is incorrect, because a bilateral contract requires both parties to perform. Response "C" is incorrect, because an option to purchase contract is not an executed contract until the buyer exercises his option. Response "D" is nonsensical.

54. C – Although there is no legal prohibition about real estate agents lending money for mortgages, as long as their state statutes are followed, of the responses listed, the agent is the least likely one to make the loan. Response "A" may appear to be the least likely, but it is more likely that the seller would carry the financing when they sell their property than the real estate agent.

55. B – In order for a veteran to re-use her eligibility, the buyer must use his eligibility when assuming the loan. Responses "A" and "D" are irrelevant to the question. Response "C" is a misstatement of the law.

56. C – The escalation clause in the promissory note and mortgage is the clause that allows the rate to increase. An acceleration clause (Response "A") refers to the clause that is necessary in a mortgage or lease to permit the mortgagor or lessor to declare the entire balance due and payable when a default has occurred. Prepayment clauses (Response "B") is the term in a promissory note and mortgage that states whether or not the borrower may pay off the debt before it is due. A subordination clause (Response "D") reverses the order of lien priorities.

57. D – Although all of the responses may be things that agents would enjoy receiving from their broker, this Response is the one that is most beneficial to them. Agents, whether they have been in the business for a short period or a long one, often need help in situations that arise daily. A sponsoring broker who is available is a valuable asset for the agents in the office.

58. A – Good accounting principles recommend that more than one person be involved in writing the checks, signing the checks, and balancing the accounts. It is too easy for someone who has complete control to embezzle money from the accounts. Response "B" is incorrect, because there is no requirement for two signatures on a trust account. However, this is a good idea. Response "C" is not correct, because a report written by the person who is in complete control of the accounts is no guarantee that the accounts are being handled properly. Response "D" is incorrect, because bonding companies require good accounting practices. If there is a claim and those practices have not been followed, the company may not pay any loses.

59. C – By definition, property that is pledged to secure repayment of a debt is known as collateral. Response "A," an appurtenance, is anything that is attached to the land. Responses "B" and "D" are other terms for personal property.

60. B – A securities license is required when one person is advising a group of people on pooling money to make an investment. Someone giving legal advise is required to have a license to practice law (Response "A"). The broker who is authorized to run a real estate brokerage by the licensing agency is some states must have a principal broker's license (Response "C"). Bankers need banking licenses (Response "D").

61. C – These three parties are the ones that must sign the HUD-1 closing statement. Unless the real estate agents, real estate brokers, and mortgage brokers are acting in the dual role of either the

buyer, seller, or settlement agent, they do not sign the statement.

62. B – To work this problem, you must first remember that land value is not depreciated. Therefore, subtract the land value of $175,000 form the total value of $975,000. Then, divide the $975,000 by 39 years, the number of years the property will be depreciated. $975,000 - $175,000 = $800,000 ÷ 39 – $20,512.82. Response "A" is found by dividing the land value by 39 years. Response "C" is found by dividing the total value by 39 years. Response "D" is found by adding the total value to the land value then dividing by 39 years. Notice that you can arrive at the other three Responses by working the problem incorrectly. Remember, just because your answer matches one of the choices doesn't mean you have the correct answer. The test writers know where you will go wrong and supply you with an answer.

63. C – The key to this question is the type of listing. With an open listing, the seller retains the right to sell the property without paying the commission. In order for Response "A" to be correct, the listing would have had to be an exclusive right to sell listing. Response "B" would only be correct, if the listing was an exclusive right to sell listing that provided for a reduction in commission if the seller sold the property himself. Response "D" is simply incorrect.

64. C – Because it is unlikely, based on the CMA, that the property would sell for enough to pay the sellers expenses, plus the real estate commission, he should discuss it with his broker. Agents must look at the reality of situations before taking listings that will likely lead

to problems. This is a good example of when it's a good idea to talk to the principal broker. Response "A" is not helpful, because selling the property quickly will not make it worth more. Response "B" will be a waste of time, because a property is only worth what it's worth. Response "D" is not a good solution, because real estate agents should not be practicing law. Calling the mortgage company to negotiate a lower pay-off would be practicing law.

65. A – Because an encumbrance stays with the property, it will affect the title for the new buyer (this is also why Response "D" is incorrect). Responses "B" and "C" are incorrect statements of the law.

66. A – Agents should provide a marketing plan to the seller to show the seller how the agent intends to get the best price for the seller in the shortest amount of time. Although agents will promote their company as suggested in Response "B," that is not going to be the one thing that swings the buyer in the agent's favor, because all agents make that statement. Response "C" will lead to a disappointed seller and agent – a property is worth what it's worth. As suggested in Response "D" the broker can set her company commission rate lower than the competition, but this may not be the one thing that gets the seller's listing.

67. A – This is a correct statement of the appraisal standards. The other responses are incorrect statements of the appraisal standards.

68. B – Unless the seller specifically gives the agent permission to leave prospects at a property unattended (a

rather unlikely event), an agent should never leave prospects in the property alone. Response "A" may be correct, but it is not the main problem. Response "C" may be correct, but it still not appropriate to leave them alone at the property. Response "D" is an incorrect statement of the seller's position.

69. C – The sponsoring broker sets policy for his office that the agents must follow. Not using the approved form violates office policy, but is not illegal. Responses "A" and "B" are true statements, but are not responsive to the question. Response "D" is simply incorrect.

70. B – This is a math problem with several steps. Take your time in working the problem. First, find the total income for a month: 60 (units) x $985 (monthly rent) = $59,100 (monthly gross rent). Then, calculate the gross rent after vacancy: $59,100 (gross rent before vacancy) x .95 (if vacancy rate is 5%, then occupancy rate is 95) = $56,145 (gross rent after vacancy). Then, find the gross rent for the year: $56,145 x 12 (months) = $673,740 (gross rent for year after vacancy). Calculate the vending machine income for the year: $600 x 12 = $7,200 (vending income for the year). Calculate the fixed expenses: $30,141 x 12 = $361,692 (fixed expenses for the year). Begin with the gross income after vacancy, add the vending machine income, and subtract the fixed expenses: $673,740 + $7,200 - $361,692 = $319,248 (projected operating income for the year).

71. D – This is a fair housing question, an example of discrimination based on familial status, and an example of

steering. Property managers must not look at a prospective tenant and decide the best place for the tenant to live. Each person has a right to choose where he wants to live, and in this example, if the prospect wanted to live near the pool, even if he has small children, he has a right to make that decision. The other responses all violate the fair housing laws.

72. A – The date and time of recording establishes the lien priority. People often think the federal or state tax liens take priority over privately held liens – they do not.

73. B – This is an example of a vendor's lien. The other Responses are examples of seller financing, those documents are not contained in the deed.

74. B – Although all of the Responses are functions of a sponsoring broker, by law, the main duty of the sponsoring broker is to supervise the associates.

75. C – Compensation paid to an agent may not be paid by the seller. Agents must receive their commission through their sponsoring broker. All of the other Responses are examples of permissible compensation arrangements between the sponsoring broker and her agents.

76. C – A due-on-sale clause is placed in a mortgage to prevent the mortgagor from conveying the property without paying the balance of the debt owed to the mortgagee. The mortgagee has approved the mortgagor for credit and is not willing to take the risk that a new owner will pay the debt as agreed. Response "A" is incorrect, because, although mortgages often require money received by the mortgagor as a result of

something happening with the property be used to reduce the principal, that is not the situation in this question. An example of the mortgagor having to use money to reduce the principal balance would be if part of the property was taken in a condemnation action. Response "B" is incorrect, because mortgages cannot prohibit the mortgagor from conveying the property as long as the debt is paid. Response "D" may be a clause contained in some mortgages, but it would be very unlikely.

77. D – By definition, to obtain property insurance, the insured must have an insurable interest. Insurance companies do not sell insurance to people who do not stand to have a monetary loss if the property is damages or destroyed. Response "A" is incorrect, because someone can have an insurable interest that does not have title to the property. For example, a tenant has an insurable interest if the lease requires her to carry the insurance. Responses "B" and "C" give a person an insurable interest, but insurable interests may arise in other ways; therefore, these responses are not the best answer. Always look for the best answer when selecting among responses.

78. A – When representing clients, whether buyers or tenants, the agent should anticipate questions that will be asked and find out the answers. Response "B" is not being very helpful to the prospective tenant. Response "C" is incorrect, because although agents must always be aware of fair housing laws, that is irrelevant in this situation. Response "C" is incorrect, because although agents are always concerned about liability when giving their opinions, the location of the subway is a fact not an opinion.

79. A – Agents receiving compensation other than their real estate commission must disclose that information to the buyers and sellers. Disclosure is important when representing clients. Failure to disclose this information could easily be construed as a breach of fiduciary duty or a conflict of interest.

80. C – Although agents often know accounting principles, they must not practice accounting without a license to do so. A real estate license and/or classes on an accounting subject does not qualify the licensee to give accounting advise. Response "A" may be true, but is still not an appropriate answer. Response "B" is a misstatement of the fiduciary duty of accounting. The fiduciary duty of accounting refers to protecting funds that belong to a client. Response "D" is true in that it would be a material misrepresentation if the information is incorrect, but it is not the best answer for this question.

81. C – Sales contracts must be signed by the legally competent party. That is, the person with the right to sell or buy the property. If it is signed by someone who is not the competent party, the contract is invalid. The other Responses are incorrect statements of the law.

82. A – Because the ownership interests are not equal, the only way they could hold title is as tenants in common. The other forms of joint tenancy require the interests to be equal.

83. A – Building codes are written to require the builder to meet minimum standards. Penalties for violation of the

building codes are assessed against the builder. Discovery of building code violations may lead to disclosure and marketability problems for the seller and real estate agent, but they are not responsible under the law for violation of the building code unless, of course, they are also the builder.

84. A – By definition, a metes and bounds description must "close," meaning that the beginning point and the ending point must be the same point. Response "B" refers to a lot and block legal description. Response "C" refers to a government survey legal description. Many areas require the mailing address (Response "D") in a deed that uses a metes and bounds description, but that is not part of the description.

85. D – This was a net listing and is illegal in most states. All of the other Responses may be true, but that does not remove the fact that the net listing was inappropriate because it was likely illegal.

86. B – Because of the legal consequences to lessees who lease property that may have environmental problems, it is important for lessees to protect themselves from potential liability. Underground storage tanks are one item that often lead to lessee and lessor liability. Response "B" is partially correct, in that a chattel search should be conducted, but not by Chuck. Response "C" is incorrect, because the lessee needs to protect his own interests. Response "D" is an incorrect statement of the law; in fact, most of the time, trade fixtures do not stay with the property unless included in the lease.

87. B – When a seller wants to sell part of a larger parcel of real estate, the first thing the agent should advise is for the seller to obtain a survey that will how the boundaries of the land being sold. Response "A" is incorrect, because an appraiser cannot appraise the property without knowing its boundaries. Response "C" is good advice, but not the best advice to get started. Response "D" may be true, but again, without a survey, an auctioneer would not know what was being sold.

88. A – When an agent makes a misrepresentation, both he and his broker may be liable. Response "B" is incorrect, because, although the broker did not make the representation, he is responsible for supervising the agent. Response "C" is correct, but not the best answer. Response "D" will be the defense used by Sam and his broker, but may not be the winning the defense.

89. C – A condominium association cannot pass bylaws that discriminate against owners or prospective owners, even if it claims the rule is to protect the other owners. Response "A" is incorrect, because although agents must follow the legal instructions of their principals, the principal's instructions in this scenario were illegal. Response "B" is correct in that prospective buyers need to know about association bylaws, but incorrect as a response to this question. Response "D" is incorrect, because the association is not required to make changes to the units. However, if the prospect purchased the unit and wanted to add fencing, that would likely be a reasonable accommodation that the association could not prohibit.

90. C – Real estate agents must use form contracts. Response "A" is incorrect, if the agent is not a party to the contract. A party may draft his own contract, but in this question the agent was not a party. Response "B" is incorrect, because it is irrelevant if a fee is paid for the service. Response "D" is incorrect, because no one can approve an agent practicing law without a license.

91. B – Offers and counteroffers may be withdrawn before they are accepted regardless of the expiration time on the offer or counteroffer. The expiration time is when the offer expires and can no longer be accepted by the offeree. It is not a guarantee the offeror will leave the offer or counteroffer open for that period of time. Response "A" is incorrect, because there is no waiting period for withdrawing an offer of counteroffer. Responses "C" and "D" are misstatements of the law.

92. A – Corporations may hold title to real estate. When corporations hold title, the name of the corporation, and not the shareholder's name, is in the deed. In some states Response "B" would be illegal for an agent to do, and in all states it would be risky for the real estate agent. There are other types of agents who may buy property in this manner, but that discussion is beyond the scope of this examination. Response "C" would certainly not be the best idea, because all states have laws on how a minor child can hold property. Response "D" would be a way to hold title, but the legal documentation for a trust is typically much more complex than for a simple corporation.

93. B – One of the best ways for an agent to be successful in the real estate business is to have informed buyers. An informed buyer is more likely to purchase property and less likely to sue the agent after the transaction closes. Responses "A" and "D" are important steps, but not the first step in successfully representing buyers. Response "C" is becoming more and more important, because of safety issues for real state agents. However, this isn't the best response, because it will not be necessary in every case.

94. C – To calculate the rate of return, you must calculate the potential gross income (monthly rent x 12), then subtract the projected vacancy, then subtract the expenses and debt service, then divide by the equity. In this question: $1,125 (monthly rent) x 12 (months) = $13,500 (annual projected income) $13,500 (annual projected rent) x .99 (occupancy rate) = $13,365 (rent after vacancy) $13,365 (rent after vacancy) x .92 (after 8% expenses for year) = $12,295.80 (rent after vacancy and expenses) $750 (monthly debt service) x 12 (months) = $8,400. $12,295.80 (rent after vacancy and expenses) – (8,400) debt service = $3,895.80 (net income) $3,895.80 (net income) ÷ $22,000 (cash investment or equity) = .0175 x 100 = 17.5%

95. B – The broker should recognize the fact that there may be capital gains tax consequences to selling the property. Although brokers should not advise on tax matters, unless they are also CPAs, they should recognize the issue and recommend the client seek accounting advice. The other Responses are marketing statements and only the opinion of the broker.

96. C – Lender's title insurance is for the protection of the lender and not the buyer. There may be defects in title that would affect the buyer, but not the lender. If the defect does not affect the lender, the title insurer will not become involved in the dispute over the defect. Response "A" is incorrect, because the attorney may or may not liable. The attorney's liability is determined by the type of defect and who the attorney was representing when performing the title examination. Response "B" is incorrect and explained above. Response "D" is incorrect, because a title examination must be performed before a title insurance policy is written.

97. A – this is a correct statement of the covenant of warranty forever. Response "B" is incorrect, because the obligation to pay legal fees only arises if the claim dispossess the owner of the title. Response "C" is incorrect, because payment of legal fees must relate to a claim against the title. Response "D" is incorrect because if legal fees are payable they include those that arose prior to grantor's ownership.

98. A – One of the elements required for a contract is offer and acceptance. The offeree must accept what the offeror is offering. In this scenario, the buyer thought he was purchasing three mobile homes and the seller thought he was selling two mobile homes. It is possible that a court could rule there was no offer and acceptance, and without offer and acceptance there is no contract. Response "B" is incorrect, because the consideration in the contract is not the issue in this situation. Response "C" is incorrect, because a buyer is not required to perform a defective contract. Response "D" raises issues on what

should have been discussed between the parties, but is not the definitive answer for this question.

99. D – With a partially amortized loan, the payments do not contain enough principal to reduce the debt to zero on the last payment. Failure to fully amortize the loan will result in a balloon payment. Neither of the other Responses are necessarily true with a partially amortized loan.

100. C – This is a math problem with a number of steps. First find the amount of the loan: $185,000 (purchase price) x .75 (loan to value ratio) = $138,750 (loan amount). Subtract the $138,750 from the $185,000 = $46,250 (the amount of the down payment). Now determine the closing costs (remember that closing costs are calculated on the loan amount, not the purchase price). $138,750 (loan amount) x .05 (closing costs) = $6,937.50. This brings you to the total cost to the seller: $46,250 (down payment) + $6,937.50 (closing costs) = $53,187.50. Now subtract the credits for the buyer: $53,187.50 - $2,000 (earnest money deposit) - $1,500 (repair credit) = $49,687.50. Response "D" is incorrect, because it does not subtract either the earnest money or repair credit.

Note: There are no additional key term match exercises for Professional Responsibilities, Fair Practice/Administrative

Listing Property 1

Terms

A. Below grade

B. Building code

C. Constructive notice

D. Alluvion

E. Brokerage fee

F. Clear title

G. Evidence of title

H. Certificate of Occupancy

I. Building permit

J. Bylaws

K. Deed

L. Assessed value

M. Anti-trust Laws

Definitions

1. _____ The notice to the world given by recording documents in the county clerk's office in the county where the real property is located.

2. _____ A fee paid to a real estate broker for services relating to the sale or purchase of property.

3. _____ The part of the improvement that is built below ground level.

4. _____ Sand, soil and gravel that are deposited along the banks of flowing water.

5. _____ A legal document used by condominium associations, homeowner's associations, corporations, and incorporated associations that includes the rules, regulations, and management processes that will be followed by the organization and its members.

6. _____ The value placed on property by the property valuation administrator on which the annual property tax is based.

7. _____ Governmental regulations that establish the minimum requirements for building construction in the area.

8. _____ Federal and state laws that are designed to keep the market place competitive by preventing collusion among providers of goods and services who may unlawfully attempt to restrain trade by fixing prices, boycotting, and creating monopolies.

9. _____ Document that must be obtained by a property owner from the local government before constructing an improvement on the land.

10. _____ Document that must be obtained from the local government once construction is complete to show that the property has been built in compliance with the building code.

11. _____ The written instrument signed by the grantor conveying real property to the grantee.

12. _____ A system for measuring land that uses principal meridians and baselines to create quadrangles and townships. Also referred to as the rectangular survey method.

13. _____ A written legal document that shows

N. Cloud on title

O. Government Survey legal
    description

ownership of property.

14. _____ A defect in the title to property that would
make it unacceptable to a grantee, and would keep a court
from compelling a buyer to accept it if the contract
provides for a marketable title.

15. _____ Title to real property that does not contain
defects or other conditions that would be
objectionable to a grantee. Sometimes referred to as
a clean title or a marketable title.

Listing Property 2

Terms

A. Zoning

B. Percolating water

C. License

D. Exclusive Right to Sell
Listing

E. Littoral water

F. Front foot

G. Assessment

H. Listing contract

I. Exclusive Agency Contract

J. Lien

K. Gross living area

L. Judgment

M. Ad Valorem taxes

N. Easement by prescription

O. Improvement

Definitions

1. _____ A listing contract in which the broker is entitled to a commission regardless of who sells, including the seller.

2. _____ Water along land bordering a sea or ocean that is affected by the tides.

3. _____ Government process used to control the way land is used by the owner.

4. _____ The final decision and order of the court stating which party wins the legal action and the amount of any damages owed.

5. _____ Lineal footage running along the front property line that will always be stated first when giving property dimensions.

6. _____ Water that collects underground.

7. _____ An encumbrance on real estate that gives a third party a claim against the property.

8. _____ An easement that arises when someone claims an easement over the objections of the property owner.

9. _____ A listing contract that grants the broker the right to market real property while the owner retains the right to sell the property without paying the broker a fee.

10. _____ Total livable square footage in an improvement that is above grade level.

11. _____ The agreement between the seller and broker retaining the broker's services to sell the real property that is the subject of the agreement.

12. _____ The value placed on property by the property valuation administrator on which the annual property tax is based.

13. _____ Annual property taxes that are collected by the property valuation administrator that are used to help support state and local governments as well as the school systems.

14. _____ (1) State authorization to practice real estate brokerage. (2) The term used to describe the relationship between a property owner and another person who is using the property for a specific purpose.

15. _____ Any structure built on the land that is designed to add value.

Listing Property 3

Terms

A. Principal broker

B. Restrictive covenants

C. Agency relationship

D. Multiple listing service

E. Open listing

F. Grantor

G. Subdivision restrictions

H. Independent contractor

I. Reliction

J. Road frontage

K. Grantee

L. Homeowners association

M. Fair market value

N. Master Deed

O. Net listing

Definitions

1. _____ The broker in the office who is responsible for managing the brokerage and supervising the affiliated real estate licensees.

2. _____ Limitations, that run with the land, placed on the land by grantors that restrict how the land may be used in the future.

3. _____ The party that conveys title to real property by deed.

4. _____ The party that receives title to real property by deed.

5. _____ The value of property determined by negotiations between a willing seller and a willing buyer when both are knowledgeable, prudent, and neither is acting under duress.

6. _____ In this contract the seller agrees to pay a commission to any broker that sells the property, but retains the right to sell the property himself and not pay a commission.

7. _____ A person retained to perform a certain service for another who is not an employee and who is neither under the direction nor control of the person receiving the services.

8. _____ A group of real estate brokers who agree to cooperate with each other by sharing access to their listings, and agree to compensate the cooperating brokerage that actually sells/leases the property.

9. _____ A listing, illegal in most states, that pays the seller a minimum amount and sets the broker's commission as all money received over that amount.

10. _____ The governing document for a condominium or homeowner's association.

11. _____ Footage that runs along the front of the property along a highway, road, street, or other passageway.

12. _____ Limitations, that run with the land, that are placed on land when it is subdivided by the developer.

13. _____ A legal relationship in which one party represents another party in dealing with a third party.

14. _____ The process of water receding from the land along the bank, effectively creating more land.

15. _____ The organization created by the subdivision covenants, or master deed in a condominium regime, comprised of the property owners who are charged with maintaining common areas and enforcing the restrictive covenants.

Listing Property 4

Terms

A. Square footage

B. Principal Meridian

C. Surface water rights

D. Township

E. Sponsoring Broker

F. Lot and Block legal description

G. Metes and Bounds legal description

H. Range

I. Legal description

J. Riparian water rights

K. Geodetic Survey legal description

L. Section

M. Meridians

N. Subdivision

O. Covenants

Definitions

1. _____ This term is used in two ways: (1) as the broker who is in charge of running the brokerage and supervising the licensed associates in the brokerage, sometimes referred to as the principal broker; (2) the broker who agrees to accept the sales associate into the brokerage once he passes the license examination.

2. _____ One of the measurements used in the government survey method that measures one square mile of land and contains 640 acres.

3. _____ An owner's right to use and re-direct water that flows across her land.

4. _____ The generic term used to describe real property so that it cannot be confused with any other parcel of land in the world.

5. _____ Process of dividing land into smaller parcels with the intention of conveying the parcels to other owners.

6. _____ Promises, that run with the land, between two or more owners in which each party agrees to perform or refrain from performing certain acts relative to the property.

7. _____ A legal description that describes the boundaries of the property that has a beginning point and an ending point, which two points must be the same.

8. _____ Used in the government survey method as the prime meridian for numbering ranges.

9. _____ A measurement of land used in the government survey method of legal description that is six miles wide, running both east and west of the principal meridian.

10. _____ The landowner's rights to use water that flows by or through his land.

11. _____ A system for measuring land that includes bench marks that are located by latitude and longitude.

12. _____ Land description that identifies parcels of land designated on a plat by the lot number, block, and subdivision name.

13. _____ Measurement of land or improvement that is calculated by multiplying the length times the width.

14. _____ Lines that run north and south used to describe property in the government survey method.

15. _____ One of the measurements in the government survey method that is a six-mile square containing 36 one-mile- sections.

Listing Property 5

Terms	Definitions

Terms

A. Comparison approach

B. Income approach

C. Expectation value

D. Depreciation

E. Investment property

F. Cost approach

G. Fair market value

H. Appreciation

I. Comparables

J. Investment value

K. Split level

L. Two-story

M. Appraisal

N. Book value

O. Speculative value

Definitions

1. _____ Value of property for accounting purposes.

2. _____ Properties that have similar physical characteristics located nearby that have sold or leased in similar market conditions.

3. _____ Value of property based on assumption that changes are going to occur for the property being valued or for adjacent property that will either increase or decrease the value.

4. _____ The value of property determined by negotiations between a willing seller and a willing buyer when both are knowledgeable and prudent, and neither is acting under duress.

5. _____ Process for determining the fair market value of property by using its net income over its remaining economic life.

6. _____ Value of property to a purchaser who intends to hold the property to make a profit at some point in the future.

7. _____ Improvement on property that has two livable floors above grade.

8. _____ Decrease in value of property.

9. _____ Property purchased with the expectation of earning income or making a profit.

10. _____ Process for determining value of real property by calculating the amount of money needed to replace or reproduce it.

11. _____ An opinion of the fair market value of property placed on the property by using either the replacement cost, income, or comparative market analysis approach to appraising.

12. _____ Increase in the fair market value of property due to economic conditions.

13. _____ Process of comparing the subject property to other similar properties that have sold recently for the purpose of estimating the fair market value of the subject property.

14. _____ A house that has two levels directly over each other with one or more other levels adjacent to those two levels.

15. _____ The fair market value of property to a particular investor.

Listing Property 6

Terms

A. Market data approach

B. Incurable

C. Liquidation value

D. Physical depreciation

E. Scarcity

F. Physical deterioration

G. Appraiser

H. Curable depreciation

I. Utility

J. External obsolescence

K. Mortgage loan value

L. Functional obsolescence

M. Transferability

N. Value in use

O. Valuation

Definitions

1. _____ An economic principle that gives value to real property based on the usefulness of the property.

2. _____ Depreciation of property that is not reasonable or economically feasible to repair or correct.

3. _____ Fair market value of property for the purpose of obtaining a mortgage loan.

4. _____ Process for estimating the fair market value of property by comparing it to other properties that are similar and that have been leased or sold recently.

5. _____ Decline in value of property because the improvement has physically deteriorated.

6. _____ The economic principle that gives value to real property because it can be transferred from owner to another.

7. _____ Fair market value of property as it is currently being used.

8. _____ An opinion of value based on objective criteria.

9. _____ Incurable depreciation of property created by changes outside the property, including those of an economic, social, and environmental nature.

10. _____ Curable and incurable depreciation caused by outdated or poor design features.

11. _____ Fair market value of property sold at a distress.

12. _____ Reduction in use or value of a property because its physical condition has declined.

13. _____ One of the economic principles that increases the value of real property when it is in short supply.

14. _____ The person who renders an opinion on the fair market value of property.

15. _____ Determination that it is reasonable and economically feasible to make

Listing Property 7

Terms	Definitions

Terms

A. Steering

B. Spot zoning

C. Redlining

D. Buffer zoning

E. Planning

F. Nonconforming use
G. Fair Housing Act of 1968

H. Bulk zoning

I. Zoning ordinances

J. Aesthetic zoning

K. Police power

L. Blockbusting

M. Variance

N. Civil Rights Act of 1866

O. Zoning classification

Definitions

1. _____ Regulations created by zoning that keep land from being too densely developed in order to prevent overloading of public services and facilities.

2. _____ Local laws that implement and enforce the comprehensive plan.

3. _____ Zoning that requires a strip of land between adjacent incompatible land uses.

4. _____ An illegal practice of mortgage lenders in which the companies refuse to make loans in a certain area, not because of the creditworthiness of the borrowers, but because of the area where the property is located.

5. _____ Use of property that does not conform to the current zoning classification but that is permitted to remain for a period of time because it existed before the zoning designation was changed.

6. _____ The specific zoning designation for each area.

7. _____ The process of rezoning a small parcel of land that lies in an area with a different zoning designation.

8. _____ An illegal practice of channeling home purchasers or renters to certain areas for the purpose of violating fair housing laws.

9. _____ An illegal tactic used to encourage owners in an area to sell their property by informing them that there will be a change in the neighborhood relating to the race, religion, sex, color, or national origin of new people purchasing property in the area.

10. _____ An agency of local government organized to develop a master plan for the use and development of the land.

11. _____ The law that prohibits discrimination in housing based on the protected classes of race, color, religion or national origin that has been amended to add sex, handicap, and familial status as protected classes.

12. _____ The constitutional right of the government to adopt and enforce laws that promote the public health, safety and welfare.

13. _____ Zoning designation designed to benefit property by keeping it attractive instead of zoning it for a certain utility.

14. _____ This is the first federal law written to prevent racial discrimination.

15. _____ Permission by the appropriate governmental body to use the land in a manner not permitted under its zoning classification.

Listing Property 8

Terms

A. Leasehold interest

B. Estate for Years

C. Transfer taxes

D. Prorated taxes

E. Deed restrictions

F. Settlement

G. Leasehold estate

H. Limited service brokers

I. Estate at will

J. Lock box

K. Estate from period to period

L. Lead based paint disclosure

M. Estate at sufferance

N. Extender clause

O. Comparative Market Analysis

Definitions

1. _____ The federal government requires that this form must be completed for properties built before 1978.

2. _____ The instrument placed on the door of a seller's house that holds the key

3. _____ A personal property right created by contract between the lessor and lessee that gives the lessee the right to possess and use the real property.

4. _____ The state tax that must be paid when property is conveyed.

5. _____ A tenancy created when the tenant occupies the property with permission of the landlord for an unspecified and uncertain period of time.

6. _____ The tenant's non-freehold interest in the property which gives the tenant the personal property right to use the land.

7. _____ A clause included in the listing contract that operates after the listing contract has expired obligating the seller to pay the real estate commission to the broker if the seller sells the property to a buyer who has been introduced to the property during the term of the listing.

8. _____ Division of property taxes between the seller and buyer based on their period of ownership.

9. _____ A method for determining the fair market value of real estate that compares a specific piece of property with similar properties that have sold in the same geographic area during a certain time period.

10. _____ Tenancy for a definite period that automatically renews at the end of the period.

11. _____ The tenancy created when a tenant wrongfully holds over after the termination of the lease without the landlord's consent.

12. _____ A term used to describe the time when the purchaser delivers the purchase price to the seller and the seller delivers the deed to the purchaser.

13. _____ A lease that has a definite beginning date and ending date.

14. _____ A business model in which the real estate brokerage provides certain services to the seller for a fee and the seller performs the remainder of the services necessary to market the property.

15. _____ Covenants contained in a deed that prohibits or requires the owner to use his property in a certain way.

Listing Property 9

Terms

A. Uniform Standards of Professional Appraisal Practice

B. National Flood Insurance Act of 1968

C. Capitalization rate

D. Fixed expenses

E. Operating expenses

F. Net Income

G. Replacement reserve

H. Federal Home Loan Mortgage Corporation

I. Fee for service brokerage

J. Operating Statement

K. Government National Mortgage Association

L. Federal National Mortgage Association

M. Federal Deposit Insurance Corporation

N. Net proceeds

O. Federal Emergency Management Agency

Definitions

1. _____ The largest secondary mortgage market.

2. _____ A secondary mortgage market for savings and loan associations.

3. _____ Expenses that do not vary.

4. _____ Standards of professional practice that must be followed by licensed and certified real estate appraisers relating to the development and communicating of appraisals.

5. _____ The rate of return on an investment stated as a percentage.

6. _____ This is a HUD agency that participates in the secondary mortgage market by financing special high risk government programs, including projects for urban renewal and housing for the elderly.

7. _____ A federal program that provides flood insurance for owners who have property damaged as a result of a flood.

8. _____ A federal agency that provides assistance in advising on building codes, flood plain management, preparing for disasters, training emergency managers supporting fire national fire service, administering flood and crime insurance, and assisting in disasters.

9. _____ Periodic expenses, that vary in amount, incurred for investment property, including utilities, management, maintenance, supplies, and professional fees.

10. _____ An independent agency within the executive branch of the federal government established to insure deposits held in nationally chartered banks.

11. _____ Income after all expenses and deductions are taken from the gross income.

12. _____ Amount of money that is due the seller once all costs and expenses are deducted from the gross sales price.

13. _____ Funds that are deposited by the property owners over a period of time and held for replacing assets as needed.

14. _____ A detailed statement showing the income and expenses of a business over a period of time.

15. _____ A brokerage practice in which the principal broker charges sellers and buyers a fee for services based on the individual service being performed.

Listing Property 10

Terms

A. Patent defect

B. Fixtures

C. Counteroffer

D. Lease

E. Trade fixtures

F. Licensee

G. Panic Peddling

H. Protection clause

I. Personal property

J. Intangible personal property

K. Bill of sale

L. Latent defect

M. Emblements

N. Real property

O. Licensor

Definitions

1. _____ Personal property that you cannot touch.

2. _____ A term in the listing contract which provides for the seller to pay the real estate commission to the broker if someone, who has been introduced to the property during the listing period, purchases the property during a specified period of time after the listing contract expires.

3. _____ (1) A person with either a broker or sales associate's license granted by the state regulatory agency, and (2) the person who enters into a license agreement with the owner of property.

4. _____ The illegal practice of making statements to property owners, either in writing or orally, that a member of a protected class is moving into the area for the purpose of depreciating property values.

5. _____ (1) The state regulatory agency that issues real estate licenses to brokers and sales associates, and (2) the owner of property that enters into a license agreement, allowing someone to use her property for a specific purpose.

6. _____ Personal property that becomes affixed to real property in such a way that it becomes part of the real property.

7. _____ All property in the world that is not real property.

8. _____ An obvious defect in property.

9. _____ The process in which an offer is made by the offeror that is not acceptable to the offeree, the offeree may reject that offer and make an offer back to the offeror.

10. _____ Personal property and equipment used in a trade or business that is affixed or attached to leased real estate in such a way that it becomes part of the real estate.

11. _____ Annual growing crops that may be harvested even if the property has transferred owners before time to harvest the crops.

12. _____ Hidden defects that may or may not be known to the owner, but not easily discoverable by the purchaser.

13. _____ An agreement, either oral or written, that creates a landlord and tenant relationship giving the tenant possession of the landlord's property.

14. _____ A document used to transfer personal property from one owner to another owner.

15. _____ The physical land, including what is beneath the surface and what is above the surface, as well as improvements attached on to the land.

288

Selling Property 1

Terms

A. Severalty

B. Limited partnership

C. Limited liability company

D. Concurrent ownership

E. Cooperative

F. Life estate *pur autre vie*

G. Condominium

H. Corporation

I. Life estate

J. Joint venture

K. Joint tenants with right of survivorship

L. Interval ownership

M. Joint ownership

N. General partnership

O. Co-tenant

Definitions

1. _____ Ownership of property by more than one person at the same time.

2. _____ Concurrent ownership of property by two or more people.

3. _____ A form of multiple ownership of property in which each owner owns a portion of the property individually and a portion of the property jointly in common with the other owners.

4. _____ Concurrent ownership of property by two or more people that passes to the survivor.

5. _____ A form of property ownership in which individuals own shares of a corporation which in turn owns the real estate.

6. _____ A form of condominium ownership in which the purchaser owns the property for a specified time interval each year.

7. _____ A legal entity that is created to afford liability protection to the shareholders.

8. _____ A business relationship created by contract, either written or oral, in which the partners share in the profits, losses, and management of the business.

9. _____ A co-owner of property.

10. _____ A general partnership formed for a specific business purpose that terminates once the project is complete.

11. _____ An estate in land that is limited to the duration of someone's life, known as the life tenant or measuring live.

12. _____ A business form with one general partner and one or more limited partners.

13. _____ A life estate that exists for the life of someone other than the life tenant.

14. _____ Individual or sole ownership of property.

15. _____ A business form that resembles a partnership that has the liability protection of a corporation.

Selling Property 2

Terms	Definitions
A. Risk of loss	1. _____ The holder of the life estate.
B. Common area	2. _____ In a life estate, the person whose life determines the duration of a life estate.
C. Real Estate Investment Trust	3. _____ A promise conditioned upon some requested or asked for act or promise, demonstrating the intent of one party to form a contract with another party.
D. Paint-to-paint	4. _____ An arrangement by which two or more people are assembled for the purpose of raising equity capital for purchasing real estate or other types of investments.
E. Bundle of rights	5. _____ Rights to property that is owned and occupied as a family home.
F. Counteroffer	6. _____ Ownership rights in land, including the degree, nature, quantity, and extent of the ownership interest, and including the owner's right to use, control and transfer the land.
G. Community property	7. _____ The wife's interest in her husband's property that he owns during their marriage.
H. Curtesy	8. _____ The husband's interest in his wife's property that the wife owns during their marriage.
I. Life tenant	9. _____ Property ownership in which each spouse has an equal interest in the property acquired by the efforts of either party during the marriage.
J. Syndications	10. _____ This phrase refers to all of the legal rights, interests, and privileges that an owner has in real property.
K. Measuring life	11. _____ Areas in a condominium, or other development with co-owners or co-tenants, that may be used by all co-owners or co-tenants.
L. Homestead rights	12. _____ When an offer is made by the offeror that is not acceptable to the offeree, the offeree may reject that offer and make an offer back to the offeror.
M. Offer	13. _____ A phrase used in condominium ownership that indicates that condominium owners own the inside of their units individually while owning everything beyond the paint in common with the other owners.
N. Estate in land	14. _____ An investment vehicle, made up of numerous individual investors, that holds title to real estate.
O. Dower	15. _____ This phrase refers to the person who bears the financial loss when property is destroyed by fire or other casualty.

Selling Property 3

Terms

A. Unities

B. Timeshares

C. Warranty

D. Tenants in common

E. Stigmatized property

F. Sales

G. Tenants by the entirety

H. Sole proprietorship

I. Planned Unit Development

J. Good faith deposit

K. Material facts

L. Financing contingency

M. Appraisal report

N. Default clause

O. Home inspector

Definitions

1. _____ A clause in a contract that specifically sets forth what will happen in the event one party to the contract fails to perform as agreed.

2. _____ A written report submitted by the appraiser to support and document her opinion of value.

3. _____ A contingency in a purchase/sale contract that allows the purchaser to terminate the contract if he can not obtain financing to purchase the property.

4. _____ A deposit made by the buyer when entering into a sales and purchase contract.

5. _____ Important fact that would influence a person's opinion and actions relative to entering into a contract and purchasing or selling real property.

6. _____ High density housing that provides for maximum use of common space where each owner owns the land under his unit while the common area is owned and maintained by the community association.

7. _____ The contract used by buyers and sellers to purchase and sell real estate containing the entire agreement between the parties.

8. _____ Property where an event has occurred that does not damage the physical property, but rather gives it a negative reputation.

9. _____ A form of business ownership in which one person owns the business.

10. _____ A promise or guarantee that certain facts are true.

11. _____ Joint ownership of real property by a husband and wife.

12. _____ The right to use and occupy property for a recurring block of time.

13. _____ Jointly owned property that does not include the right of survivorship.

14. _____ Common law requirements necessary to create concurrent ownership of property.

15. _____ A person who inspects real estate for the purpose of determining if there are defects in the property, including whether or not it meets minimum structural and code standards.

Selling Property 4

Terms

A. Lead based paint disclosure form

B. Disclosure of property condition form

C. Unity of Title

D. Unity of Time

E. Home protection plan

F. Surveyor

G. Property inspector

H. Unity of Possession

I. Survey report

J. Unity of Interest

K. Inspection report

L. Pinned and staked survey

M. Survey

N. Earnest money deposit

O. Appraiser

Definitions

1. _____The form, required by the federal government, completed by sellers or lessors of property built before 1978, that discloses known presence of lead based paint.

2. _____Forms that are designed to be completed by sellers informing prospective purchasers about conditions relating to the property.

3. _____The written report of the home inspector's findings.

4. _____All owners must take title in the same deed or will.

5. _____The process used to determine property boundaries that is performed by a registered professional engineer or registered land surveyor.

6. _____A person who inspects real estate for the purpose of determining if there are defects in the property, including whether or not it meets minimum structural and code standards.

7. _____The process followed by a registered land surveyor or registered engineer that marks the corners of property by placing a permanent pin in the ground and a wooden stake on the surface to give a visual of the boundaries.

8. _____All owners must receive their title at the same time.

9. _____A drawing by the surveyor that shows the property boundaries and the improvements on it.

10. _____When a buyer enters into a sales contract to purchase property, the buyer generally gives the seller a deposit to show he is acting in good faith.

11. _____All owners have the right to possess the property at the same time.

12. _____The person who performs a survey of real property.

13. _____All owners hold an equal interest in the property.

14. _____A warranty that is purchased by the buyer or seller where the company agrees, for a certain period of time after the closing, to repair items.

15. _____The person who renders an opinion on the fair market value of property.

Property Management 1

Terms	Definitions

Terms

A. Construction maintenance

B. Strip center

C. Preventative maintenance

D. Resident manager

E. Property manager

F. Corrective maintenance

G. Management proposal

H. Handicap/Disability status

I. Routine maintenance
J. Reasonably achievable accommodations

K. Management agreement

L. Multi-peril insurance

M. Anchor store

N. Insurable interest
O. Marketing plan

Definitions

1. _____A contract between the owner of real property and a property manager that includes the scope of the duties and responsibilities of the property manager and the obligations of the owner to pay for the services.

2. _____An outline submitted to the property owner showing how the property manager intends to manage the property if she is retained to do so.

3. _____A retail center containing four or more stores that are easily accessible with ample parking.

4. _____A popular retail business placed in a shopping center used to generate customers for all of the other stores in the shopping center.

5. _____A plan that specifically details the marketing strategy to rent or sell real estate.

6. _____The maintenance performed after the preventative, corrective, and routine maintenance is completed, including remodeling, interior decorating, and new capital improvements.

7. _____A person employed to manage a building who lives on the premises and is paid a salary.

8. _____A person retained, either as an employee or independent contractor, by a property owner to advertise the property, negotiate leases, collect rents, maintain the property, and perform other necessary management services.

9. _____Day-to-day maintenance of the property.

10. _____The American with Disabilities Act defines this as modifications on a property that are easily accomplishable and able to be carried out without much difficulty or expense.

11. _____An interest or right in property that would cause the person who has the right or interest to have a monetary loss if the property were damaged or destroyed.

12. _____Periodic work and upkeep performed on and to the property, its improvements, and equipment to keep it in order for the building and equipment to function as they should.

13. _____One of the fair housing classes, defined as someone who has a physical or mental impairment, that substantially limits one or more major life activities.

14. _____Repairs to nonfunctioning equipment.

15. _____Insurance for commercial property that insures against many perils in one policy, such as fire, acts of God, liability, and casualty.

Property Management 2

Terms	Definitions
A. Fiduciary relationship	1. _____Funds set aside each year for the future replacement of major items in apartment complexes, shopping centers, and condominiums.
B. Cash reserve fund	2. _____The right to use leased property without interference by others claiming the right to use the same property.
C. Escrow account	3. _____A leasehold estate that grants the lessee the right to use the property, but does not create ownership rights.
D. Nonfreehold estate	4. _____An economic principle stating that the lower the demand and the higher the supply, the lower the price, and the higher the demand and lower the supply, the higher the price.
E. Surety bond	5. _____A separate account used to hold client's money and money belonging to others.
F. Warranty of quiet enjoyment	6. _____The account that must be maintained by principal brokers to hold earnest money deposits and property management funds coming into the brokerage.
G. Trust account	7. _____ Form that sellers of one-to four-family residential properties built before 1978 are required to give buyers.
H. Supply and demand	8. _____ An agreement between an insurance or bonding company and a person obligated to perform certain tasks whereby the company assumes the responsibility for the performance of the insured party and agrees to pay a third party in the event the insured party fails to perform.
I. Warranty of habitability	9. _____A relationship of trust between a principal and agent.
J. Lead-based paint disclosure	10. _____ Federal law that prohibits discrimination against individuals with disabilities in equal access to jobs, public accommodations, public transaction, telecommunications, and government services.
K. Disability	11. ____ Division of taxes, insurance, assessments, and other items relating to the property transaction between the seller and buyer or lessor and lessee.
L. Americans With Disabilities Act (ADA)	12. _____When used in a lease, an option gives the tenant to right to lease the property for some future period at an agreed upon rate under the same terms and conditions as the original lease.
M. Familial status	13. _____One of the protected classes under the fair housing laws that includes one or more individuals, who have not obtained the age of 18 years (being domiciled with a parent or another person having legal custody of such individual or individuals or the designee of such parent or other person having such custody of such individual or individuals).
N. Pro-rations	14. ____This is the agreement of a landlord to keep the property in good condition during the term of the lease.

O. Option

15. _____One of the fair housing classes, defined as someone who has a physical or mental impairment that substantially limits one or more major life activities.

Property Management 3

Terms	Definitions
A. Vacancy loss	1. _____ A detailed statement of the income and expenses which gives the financial picture of a business as of a certain date.
B. Statutory year	2. _____ A year with 360 days.
C. Security deposit	3. _____ When someone that has entered upon the property, either legally or illegally, refuses to leave once asked to do so.
D. Rate of Return (ROI)	4. _____ The estimated amount of lost rental revenue because of vacancies.
E. Profit and loss statement	5. _____ The owner of leased property.
F. Potential gross income	6. _____ Money deposited with the landlord to secure the landlord against financial loss due to damage to the premises occasioned by the tenant's occupancy, other than ordinary wear and tear.
G. Operating budget	7. _____ Expenses that are a known amount and that do not vary from month to month, such as property taxes, insurance, and licensing fees.
H. Net operating income	8. _____ The ratio between the equity invested and the net income stated as a percentage.
I. Lessor	9. _____ An agreement between an insurance or bonding company and a person obligated to perform certain tasks whereby the company assumes the responsibility for the performance of the insured party and agrees to pay a third party in the event the insured party fails to perform.
J. Forcible entry and detainer	10. _____ Insurance that provides for loss or injury suffered as a result of a breach of contract.
K. Fixed expenses	11. _____ Total amount of gross receipts if all rental units are leased and all tenants pay their rent.
L. Lessee	12. _____ The person who leases property.
M. Fidelity bond	13. _____ Insurance that pays in the event of a flood that damages real property and its improvements.
N. Consequential loss	14. _____ The amount of income left after deducting expenses of a building or investment gross income.
O. Flood insurance	15. _____ An annual budget prepared by the property manager showing the income and expenses for the property.

Settlement/Transfer of Ownership 1

Terms

A. Tax shelter

B. Special assessment

C. Party of the Second Part

D. Straight-line depreciation

E. Bill of Sale

F. Recording

G. Capital improvement

H. Quiet title action

I. Party of the First Part

J. Grantee

K. Discount points

L. 1031 tax deferred exchange

M. Subject-to

N. Grantor

O. Deed

Definitions

1. _____ Anytime in a real estate transaction in the grantee takes title to real estate that has existing liens, thereby agreeing that the property will be liable for those liens.

2. _____ An assessment levied against property by a local taxing authority when the government makes additions to the property that benefit the public.

3. _____ A permanent improvement added to real estate for the purpose of increasing its useful life and/or increasing its value.

4. _____ A legal way for a taxpayer to shield or reduce income or capital gain from tax liability.

5. _____ In a deed or easement, another name for the grantee.

6. _____ A legal way to defer capital gains taxes on investment property by exchanging one qualified property for another qualified property.

7. _____ A method for depreciating investment property that is computed by dividing the adjusted basis of the property by a set number of years so that each year the property is depreciated by the same amount.

8. _____ The party that conveys title to real property by deed.

9. _____ The process of filing records in the county court clerk's office in the county where the property is located to give constructive notice of an interest in land.

10. _____ Prepaid interest.

11. _____ A lawsuit filed by a property owner to remove a cloud or claim that has been placed on the title to property.

12. _____ In a deed or easement, another name for the grantor.

13. _____ The party that receives title to real property by deed.

14. _____ A written instrument used to transfer ownership of personal property in contrast to real property which is transferred by a deed.

15. _____ The written instrument signed by the grantor conveying real property to the grantee.

Settlement/Transfer of Ownership 2

Terms	Definitions

Terms

A. Real Estate Settlement Procedures Act (RESPA)

B. Good faith estimate

C. Grant, bargain, and sale deed

D. Quitclaim Deed

E. Grant deed

F. General warranty

G. Debit

H. Credit

I. Covenant of warranty forever

J. Covenant of seisin

K. Covenant of right to convey

L. Covenant of quiet enjoyment

M. Covenant of further assurance

N. Covenant against encumbrances

Definitions

1. _____ A promise by the grantor that no one has superior title to that of the grantor and assures the grantee of peaceful possession without fear of someone making a claim to the property that is superior to the grantee's claim.

2. _____ A mutual exchange of promises in the deed between the grantor and grantee, including, but not limited to, the amount of money paid by the grantee to the grantor and the transfer of the property from the grantor to the grantee.

3. _____ A promise by the grantor in the deed which provides the assurance that no encumbrances exist other than those specified in the deed.

4. _____ An estimate of the buyer's closing costs which, under the Real Estate Settlement Procedures Act (RESPA), must be given to the applicant by the lender within three days of the loan application.

5. _____ A promise by the grantor that he will underwrite the legal expenses if any person establishes a superior claim to the title conveyed by the grantor.

6. _____ A promise by the grantor that he will perform reasonably necessary acts in the future to correct any defects in the title or in the deed instrument itself.

7. _____ In a real estate transaction, the dollar amounts shown on the closing statement that have either been paid by one of the parties or is due to one of them.

8. _____ A promise by the grantor that the grantor has the exact estate in the quantity and quality which is being conveyed to the grantee.

9. _____ A federal law that requires lenders to disclose good faith estimates of costs to borrowers and prohibits kickbacks from and to service providers.

10. _____ In a real estate transaction, a dollar amount on the closing statement that shows money is owed at closing.

11. _____ A promise by the grantor to defend the title forever even if the defect was created before the grantor's ownership.

12. _____ A promise by the grantor that she has the right, power, and authority to convey the title that she is conveying.

13. _____ A deed that conveys only the interest, if any, that the grantor has in the property and contains no warranties.

14. _____ A deed that includes warranties set forth in the statute.

O. Consideration in deed

15. _____ A deed that warrants the title is free from encumbrances created by the grantor.

Settlement/Transfer of Ownership 3

Terms

A. Unilateral contract

B. Valid contract

C. Voidable contract

D. Reality of consent

E. Offeror

F. Offeree

G. Offer and acceptance

H. Implied contract

I. Express contract

J. Executory contract

K. Executed contract

L. Enforceable contract

M. Contingency contract

N. Bilateral contract

O. Void contract

Definitions

1. _____ The person making the offer.

2. _____ Mutual agreement of the parties to a contract about the terms and conditions of the contract.

3. _____ The person receiving the offer.

4. _____ A contract created in whole, or part, by the actions of the parties.

5. _____ A contract that is in the process of being performed.

6. _____ A contract that contains a provision or condition that must be completed by a certain act or the occurrence of a certain event before the contract becomes binding.

7. _____ A contract appearing to be valid and enforceable but legally does not exist.

8. _____ A contract with at least two parties, containing promises to be performed by both parties.

9. _____ A contract that a court would require to be performed by the parties.

10. _____ A contract in which the obligations have been performed by all of the parties and nothing is left to be completed.

11. _____ An express agreement between the parties that may be oral or in writing.

12. _____ An essential element of contract formation that requires the offeree accept the offer without any changes.

13. _____ A contract that may be terminated by one of the parties, although it appears on its face to be valid and enforceable.

14. _____ A contract that includes all of the essential elements required to create a contract.

15. _____ A contract that has only one party who promises to perform under the contract.

Settlement/Transfer of Ownership 4

Terms	Definitions

Terms

A. Writ of attachment

B. Taking

C. Securities

D. Promissory note

E. Lis pendens

F. Legal competency

G. Just compensation

H. Eminent domain

I. Condemnation

J. Adverse Possession

K. Truth-in-lending

L. Tacking

M. Paint-to-paint

N. Land contract

O. Warrantor

Definitions

1. _____ The law that requires creditors to give meaningful credit disclosures to borrowers and requires lenders to include certain information in their advertising.

2. _____ Refers to a person's legal ability to enter into contracts and to acquire legal rights and liabilities.

3. _____ A notice recorded in the chain of title to real property to warn anyone taking an interest in the property that the property is the subject matter of litigation and that any interests acquired during the pendency of the lawsuit are subject to its outcome.

4. _____ A legal process in which one person can intentionally take another's real property by using the property in an actual, open, notorious, hostile, continuous, visible, and exclusive manner for a set period of time based on state law.

5. _____ The legal process used by the government in eminent domain actions to take privately owned property to be used for the common good.

6. _____ The borrower's personal promise to repay.

7. _____ The right of federal, state, and local governments to take private property for a use that will benefit the public.

8. _____ The amount of money the government must pay the landowner when the owner's property is taken in an eminent domain action for the common good.

9. _____ Evidence of obligations to pay money or of rights to participate in earnings and distribution of corporate, trust, or other property.

10. _____ The term used in eminent domain proceedings when the government acquires ownership of real property to be used for the common good.

11. _____ The legal process of seizing the real or personal property of a defendant in a lawsuit by court order.

12. _____ Adding consecutive periods of ownership to qualify for adverse possession.

13. _____ Expression to indicate ownership of interior space in a condominium regime.

14. _____ A method of seller financing.

15. _____ Person giving a warranty.

Financing 1

Terms	Definitions

Terms

A. Prepaids

B. Novation

C. Land contract

D. Down payment

E. Closing costs

F. Amortization

G. Blanket mortgage

H. Adjustable rate mortgage

I. Construction mortgage

J. Conventional loan

K. Fully amortized

L. Partially amortized

M. Nonamortized

N. Security interest

O. Statute of Frauds

Definitions

1. _____ At closings, items paid in advance by the buyer as required by the lender.

2. _____ An agreement generated by the lender substituting a new mortgagor for the original mortgagor in a loan assumption situation.

3. _____ A form of owner financing in which the seller retains title to the property and the buyer has possession of the property.

4. _____ The amount paid out-of-pocket by a purchaser that is added to the mortgage amount to equal the total sales price.

5. _____ Costs associated with the consummation of the real estate transaction.

6. _____ A loan that provides for periodic interest-only payments with payment of the principal in one lump sum.

7. _____ A method of loan repayment in which periodic payments do not reduce the outstanding loan balance to zero at maturity thereby leaving a balloon payment due at maturity.

8. _____ A loan that is fully repaid at maturity by periodic payments of principal and interest.

9. _____ A mortgage loan made without either government insurance or guarantee.

10. _____ A short-term loan which provides the funds necessary for the building or development of a real estate project.

11. _____ A mortgage that has an interest rate that may change at predetermined intervals based on a stated index.

12. _____ A mortgage in which two or more pieces of property are used to secure a single debt.

13. _____ Repayment of a debt by paying installments of the interest owed at that time plus a portion of the principal.

14. _____ An interest in property that allows the lender to foreclose on the property in the event of the borrower's default in repayment of the money owed.

15. _____ The law that requires certain contracts to be in writing to be enforceable.

Financing 2

Terms

A. Insured loan

B. Trustor

C. Collateral

D. Trustee

E. Deed of reconveyance

F. Defeasance clause

G. Primary lenders

H. Title theory

I. Legal title

J. Lien theory

K. Hypothecating

L. Equity

M. Intermediate theory

N. Deed of trust

O. Equitable title

Definitions

1. _____ In a title theory state, the owner of the property.

2. _____ A high risk loan that is insured by the government, or private insurer, and paid for by the borrower, that assures the lender that, in the event of mortgagor default, the lender will not have a loss.

3. _____ Property pledged to secure repayment of a debt.

4. _____ A provision in a mortgage that requires the real estate title returned to the borrower after the terms and conditions of the mortgage debt has been met.

5. _____ The person appointed in a trust deed to hold title to property and to reconvey it when the mortgage debt is paid.

6. _____ A document releasing an interest in real estate after a debt or other obligation has been paid.

7. _____ The ownership interest that one has in real property upon the execution of a sales contract, a land contract, or deed of trust.

8. _____ A deed used to transfer title from the trustee back to the owner-borrower (trustor or beneficiary) after the mortgage debt has been paid in full.

9. _____ States that allow the lender to hold the equitable title to the property during the term of the mortgage loan.

10. _____ Title which is complete and perfect regarding the apparent right of ownership and possession, although another person may hold equitable title.

11. _____ States that provide a mechanism for lenders to have a lien on real estate to secure repayment of the debt in the form of a mortgage.

12. _____ Lenders who make loans directly to borrowers.

13. _____ Pledging real estate as security for a debt while retaining possession of the property.

14. _____ The amount of the owner's interest in the property after subtracting mortgages and liens from the fair market value.

15. _____ A combination of the lien theory and title theory that allows the lender to receive a specific lien on the property that can be foreclosed in the event of default.

Financing 3

Terms

A. Reverse annuity mortgage

B. Farmer's Home Administration loans

C. Renegotiable rate mortgage

D. Participation mortgage

E. Federal Home Loan Mortgage Corporation

F. Federal Housing Administration loans

G. Package mortgage

H. Government National Mortgage Association

I. Open-end mortgage

J. Federal National Mortgage Association

K. Mortgage insurance

L. Buydown mortgage

M. Guaranteed loan

N. Graduated payment mortgage

O. Growing equity mortgage

Definitions

1. _____ A means by which a seller or buyer pays cash at closing to a lender who, in turn, reduces the interest rate on the buyer's mortgage loan.

2. _____ A financing arrangement whereby a lender pays the borrower a fixed annuity or periodic payment based on the owner's equity in the property.

3. _____ A mortgage that requires additional payments that are applied directly to principal reduction thereby shortening the maturity date.

4. _____ Loans made by an agency of the federal government operating within the Department of Agriculture providing financing for residential property to farmers and others purchasing rural property.

5. _____ This is a HUD agency that participates in the secondary mortgage market by financing special high risk loans.

6. _____ Financing for residential real estate in which monthly payments start lower and increase periodically over the life of the mortgage.

7. _____ Mortgages that contain future advance clauses allowing the lender to lend additional funds under the same mortgage.

8. _____ A loan that is guaranteed by the federal government.

9. _____ The largest secondary mortgage market.

10. _____ Insurance purchased by the borrower to protect the lender from a loss in the event the borrower defaults on an FHA or conventional-insured mortgage.

11. _____ A real estate loan which covers both real and personal property with one mortgage.

12. _____ Insured loans.

13. _____ A secondary mortgage market for savings and loan associations.

14. _____ A type of mortgage that provides the lender with a certain percentage of cash flow beyond the fixed rate of interest paid by the borrower.

15. _____ A mortgage that is a series of short term loans that are renegotiated at periodic intervals to adjust the interest to the current levels.

Financing 4

Terms

A. Uninsured loan

B. Secondary mortgage market

C. Second mortgage

D. Promissory note

E. Private mortgage insurance

F. Prepayment penalty

G. Origination fee

H. Mortgage liquidity

I. Mortgage

J. Interest rate cap/floor

K. Income-to-debt ratio

L. Home equity mortgage

M. Foreclosure

N. Disintermediation

O. Discount points

Definitions

1. _____ Prepaid interest paid at the closing that effectively decreases the mortgage interest rate.

2. _____ The process used to enforce a mortgage lien when the mortgagor fails to repay the money as agreed that terminates the owner's and all lien holder interests in the property.

3. _____ Low-risk loans that do not require mortgage insurance to be paid by the borrower.

4. _____ A loan secured by a mortgage on a person's home with an open line of credit based on the homeowner's equity.

5. _____ The loss of funds from financial institutions when depositors make withdrawals in order to invest the money in higher yield investments.

6. _____ A mortgage underwriting process that compares a borrower's monthly debts to his monthly gross income to determine how much money may be borrowed for a mortgage loan.

7. _____ The process of buying and selling first mortgages to provide mortgage liquidity.

8. _____ A term in an adjustable or variable rate mortgage and promissory note that sets the highest and lowest interest rate that may be charged on the loan.

9. _____ A voluntary lien given by the mortgagor to the mortgagee to secure the repayment of a debt.

10. _____ A mortgage that has a junior lien position to the first mortgage, because of the time of recording the mortgage or of the subordination of the mortgage.

11. _____ The secondary market process of turning mortgages into cash thereby enabling lenders to use the money to make more mortgage loans.

12. _____ The fees charged by a lender to pay for time and expenses incurred in arranging for a loan.

13. _____ A provision in a promissory note that provides for the borrower to pay a monetary penalty if more than what is due is paid any one time, including paying the balance in full before a specified time.

14. _____ Insurance that is paid by the borrower on a conventional mortgage insuring the lender against loss if the borrower fails to repay the debt and the property is foreclosed upon.

15. _____ In the mortgage lending process, the primary evidence of the debt and the borrower's personal promise to repay the debt.

Financing 5

Terms

A. Strict foreclosure

B. Shared-appreciation mortgage

C. Statutory redemption

D. Veterans Administration loans

E. Recourse provision

F. Wraparound mortgage

G. Escrow account

H. Nonrecourse provision

I. Conditional approval

J. Foreclosure

K. Deed in lieu of foreclosure

L. Equity of redemption

M. Default clause

N. Deficiency judgment

Definitions

1. _____ A type of mortgage foreclosure in which the lender does not have to pay the property owner equity that may be left after the debt and all expenses are paid.

2. _____ A mortgage that allows borrowers to obtain additional financing on their property without paying the current first mortgage.

3. _____ Loans that allow the buyer to get a reduced interest rate because the lender shares in the appreciation.

4. _____ A loan provision which states that the lender can take legal action against the borrower personally in case of default.

5. _____ A statutory period of time enacted in some states in which the borrower can redeem the property after foreclosure by paying the outstanding debt, interest, and legal fees.

6. _____ The account required by the lender for certain types of mortgage loans for property taxes and hazard insurance.

7. _____ A guaranteed loan that allows qualified veterans to borrow 100% of the money needed to purchase a home.

8. _____ A loan provision which states that the borrower is not personally liable for payment of the debt if the value of the property securing the loan is less than the amount necessary to repay the loan.

9. _____ The process used to enforce a mortgage when the mortgagor fails to repay the money as agreed.

10. _____ A deed used to convey title to the lender after a borrower's default to avoid a foreclosure action.

11. _____ Once the loan is approved, the underwriter may require that certain criteria be met prior to the closing.

12. _____ The right of the borrower to reclaim his or her property by paying the outstanding loan, interest, and court costs prior to a foreclosure sale.

13. _____ A clause in a contract that specifically sets forth what will happen in the event one party to the contract fails to perform as agreed. These clauses are found in listing contracts, sales contracts, mortgages, and leases.

14. _____ The judgment a mortgagee may request from the court after a foreclosure by judicial sale if the mortgagee does not receive all money owed to it from the sale.

O. Annual percentage rate

15. _____ The amount of interest paid by borrowers after the lender's costs for borrowing the money is added to the stated interest rate.

Financing 6

Terms	Definitions
A. Subordination	1. _____ A clause that may be included in a mortgage requiring the mortgagor to repay the debt in full if the property is transferred to another person.
B. Prepayment privilege	2. _____ The order in which liens will be paid in the event of a foreclosure action.
C. Maturity date	3. _____ A clause informing the mortgagor whether or not he can prepay the principal balance prior to its due date.
D. Regulation Z	4. _____ The person that reviews the loan application and all other documentation supplied by the borrower to determine the lender's risk in extending the mortgage loan to the buyer.
E. Equal Credit Opportunity Act	5. _____ A clause inserted in mortgage and leases that allow for an increase in the payments at specified times under certain conditions.
F. Loan origination fee	6. _____ The law requires creditors to give meaningful credit disclosures to borrowers and re quires lenders to include certain information in their advertising.
G. Three-day right of rescission	7. _____ As used in regulation Z, terms that must be used in an advertisement to inform the borrower of the down payment, cash price of property, annual percentage rate, interest rate (if variable or adjustable, must be stated as variable or adjustable), amount of down payment, amount of each payment, date when each payment is due, and total number of payments.
H. Trigger terms	8. _____ A clause in a mortgage that gives the mortgagee the right to demand payment of the entire amount owed when the mortgagor defaults on the mortgage.
I. Truth-in-Lending	9. _____ The date that the last payment on a mortgage is due.
J. Underwriter	10. _____ The right of a borrower refinancing a personal residence.
K. Prepayment clause	11. _____ A federal regulation that covers all real estate credit extended to a natural person that is not for business, commercial or agricultural purposes.
L. Lien priority	12. _____ A federal law that prohibits discrimination in the lending process based on race, color, religion, national origin, sex, marital status, age, and dependence on public assistance.
M. Due-on-sale clause	13. _____ The amount of money charged by the lender for its work relating to obtaining the loan.
N. Escalation clause	14. _____ The right to prepay a debt before it is due.
O. Acceleration clause	15. _____ The process of reversing lien priorities.

ANSWER KEY – APPENDIX EXERCISES

Listing Property 1

1. C
2. E
3. A
4. D
5. J
6. L
7. B
8. M
9. I
10. H
11. K
12. O
13. G
14. N
15. F

Listing Property 2

1. D
2. E
3. A
4. L
5. F
6. B
7. J
8. N
9. I
10. K
11. H
12. G
13. M
14. C
15. O

Listing Property 3

1. A
2. B
3. F
4. K
5. M
6. E
7. H
8. D
9. O
10. N
11. J
12. G
13. C
14. I
15. L

Listing Property 4

1. E
2. L
3. C
4. I
5. N
6. O
7. G
8. B
9. D
10. J
11. K
12. F
13. A
14. M
15. H

Listing Property 5

1. N
2. I
3. C
4. G
5. B
6. O
7. L
8. D
9. E
10. F

11. M
12. H
13. A
14. K
15. J

Listing Property 6

1. I
2. B
3. K
4. A
5. D
6. M
7. N
8. O
9. J
10. L
11. C
12. F
13. E
14. G
15. H

Listing Property 7

1. H
2. I
3. D
4. C
5. F
6. O
7. B
8. A
9. L
10. E
11. G
12. K
13. J
14. N
15. M

Listing Property 8

1. L
2. J
3. A

4. C
5. I
6. G
7. N
8. D
9. O
10. K
11. M
12. F
13. B
14. H
15. E

Listing Property 9

1. L
2. H
3. D
4. A
5. C
6. K
7. B
8. O
9. E
10. M
11. F
12. N
13. G
14. J
15. I

Listing Property 10

1. J
2. H
3. F
4. G
5. O
6. B
7. I
8. A
9. C
10. E
11. M
12. L
13. D

14. K
15. N

Selling Property 1

1. D
2. O
3. G
4. K
5. E
6. L
7. H
8. N
9. M
10. J
11. I
12. B
13. F
14. A
15. C

Selling Property 2

1. I
2. K
3. M
4. J
5. L
6. N
7. O
8. H
9. G
10. E
11. B
12. F
13. D
14. C
15. A

Selling Property 3

1. N
2. M
3. L
4. J

5. K
6. I
7. F
8. E
9. H
10. C
11. G
12. B
13. D
14. A
15. O

Selling Property 4

1. A
2. B
3. K
4. C
5. M
6. G
7. L
8. D
9. I
10. N
11. H
12. F
13. J
14. E
15. O

Property Management 1

1. K
2. G
3. B
4. M
5. O
6. A
7. D
8. E
9. I
10. J
11. N
12. C
13. H

14. F
15. L

Property Management 2

1. B
2. F
3. D
4. H
5. G
6. C
7. J
8. E
9. A
10. L
11. N
12. O
13. M
14. I
15. K

Property Management 3

1. E
2. B
3. J
4. A
5. I
6. C
7. K
8. D
9. M
10. N
11. F
12. L
13. O
14. H
15. G

Settlement/Transfer of Ownership 1

1. M

2. B
3. G
4. A
5. C
6. L
7. D
8. N
9. F
10. K
11. H
12. I
13. J
14. E
15. O

Settlement/Transfer of Ownership 2

1. L
2. O
3. N
4. B
5. I
6. M
7. H
8. J
9. A
10. G
11. F
12. K
13. D
14. E
15. C

Settlement/Transfer of Ownership 3

1. E
2. D
3. F
4. H
5. J
6. M
7. O
8. N
9. L

10. K
11. I
12. G
13. C
14. B
15. A

Settlement/Transfer of Ownership 4

1. K
2. F
3. E
4. J
5. I
6. D
7. H
8. G
9. C
10. B
11. A
12. L
13. M
14. N
15. O

Financing 1

1. A
2. B
3. C
4. D
5. E
6. M
7. L
8. K
9. J
10. I
11. H
12. G
13. F
14. N
15. O

Financing 2

1. B
2. A
3. C
4. F
5. D
6. N
7. O
8. E
9. H
10. I
11. J
12. G
13. K
14. L
15. M

Financing 3

1. L
2. A
3. O
4. B
5. H
6. N
7. I
8. M
9. J
10. K
11. G
12. F
13. E
14. D
15. C

Financing 4

1. O
2. M
3. A
4. L
5. N
6. K
7. B
8. J
9. I
10. C
11. H
12. G
13. F
14. E
15. D

Financing 5

1. A
2. F
3. B
4. E
5. C
6. G
7. D
8. H
9. J
10. K
11. I
12. L
13. M
14. N
15. O

Financing 6

1. M
2. L
3. K
4. J
5. N
6. I
7. H
8. O
9. C
10. G
11. D
12. E
13. F
14. B
15. A

1031 Tax Deferred Exchange A legal method of deferring capital gains taxes by exchanging one qualified property for another qualified property. When real estate for investment or for production of income is exchanged for like-kind property, a tax-free exchange can take place.

Above Grade The part of the improvement that is above the ground level.

Acceleration Clause A clause in a mortgage that gives the mortgagee the right to demand payment of the entire amount owed when the mortgagor defaults on the mortgage. These clauses may also be found in leases, and they allow the lessor the right to terminate the lease and demand payment of the remaining lease payments when the lessee defaults.

Accretion The process of acquiring additional land because of gradual accumulation of rock, sand, and soil when the land fronts on a lake, river, or ocean.

Acre A measurement of land containing 43,560 square feet.

Ad Valorem Taxes Annual property taxes that are collected by the property valuation administrator. These taxes are used to help support state and local governments as well as the school systems.

Adverse Possession A legal process in which one person can intentionally take another's real property by using the property in an actual, open, notorious, hostile, continuous, visible, and exclusive manner for a set period of time based on state law.

Aesthetic Zoning Zoning designation designed to benefit property by keeping it attractive instead of zoning it for a certain utility. An example would be zoning for a certain architectural style or zoning around a lake to keep the land natural.

Agency Disclosure Form A form mandated by the real estate licensing law that must be completed by licensees notifying buyers and sellers of agency relationships.

Agency Relationship A legal relationship where one party (the agent) represents another party (the principal) in dealing with a third party.

Alienation Clause Another term for a due-on-sale clause.

Alluvion Sand, soil and gravel that are deposited along the banks of flowing water.

Americans With Disabilities Act (ADA) Federal law that prohibits discrimination against individuals with disabilities in equal access to jobs, public accommodations, public transaction, telecommunications, and government services.

Anchor Store A popular retail business placed in a shopping center used to generate customers for all of the other stores in the shopping center.

Annexation (1) The process of adding area to a city; (2) the process of affixing personal property to real estate.

Annual Percentage Rate The amount of interest paid by borrowers after the lender's costs for borrowing the money is added to the stated interest rate.

Anti-Trust Laws Federal and state laws that are designed to keep the market place competitive by preventing collusion among providers of goods and services who may unlawfully attempt to restrain trade by fixing prices, boycotting, and creating monopolies.

Appraisal Report A written report submitted by the appraiser to support and document her opinion of value.

Appraisal An opinion of the fair market value of property, placed on the property by an appraiser, using either the replacement cost, income, or comparative market analysis approach to appraising.

Appraiser The person who renders an opinion on the fair market value of property. Appraisers may or may not be licensed or certified, and may or may not carry professional liability insurance.

Appreciation Increase in the fair market value of property due to economic conditions.

Appurtenances Everything that is attached to the real estate. Attachments include physical improvements like houses, barns, fences and road, as well as rights and interests in the land, including easements, leases, and air rights.

Appurtenant Easement An easement involving adjoining parcels of land known as the dominant estate and the servient estate. The dominant estate is the tract of land that has the right to use the easement lying across the adjoining tract, which is known as the servient estate.

Assessed Value The value placed on property by the property valuation administrator on which the annual property tax is based. Also referred to as the "assessment."

Assessment The value placed on property by the property valuation administrator on which the annual property tax is based. Also referred to as the "assessed value."

Assumable Mortgage A mortgage that can be assumed by a new mortgagor without changing its original terms.

Avulsion Loss of land caused by running water, such as a stream or creek.

Banker's Year A year with 360 days.

Below Grade The part of the improvement that is built below ground level.

Beneficiary In a title theory state, the lender in a trust deed.

Bilateral Contract A contract with at least two parties containing promises to be performed by both parties.

Bill of Sale A written instrument used to transfer ownership of personal property in contrast to real property which is transferred by a deed. A bill of sale is used when personal property is being transferred in conjunction with real property.

Blockbusting An illegal tactic used to encourage owners in an area to sell their property by informing them that there will be a change in the neighborhood relating to the race, religion, sex color, handicap, familial status, or national origin of new people purchasing property in the area. The statements are made for the purpose of driving down the property values, thereby giving the informant the opportunity to purchase the property at less than the fair market value.

Book Value Value of property for accounting purposes.

Boycotting The act of refusing to cooperate with another company in an effort to show disapproval of its policies and procedures. When boycotting is done in concert with other companies, it is a violation of the anti-trust laws.

Brokerage Accounts The operating bank account for the brokerage.

Brokerage Fee A fee paid to a real estate broker for services relating to the sale or purchase of real property.

Buffer Zoning Zoning that requires a strip of land between adjacent incompatible land uses.

Building Code Governmental regulations that establish the minimum requirements for building construction in the area.

Building Permit Document that must be obtained by a property owner from the local government before constructing an improvement on the land.

Bulk Zoning Regulations created by zoning that keep land from being too densely developed in order to prevent overloading of public services and facilities. Some of the methods used are minimum side yards and setbacks, requirements for off-street parking, and height restrictions for buildings.

Bundle of Rights This phrase refers to all of the legal rights, interests, and privileges that an owner has in real property.

Buydown Mortgage A means by which a seller or buyer pays cash at closing to a lender who, in turn, reduces the interest rate on the buyer's mortgage loan.

Bylaws A legal document used by condominium associations, homeowner's associations, corporations, and incorporated associations that includes the rules, regulations, and management processes that will be followed by the organization and its members.

Calendar Year A year with 365 days or with 366 days when there is a leap year.

Cap Rate Shorthand for capitalization rate.

Capital Improvement Any permanent improvement made to real estate for the purpose of increasing the useful life of the property or increasing the property's value.

Capitalization Rate The rate of return on an investment stated as a percentage.

Carryover Clause A clause included in the listing contract that operates after the listing contract has expired. The clause is effective for a specific period of time after the listing expires and obligates the seller to pay the real estate commission to the broker if the seller sells the property to a buyer that has been introduced to the property during the term of the listing. This clause is also referred to as a protection clause, safety clause, and extender clause.

Cash Reserve Fund Funds set aside each year for the future replacement of major items in apartment complexes, shopping centers, and condominiums. This includes replacement of items such as roofs, parking lots, and outside painting.

Casualty Insurance Insures against claims caused by injuries to people and the legal liability resulting from those injuries.

Certificate of Occupancy Document that must be obtained from the local government once construction is complete to show that the property has been built in compliance with the building code.

Civil Rights Act of 1866 This is the first federal law written to prevent racial discrimination.

Clear Title Title to real property that does not contain defects or other conditions that would be objectionable to a grantee. Sometimes referred to as a clean title or a marketable title.

Closing The time when the real estate transaction is consummated and title to the real estate passes from the seller to the buyer. This is also referred to as the settlement.

Closing Costs Costs associated with the consummation of the real estate transaction. Although costs are negotiated in the contract, certain costs are customarily paid by the seller and the buyer. The buyer pays the costs of obtaining the financing and recording the deed and mortgage, while the seller pays for preparing the deed and the state transfer tax.

Cloud on Title A defect in the title to property that would make it unacceptable to a grantee, and would keep a court from compelling the buyer to accept if the contract provides for a marketable title.

CMA Shorthand for comparative market analysis.

Collateral Property pledged to secure repayment of a debt. Should the borrower not repay the money borrowed, the property may be sold by the lender to recover the amount owed. In a real estate context, the collateral for a mortgage loan is typically the real estate being purchased.

Commingle The process of depositing client funds into the brokerage's general account, operating account, or the broker's personal account.

Common Area Areas in a condominium, or other development with co-owners or co-tenants, that may be used by all co-owners or co-tenants. Parking lots, hallways, swimming pools, tennis courts, and parks are all common areas. These areas are also referred to as "common elements."

Community Property Property ownership in which each spouse has an equal interest in the property acquired by the efforts of either party during the marriage.

Comparables Properties that have similar physical characteristics located nearby that have sold or leased in similar market conditions.

Comparative Market Analysis A method for determining the fair market value of real estate. This process compares a specific piece of property with similar properties that have sold in the same geographic area during a certain time period.

Comparison Approach Process of comparing the subject property to other similar properties that have sold recently for the purpose of estimating the fair market value of the subject property.

Comps Shorthand term for "comparables."

Concurrent Ownership Ownership of property by more than one person at the same time. Examples of this form of ownership include joint tenancy with right of survivorship, tenancy in common, and tenancy by the entireties.

Condemnation The legal process used by the government in eminent domain actions to take privately owned property to be used for the common good.

Conditional Approval Once the loan is approved, the underwriter may require that certain criteria be met prior to the closing.

Condominium A form of multiple ownership of property in which each owner owns a portion of the property individually and a portion of the property jointly in common with the other owners.

Consequential Loss Insurance that provides for loss or injury suffered as a result of a breach of contract.

Consideration in Deed A deed is a contract; therefore, must contain consideration (an essential element of a contract). In a deed the consideration is typically stated as a dollar amount (often the sales price of the property), plus "other good and valuable consideration." This last phrase shows that the parties each gave and received something of value in addition to the money that changes hands.

Construction Lien A short-term loan, sometimes referred to as interim financing, which provides the funds necessary for the building or development of a real estate project.

Construction Maintenance The maintenance performed after the preventative, corrective, and routine maintenance is completed, including remodeling, interior decorating, and new capital improvements.

Constructive Notice The notice to the world given by recording documents in the appropriate government office in the county where the real property is located. Once the document is recorded, it is presumed that anyone taking an interest in the real property has notice of another party's interest in the same property. Deeds, mortgages, leases, and easements are examples of documents recorded to give constructive notice.

Contingency Contract A provision or condition included as part of a contract which requires the completion of a certain act or the occurrence of a certain event before the contract becomes binding.

Contract Buyer's Title Insurance Title insurance that protects a buyer who purchases under an installment sales contract against defects in the seller's title prior to the contract.

Contract A promise or a set of promises between two parties.

Cooperating Broker When the listing broker permits another broker to sell his listed property, the broker bringing the buyer to the transaction is known as the cooperating broker. The cooperating broker has no contractual relationship with the seller of the property and is paid his commission by the listing broker.

Cooperative A form of property ownership in which individuals own shares of a corporation which in turn owns the real estate.

Corporation A legal entity that is created to afford liability protection to the shareholders.

Corrective Maintenance Repairs to nonfunctioning equipment.

Cost Approach Process for determining value of real property by calculating the amount of money needed to replace or reproduce it.

Co-Tenant A co-owner of property.

Counteroffer When an offer is made by the offeror that is not acceptable to the offeree, the offeree may reject that offer and make an offer back to the offeror known as a counteroffer.

Covenant Against Encumbrances A covenant which provides the assurance that no encumbrances other than those specified in the deed exist.

Covenant of Further Assurance A promise by a grantor that he or she will perform further acts reasonably necessary to correct any defects in the title or in the deed instrument.

Covenant of Quiet Enjoyment A promise that no one has superior or paramount title to that of the grantor and assurance to the grantee of peaceful possession without fear of being ousted by a person with a superior claim to the property.

Covenant of Right to Convey The assurance that the grantor has the right, power, and authority to convey the title being granted.

Covenant of Seisin A covenant which gives the assurance that the grantor has the exact estate in the quantity and quality which in fact is being conveyed. This covenant may also be spelled "seizing."

Covenant of Warranty Forever Sometimes called *warranty of title*, this covenant is the assurance that the grantor will underwrite the legal expenses if any person establishes a claim superior to the title given by the grantor.

Covenants Promises between two or more owners where each party agrees to perform or refrain from performing certain acts.

Credit In a real estate transaction, the dollar amounts on the closing statement that have either been paid by one of the parties or that is due to one of them. The purchase price is a credit to the seller because the seller is receiving that amount, while the earnest money deposit is a credit to the buyer because the buyer has paid that amount when entering into the sales contract. Credits are amounts received at the closing, while debits are amount that are paid at the closing.

Credit Scores A method used by credit reporting agencies to determine the creditworthiness of an individual. The score is determined by a formula using the individual's past credit history, amount of open credit lines, and other factors that show the individual's potential for repaying money as agreed. Mortgage lenders use these credit scores when underwriting a mortgage loan.

Curable Depreciation Determination that it is reasonable and economically feasible to make necessary repairs; i.e. cost to repair does not exceed the increase in the value of the property.

Curtesy The husband's interest in his wife's property that she owns during the marriage.

Debit In a real estate transaction, a dollar amount on the closing statement that shows money is owed at closing. The purchase price will be a debit to the purchaser because the money is owed at closing, while the seller's existing mortgage payoff will be shown as a debit to the seller because the seller must pay it at closing. Debits are paid at the

closing while credits are amounts received at the closing.

Declaration of Restrictions A recordable document, generally prepared and recorded by the developer, that prohibits or requires the owners of the property developed to use the property in a certain way.

Declaratory Judgment When the court enters a judgment based solely on the law, because the parties agree to the facts and the only issue is how the facts will be interpreted under the current law.

Deed Restrictions Covenants contained in a deed that prohibits or requires the owner to use his property in a certain way. Improvements on the property may be required to be a certain size, have a particular façade, or have certain amenities. These are sometimes referred to as restrictive covenants.

Deed The written instrument signed by the grantor conveying real property to the grantee.

Deed in Lieu of Foreclosure A deed used to convey title to the lender after a borrower's default to avoid a foreclosure action.

Deed of Reconveyance A deed used to transfer title from the trustee back to the owner borrower (trustor or beneficiary) after the mortgage debt has been paid in full.

Deed of Release A document releasing an interest in real estate after a debt or other obligation has been paid.

Deed of Trust A deed used to secure

repayment of a debt in which title to real estate is transferred to the trustee until the debt is paid in full.

Default Clause A clause in a contract that specifically sets forth what will happen in the event one party to the contract fails to perform as agreed. These clauses are found in listing contracts, sales contracts, mortgages, and leases.

Defeasance Clause A provision in a mortgage that requires the real estate title returned to the borrower after the terms and conditions of the mortgage debt have been met.

Deficiency Judgment The judgment a mortgagee may request from the court after a foreclosure by judicial sale if the mortgagee does not receive all money owed to it from the sale. A mortgagee may use the deficiency judgment to collect the additional debt from the mortgagor from assets other than the mortgaged property.

Depreciation Decrease in value of property.

Disability One of the fair housing classes, defined as someone who has a physical or mental impairment that substantially limits one or more major life activities.

Disclosure of Property Condition Form Forms that are designed to be completed by sellers informing prospective purchasers about conditions relating to the property.

Discount Points Prepaid interest paid at the closing that effectively decreases the interest rate

used in the promissory note, but increases the yield to the lender.

Disintermediation The loss of funds from financial institutions when depositors make withdrawals in order to invest the money in higher yield investments.

Doctrine of Prior Appropriation A water system found in dryer states that gives the government control over water adjacent to property. The government establishes a permit system for the water usage.

Double Net Lease A commercial lease that requires the tenant to pay a base rent plus two of the following: property insurance, property taxes, or property maintenance. Also referred to as a net net lease.

Dower The wife's interest in her husband's property that he owns during their marriage.

Down Payment The amount paid out-of-pocket by a purchaser that is added to the mortgage amount to equal the total sales price.

Dual Agent Occurs in a real estate transaction in which the real estate broker represents both the seller and the buyer.

Due-on-Sale Clause An acceleration clause that may be included in a mortgage requiring the mortgagor to repay the debt in full if the property is transferred to another person. Depending on the specific language used in the mortgage, this clause may become effective when interest in the property is conveyed by deed, by will, by descent, by installment sale contract, be lease, or by lease option.

Duty of Accounting The fiduciary duty of the agent to inform the principal about all monies received and disbursed by the agent on behalf of the principal.

Duty of Confidentiality The fiduciary duty of the agent to keep all of the principal's personal information confidential.

Duty of Disclosure The fiduciary duty of the agent to inform the principal about all material facts surrounding the property and the transaction.

Duty of Due Care and Diligence The fiduciary duty of the agent to use at least the same level of skill and effort in representing the principal as another agent would use.

Duty of Loyalty The fiduciary duty of the agent to protect the interests of the principal above the interests of all others, including those of the agent.

Duty of Obedience The fiduciary duty of the agent to follow all legal instructions of the principal even if the agent does not agree with the instructions.

Earnest Money Deposit When a buyer enters into a sales contract to purchase property, the buyer generally gives the seller a deposit to show he is acting in good faith.

Easement by Necessity An easement granted by the court for ingress and egress that will prevent a property from being landlocked. Two requirements are that both parcels must

have a common grantor and the easement must be necessary, not just convenient.

Easement by Prescription An easement by prescription arises when someone claims an easement over the objections of the property owner. In order to establish the easement, the person must prove that the easement was used in an actual, open, notorious, forcible, exclusive, and hostile way for a statutory period of time set by state law.

Easement in Gross The personal right to use someone else's property. Utility easements are examples of easements in gross.

Emblements Annual growing crops that may be harvested by the owner even if he has transferred the property to a new owner prior to the time to harvest the crops. Emblements are personal property.

Eminent Domain The right of the federal, state, and local governments to take private property for a use that will benefit the public.

Encroachment An improvement that crosses the boundary line. Encroachments are encumbrances and include fences, trees, buildings, driveways, and garages.

Encumbrance A limitation on the owner's rights in his real property. Encumbrances include liens, mortgages, easements, taxes, and leases.

Enforceable Contract A contract that a court would require performed by the parties.

Equal Credit Opportunity Act A federal law that prohibits discrimination in the lending process based on race, color, religion, national origin, sex, marital status, age, and dependence on public assistance.

Equitable Title The ownership interest that one has in real property upon the execution of a sales contract, a land contract, or deed of trust.

Equity The amount of the owner's interest in the property after subtracting mortgages and liens from the fair market value. If the fair market value is $200,000 and the mortgages and liens total $160,000, the owner's equity is $40,000.

Equity of Redemption The right of the borrower to reclaim his or her property by paying the outstanding loan, interest, and court costs prior to a foreclosure sale.

Escalation Clause A clause inserted in mortgage and leases that allow for an increase in the payments at specified times under certain conditions.

Escrow Account (1) The account that must be maintained by principal brokers to hold earnest money deposits and property management funds coming into the brokerage. Also referred to as a trust account. (2) Accounts established by lenders for most secondary market loans that hold the property taxes, hazard insurance, and assessments that are paid by the mortgagor each month.

Estate at Sufferance The tenancy created when a tenant wrongfully holds over after the termination of the lease without the landlord's consent. A landlord cannot accuse the tenant of trespassing and the tenant cannot adversely possess the property.

Estate at Will A tenancy created when the tenant occupies the property with permission of the landlord and either the landlord or tenant may terminate the tenancy when they choose to do so by giving proper notice as required by state law.

Estate for Years A lease that has a definite beginning date and ending date. The lease begins on a certain date and ends on a certain date, and the tenant is expected to vacate the premises on that date without either party giving the other notice that the lease is terminating. Also referred to as a tenancy for years.

Estate from Period to Period Tenancy for a definite period that automatically renews at the end of the period. An example would be a month-to-month lease. Sometimes referred to as tenancy from month to month and tenancy from year to year, even if a month or year is not the period of time.

Estate in Land Ownership rights in land, including the degree, nature, quantity, and extent of the ownership interest, and including the owner's right to use, control and transfer the land.

Evidence of Title A written legal document that shows ownership of property. Deeds, last wills and testaments, and affidavits of title are examples.

Exclusive Agency Contract A listing contract that grants the broker the right to market real property while the owner retains the right to sell the property without paying the broker a fee.

Exclusive Right to Sell Listing A listing contract in which the broker is entitled to a commission regardless of who sells the property, including the seller. Under the exclusive right to sell listing contract, once the seller signs the agreement, the broker earns a commission even if he does not bring the buyer and seller together, as long as the property sells during the term of the listing.

Executed Contract A contract in which the obligations have been performed on both sides of the contract and nothing is left to be completed. An example is a purchase/sale contract that has been completed and the transaction has closed.

Executory Contract A contract that is in the process of being performed. An example would be a purchase/sale contract that has not yet closed.

Expectation Value Value of property based on assumption that changes are going to occur for the property being valued or for adjacent property that will either increase or decrease the value of the subject property.

Express Contract An express agreement between the parties that may be oral or in writing. This contract is opposite of an implied contract which is created by the actions of the parties.

Extended Coverage Insurance Insurance that extends a standard fire insurance policy to cover damages resulting from wind, rain, and other perils.

Extender Clause A clause included in the listing contract that operates after the listing contract has expired. The clause is effective for a specific period of time after the listing expires and obligates the seller to pay the real estate commission to the broker if the seller sells the property to a buyer that has been introduced to the property during the term of the listing. This clause is also referred to a carryover clause, safety clause, or protection clause.

Fair Housing Act of 1968 The law that prohibits discrimination in housing based on the protected classes of race, color, religion or national origin. Sex was added as a protected class in 1974, and in 1988 the protected classes of handicap and familial status were added to the fair housing laws.

Fair Market Value The value of property determined by negotiations between a willing seller and a willing buyer when both are knowledgeable, prudent, and neither is acting under duress.

Familial Status One of the protected classes under the fair housing laws that includes one or more individuals, who have not obtained the age of 18 years (being domiciled with a parent or another person having legal custody of such individual or individuals or the designee of such parent or other person having such custody of such individual or individuals).

Farmer's Home Administration Loans
Loans made by the Farmer's Home Administration, an agency of the federal government operating within the Department of Agriculture providing financing for residential property to farmers and others purchasing rural property.

FDIC Acronym for the Federal Deposit Insurance Corporation.

Federal Deposit Insurance Corporation An independent agency within the executive branch of the federal government established to insure deposits held in nationally chartered banks.

Federal Emergency Management Agency (FEMA) A federal agency that provides assistance in advising on building codes, flood plain management, preparing for disasters, training emergency managers, supporting national fire service, administering flood and crime insurance, and assisting in disasters.

Federal Home Loan Mortgage Corporation (FHLMC) A secondary mortgage market for savings and loan associations. Sometimes referred to as "Freddie Mac."

Federal Housing Administration Loans Insured loans made by FHA approved lenders on real estate that meets FHA minimum standards.

Federal National Mortgage Association (FNMA) The largest secondary mortgage market. Sometimes referred to as "Fannie Mae."

Fee for Service Brokerage A brokerage practice in which the principal broker charges sellers and buyers a fee for services based on the individual service being performed. The broker may charge one fee for advertising the property, one fee for showing the property, and one fee for negotiating the contract. This is unlike the traditional brokerage fee that includes all services for one fee. Fee for service brokers are sometimes referred to as "limited services brokers" and are said to offer "unbundled services."

FEMA Acronym for the Federal Emergency Management Agency.

FHLMC Acronym for the Federal Home Loan Mortgage Corporation.

FNMA Acronym for the Federal National Mortgage Association. The largest secondary mortgage market. Sometimes referred to as "Fannie Mae."

Fidelity Bond An agreement between an insurance or bonding company and a person obligated to perform certain tasks whereby the company assumes the responsibility for the performance of the insured party and agrees to pay a third party in the event he insured party fails to perform. May also be used to insure employees entrusted with cash or other valuables. Also referred to as a surety bond.

Fiduciary Duties Responsibilities that arise in a fiduciary relationship of trust between the agent and the principal. Duties owed by the agent to the principal include loyalty, confidentiality, accounting, care and diligence, accounting, obedience to lawful instructions, and full disclosure.

Fiduciary Relationship A relationship of trust between a principal and agent.

Financing Contingency A contingency in a purchase/sale contract that allows the purchaser to terminate the contract if he can not obtain financing to purchase the property.

Fire and Hazard Insurance A basic fire insurance policy covering losses caused by fire or lightning.

Fixed Expenses Expenses that are a known amount and that do not vary from month to month.

Fixtures Personal property that becomes affixed to real property in such a way that it becomes part of the real property.

Flipping The practice of purchasing real estate for a low dollar amount with the intention of quickly transferring it to another buyer for a hefty profit.

Flood Insurance Insurance that pays in the event of a flood that damages real property and its improvements. This insurance is required for properties that are financed though federally regulated lenders.

FNMA Acronym for the Federal National Mortgage Association.

Forcible Entry and Detainer When someone that has entered upon the property, either legally or illegally, refuses to leave once asked to do so.

Foreclosure The process used to enforce a mortgage when the mortgagor fails to repay the money as agreed. This process terminates the owner's and all lien holder interests in the property.

Front Foot Lineal footage running along the front property line that will always be stated first.

FSBO Acronym for "For Sale By Owner." Sometimes "FISBO."

Functional Obsolescence Curable and incurable depreciation caused by outdated or poor design features.

General Lien Liens that, once recorded, become a lien on all personal and real property owned by the licensee.

General Partnership A business relationship created by contract, either written or oral, in which the partners share in the profits, losses, and management of the business.

General Warranty A promise by the grantor to defend the title forever. The warranty protects against defects in title that were created during the grantor's ownership as well as those that existed before his ownership, regardless of when they arise.

Geodetic Survey Legal Description A system for measuring land that includes bench marks that are located by latitude and longitude. Sometimes referred to as the government survey method.

GNMA Acronym for Government National Mortgage Association. Sometimes referred to as "Ginnie Mae."

Good Faith Deposit A deposit made by the buyer when entering into a sales and purchase contract.

Good Faith Estimate An estimate of the buyer's closing costs which, under the Real Estate Settlement Procedures Act, must be given by the lender within three days of loan application.

Government National Mortgage Association This is a HUD agency that participates in the secondary mortgage market by financing special high risk government programs, including projects for urban renewal and housing for the elderly. Sometimes referred to as "Ginnie Mae."

Government Survey Legal Description A system for measuring land that uses principal meridians and baselines to create townships. Also referred to as the rectangular survey method.

Graduated Payment Mortgage Financing for residential real estate in which monthly payments start lower and increase periodically over the life of the mortgage.

Grant Deed A deed that includes warranties set forth in the statute.

Grant, Bargain, and Sale Deed A deed that warrants the title is free from encumbrances created by the grantor.

Grantee The party that receives title to real property by deed.

Grantor The party that conveys title to real property by deed.

Gross Living Area Total livable square footage in an improvement that is above grade level.

Growing Equity Mortgage A mortgage that requires additional payments that are applied directly to principal reduction thereby shortening the maturity date.

Guaranteed Loan A loan that guaranteed by the federal government.

Handicap/Disability Status One of the fair housing classes, defined as someone who has a physical or mental impairment that substantially limits one or more major life activities.

Hidden Defect A defect in property that would not be obvious to a prospective purchaser.

Holder The person in legal possession of a promissory note with the right to receive payment of the amount owed.

Home Equity Mortgage A loan secured by a mortgage on a person's home with an open line of credit based on the homeowner's equity.

Home Inspector A person who inspects real estate for the purpose of determining if there are defects in the property, including whether or not it meets minimum structural and code standards. Sometimes referred to as a property inspector.

Home Protection Plan A warranty that is purchased by the buyer or seller where the company agrees, for a certain period of time after the closing, to repair items. Examples of warranted items include the roof, the heating and cooling systems, and the appliances.

Home Warranty A contract between a warranty company and the homeowner in which the company agrees to repair certain items for a set period of time after the construction of the house. The time periods go from one year for numerous repairs to ten years for structural defects.

Homeowners Association The organization created by the subdivision covenants, or master deed in a condominium regime, comprised of the property owners who are charged with maintaining common areas and enforcing the restrictive covenants.

Homestead Rights Rights to property that is owned and occupied as a family home. Some states protect these rights from general creditors, and some states provide reduced tax values for home owners over a certain age.

Hypothecating Pledging real estate as security for a debt while retaining possession of the property.

Implied Contract A contract created in whole, or part, by the actions of the parties.

Improvement Any structure built on the land that is designed to add value.

Income Approach Process for determining the fair market value of property by capitalizing its net income over its remaining economic life.

Income Shelter A legal way for a taxpayer to shield or reduce income taxes on ordinary income or capital gain. Sometimes referred to as a tax shelter.

Income-to-Debt Ratio A mortgage underwriting process that compares a borrower's monthly debts to his monthly gross income to determine how much

money may be borrowed for a mortgage loan.

Incurable Depreciation of property that is not reasonable or economically feasible to repair or replace.

Independent Contractor A self-employed person retained to complete a certain task and is subject to the control of the hiring person only as the final result of the work effort. Most real estate licensees work as independent contractors.

Informed Consent Consent that is given after the parties understand all of the pros and cons of a particular action.

Inspection Report The written report of the home inspector's findings.

Installment Sales Contract A form of owner financing in which the seller retains title to the property and the buyer has possession of the property. The buyer makes payments to the seller, and at some point designated in the contract, the seller conveys title to the buyer. These contracts are also referred to as land contracts, contract for deed, bond for title, land sales contract, and articles of agreement for warranty deed.

Insurable Interest The relationship to the object or the person to be insured that one must show in order to take out an insurance policy.

Insurable Title Title to real estate that is clear enough of defects to allow the owner to obtain title insurance.

Insured Loan A high risk loan that is insured by the government, or private insurer, and paid for by the borrower, that assures the lender that, in the event of mortgagor default, the lender will not have a loss.

Intangible Personal Property Personal property that you cannot touch. Examples include contractual rights, legal claims, or patents.

Interest Rate Cap A term in an adjustable or variable rate mortgage and promissory note that sets the highest interest rate that may be charged on the loan.

Interest Rate Floor A term in an adjustable or variable rate mortgage and promissory note that sets the lowest interest rate that may be charged on the loan.

Intermediate Theory A combination of the lien theory and title theory that allows the lender to receive a specific lien on the property that can be foreclosed in the event of default.

Interval Ownership A form of condominium ownership in which the purchaser owns the property for a specified time interval each year.

Investment Property Property purchased with the expectation of earning income or making a profit.

Investment Value The fair market value of property to a particular investor.

Joint Ownership Concurrent ownership of property by two or more people.

Joint Tenants with Right of Survivorship Concurrent ownership of property by two or more people

known as tenants. Upon the death of one tenant, the surviving tenant automatically receives the share of the deceased tenant.

Joint Venture A general partnership formed for a specific business purpose that terminates once the project is complete. Also referred to as joint adventure.

Judgment Lien A statutory general lien that may be filed against a judgment debtor by the judgment creditor once the court enters its final decision.

Judgment The final decision and order of the court stating which party wins the legal action and the amount of any damages owed.

Junior Lienholder A holder of a lien that is second in priority to a previously recorded lien.

Just Compensation The amount of money the government must pay the landowner when the owner's property is taken in an eminent domain action for the common good. This amount is either negotiated between the government and owner, or decided by a jury when the parties cannot agree as to what is "just."

Latent Defect Hidden defects that may or may not be known to the owner, and that are not easily discovered by someone looking at the property.

Lead Based Paint Disclosure Under the federal law, sellers of one to four-family residential properties built before 1978 are required to inform buyers of the existence of any known lead based paint used in the property and are required to provide the buyer with any reports or other documentation in the seller's possession relating to the existence of such paint. Sellers must give buyers a ten-day opportunity to have a risk assessment made of the property; however, the law does not require sellers to test for the presence of lead based paint, nor are they required to remove it. Real estate agents are required to insure compliance with the law by the seller by asking the seller to complete a disclosure form, and are required to pass out to buyers the pamphlet entitled: "Protect Your Family From Lead In Your Home."

Lease Agreement An agreement, either oral or written, that creates a landlord and tenant relationship.

Lease Option A contract between a seller and buyer that gives the buyer the right to purchase the property at some point in the future upon the terms contained in the contract and giving the buyer the right to lease the property while deciding whether or not to purchase it.

Lease An agreement, either oral or written, that creates a landlord and tenant relationship giving the tenant possession of the landlord's property.

Leased Fee Interest The lessor's interest in leased property.

Leasehold Estate An interest in land that grants the lessee the right to use the property, but does not create ownership rights.

Leasehold Interest A personal property right created by contract between the lessor and lessee that gives the lessee the right to possess and use the real property. Sometimes referred to as a leasehold estate.

Leasehold Title Insurance Protects the lessee against defects in the lessor's title that may interfere with the lessee's quiet enjoyment of the property.

Legal Competency Recognition which the law gives that a person has the ability to incur legal liability or acquire legal rights.

Legal description A way to describe real property so that it cannot be confused with any other parcel of land in the world.

Legal Title Title which is complete and perfect regarding the apparent right of ownership and possession, although another person may hold equitable title.

Lender's Title Insurance Insurance that protects only the mortgagee's interest in the mortgagor's property during the term of the mortgage.

Lessee The person who leases property. Also referred to as the tenant.

Lessor The owner of leased property. Also referred to as the landlord.

Liability Insurance Insurance that protects a party against liability or losses suffered by a third party.

License (1) State authorization to practice real estate brokerage. That permission is in the form of a license. (2) The term used to describe the relationship between a property owner, known as the licensor, and another person, known as the licensee, who is using the property for a specific purpose.

Licenses are similar to easements, but they do not transfer an interest in the land and they do not "run with the land."

Licensee A person with either a broker or sales associate's license granted by the state regulatory agency. Also the person who enters into a license agreement with the owner of property.

Licensor The regulatory agency that issues real estate licenses to brokers and sales associates. Also, the owner of property that enters into a license agreement, allowing someone to use her property for a specific purpose.

Lien An encumbrance on real estate that gives a third party a claim against the property.

Lien Priority The order in which liens will be paid in the event of a foreclosure action.

Lien Theory States that provide a mechanism for lenders to have a lien on real estate to secure repayment of the debt in the form of a mortgage. This is different from title theory states where the lenders take title to the property by a deed of trust.

Life Estate Pur Autre Vie A life estate that exists for the life of someone other than the life tenant. This third party is known as the measuring life, and the life estate terminates when the measuring life dies, at which time title passes to the remainderman.

Life Estate An estate in land that is limited to the duration of someone's life, known as the life tenant or measuring live. Upon the death of the life tenant, title to the property passes to the remainderman.

Life Tenant The holder of the life estate.

Limited Liability Company A business form that resembles a partnership that has the liability protection of a corporation. The owners of the company are called members.

Limited Partnership A business form with one general partner and one or more limited partners.

Limited Service Brokers A business model where the real estate brokerage provides certain services to the seller for a fee and the seller performs the remainder of the services necessary to market the property.

Liquidation Value Fair market value of property sold at a distress sale.

Lis Pendens A notice recorded in the chain of title to real property to warn anyone taking an interest in the property that the property is the subject matter of litigation and that any interests acquired during the pendency of the lawsuit are subject to its outcome. A lien filed after the lis pendens is filed has an inferior position to all liens filed prior to the lis pendens.

Listing Contract The agreement between the seller and broker retaining the broker's services to sell the real property that is the subject of the agreement. Sometimes referred to simply as a listing.

Littoral Water Water that is along land bordering a sea or ocean and that is affected by the tides.

Loan Origination The amount of money charged by the lender for its work relating to obtaining the loan.

Lock Box An instrument placed on the door of a seller's house that holds the key.

Lot and Block Legal Description Land description that identifies parcels of land designated on a plat by the lot number, block, and subdivision name.

Maker The person who signs a promissory note and who is liable to repay the debt.

Management Agreement A contract between the owner of real property and a property manager that includes the scope of the duties and responsibilities of the property manager and the obligations of the owner to pay for the services. Also referred to as a Property Management Agreement.

Management Proposal An outline submitted to the property owner showing how the property manager intends to manage the property if she is retained to do so.

Market Data Approach Process for estimating the fair market value of property by comparing it to other properties that are similar and that have been leased or sold recently. Sometimes referred to as the comparable market approach.

Marketing Plan A plan that specifically details the marketing strategy to rent or sell real estate.

Master Deed The governing document for a condominium or homeowner's association.

Material Facts Important fact that would influence a person's opinion and actions relative to entering into a contract and purchasing or selling real property.

Maturity Date The date that the last payment on a mortgage is due.

Measuring Life The person whose life determines the duration of a life estate.

Mechanic and Materialman's Lien A statutory lien that may be filed by mechanics and materialmen when they are not paid for their services and supplies. The lien rights are very specific and must be followed exactly or the lien will not be enforceable.

Meridians Lines that run north and south used to describe property in the government survey method.

Metes and Bounds Legal Description A legal description that describes the boundaries of the property that has a beginning point and an ending point, which two points must be the same.

Mineral Rights Landowner's rights to the subsurface minerals. These rights include leaving the minerals where they are located, as well as the right to remove the minerals and profit from their sale. Mineral rights stay with the surface rights unless they are severed by conveyance of the surface to one owner and conveyance of the subsurface to another.

Mortgage A voluntary lien given by the mortgagor to the mortgagee to secure the repayment of a debt.

Mortgage Banker A person who works for a company that makes real estate loans and services them.

Mortgage Broker A person who brokers money by bringing together a borrower and a lender for a fee.

Mortgage Company A company who brings borrowers and lenders together, makes loans, packages them, and sells the packages to both primary and secondary investors.

Mortgage Insurance Insurance purchased by the borrower to protect the lender from a loss in the event the borrower defaults on an FHA or conventional-insured mortgage.

Mortgage Liquidity The secondary market process of turning mortgages into cash thereby enabling lenders to use the money to make more mortgage loans.

Mortgage Loan Value Fair market value of property for the purpose of obtaining a mortgage.

Mortgagee The lender.

Mortgagor The borrower.

Multi-Peril Insurance Insurance for commercial property that insures against many perils in one policy, such as fire, acts of God, liability, and casualty.

Multiple Listing Service A group of real estate brokers who agree to cooperate with each other by sharing access to their listings, and agree to compensate the cooperating brokerage who actually sells/leases the property.

Mutual Savings Bank A primary source of financing residential real estate that is chartered and regulated by the state where they do business.

National Flood Insurance Act of 1968 A federal program that provides flood insurance for necessary repairs; i.e. cost to repair does not exceed value of property.

Net Income Income after all expenses and deductions are taken from the gross income.

Net Lease A commercial lease in which the tenant pays a base rent plus either the property taxes, the maintenance, or the property insurance.

Net Listing A listing, illegal in most states, that pays the seller a minimum amount and sets the broker's commission as all money received over that amount.

Net Operating Income The amount of income left after deducting expenses of a building or investment gross income.

Net Proceeds Amount of money that is due the seller once all costs and expenses are deducted.

Non-Assumable Mortgage A mortgage that contains a due-on-sale clause.

Nonconforming Use Use of property that does not conform with the current zoning classification but that is permitted to remain for a period of time because it existed before the zoning designation was changed.

Nonfreehold Estate A leasehold estate that grants the lessee the right to use the property, but does not create ownership rights.

Nonrecourse Provision A loan provision which states that the borrower is not personally liable for payment of the debt if the value of the property securing the loan is less than the amount necessary to repay the loan.

Novation An agreement generated by the lender substituting a new mortgagor for the original mortgagor in a loan assumption situation.

Offer and Acceptance An essential element of contract formation that requires the offeree accept the offer without any changes.

Offer A promise conditioned upon some requested or asked for act or promise, demonstrating the intent of one party to form a contract with another party.

Offeree The person receiving the offer.

Offeror The person making the offer.

Open-End Mortgage Mortgages that contain future advance clauses allowing the lender to lend additional funds under the same mortgage.

Open Listing In this contract the seller agrees to pay a commission to any broker that sells the property, but retains the right to sell the property himself and not pay a commission.

Operating Budget An annual budget prepared by the property manager showing the income and expenses for the property.

Operating Expenses Periodic expenses, that vary in amount, incurred for investment property,

Operating Statement A detailed statement showing the income and expenses of a business over a period of time. Sometimes referred to as a profit and loss statement or an income statement.

Option When used in a lease, an option gives the tenant to right to lease the property for some future period at an agreed upon rate under the same terms and conditions as the original lease.

Origination Fee The fees charged by a lender to pay for time and expenses incurred in arranging for a loan.

Owner's Title Insurance Protects the new owner's interest in real property from defects in title that existed before conveyance to the new owner.

Package Mortgage A real estate loan which covers both real and personal property with one mortgage.

Paint-to-Paint A phrase used in condominium ownership that indicates that condominium owners own the inside of their units individually while owning everything beyond the paint in common with the other owners.

Panic Peddling The illegal practice of making statements to property owners, either in writing or orally, that a member of a protected class is moving into the area for the purpose of depreciating property values. Sometimes referred to as blockbusting.

Participation Mortgage A type of mortgage that provides the lender with a certain percentage of cash flow beyond the fixed rate of interest paid by the borrower.

Party of the First Part In a deed or easement, the grantor.

Party of the Second Part In a deed or easement, the grantee.

Patent Defect An obvious defect in property.

Percolating Water Water that collects underground.

Personal Property All property that cannot be classified as real property.

Physical Deterioration Reduction in use or value of a property because its physical condition has declined. This condition is either curable or incurable depending on the economic feasibility of making the necessary repairs.

Pinned and Staked Survey The process followed by a registered land surveyor or registered engineer that marks the corners of property by placing a permanent pin in the ground and a wooden stake on the surface to give a visual of the boundaries.

Planned Unit Development High density housing that provides for maximum use of common space where each owner owns the land under his unit while the common area is owned and maintained by the community association.

Planning An agency of local government organized to develop a master plan for the use and development of the land.

Plat A map of a city, town, subdivision, or other parcel of land that has been divided into lots. The boundaries of the lots are determined by a surveyor and include the name of the subdivision, the lot number, the dimensions of the lots, the easements, the building lines, and other requirements that may be placed by the local government on the lot.

Police Power The constitutional right of the government to adopt and enforce laws that promote the public health, safety and welfare.

Policy Manual A booklet prepared by the Sponsoring Broker (or Principal Broker) of a company setting out the policies and procedures that are to be followed by those associated with the company.

Potential Gross Income Total amount of gross receipts if all rental units are leased and all tenants pay their rent.

Predatory Lending A recent development in lending practices that includes deception and fraud by lenders. Borrowers are manipulated through aggressive sale techniques that lead to them borrowing more money at higher interest rates than they can afford to repay. Lenders costs are extremely high and borrowers are not adequately informed of the costs and the risks of losing not only the equity in their property, but actually losing the property through foreclosure. Victims of these lending schemes are often minorities, elderly, uneducated, and unsophisticated in business practices. Buyers, sellers, and agents should be on guard for lenders that ask for sales contracts to be changed after they are signed, ask for money to be paid outside of closing that does not appear on the closing statement, and ask that inaccurate information be included on the settlement statement. Although these requests may be legitimate, they are signals that predatory lending practices may be happening.

Prepaids At closings, items paid in advance by the buyer as required by the lender. These items include interim interest, mortgage insurance premiums (MIP and PMI), and homeowner's insurance.

Prepayment Clause Prepayment clauses inform the mortgagor whether or not he may prepay the principal balance prior to its due date.

Prepayment Penalty A provision in a promissory note that provides for the borrower to pay a monetary penalty if more than what is due is paid any one time, including paying the balance in full before a specified time.

Prepayment Privilege The right to prepay a debt before it is due.

Presentation The process where the real estate agent, while representing the seller or buyer, delivers, explains, and assists in responding, to an offer or counteroffer.

Preventative Maintenance Periodic work and upkeep performed on and to the property, its improvements, and equipment to keep it in order for the building and equipment to function as they should.

Price Fixing The illegal practice of conspiring to fix fees or prices for services rendered or goods sold in an effort to protect the service or goods provider.

Principal Broker The broker in the office who is responsible for managing the brokerage and supervising the affiliated real estate licensees. Some states refer to this person as the sponsoring broker.

Principal Meridian Used in the government survey method as the prime meridian for numbering ranges.

Private Mortgage Insurance Insurance that is paid by the borrower on a conventional mortgage insuring the lender against loss if the borrower fails to repay the debt and the property is foreclosed upon.

Profit and Loss Statement A detailed statement showing the income and expenses of a business over a period of time. Sometimes referred to as an operating statement or an income statement.

Promissory Note The promissory note is the primary evidence of the debt. The promissory note is the borrower's personal promise to repay the debt. That promise is secured by a lien on the real property in the form of a mortgage.

Property Inspection Inspection of property obtained by buyers prior to the closing.

Property Inspector A person who inspects real estate for the purpose of determining if there are defects in the property, including whether or not it meets minimum structural and code standards. Sometimes referred to as a home inspector.

Property Management Agreement A contract between the owner of real property and a property manager that includes the scope of the duties and responsibilities of the property manager and the obligations of the owner to pay for the services. Also referred to as a Management Agreement.

Property Manager A person retained, either as an employee or independent contractor, by a property owner to advertise the property, negotiate leases, collect rents, maintain the property, and perform other necessary management services.

Prorated Taxes Division of property taxes between the seller and buyer based on their period of ownership.

Pro-Rations Division of taxes, insurance, assessments, and other items relating to the property transaction between the seller and buyer or lessor and lessee.

Protection Clause A clause included in the listing contract that operates after the listing contract has expired. The clause is effective for a specific period of time after the listing expires and obligates the seller to pay the real estate commission to the broker if the seller sells the property to a buyer that has been introduced to the property during the term of the listing. This clause is also referred to a carryover clause, safety clause, or an extender clause.

PUD Acronym for Planned Unit Development.

Purchase Contract A contract for the purchase and sale of real property in which the buyer agrees to purchase and the seller agrees to sell. This is sometimes referred to as the sales contract.

Purchase Money Mortgage A loan to a buyer to cover all or part of the purchase price.

Quiet Title Action A lawsuit filed by a property owner to remove a cloud or claim that has been placed on the title to property.

Quitclaim Deed A deed that conveys only the interest, if any, that the grantor has in the property and contains no warranties. This deed does not imply that the grantor has an interest to convey.

Ranch A one-story house that may or may not have a basement.

Range A measurement of land used in the government survey method of legal description that is six miles wide running both east and west of the principal meridian.

Rate of Return (ROI) The ratio between the equity invested and the net income stated as a percentage.

Real Estate Investment Trust An investment vehicle, made up of numerous individual investors, that holds title to real estate. Investors receive income from the trust and also certain tax advantages. Sometimes referred to by the acronym of "REIT."

Real Estate Settlement Procedures Act (RESPA) A federal law that became effective in 1974 after Congress found that significant reforms were needed in the real estate settlement process. RESPA applies to federally-related one to four-family residential transactions. The purpose of the act is to: (1) require more effective advance disclosure to buyers and sellers of settlement costs; (2) eliminate kickbacks or referral fees in the delivery of settlement services; (3) reduce the amount of money home buyers are required to place in escrow accounts for real estate taxes and property insurance; and (4) reform and modernize local record keeping of land title information. Lenders must provide a special information booklet that explains the settlement process and costs to all applicants within three business days after a mortgage loan application is received or prepared. This booklet generally explains the mortgage process and gives the borrower a "good faith estimate" of the settlement costs they will likely incur. Settlement costs, also referred to as closing costs, include services provided by the lender, the attorney, the settlement agent, the appraiser, the inspector, the surveyor, the real estate agent, the insurance agent, and the credit reporting agency. Basically, this includes all costs that the borrower is required to pay because he/she is borrowing money to purchase residential real estate. The HUD-1 closing statement must used for all closings that fall under RESPA, and the borrower has the right to inspect the

HUD-1 one business day before the closing. Under RESPA, the settlement agent is required to provide true and accurate information on the HUD-1. Borrowers, sellers, and the settlement agent all sign the HUD-1, stating that the information on the form is true and correct. In the event the information is not correct, all three parties are subject to penalties. Under RESPA, no person shall give or accept a "fee, kickback, or thing of value" for referring business incidental to the settlement services. Also prohibited is the giving or accepting of any portion, split, or percentage of the fees paid for rendering a service in the settlement process. Anyone violating this prohibition may be fined up to $10,000 and be imprisoned for up to one year or both. In addition, the consumer who paid the fee for service that involved the kickback is entitled to receive an amount equal to three times the amount paid for the service. This award may be collected by the borrower from either the party that paid the kickback or the one that received it.

Real Property The physical land, including what is beneath the surface and what is above the surface, as well as improvements attached on to the land. Improvements include structures, easements, licenses, roads, sewers and anything else attached to the surface, beneath the surface , or above the land. Also referred to as realty and real estate.

Reality of Consent Mutual agreement of the parties to a contract about the terms and conditions of the contract.

Reasonably Achievable Accommodations The American with Disabilities Act defines this as modifications on a property that are easily accomplishable and able to be carried out without much difficulty or expense.

Recording The process of filing records in the county court clerk's office in the county where the property is located to give constructive notice of an interest in land. Deeds, mortgages, liens, releases, corporation documents, and wills are all examples of documents that are recorded.

Recourse Provision A loan provision which states that the lender can take legal action against the borrower personally in case of default.

Rectangular Survey Legal Description A system for measuring land that uses principal meridians and baselines to create townships. Also referred to as the government survey method.

Redlining An illegal practice of mortgage lenders in which the companies refuse to make loans in a certain area, not because of the creditworthiness of the borrowers, but because of the area where the property is located. This is a discriminatory practice, because many of the people who live in these areas are racially diverse.

Referral Fee The fee received for recommending someone to a service provider. Real estate brokers may refer buyers and sellers to other real estate brokers and receive a fee for the referral if the other broker has a real estate license. Licensees may not pay referral fees to unlicensed individuals for leads. Under the Real Estate Settlement Procedures Acts some referrals are inappropriate and may be considered as illegal kickbacks.

Regulation Z A federal regulation that covers all real estate credit extended to a natural person that is not for business, commercial or agricultural purposes. It is often referred to as the Truth-in-Lending and is enforced by the Federal Trade Commission. When real and personal property used, or intended to be used, as a principal dwelling is taken by the lender as collateral to secure a loan, the regulation applies. Certain information must be given the borrower: finance charge, annual percentage rate, disclosure statement, and, in the event of a second mortgage or refinance of a personal residence, information regarding the right to rescind the transaction. The finance charge is the total of all costs the borrower must pay for obtaining the credit. These charges include loan origination fees, prepaid interest, and discount points. Finance charges do not include monies that would have to be paid in a real estate transaction if no credit had been extended.

Regulatory Agency The governmental agency that licenses, regulates, educates, and disciplines real estate agents.
REIT Acronym for Real Estate Investment Trust.

Release The discharge or relinquishment of a right, claim, or privilege.

Reliction The process of water receding from the land along the bank, effectively creating more land.

Remainder Interest A future interest in real estate that is created simultaneously with the present interest. An example would be the remainder interest created by a life estate.

Renegotiable Rate Mortgage A mortgage that is a series of short term loans that are renegotiated at periodic intervals to adjust the interest to the current levels.

Replacement Reserve Funds that are deposited by the property owners over a period of time and held for replacing assets as needed. An example would be a condominium association that has a reserve to replace the roof and parking lot in the future.

Resident Manager A person employed to manage a building who lives on the premises and is paid a salary.

Restrictive Covenants Limitations placed on the land by grantors that restrict how the land may be used in the future. These restrictions run with the land. Examples of these restrictions include number, size, and type of structures that may be built on the land; use of the land for keeping livestock and other animals; limitations on parking vehicles, boats, and trailers on the property; and construction of fences, swimming pools, and garages. Restrictive covenants may be placed on the land by the owner through the use of recorded subdivision restrictions and deeds of restrictions.

Reverse Annuity Mortgage A financing arrangement whereby a lender pays the borrower a fixed annuity or periodic payment based on the owner's equity in the property.

Riparian Water Rights The landowner's rights to use water that flows by or through his land.

Risk of Loss This phrase refers to the person who bears the financial loss when property is destroyed by fire or other casualty.

Road Frontage Footage that runs along the front of the property along a highway, road, street.

Routine Maintenance Day-to-day maintenance of the property.

Run with the Land Encumbrances that remain with the land regardless of who owns it are said to run with the land. Examples are easements, deed restrictions, and property taxes. This may also be referred to as "running with the land."

Sales Contract The contract used by buyers and sellers to purchase and sell real estate containing the entire agreement between the parties. This is sometimes referred to as the purchase contract.

Savings & Loan Association A primary supplier of mortgages for new construction and the purchase of existing properties, primarily in the residential real estate market.

Scarcity One of the economic principles that increases the value of real property when it is in short supply.

Second Mortgage A mortgage that has a junior lien position to the first mortgage, because of the time of recording the mortgage or of the subordination of the mortgage.

Secondary Mortgage Market The process of buying and selling first mortgages to provide mortgage liquidity.

Section One of the measurements used in the government survey method that measures one square mile of land and contains 640 acres.

Securities Evidence of obligations to pay money or of rights to participate in earnings and distribution of corporate, trust, or other property. Examples include stocks, bonds, and promissory notes.

Security Deposit Money deposited with the landlord to secure the landlord against financial loss due to damage to the premises occasioned by the tenant's occupancy, other than ordinary wear and tear.

Senior Lienholder A holder of a lien that has higher priority than other liens.

Settlement A term used to describe the time when the purchaser delivers the purchase price to the seller and the seller delivers the deed to the purchaser. Sometimes referred to as a "closing."

Severalty Individual or sole ownership of property.

Shared-Appreciation Mortgage Loans that allow the buyer to get a reduced interest rate because the lender shares in the appreciation.

Sherman Anti-Trust Act A federal statute prohibiting price-fixing, certain types of boycotts, tying arrangements and market allocation schemes.

Sole Proprietorship A form of business ownership in which one person owns the business.

Special Assessment An assessment levied against property by a local taxing authority when the government makes additions to the property that benefit the public. Examples include sewers, sidewalks, and street lights.

Special Warranty Deed A deed in which the grantor warrants that he owns the property, has the right to convey it, and that it is free of encumbrances. The grantor's warranty only extends to claims that arise for the period of time he owned the property and does not extend to the period of time before his ownership. Defects in title that arise prior to his ownership are not included in his warranty.

Specific Lien A lien that is filed against a certain parcel of real estate and does not attach to other property owned by the debtor. These liens may be voluntary, like mortgages, and may be involuntary, like property mechanic's and materialman's liens and property tax liens.

Speculative Value Value of property to a purchaser who intends to hold the property to make a profit at some point in the future.

Split Level A house that has two levels directly over each other with one or more other levels adjacent to those two levels.

Sponsoring Broker This term is used in two ways: (1) as the broker who is in charge of running the brokerage and supervising the licensed associates in the brokerage, sometimes referred to as the principal broker; (2) the broker who agrees to accept the sales associate into the brokerage once he passes the license examination.

Spot Zoning The process of rezoning a small parcel of land that lies in an area with a different zoning designation.

Square Footage Measurement of land or improvement that is calculated by multiplying the length times the width.

Statutory Redemption A statutory period of time enacted in some states in which the borrower can redeem the property after foreclosure by paying the outstanding debt, interest, and legal fees.

Statutory Year A year with 360 days.

Steering An illegal practice of channeling home purchasers or renters to or away from certain areas for the purpose of violating fair housing laws.

Stigmatized Property Property where an event has occurred that does not damage the physical property, but rather gives it a negative reputation. Examples include houses where there has been a murder or suicide, or where a ghost is said to reside.

Straight-Line Depreciation A method for depreciating investment property that is computed by dividing the adjusted basis of the property by a set number of years so that each year the property is depreciated by the same amount.

Strict Foreclosure A type of mortgage foreclosure in which the lender does not have to pay the property owner equity that may be left after the debt and all expenses are paid.

Strip Center A retail center containing four or more stores that are easily accessible with ample parking.

Subdivision Restrictions Limitations placed on lots in the subdivision by the developer. Purchasers of the lots may be required to build houses that have a minimum square footage, certain facades, and specific paint colors. The restrictions may prohibit detached garages, fences, livestock in the yards, swimming pools, or clothes lines. These restrictions run with the land and may be enforced by either the developer or other property owners in the subdivision.

Subdivision Process of dividing land into smaller parcels with the intention of conveying the parcels to other owners. Parcels may be referred to a lots, units, or sections.

Subject-to The grantee takes title to real estate that has existing liens, thereby agreeing that the property will be liable for those liens.

Sublease A lease entered into between a lessee, known as the sublessor, and a third person, known as the sublessee, that transfers part of the leasehold interest to the sublessee with a reversionary interest to the sublessor at the end of the sublease. The contractual relationship is between the sublessor and sublessee, and not between the sublessee and the landlord. The sublessor remains liable to the landlord for rents due under the lease.

Subordination Clause The process of reversing lien priorities. A first mortgage holder may agree to allow another mortgage holder to have the first lien position. Subordination may be accomplished by a clause in an already recorded document in which the lienholder agrees in advance to take a lower lien priority in certain situations or by a later executed document in which the lienholder agrees to relinquish its higher priority.

Subsurface Rights Ownership of land below the surface, including minerals and water.

Supply and Demand An economic principle stating that the lower the demand and the higher the supply, the lower the price, and the higher the demand and lower the supply, the higher the price.

Surety Bond An agreement between an insurance or bonding company and a person obligated to perform certain tasks whereby the company assumes the responsibility for the performance of the insured party and agrees to pay a third party in the event the insured party fails to perform. May also be used to insure employees entrusted with cash or other valuable. Also referred to as a fidelity bond.

Surface Water Rights An owner's right to use and re-direct water that flows across her land.

Survey Report A drawing by the surveyor that shows the property boundaries and the improvements on it.

Survey The process used to determine property boundaries that is performed by

a registered professional engineer or registered land surveyor.

Surveyor The person who performs a survey of real property.

Syndications An arrangement by which two or more people are assembled for the purpose of raising equity capital for purchasing real estate or other types of investments.

Taking The term used in eminent domain proceedings when the government acquires ownership of real property to be used for the common good.

Tangible Personal Property Things that can be touched that are not real property.

Tax Shelter A means by which a taxpayer can legally shield or reduce income or gain from tax liability.

Tenants by the entirety Joint ownership of real property by a husband and wife. At the time of death of one spouse, the surviving spouse has individual or sole ownership of the property.

Tenants in Common Concurrent ownership of property in which each owner owns an undivided ownership interest in the whole property. Each owner has a percentage ownership interest, which may or may not be a percentage equal to the other owners. An example would be three cotenants, one of which has a 90% interest, one nine percent, and the other one percent. As long as the total ownership equals 100%, the fractional ownership can be any amount stated in the legal document creating the ownership. Each owner has the right to the possession and use of the entire property, subject to the rights of the co-tenants.

Territorial Allocations The illegal practice used by companies with a large market share to prevent other companies from coming into their area of town to do business.

Three-Day Right of Rescission The legal mechanism for setting aside a contract and placing the parties back in their original positions prior to the contract being entered into. Rescission may take place by mutual agreement of the parties or by court order. It may occur before the contract is consummated or after the contract is consummated.

Timber Rights Ownership rights to timber both before and after it is severed from the land.

Timeshares The right to use and occupy property for a recurring block of time.

Title Abstract A condensed chronological history of all recorded instruments in the chain of title which affect the title.

Title Examination The process of reviewing all recorded documents relating to a specific parcel of property to locate the names of the current and prior owners, to determine if the property is subject to any liens or other encumbrances, and to review all recorded documents that may affect the marketability of the property.

Title Theory States that allow the lender to hold the equitable title to the property during the term of the mortgage loan. These states ask borrowers to sign trust deeds instead of mortgages.

Trigger Terms As used in regulation Z, terms that must be used in an advertisement to inform the borrower of the down payment, cash price of property, annual percentage rate, interest rate (if variable or adjustable, must be stated as variable or adjustable), amount of down payment, amount of each payment, date when each payment is due, and total number of payments.

Township One of the measurements in the government survey method of legal description; the township is a six-mile square containing 36 one-mile-square sections.

Trade Fixtures Personal property and equipment used in a trade or business that is affixed or attached to leased real estate in such a way that it becomes part of the real estate. Generally, fixtures cannot be removed; however, property that is specifically designated as trade fixtures may be removed at the end of the lease unless the lease agreement states otherwise.

Transfer Taxes The state tax that must be paid when property is conveyed. This tax is sometimes referred to as "deed stamps."

Transferability The ability to transfer real estate from one owner to another. This is one of the economic principles that gives value to real property.

Triple Net Lease A commercial lease in which the tenant pays a base rent, plus the property taxes, insurance, and maintenance. Also referred to as a net, net, net lease.

Trust Account A separate account used to hold client's money and money belonging to others. Sometimes referred to as an escrow account.

Truth-in-Lending On July 1, 1969, the National Consumer Credit Protection Act became effective. This Act is commonly referred to as "Truth-in-Lending" or "Regulation Z." All real estate transactions are covered. The law requires creditors to give meaningful credit disclosures to borrowers and requires lenders to include certain information in their advertising. Creditors under this Act are those lenders who regularly extend consumer credit. Finance charges must be disclosed and the annual percentage rate (APR) must be provided. Owners who are refinancing their homes or placed junior liens (second mortgages, third mortgages, etc) must be given three business days after signing the mortgage documents to cancel the transaction.

Trust Deed A deed conveying property owned by the trust that is executed by the trustee on behalf of the trust. Term may also be used to describe the instrument used to secure repayment of a promissory note in a title theory state.

Trustee The person appointed in a will or trust to administer the provisions of the trust and to disburse the funds as directed by the terms of the will or trust. Term may also be used to describe the holder of title in a deed of trust in a title theory state.

Trustor In a title theory state, the owner of the property.

Two-story Improvement on property that has two livable floors above grade.

Tying agreements The illegal practice of requiring the consumer to purchase goods and services as a bundle in an effort to keep prices high and to prevent comparison shopping.

Underwriter The person that reviews the loan application and all other documentation supplied by the borrower to determine the lender's risk in extending the mortgage loan to the buyer. Lending guidelines are reviewed by the underwriter, and the borrower's creditworthiness is analyzed to determine the risk to the lender in making the loan.

Underwriting The process of assessing the risk to the lender when making a mortgage loan.

Uniform Standards of Professional Appraisal Practice Standards of professional practice that must be followed by licensed and certified real estate appraisers relating to the development and communicating of appraisals. Sometimes referred to by the acronym of "USPAP."

Unilateral Contract A contract that has only one party who promises to perform under the contract. Examples of unilateral contracts are option contracts requiring only the seller to perform if the buyer chooses to buy the property at some future time and open listing contracts that require the seller to pay the broker if the property sells, but do not require the broker to attempt to sell the property.

Uninsured Loan Low-risk loans that do not require mortgage insurance to be paid by the borrower.

Unities of Title Common law requirements necessary to create concurrent ownership, including, unity of interest, unity of marriage, unity of time, unity of title, and unity of possession.

Unity of Interest All owners hold an equal interest in the property.

Unity of Marriage Owners must be married to hold title. This is the requirement to hold title as tenants by the entirety.

Unity of Possession All owners have the right to possess the property at the same time. This unity is required for ownership as tenants by the entirety, joint tenants with right of survivorship, and as tenants in common.

Unity of Time All owners must receive their title at the same time.

Unity of Title All owners must take title in the same deed or will.

Use and Occupancy Insurance Insurance for commercial property that insures against lost rent.

USPAP Acronym for the Uniform Standards of Professional Appraisal Practice.

Utility An economic principle that gives value to real property based on the usefulness of the property.

Vacancy Loss The estimated amount of lost rental revenue because of vacancies.

Valid Contract A contract that in all respects complies with the provisions of contract law.

Valuation An opinion of value based on objective criteria.

Value in Use Fair market value of property as it is currently being used.

Variance Permission by the appropriate governmental body to use the land in a manner not permitted under its zoning classification.

Vendor's Lien A form of seller financing in which the seller conveys title to the buyer by deed, but retains a lien in the deed.

Veterans Administration Loans A guaranteed loan that allows qualified veterans to borrow 100% of the money need to purchase a home.

Void Contract A contract appearing to be valid and enforceable that legally does not exist. This situation arises when the contract is missing one of its essential terms. Those essential terms include offer and acceptance, consideration, legal purpose, and competent parties. Unlike voidable contracts that may be ratified, void contracts have never existed; therefore, they cannot be ratified. A real estate contract entered into by a mentally disabled individual is void because the individual does not have the legal competency to enter into a contract.

Voidable Contract A contract that may be terminated by one of the parties, although it appears on its fact to be valid and enforceable. An example would be a real estate contract entered into by a minor. Once the minor reaches majority age, he may choose to ratify the contract or he may choose to terminate the contract.

Walk-through inspection The physical inspection of property that takes place immediately prior to closing to determine that the property is in the same physical condition as when the sales contract was signed.

Warranty of Habitability This is the agreement of a landlord to keep the property in good condition during the term of the lease.

Warranty of Quiet Enjoyment The right to use leased property without interference by others claiming the right to use the same property.

Warranty of Title Grantor's promise to warrant and defend the title to the grantee against the lawful claims of all persons.

Warranty A promise or guarantee that certain facts are true.

Wood-Destroying Organisms Inspections An inspection obtained by the seller or buyer from a pest control company to determine if wood destroying organisms are active in the property.

Wraparound Mortgage A mortgage that allows borrowers obtain additional financing on their property without paying off the current first mortgage.

Writ of Attachment The legal process of seizing the real or personal property of a defendant in a lawsuit by levy or judicial order, and holding it in the custody of the court as security for satisfaction of a judgment.

Zoning Classification The specific zoning designation for each area.

Zoning Ordinances Local laws that implement and enforce the comprehensive plan. These ordinances consist of two parts. The zoning map shows the designated zones and the zoning ordinance is a narrative that sets the use permitted in each zone.

Zoning Government process used to control the way land is used by the owner.